P9-CCU-828

Stephen L. Pevar is Regional Counsel for the Mountain States Office of the American Civil Liberties Union, a position he has held since 1976. He is also staff counsel to the ACLU's Indian Rights Committee. In addition, Mr. Pevar is an Adjunct Professor at the University of Denver School of Law, where he teaches a course entitled Indian Law. From 1971 through 1974 Mr. Pevar was a Legal Services attorney on the Rosebud Sioux Indian Reservation in South Dakota. He has litigated many Indian rights cases. Mr. Pevar graduated from Princeton University in 1968 and from the University of Virginia School of Law in 1971.

AN AMERICAN CIVIL LIBERTIES UNION HANDBOOK

THE RIGHTS OF INDIANS AND TRIBES

THE BASIC ACLU GUIDE TO INDIAN AND TRIBAL RIGHTS

SECOND EDITION
Completely Revised and Up-to-Date

Stephen L. Pevar

General Editor of the Handbook Series
Norman Dorsen, President, ACLU 1976–1991

SOUTHERN ILLINOIS UNIVERSITY PRESS
CARBONDALE AND EDWARDSVILLE

*To the Pevars and Hoskins of Connecticut
and the Antoines
of the Rosebud Sioux Indian Reservation
and to everyone who seeks peace
and justice*

Copyright © 1992 by the American Civil Liberties Union
All rights reserved
Printed in the United States of America
Production supervised by New Leaf Studio

99 98 97 96   7 6 5 4

Library of Congress Cataloging-in-Publication Data

Pevar, Stephen L.
  The rights of Indians and tribes: the basic ACLU guide to Indian
and tribal rights / Stephen L. Pevar.—2d ed., completely
rev. and up-to-date.
      p.   cm. — (An American Civil Liberties Union handbook)
    1. Indians of North America—Civil rights.   2. Indians of North
America—Legal status, laws, etc.   I. Title.   II. Series.
KF8210.C5P48   1992
342.73'0872—dc20
[347.302872]   91-11872
ISBN 0-8093-1768-0   CIP

The paper used in this publication meets the minimum requirements of
American National Standard for Information Sciences—Permanence of
Paper for Printed Library Materials, ANSI Z39.48-1984. ∞

Contents

Preface

This guide sets forth your rights under the present law and offers suggestions on how they can be protected. It is one of a continuing series of handbooks published in cooperation with the American Civil Liberties Union (ACLU).

Surrounding these publications is the hope that Americans, informed of their rights, will be encouraged to exercise them. Through their exercise, rights are given life. If they are rarely used, they may be forgotten and violations may become routine.

This guide offers no assurances that your rights will be respected. The laws may change, and in some of the subjects covered in these pages they change quite rapidly. An effort has been made to note those parts of the law where movement is taking place, but it is not always possible to predict accurately when the law *will* change.

Even if the laws remain the same, their interpretations by courts and administrative officials often vary. In a federal system such as ours, there is a built-in problem, since state and federal law differ, not to speak of the confusion between states. In addition, there are wide variations in the ways in which particular courts and administrative officials will interpret the same law at any given moment.

If you encounter what you consider to be a specific abuse of your rights, you should seek legal assistance. There are a number of agencies that may help you, among them ACLU affiliate offices, but bear in mind that the ACLU is a limited-purpose organization. In many communities, there are federally funded legal service offices that provide assistance to persons who cannot afford the costs of legal representation. In general, the rights that the ACLU defends are freedom of inquiry and expression; due process of law; equal protection of the laws; and privacy. The authors in this series have discussed other rights (even though they sometimes fall outside the ACLU's usual concern) in order to provide as much guidance as possible.

These books have been planned as guides for the people directly affected: thus the question-and-answer format. (In

some areas there are more detailed works available for experts.)
These guides seek to raise the major issues and inform the
nonspecialist of the basic law on the subject. The authors of
these books are themselves specialists who understand the
need for information at "street level."

If you encounter a specific legal problem in an area discussed
in one of these handbooks, show the book to your attorney. Of
course, he or she will not be able to rely exclusively on the
handbook to provide you with adequate representation. But if
your attorney hasn't had a great deal of experience in the
specific area, the handbook can provide helpful suggestions on
how to proceed.

> Norman Dorsen, Stokes Professor of Law,
> New York University School of Law

The principal purpose of this handbook, as well as others
in this series, is to inform individuals of their legal rights.
The authors from time to time suggest what the law
should be, but their personal views are not necessarily
those of the ACLU. For the ACLU's position on the
issues discussed in this handbook, the reader should write
to Public Education Department, ACLU, 132 West 43d
Street, New York, N.Y. 10036.

Acknowledgments

I would like to thank the people whose encouragement and support were so instrumental to the completion of this book. They include my immediate family—Laurel, Micki, Nathan, Peter, and Jeffrey—and my friends—Sara Seibert, Stephen Metcalf, Mark Perkell, Barbara Barton, King Golden, Larry Nault, Mike Butyn, and Hap Patz. I also wish to acknowledge some terrific people with whom I have had the pleasure of working for several years—Dorothy Davidson, Carolyn Daly, and Carol Hamilton. Finally, I wish to thank James B. Page for his helpful editorial assistance.

Introduction

The subject of Indian rights is complex and terribly confusing. There are thousands of treaties, statutes, executive orders, court decisions, and agency rulings that play integral roles. Indian law is a subject unto itself, having few parallels. As a subcommittee of the U.S. Senate noted in 1977:

> It is almost always a mistake to seek answers to Indian legal issues by making analogies to seemingly similar fields. General notions of civil rights law and public land law, for example, simply fail to resolve many questions relating to American Indian tribes and individuals. This extraordinary body of law and policy holds its own answers, which are often wholly unexpected to those unfamiliar with it.[1]

The subject of Indian rights is also highly controversial. Everyone familiar with it seems to have a strong opinion about it. Some people resent the fact that Indians have special hunting, fishing, and water rights, for example. Others feel that Indians are simply exercising rights which have always been theirs.

This book is not written with the idea that Indians deserve better treatment than other people do. It is dedicated instead to a principle: Every right you and I have was acquired at a significant cost, paid for either by us or by others to whom that right was worth fighting for. Yet unless we know what our rights are, we cannot exercise them, and unless we exercise them, we will lose them. The goal of this book is to help Indians and tribes exercise their rights, in the same way that everyone else is entitled to exercise theirs.

NOTE

1. American Indian Policy Review Commission, *Final Report* p. 99 (Washington, DC: Government Printing Office, 1977).

THE RIGHTS OF
INDIANS AND TRIBES

I

A History of Federal Indian Policy

More than four hundred independent nations were prospering in what is now the United States when Europeans first arrived there. By 1900 war and disease had reduced a population of nearly one million Indians* to three hundred thousand. Since 1900 the Indian population has increased to 1.5 million, nearly a third of whom are less than fifteen years old.[1]

Indians live in every state in the country and nearly half of the population lives on or near Indian reservations. There are some three hundred Indian reservations in the United States covering 52.4 million acres of land in twenty-seven states. Reservations range in size from the 15.4 million-acre Navajo reservation (about the size of West Virginia) to the one-quarter-acre Golden Hill reservation in Connecticut. Most Indians live west of the Mississippi River, but 25 percent live in the Northeast, and North Carolina has the fifth-largest Indian population of any state.[2]

Indians have the lowest life expectancy of any group in the country; as a whole, Indians live only two-thirds as long as the non-Indian population. Indians also suffer from a high rate of unemployment (which exceeds 70 percent on many reservations), and they fall well below the national average in income, quality of housing, and education (half the Indian population lacks a high school diploma).[3] "The red man continues to be the most poverty stricken and economically deprived segment of our population, a people whose plight dwarfs the situation of any other Americans, even those in the worst big city ghettos."[4]

---

* Considerable thought was given to using "Native American" rather than "Indian" in this book. Indian was chosen for several reasons. First, most Indians use Indian and Native American interchangeably, and most Indian organizations, including the National Congress of American Indians and the American Indian Movement, use Indian in their titles. Second, virtually all federal laws, such as the Indian Reorganization Act, and federal agencies, such as the Bureau of Indian Affairs, use Indian. Lastly, Native Americans include Hawaiians, and this book does not address their legal rights, but only the rights of Indians and their tribes.

Although conditions for Indians have improved somewhat in recent years, dramatic changes in the near future are unlikely due to the many problems associated with reservation life, cultural differences and persistent racial discrimination.

A central problem that Indians face today is the complex and confusing pattern of laws, especially federal laws, that dominate their lives. No other ethnic or cultural group is so heavily regulated. Although some federal laws were intended to benefit Indians, as a whole they have placed Indians in a political and economic straightjacket. Indians and Indian tribes are in such a precarious position today that economic survival would be difficult without major support from the federal government. This sad state of affairs is the result of two hundred years of federal government regulation.

The subject of this book is federal Indian law—the federal statutes, court decisions, and policies which influence or control so much of Indian life. This subject can be understood more easily if it is placed in historical perspective.[5] First it must be recognized that there has never been a consistent federal Indian policy. On the contrary, federal policy with respect to Indians has shifted during the past two hundred years from regarding tribes as sovereign equals, to relocating tribes, to attempts to exterminate or assimilate them, and currently, to encouraging tribal self-determination. These policy changes have often been rapid and are usually highly disruptive. Until recently, the most striking feature of federal Indian policy was the total lack of Indian involvement or consent in its formulation. A brief summary of these policy shifts will help to place current Indian law in its context.

A. 1492–1787: TRIBAL INDEPENDENCE

North America was inhabited by over four hundred independent nations when it was "discovered" by Columbus in 1492. Each nation controlled its own territory and had its own government, culture, and language. Columbus mistakenly thought that he had landed in the Indies and therefore the native peoples were called "Indians."

Most Indian tribes welcomed the arrival of the Europeans and allowed them to settle on their land. Treaties and agreements were made between the settlers and neighboring tribes in which European goods were exchanged for Indian land and friendship. Few settlements could have survived without the active support and protection of the Indians.

As these settlements grew in number, fights erupted over the control of land, especially between settlements occupied by different European countries. Invariably, each settlement attempted to enlist the support of nearby Indian tribes. A war erupted in 1763 between English and French settlers, known as the French and Indian War. The Iroquois Confederacy,[6] the most powerful group of Indians north of Mexico, sided with the English. Had they chosen differently, people in the United States might speak French today.[7]

B. 1787–1828: AGREEMENTS BETWEEN EQUALS

In the years immediately following the Revolutionary War, the United States government regarded Indian tribes as having the same status as foreign nations and every effort was made to obtain their allegiance. As the U.S. Supreme Court said in 1832, "[t]he early journals of Congress exhibit the most anxious desire to conciliate the Indian nations. . . . The most strenuous exertions were made to procure those supplies on which Indian friendships were supposed to depend; and everything which might excite hostility was avoided."[8] The Northwest Ordinance of 1787, ratified by Congress in 1789, declared: "The utmost good faith shall always be observed towards Indians; their land and property shall never be taken from them without their consent."[9]

The First Congress passed a number of laws to protect Indians from non-Indians. In 1790 Congress passed laws requiring that persons who wished to trade with Indians must obtain a federal license, authorizing the prosecution of non-Indians who committed certain crimes against Indians, and prohibiting non-Indians from obtaining Indian land without the consent of the United States.[10] In 1793 Congress prohibited non-Indians from settling on Indian lands, prohibited federal employees from trading with Indians, and exempted Indians from complying with state trade regulations.[11]

Unfortunately, few of these laws were enforced, particularly those which might have discouraged settlers from moving westward. The government consistently overlooked the forcible and illegal taking of Indian land. "The government meant to restrain and govern the advance of the whites, not to prevent it forever."[12]

C. 1828–87: RELOCATION OF THE INDIANS

Federal Indian policy changed abruptly in 1828 when Andrew Jackson became President of the United States. Jackson was well known for his military campaigns against Indians. Under Jackson's administration, what previously had been an unspoken policy now became a publicly stated goal: removal of the eastern Indian tribes to the West. This removal policy became "the dominant federal Indian policy of the nineteenth century."[13]

In 1830 Congress passed the Indian Removal Act,[14] which authorized the President to "negotiate" with eastern tribes for their relocation west of the Mississippi River. Between 1832 and 1843 most of the eastern tribes either had their lands reduced in size or were coerced into moving to the West. Many tribes, at first given "permanent" reservations in Arkansas, Kansas, Iowa, Illinois, Missouri, and Wisconsin, were forced to move even farther west to the Oklahoma Indian Territory. Indian treaties were broken by the government almost as soon as they were made.

The discovery of gold in California in 1848 brought thousands of settlers to the West and increased the desire for Indian land. Western tribes soon suffered the same fate as the eastern Indians: impoverished by military campaigns, they were forced to accept reservation life and became increasingly dependent upon government rations for survival.

Congress passed a number of laws during the mid-nineteenth century in order to increase federal control over Indians and to promote the Indians' assimilation into white society. Particular emphasis was placed on "educating" and "civilizing" Indian youth. By 1887 more than two hundred Indian schools had been established under federal supervision, with an enrollment of over fourteen thousand Indian students. The history of their authoritarian rule is notorious; for example, students were severely punished if they spoke their native language or practiced their traditions.[15] In addition, Congress placed federal agents on Indian reservations in order to increase its supervision over Indian activities and authorized federal courts to prosecute Indians who committed certain crimes against other Indians.[16]

Nearly a century after Congress passed the Northwest Ordinance in 1787, which acknowledged the sovereign integrity of Indian tribes, Congress passed a law which reflects the degree to which the tribes' status had diminished. In 1871 Congress eliminated the practice of making treaties with Indian tribes.[17] The federal government no longer considered Indian tribes as independent nations. Thereafter, Congress would deal with Indians by passing statutes, which, unlike treaties, did not require tribal consent.

D. 1887–1934: ALLOTMENT AND ASSIMILATION

In 1887 Congress passed the General Allotment Act,[18] also known as the Dawes Act. The ultimate purpose of the Dawes Act was to break up tribal governments, abolish Indian reservations, and force Indians to assimilate into white society.[19] Congress felt that Indians should learn how to farm. To accomplish this, Congress decided to divide communally held tribal lands into separate parcels, give each tribal member a parcel, and sell "surplus" parcels to white farmers. Congress hoped that this process would not only break up tribal relationships but that, if whites settled on Indian reservations, Indians would learn and adopt white ways.

The effect of the General Allotment Act on Indians was catastrophic. Most Indians did not want to abandon their communal society and adopt the way of life of a farmer. Further, much of the tribal land was unsuitable for small scale agriculture. Thousands of impoverished Indians sold their parcels of land to white settlers or lost their land in foreclosures when they were unable to pay state real estate taxes. Moreover, tribal government was seriously disrupted by the sudden presence of so many non-Indians on the reservation and by the huge decrease in the tribe's land base. Of the 140 million acres of land which tribes collectively owned in 1887, only 50 million acres remained in 1934 when the allotment system was abolished. Although Congress extended United States citizenship to all Indians in 1924,[20] this did little or nothing to improve their situation.

E. 1934–53: INDIAN REORGANIZATION

In the early 1930s federal Indian policy abruptly changed and a more humane and considerate approach was adopted. A number of factors precipitated the change. For one thing, the onset of the Great Depression all but eliminated the desire of whites to obtain additional Indian lands. It also had become widely recognized that the General Allotment Act was very harmful to the Indians, disrupting their reservations, their culture, and their well-being. Mounting public criticism of the federal government's Indian policies encouraged President Franklin D. Roosevelt to make some radical changes.[21]

In 1933 John Collier was appointed by Roosevelt as Commissioner of Indian Affairs. Collier, who had been personally involved in the Indian reform movement for more than a decade, declared in 1934: "No interference with Indian religious life or expression will hereafter be tolerated. The cultural history of Indians is in all respects to be considered equal to that of any non-Indian group."[22]

In June 1934 Congress passed the Indian Reorganization Act (IRA),[23] also known as the Wheeler-Howard Act. The express purpose of the IRA was "to rehabilitate the Indian's economic life and to give him a chance to develop the initiative destroyed by a century of oppression and paternalism."[24]

The IRA not only prohibited the further allotment of tribal land to individual Indians, it also authorized the Secretary of the Interior to add lands to existing reservations, to create new reservations for landless tribes, and to restore to tribal ownership any land that had been removed as surplus under the General Allotment Act and not as yet sold to non-Indians. Indian tribes were encouraged to adopt their own constitutions, to become federally chartered corporations, and to assert their inherent powers of local self-government. The act established a $10 million revolving credit fund from which loans could be made to incorporated tribes. Finally, the act required the

Secretary of the Interior to give Indians a preference in employment within the Bureau of Indian Affairs. This way, Indians would have some influence in administering, if not in formulating, federal Indian policy.

Between 1935 and 1953 Indian landholdings increased by over two million acres, and federal funds were spent for on-reservation health facilities, irrigation works, roads, homes, and community schools. Unfortunately, the onset of World War II diverted the federal government's attention to other problems, and Indian economic well-being once again began to decline.

F. 1953–68: TERMINATION

During the 1950s Congress made another abrupt change in policy, abandoning the goals of the Indian Reorganization Act and ending its efforts to improve Indian economic life. The new policy Congress adopted brought Indian tribes to the brink of economic collapse. This new policy was called *termination*: the termination of federal benefits and support services to certain Indian tribes and the forced dissolution of their reservations.[25]

In 1953 Congress adopted House Concurrent Resolution No. 108, which declared that federal benefits and services to various Indian tribes should be ended "at the earliest possible time." In the decade that followed, Congress terminated its assistance to over one hundred tribes. Each of these tribes was ordered to distribute its land and property to its members and to dissolve its government.

In an effort to reduce federal responsibility even further, Congress passed Public Law 83–280,[26] generally known as P.L. 280. This statute conferred upon certain designated states full criminal and some civil jurisdiction over Indian reservations and consented to the assumption of such jurisdiction by any additional state that chose to accept it. State governments had long resented the notion of tribal sovereignty and had made repeated efforts to gain control over Indian resources and people. P.L. 280 thus gave powers and responsibilities to the states—the traditional enemy of Indian tribes—that previously had been assumed by the federal government.

G. 1968– : TRIBAL SELF-DETERMINATION

In 1968 President Johnson declared: "We must affirm the rights of the first Americans to remain Indians while exercising their rights as Americans. We must affirm their rights to freedom of choice and self-determination."[27]

Federal Indian policy thus shifted its course once again. President Nixon, who had been Vice-President during the termination era, expressly denounced the termination policy in 1970 and stated: "This, then, must be the goal of any new national policy toward the Indian people: to strengthen the Indian sense of autonomy without threatening his sense of community."[28]

Since the late 1960s, Congress has passed a number of statutes that foster Indian self-determination and economic development. In 1968 Congress prohibited states from acquiring any authority over Indian reservations without the consent of the affected tribe.[29] An Indian Business Development Fund was created by Congress to stimulate Indian business and employment.[30] The Indian Financing Act,[31] which established a revolving loan fund, and the Native American Programs Act,[32] another loan program, were designed to develop Indian resources. The Indian Self-Determination and Education Assistance Act of 1975,[33] perhaps the single most important piece of Indian legislation since the Indian Reorganization Act, allows Indian tribes to administer the federal government's Indian programs on their reservation, and many tribes have used this opportunity to rid themselves of unnecessary federal domination. The Indian Mineral Development Act of 1982[34] gives tribes the flexibility to enter into joint-venture agreements with mineral developers in order to maximize the tribes' financial return from their mineral resources. The Indian Tribal Government Tax Status Act of 1982[35] extends to Indian tribes many of the tax advantages enjoyed by the states, such as the ability to issue tax exempt bonds to finance government programs. The Indian Gaming Regulatory Act of 1988[36] authorizes Indian tribes to engage in gaming, such as bingo, to raise revenue and promote economic development.

Thus, Congress has repudiated the termination policies of the 1950s. As the Supreme Court noted in 1983, "both the tribes and the federal government are firmly committed to the goal of promoting tribal self-government, a goal embodied in numerous federal statutes."[37]

H. THE FUTURE

The future of federal Indian policy is impossible to predict. During the past forty years alone, Congress has radically altered its Indian policies three times. Although current policy is aimed at strengthening tribal self-government, this can change at any time.

In recent years Indian tribes have increasingly asserted their treaty and statutory rights. Such activity is bitterly opposed by certain non-Indian groups, some of which are aggressively seeking the enactment of federal laws abolishing Indian and tribal rights. In fact, the failure of these groups, some of which are well financed, to push through harmful Indian legislation is itself a significant victory for Indian interests. A recent Senate commission report endorses the continued strengthening of tribal governments:

> The long-term objective of Federal-Indian policy [should] be the development of tribal governments into fully operational governments exercising the same powers and shouldering the same responsibilities as other local governments. This objective should be pursued in a flexible manner which will respect and accommodate the unique cultural and social attributes of the individual Indian tribes.[38]

In 1983 President Reagan reaffirmed the federal government's policy of promoting tribal self-determination: "This administration intends to restore tribal governments to their rightful place among governments of this nation and to enable tribal governments, along with State and local governments, to resume control over their own affairs."[39] This policy should be pursued in the future.

NOTES

1. American Indian Policy Review Commission, *Final Report* pp. 89–90 (Washington, DC: Government Printing Office, 1977).

2. *Id.*, pp. 90–91.

3. *Id.*, pp. 91–93.

4. R. Strickland, *Genocide-At-Law: An Historic and Contemporary View of the Native American Experience*, 34 U. Kan. L. Rev. 713, 716 (1986).

5. For additional information on the history of federal Indian policy, see F. Prucha, *The Great Father: The United States Government and the American Indians* (Lincoln: Univ. of Nebraska Press, 1984); S. L. Tyler, *A History of Indian Policy* (Washington, DC: Government Printing Office, 1973), and the extensive bibliography cited at 281–309.

6. The composition and influence of the Iroquois Confederacy is discussed in ch. 15, sec. D.

7. *See* C. Colden, *History of the Five Indian Nations* (Ithaca, NY: Cornell Univ. Press, 1958).

8. *Worcester v. Georgia,* 31 U.S. 515, 548 (1832).

9. Act of Aug. 7, 1789, 1 Stat. 50.

10. 1 Stat. 137, codified as 25 U.S.C. Secs. 68 and 177.

11. 1 Stat. 329.

12. F. Prucha, *American Indian Policy in the Formative Years* p. 187 (Cambridge, MA: Harvard Univ. Press, 1962). *See also* Tyler, note 5 above, pp. 48–51.

13. V. Deloria, *American Indian Policy in the Twentieth Century* p. 242 (Norman, OK: Univ. of Oklahoma Press, 1985).

14. 4 Stat. 411.

15. Tyler, note 5 above, p. 88; Strickland, note 4 above, p. 729.

16. 23 Stat. 362, 385, codified with amendments as 18 U.S.C. Sec. 1153.

17. 16 Stat. 544, 566 codified as 25 U.S.C. Sec. 71.

18. 24 Stat. 388, as amended, 25 U.S.C. Secs. 331–58.

19. For an extended discussion of the General Allotment Act see Tyler, note 5 above, pp. 95–104; D. Otis, *The Dawes Act and the Allotment of Indian Lands* (1973). *See also Hodel v. Irving,* 481 U.S. 704 (1987).

20. 43 Stat. 253, codified as 8 U.S.C. Sec. 1401(a)(2).

21. *See* Tyler, note 5 above, pp. 112–22.

22. *Annual Report,* Commissioner of Indian Affairs, 1934, p. 90.

23. 48 Stat. 984, codified as 25 U.S.C. Secs. 461 *et seq.*

24. H.R. Rep. No. 1804, 73d Cong., 2d Sess., p. 6 (1934). *See also* 25 U.S.C. Sec. 450.

25. Termination is discussed in detail in ch. 5, sec. B. *See also* Tyler, note 5 above, pp. 168–81.

26. 67 Stat. 488, codified as 18 U.S.C. Sec. 1162, 28 U.S.C. Sec. 1360. P.L. 280 is discussed at length in ch. 7.

27. Presidential Documents, Weekly Compilation of, 1968, vol. IV, no. 10 (Washington, DC: Government Printing Office).

28. Message from the President of the United States, 1970, "Recommendations for Indian Policy" (Washington, DC: Government Printing Office).

29. 25 U.S.C. Sec. 1322.

30. 25 U.S.C. Secs. 1521 *et seq.*

31. 25 U.S.C. Secs. 1451 *et seq.*

32. 42 U.S.C. Secs. 2991 *et seq.*

33. Pub. L. No. 93–638, codified as 25 U.S.C. Secs. 450f *et seq.* and in scattered sections of 5, 25, 42, and 50 U.S.C.

34. 25 U.S.C. Secs. 2101–8.

35. Pub. L. No. 97–473, 96 Stat. 2607 (codified as amended in scattered sections of 26 U.S.C.).

36. 25 U.S.C. Secs. 2701–21.

37. *New Mexico v. Mescalero Apache Tribe,* 462 U.S. 324, 334–35 (1983).

38. *Final Report,* note 1 above, p. 13.

39. President's Statement on Indian Policy, 1983, Pub. Papers 96, 99 (1984).

II

Definitions: "Indian," "Indian Tribe," "Indian Country," and "Indian Title"

A. "INDIAN"

Who is an "Indian"?

There is no universally accepted definition of the term "Indian." Therefore, determining who is an Indian is difficult. For example, people who have one-quarter Indian blood and three-quarters Caucasian blood could call themselves either Indian or Caucasian.

The term "Indian" can be defined in either an ethnological (racial) or in a legal sense.[1] Indians are a distinct race of people, as are Caucasians. Ethnologists would classify a person as being an Indian only if that person has more than one-half Indian blood.

Although there is one ethnological definition of Indian, there are many legal definitions. Different laws use different definitions. Some federal laws define an Indian as anyone of Indian descent, while other laws require one-fourth or one-half Indian blood in order to be considered as an Indian for purposes of those laws. Still other federal laws define Indian as anyone who has been accepted as a member of a "federally recognized" Indian tribe.[2]

Many federal laws use the word "Indian" without defining it. This allows federal agencies to decide who is an Indian under those laws. Some agencies have been accused of defining Indian too narrowly, thereby depriving people of benefits that Congress intended them to receive.[3] When Congress has not defined the term, courts have used a two-part test to determine who is an Indian. First, the person must have some Indian blood, that is, some identifiable Indian ancestry. Second, the Indian community must recognize this person as an Indian.[4]

These varying legal standards have caused confusion and inconsistency. As an example, a person may qualify as an "Indian" for educational benefits and not qualify for health benefits. The Census Bureau takes a simple approach to these problems. The bureau lists every person as an Indian who claims to be one.

Each Indian tribe has eligibility requirements for enrollment. Most tribes require that a person have at least one-fourth tribal blood to become a member. Some tribes require as much as one-half tribal blood, while others require one-sixteenth. Although these requirements determine tribal membership, they do not necessarily determine who is an Indian for other purposes. To be considered an Indian for federal purposes, an individual must have some Indian blood. A non-Indian who is adopted into an Indian tribe is not an Indian under federal law.[5] However, under certain federal laws small amounts of Indian blood, together with recognition as an Indian by the Indian community, will qualify a person as an Indian.[6]

The fact that the federal government does not recognize a person as an Indian does not prevent a tribe from considering that person an Indian for tribal purposes.[7] Similarly, lack of tribal membership does not prevent a person from being recognized as an Indian under most federal laws.[8] Most federal laws require only that a person have one-fourth or more Indian blood to be considered an Indian. Thus, a person can have more Caucasian blood than Indian blood and still be an Indian for federal purposes.

Are the native people of Alaska, including the Eskimos and Aleuts, considered Indians?

The native people of Alaska are comprised of three groups: Eskimos, Aleuts, and American Indians. Eskimos and Aleuts are ethnologically distinct from, but related to, the American Indian. Eskimos and Aleuts constitute the majority of Alaska's native population.

Most federal laws relating to Indians expressly apply to Eskimos and Aleuts also.[9] The Supreme Court has held that Congress has the same authority to regulate Eskimos and Aleuts as it does the Indians.[10] Throughout this book, and in other books discussing federal Indian law, the term "Indian" generally applies to the Eskimo and Aleut as well as the American Indian. There are a number of laws, however, which apply only to Alaska natives. These are discussed in chapter 15, section B.

Can an Indian be a citizen of both the United States and of an Indian tribe?

Yes. In 1924 Congress extended United States citizenship to all Indians born in the United States.[11] Many Indians had become citizens before this time by treaty or federal statute. In 1905 the Supreme Court held that Indians who had been granted U.S. citizenship could not participate in federal Indian programs.[12] Eleven years later, the Court reversed that decision.[13] It is now established that an Indian can be both a citizen of the United States and a member of an Indian tribe and have all the benefits and obligations that arise out of that dual capacity.

B. "INDIAN TRIBE"

What constitutes an "Indian tribe"?

As with the term "Indian," the term "Indian tribe" has more than one definition. Ethnologists define an Indian tribe as a group of Indians who share a common heritage and speak a distinct language. However, the legal definition is open to debate. The federal government does not recognize many groups that claim to be Indian tribes. In fact, the federal government officially recognizes less than three hundred of the more than four hundred tribes that claim to exist.[14]

A tribe normally will be recognized by the federal government if Congress or the President at some point created a reservation for the tribe and the United States has had some continuing political relationship with the tribe.[15] Tribes may be denied federal recognition for several reasons. Some tribes were terminated, as explained in the previous chapter, and therefore are ineligible for federal recognition. Other tribes, in the opinion of the federal government, at some point lacked a unifying leadership or lost their tribal identity and thereby lost their tribal status. The government will not recognize these tribes even though their descendants today wish to pursue the tribe's heritage.[16] The government's refusal to recognize certain tribes has caused great controversy and bitterness.

A group of Indians can call itself a tribe and be recognized as such by other tribes. However, to qualify for the many benefits which Congress has made available to federally recognized tribes, the group must satisfy the requirements for recognition established by the Department of the Interior. (These requirements are discussed in chapter 15, section E.)

Federal recognition by the Interior Department guarantees that an Indian tribe can participate in federal Indian programs. However, a denial of federal recognition does not necessarily disqualify a tribe from all of these programs. Indians, for instance, can still enforce a treaty that their ancestors made with the United States even though the federal government refuses to recognize the continued existence of the tribe.[17] Similarly, tribes not officially recognized by the Department of the Interior may participate in some federal programs that do not limit eligibility to "recognized" tribes.[18]

Tribes may also be defined in terms of their political identity. On occasion the federal government has placed different ethnological tribes on the same reservation, and these tribes have taken on a single political identity.[19] An example is the Fort Belknap Indian Community in Montana, which, though viewed as one tribe politically, is composed of the culturally distinct Gros Ventre and Assiniboine tribes. Also, single ethnological tribes that were divided and placed on different reservations have obtained separate political identities. Various bands of Sioux, Chippewa, and Shoshone were placed on separate reservations and are now treated as different tribes politically.

Is an Indian "nation" different from an Indian "tribe"?

The terms "nation," "tribe," and "band" have been used interchangeably in Indian treaties and statutes. The term "nation" usually refers to a government independent from any other government, possessing the power of absolute dominion over its territory and people.

Technically, Indian tribes are no longer nations because their governmental authority has been restricted by the United States government.[20] Some tribal governments, however, continue to call themselves "nations" rather than "tribes." This designation reflects the belief, shared by a number of people, that the United States has no right to exercise any power or authority over Indian tribes. This subject is further discussed in chapter 5.

C. "INDIAN COUNTRY"

Broadly speaking, Indian country is all the land under the supervision of the United States government that has been set aside primarily for the use of Indians. This would include all Indian reservations as well as any other areas under federal jurisdiction and designated for Indian use. As a general rule, state jurisdiction does not extend to Indian country and, instead, tribal and federal law governs. If someone says, "The crime took place in Indian country," this implies that tribal or federal law governs the crime, and the state has no jurisdiction. Thus, a great deal depends on whether an area is Indian country or not. The Indian country designation "is the benchmark for approaching the allocation of federal, tribal, and state authority with respect to Indians and Indian lands."[21]

The term "Indian country" was first used by Congress in 1790 to describe the territory controlled by Indians.[22] Today a federal statute concerning criminal jurisdiction provides the federal government's definition of this term. This law, Title 18, U.S. Code, section 1151 (18 U.S.C. § 1151), states:

> "Indian country" . . . means (a) all land within the limits of any Indian reservation under the jurisdiction of the United States government, notwithstanding the issuance of any patent, and including rights-of-way running through the reservation, (b) all dependent Indian communities within the borders of the United States whether within the original or subsequently acquired territory thereof, and whether within or without the limits of a state, and (c) all Indian allotments, the Indian titles to which have not been extinguished, including rights-of-way running through the same.

Although "Indian country" is defined in a criminal law, the concept of Indian country also applies to noncriminal (civil) cases as well. Just as most crimes by Indians within Indian country are governed by tribal or federal and not state law, so are such civil matters as divorce, inheritance, taxation, child custody, and contract disputes, where Indians are involved.[23] Proof that an area is Indian country often involves complicated historical facts; such proof is an issue of law to be decided by a judge rather than a jury.[24]

Section 1151 identifies three areas as being "Indian country." First, Indian country includes *all* lands within the boundaries of an Indian reservation, regardless of ownership. Thus, land located within a reservation but owned by a non-Indian is Indian country.[25] (There is one exception to this rule, which is discussed below.) Even rights-of-way through reservation lands, such as state or federal highways, remain a part of Indian country.[26] Thus, whenever the federal government sets aside land under federal supervision for Indians, the land becomes Indian country. This is true even if there is no official proclamation that a reservation is being created,[27] even if years go by before the tribe defends its property interests,[28] and even if the land is owned by the tribe in fee, that is, it is not federally owned trust land.[29]

Second, Indian country includes "all dependent Indian communities" within the United States.[30] A dependent Indian community is any area of land which has been set aside by the federal government for the use, occupancy or benefit of Indians, even if it is not part of a reservation.[31] The Pueblos of New Mexico, whose lands are owned by the tribes themselves but are under federal supervision, is an excellent example.[32] Other examples include tribal housing projects located on federal land[33] and federal schools operated for Indian children on federal land.[34] However, predominant Indian use by itself will not create a dependent Indian community. There must also be some evidence of federal or tribal control or supervision and an indication that the federal government intended to set the area apart primarily for Indian use.[35]

Finally, section 1151 includes as Indian country all "trust" and all "restricted" allotments of land, whether or not these allotments are inside an Indian reservation.[36] (A trust allotment is federal land which has been set aside for the exclusive use of an Indian, who is called the "allottee." A restricted allotment is land for which federal approval must be obtained before it can be sold, leased, or mortgaged, whether the land is owned by the federal government or not. These terms are further discussed in chapter 10.) Even a "non-trust" allotment outside the reservation is considered Indian country for as long as the allottee retains ownership.[37] (A non-trust allotment is land the federal government has given to an Indian with full rights of ownership, as opposed to a trust allotment, ownership of which is retained by the United States.) Thus, even if the federal government has eliminated a tribe's reservation but trust land still exists, either tribally or individually held, this trust land is Indian country.[38]

To summarize, all land within an Indian reservation is Indian country, even land owned by a non-Indian. In addition, trust and restricted Indian allotments outside a reservation are considered Indian country, and so are dependent Indian communities.

There is, however, one exception to the rule that all land within a reservation is Indian country. Privately owned land that can be classified as a "non-Indian community" is not Indian country for purposes of federal liquor laws.[39] The state, rather than the tribe or the federal government, has jurisdiction to regulate the introduction of liquor in non-Indian communities even though these communities are within the boundaries of an Indian reservation.

Exactly what constitutes a non-Indian community within a reservation is somewhat unclear. The term is not defined in the statute which uses it, nor in any other statute. Over the years several liquor stores owned by non-Indians and located within Indian reservations have claimed to be exempt from tribal liquor regulations because they were located in a non-Indian community.[40] One of these challenges reached the Supreme Court, which held that the store was not located in a non-Indian community because the majority of the people who lived in the vicinity were Indians and tribal headquarters were located nearby.[41] In another case a federal court held that a liquor establishment was located in a non-Indian community because most residents of the area were non-Indian, the area had a history of being owned and controlled by non-Indians, and no tribal offices or housing projects were located nearby.[42]

Are non-Indians permitted to live within Indian country?

Yes. Many non-Indians live within Indian country. (As explained in chapter 1, the federal government sold a large amount of reservation land to non-Indians between 1887 and 1934.) In a recent case, the Supreme Court noted that only 19 percent of the population of the Flathead Indian Reservation in Montana is Indian. Nevertheless, the entire reservation retains its status as Indian country.[43]

What is an Indian reservation?

An Indian reservation is land that has been set aside by the federal government for the use, possession, and benefit of an Indian tribe or group of Indians. Most reservations were created by some formal means, such as a treaty, presidential order, or act of Congress. Some were created by implication, when Congress took action that implied ownership of certain land by a particular tribe.[44]

All land within the boundaries of an Indian reservation is "Indian country" (with one exception, already explained). It makes no difference if the reservation was created from lands that had not been recently or continuously inhabited by Indians.[45] Although the terms "Indian reservation" and "Indian country" are often used interchangeably, they are not the same. Indian country includes Indian trust land and dependent Indian communities even when located *outside* a reservation.

D. "INDIAN TITLE"

What is "Indian title"?

The doctrine of Indian title is one of the most complicated and controversial doctrines in Indian law.[46]

Soon after the United States gained its independence from European control, the Supreme Court had to determine who owned the land still occupied by the Indians: the Indians or the United States government. The Court decided this question in *Johnson v. McIntosh* (1823).[47] The specific issue in that case was whether a non-Indian who purchased land from an Indian tribe had obtained a valid title. Obviously, the purchaser could acquire only that interest which the tribe could legally sell.

The Supreme Court held that the buyer did not acquire valid title because the land no longer was owned by the tribe. The United States government had become the owner of all the land within the United States by virtue of the European "discovery" of the North American continent and the "conquest" of its inhabitants. It did not matter to the Court, apparently, that Europeans had not discovered North America and certainly had not conquered all the Indians living there. We can assume the Court made the decision as it did because a contrary ruling would have meant that most of the United States still belonged to the Indians.

The Court went on to hold, though, that the Indians retained a "right of occupancy" in their ancestral homelands, a right which was superior to all claims other than those of the federal government. The federal government could extinguish this "Indian title" at will, but until it did so, the Indians had the right to remain on their original homelands.

Indian title is sometimes called "aboriginal title" and "Indian right of occupancy." As explained in *Johnson v. McIntosh* and in later cases, the essential principles of Indian title are the following: (1) the federal government acquired ownership of all land within the United States by discovery and conquest, (2) Indians retain a perpetual right to live on their ancestral homelands until such time as Congress decides to take this land for another purpose, (3) Indian title is a possessory interest, that is to say, Indians have a right to possess their ancestral homelands but not to own it unless Congress gives them title to it, and (4) Indian title cannot be sold by the Indians or bought by anyone else without authorization from the federal government.[48]

In order to prove Indian title, a tribe is not required to rely on a treaty or other form of official government recognition. It need only show by historical evidence that the land in question was part of its ancestral homelands and was occupied and controlled exclusively by it.[49] (A tribe can permit other tribes to share its land without losing aboriginal title to it, but lands continuously wandered over by adverse tribes cannot be claimed by any of these tribes as aboriginal lands.)[50] The tribal interest in continued occupancy is so important that the tribe is entitled to bring a court action to eject trespassers,[51] the federal government has an obligation to help the tribe eject trespassers,[52] and a court must recognize a tribe's Indian title unless it is clear that Congress intended to abolish the tribe's interest.[53] For example, even if the United States sells ancestral tribal land to a railroad, the railroad takes that land subject to aboriginal Indian title unless Congress clearly intended otherwise.[54] Indian title includes the right not only to occupy the property but the right to use such natural resources as water and timber, as well as the right to hunt and fish, on the property.[55]

Indian title is an important protection. In several recent

cases, federal courts have recognized that Indian tribes can eject persons, including state and local officials,[56] from lands claimed under Indian title, even when the non-Indian "owners" of these lands could trace their "titles" back one hundred and fifty years during which time Indians did not occupy the territory.[57] The fact is, unless aboriginal title has been extinguished by Congress, any grant or conveyance of the property, whether by the Indian tribe, the United States, a state, or any other party, is subject to the tribe's superior right of occupancy.

When the federal government extinguishes Indian title, must it compensate the tribe for destroying its occupancy rights?

Not always. Every tribe has the right to occupy its ancestral homelands until Congress decides otherwise, and this right of occupancy is known as Indian title. However, there are two kinds of Indian title—"aboriginal Indian title" and "recognized Indian title." The latter carries one legal right that the former does not: the right to compensation if the title is removed.

Indian title becomes "recognized" only when Congress has taken some action, whether by treaty, statute, or agreement, which confers upon the tribe a right to permanent occupancy. If a tribe can show clear congressional intent, such as a treaty guarantee, to grant the tribe the right to permanently occupy a specific territory, then this property interest becomes "recognized." Any subsequent "taking" of this interest must be compensated under the Just Compensation Clause of the Fifth Amendment to the U.S. Constitution.[58] For example, a tribe is entitled to be compensated if it has a treaty guarantee of permanent occupancy and the United States then places a second tribe on the reservation.[59] On the other hand, Indian title that has not been "specifically recognized as ownership" by Congress "may be extinguished by the Government without compensation."[60]

The Supreme Court has been criticized for holding that Indian title is not protected by the Fifth Amendment unless it has been recognized by some formal governmental act.[61] In enacting the Alaska Native Claims Settlement Act of 1971, Congress decided to compensate Alaska natives for all claims based upon Indian title, whether "recognized" or not.[62] In so doing, Congress decided to satisfy its moral obligations rather than take advantage of legal loopholes. Unfortunately, Congress has not always been so honorable.[63]

Can individual Indians claim Indian title to land?

Yes. Individual Indians who can show that their lineal descendants held and exclusively occupied, as individuals, a particular tract of land from time immemorial and that this title has never been extinguished by Congress have a continued possessory interest (Indian title) to that land.[64]

Can the courts reverse a Congressional decision to extinguish Indian title?

No. In 1941 a unanimous Supreme Court held that extinguishment of Indian title by Congress is not subject to review by the courts.[65] The power of Congress in this regard is supreme. Neither the manner, the method, nor the time of extinguishment can be challenged. A court can only determine whether the Indian title being extinguished is recognized title for which compensation must be paid; a court cannot prevent the extinguishment. However, only Congress can extinguish Indian title. Neither the President nor any government agency can extinguish Indian title, even aboriginal Indian title.[66]

NOTES

1. *See* F. Cohen, *Handbook of Federal Indian Law* pp. 19–24 (1982).
2. *See, e.g.,* 25 U.S.C. Sec. 479. The concept of federal recognition is discussed later in this chapter.
3. *See, e.g., Zarr v. Barlow,* 800 F.2d 1484 (9th Cir. 1986) (invalidating an agency regulation requiring one-quarter Indian blood for educational benefits). *See also* K. Funke, *Education Assistance and Employment Preference,* 4 Am. Indian L. Rev. 1 (1976).
4. *U.S. v. Broncheau,* 597 F.2d 1260, 1263 (9th Cir.), *cert. denied,* 444 U.S. 859 (1979); *U.S. v. Dodge,* 538 F.2d 770, 776 (8th Cir. 1976), *cert. denied,* 429 U.S. 1099 (1977).
5. *U.S. v. Rogers,* 45 U.S. 566 (1846); *State v. Attebery,* 519 P.2d 53 (Ariz. 1974).
6. *Sully v. U.S.,* 195 F. 113 (8th Cir. 1912); *Makah Indian Tribe v. Callam County,* 440 P.2d 442 (Wash. 1968); *Dodge,* note 4 above.
7. *Nofire v. U.S.,* 164 U.S. 657 (1897).

8. *Halbert v. U.S.*, 283 U.S. 753 (1931). Congress determines who is an Indian for federal purposes, not the tribe. *Simmons v. Eagle Seelatsee*, 244 F. Supp. 808, 813–15 (E.D. Wash. 1965), *aff'd per curiam*, 384 U.S. 209 (1966).

9. *See, e.g.*, 25 U.S.C. Sec. 479.

10. *Alaska Pacific Fisheries v. U.S.*, 248 U.S. 78 (1918).

11. 42 Stat. 253, codified as 8 U.S.C. Sec. 1401(a)(2).

12. *In re Heff*, 197 U.S. 488 (1905).

13. *U.S. v. Nice*, 241 U.S. 591 (1916).

14. American Indian Policy Review Commission, *Final Report* p. 461 (Washington, DC: Government Printing Office, 1977).

15. *See* Cohen, note 1 above, p. 6; *Mashpee Tribe v. Secretary of the Interior*, 820 F.2d 480, 484 (1st Cir. 1987).

16. *Mashpee Tribe*, note 15 above; *James v. Watt*, 716 F.2d 71 (1st Cir. 1983), *cert. denied*, 467 U.S. 1209 (1984).

17. *U.S. v. Washington*, 384 F. Supp. 312, 406 (W.D. Wash. 1974), *aff'd*, 520 F.2d 676 (9th Cir. 1975), *cert. denied*, 423 U.S. 1086 (1976).

18. *Joint Tribal Council of Passamoquoddy Tribe v. Morton*, 528 F.2d 370 (1st Cir. 1975); *State v. Dana*, 404 A.2d 551 (Me. 1979), *cert. denied*, 444 U.S. 1098 (1980); *Cook Inlet Native Ass'n v. Bowen*, 810 F.2d 1471 (9th Cir. 1987).

19. When this occurs, a member of one tribe can acquire certain rights in the other tribe that otherwise would not have been available. *See Williams v. Clark*, 742 F.2d 549 (9th Cir. 1984), *cert. denied sub nom. Elvrum v. Williams*, 471 U.S. 1015 (1985).

20. *See* ch. 5, section A.

21. *Indian Country, U.S.A., Inc. v. Oklahoma Tax Comm'n*, 829 F.2d 967, 973 (10th Cir. 1987), *cert. denied sub nom. Oklahoma Tax Comm'n v. Muscogee (Creek) Nation*, 487 U.S. 1218 (1988).

22. 1 Stat. 137.

23. Criminal jurisdiction in Indian country is discussed in ch. 8 and civil jurisdiction in ch. 9.

24. *U.S. v. Levesque*, 681 F.2d 75, 78 (1st Cir.), *cert. denied*, 459 U.S. 1089 (1982); *U.S. v. Sohappy*, 770 F.2d 816 (9th Cir. 1985), *cert. denied*, 477 U.S. 906 (1986). *See also Alaska v. Native Village of Venetie*, 856 F.2d 1384 (9th Cir. 1988).

25. 18 U.S.C. Sec. 1151(a). *See Seymour v. Superintendent*, 368 U.S. 351 (1962); *U.S. v. John*, 437 U.S. 634 (1978).

26. 18 U.S.C. Sec. 1151(c). *See Gourneau v. Smith*, 207 N.W.2d 256 (N.D. 1973).

27. *U.S. v. John*, 437 U.S. 634 (1978); *Langley v. Ryder*, 778 F.2d 1092, 1094–95 (5th Cir. 1985).

28. *Indian Country, U.S.A.*, note 21 above.

29. *Id.*
30. 18 U.S.C. Sec. 1151(b).
31. *U.S. v. Sandoval*, 231 U.S. 28 (1913); *U.S. v. McGowan*, 302 U.S. 535 (1938); *U.S. v. Martine*, 442 F.2d 1022 (10th Cir. 1971).
32. *Sandoval*, note 31 above; *State v. Warner*, 379 P.2d 66 (N.M. 1963).
33. *U.S. v. South Dakota*, 665 F.2d 837 (8th Cir. 1981), *cert. denied*, 459 U.S. 823 (1983); *Martine*, note 31 above.
34. *C.M.G. v. Oklahoma*, 594 P.2d 798 (Okla. Ct. App.), *cert. denied*, 444 U.S. 992 (1979).
35. *U.S. v. South Dakota*, note 33 above; *Martine*, note 31 above; *Levesque*, note 24 above.
36. 18 U.S.C. Sec. 1151(c). *See U.S. v. Ramsey*, 271 U.S. 467 (1926); *Beardslee v. U.S.*, 387 F.2d 280 (8th Cir. 1967).
37. *State v. Moss*, 471 P.2d 333 (Wyo. 1970); *Hollow Horn Bear v. Jameson*, 95 N.W.2d 181 (S.D. 1959).
38. *DeCoteau v. District County Court*, 420 U.S. 425, 427, 429 (1975); *Oklahoma Tax Comm'n v. Citizen Band Potawatomi Indian Tribe*, 111 S.Ct. 905 (1991); *Ahboah v. Housing Authority of Kiowa Tribe*, 660 P.2d 625 (Okla. 1983); *Ramsey*, note 36 above.
39. 18 U.S.C. Secs. 1151(a), 1154(c), and 1156.
40. *U.S. v. Mazurie*, 419 U.S. 544 (1975); *Berry v. Arapaho and Shoshone Tribes*, 420 F. Supp. 934 (D. Wyo. 1976); *U.S. v. Morgan*, 614 F.2d 166 (8th Cir. 1980).
41. *Mazurie*, note 40 above.
42. *Morgan*, note 40 above. *See also Blatchford v. Gonzales*, 670 P.2d 944 (N.M. 1983), *cert. denied*, 464 U.S. 1033 (1984).
43. *Moe v. Confederated Salish and Kootenai Tribes*, 425 U.S. 463 (1976).
44. *Minnesota v. Hitchcock*, 185 U.S. 373, 390 (1902); *Sac and Fox Tribe of Mississippi*, 596 F.2d 145 (8th Cir. 1978), *cert. denied*, 439 U.S. 955 (1978).
45. *Donnelly v. U.S.*, 228 U.S. 243 (1913); *Alaska Pacific Fisheries*, note 10 above.
46. *See* J. Y. Henderson, *Unraveling the Riddle of Aboriginal Title*, 5 Am. Indian L. Rev. 75 (1977).
47. 21 U.S. 543 (1823).
48. *See U.S. v. Santa Fe Pacific R.R. Co.*, 314 U.S. 339 (1941); *Tee-Hit-Ton Indians v. U.S.*, 348 U.S. 272 (1955); *Oneida Indian Nation v. County of Oneida*, 414 U.S. 661 (1974). For a critical review of these decisions, see Henderson, note 46 above.
49. *Santa Fe*, note 48 above. *See also Six Nations v. U.S.*, 173 Ct. Cl. 899, 911 (1965).
50. *Santa Fe*, note 48 above, 314 U.S. at 345.
51. *Oneida Indian Nation*, note 48 above.

52. *Santa Fe*, note 48 above; *Tee-Hit-Ton*, note 48 above.

53. *Santa Fe*, note 48 above.

54. *Id. See also Lac Courte Oreilles Band of Lake Superior Chippewa Indians v. Voight*, 700 F.2d 341 (7th Cir.), *cert. denied*, 464 U.S. 805 (1983).

55. *See* cases cited in *U.S. v. Adair*, 723 F.2d 1394, 1413–14 (9th Cir. 1983), *cert. denied*, 467 U.S. 1252 (1984).

56. *Oneida Indian Nation*, note 48 above.

57. *Catawba Indian Tribe v. South Carolina*, 718 F.2d 1291 (4th Cir.), *cert. denied*, 109 S.Ct. 3190 (1989). *But see Oneida Indian Nation of New York v. New York*, 860 F.2d 1145 (2d Cir. 1988), *cert. denied*, 110 S.Ct. 200 (1989) (during the pre-Constitution Confederal period, a state could extinguish Indian title.)

58. *Tee-Hit-Ton*, note 48 above; *Shoshone Tribe of Indians v. U.S.*, 299 U.S. 476 (1937). However, once the tribe has been paid, Indian title is extinguished. *United States v. Dann*, 873 F.2d 1189, 1194 (9th Cir. 1989).

59. *Shoshone Tribe*, note 58 above. *See also Santa Fe*, note 48 above.

60. *Tee-Hit-Ton*, note 48 above, 348 U.S. at 289. *See also Inupiat Community of the Arctic Slope v. U.S.*, 680 F.2d 122 (Ct. Cl. 1982), *cert. denied*, 459 U.S. 969 (1982).

61. *See, e.g.*, F. Cohen, *The Legal Conscience* (1958), pp. 264–67; Henderson, note 46 above. *See also Shoshone Indians v. U.S.*, 324 U.S. 335, 359 (1945) (Douglas, J., dissenting).

62. 42 U.S.C. Secs. 1601 *et seq.* For a further discussion of this act, see ch. 15, sec. B.

63. *See, e.g.*, *Shoshone Indians*, note 61 above; *Tee-Hit-Ton Indians*, note 48 above.

64. *U.S. v. Dann*, note 58 above; *U.S. v. Dann*, 470 U.S. 39, 50 (1985).

65. *Santa Fe*, note 48 above.

66. *Id.*; *U.S. v. Dann*, note 58 above, 873 F.2d at 1195 n.5.

III

The Trust Responsibility

What is the "doctrine of trust responsibility"?

The Supreme Court recently reaffirmed a principle that "has long dominated the government's dealings with Indians." That principle is "the undisputed existence of a general trust relationship between the United States and the Indian people."[1] This relationship is one of the most important concepts in Indian law.

The Supreme Court first recognized the existence of a trust relationship between the federal government and Indian people in its early decisions interpreting Indian treaties.[2] Between 1787 and 1871 the United States entered into hundreds of treaties with Indian tribes. In almost all of these treaties, the Indians gave up land in exchange for promises. These promises included a guarantee that the United States would create a permanent reservation for the tribe and would protect the safety and well-being of tribal members.[3] The Supreme Court has held that such promises create a trust relationship. This relationship is "marked by peculiar and cardinal distinctions which exist nowhere else" and "resembles that of a ward to his guardian."[4] These promises create a "duty of protection" toward the Indians.[5]

The foundation of this unique relationship is one of trust: the Indians trust the United States to fulfill the promises which were given in exchange for their land. The federal government's obligation to honor this trust relationship and to fulfill its treaty commitments is known as its *trust responsibility*.[6]

Although it was originally created to enforce treaty commitments, the courts have extended the trust responsibility in three respects. First, federal statutes, agreements,[7] and executive orders can create trust obligations in the same way that a treaty can.[8] For example, a federal statute enacted in 1790 to protect Indian lands created a trust responsibility of the federal government to enforce the law that continues even today.[9]

Second, the trust obligation may include implied, not just express, commitments. For example, when a treaty promises a tribe that it can use its reservation "for Indian purposes," this obligates the government to protect the Indians' right to hunt and fish on that land.[10] Similarly, a guarantee that Indians can hold their reservation "as Indian lands are held" obligates the United States to protect the reservation's water supply, even though the treaty says nothing about water rights.[11]

Finally, the trust responsibility imposes an independent obligation upon the federal government to remain loyal to the Indians and to advance their interests, including their interest in self-government.[12] The modern view is that to the maximum extent possible the trust doctrine should recognize and encourage the autonomy of Indian tribes. In 1977 a Senate commission expressed this obligation as follows:

> The purpose behind the trust doctrine is and always has been to ensure the survival and welfare on Indian tribes and people. This includes an obligation to provide those services required to protect and enhance Indian lands, resources, and self-government, and also includes those economic and social programs which are necessary to raise the standard of living and social well-being of the Indian people to a level comparable to the non-Indian society.[13]

The Supreme Court has used such terms as "solemn," "special," and "trust" to describe the government's relationship with Indian tribes.[14] The federal government is the "fiduciary" of tribal resources, which means "that it must act with good faith and utter loyalty to the best interests" of the Indians.[15]

The federal government always has a duty of loyalty to Indians. However, specific tasks are not necessarily required. That is, Indians and tribes cannot force the government to undertake a specific activity unless a treaty, statute, or agreement expressly imposes or clearly implies that obligation. This principle is illustrated by *United States v. Mitchell* (1980)[16] ("*Mitchell I*") and *United States v. Mitchell* (1983)[17] ("*Mitchell II*").

In *Mitchell I*, a tribe sought damages from the federal government for mismanaging the tribe's timber resources. The tribe claimed that the General Allotment Act of 1887 required the government to manage these resources wisely. The Supreme Court held that, although this act, like other federal Indian laws, creates a trust relationship, that relationship is limited to the provisions in the act. The Court dismissed the tribe's claim for damages because nothing in the act imposed any specific duty regarding the management of timber.

The tribe tried again in *Mitchell II*. This time the tribe relied upon federal statutes and regulations that give federal officials comprehensive control over the management of tribal timber. These statutes and regulations, the Court held, impose specific duties, and therefore, specific trust obligations. The Court permitted the tribe to recover damages from the federal government for violating these fiduciary responsibilities.

Thus, the more specific the obligation, the higher the duty of care. "The United States undoubtedly owes a strong fiduciary duty" to Indians, the Supreme Court stated in 1983,[18] but this duty is only a general one unless a treaty, statute, or agreement requires something more specific. For instance, a statute that allows but does not require the federal government to purchase land for Indian tribes does not create a trust obligation to purchase land for a particular tribe.[19] On the other hand, where a statute places Indian property under the control of a federal agency, the courts generally impose a fiduciary duty on that agency to act with a high degree of care and responsibility.[20] If a tribe claims that a federal agency mismanaged tribal property under its control, the agency must produce clear and accurate accounts of its transactions. If these records reveal that the agency's conduct fell short of this high standard, the tribe can recover damages to compensate for any loss caused by the government's mismanagement.[21]

How can a statute create a trust responsibility?

It is easy to understand how an Indian treaty can create a trust obligation. In a treaty, the tribe has traded land for promises, and these promises must be kept. It is not as easy to see how a statute can create a trust obligation because that same kind of exchange may not be obvious.

However, Congress often chooses to enforce its treaty obligations through statutes. In these situations, Indians have the right to expect that these statutes will be enforced. Moreover, many federal statues give federal agencies enormous control over Indian property. It is unfair, the courts have recognized, to permit an agency to control tribal property without also requiring that the agency manage that property in the tribe's best interests.

Does the United States have a trust relationship with every Indian tribe?

A broad interpretation of the federal government's trust responsibility would create a trust relationship with every Indian tribe. Unfortunately, the Department of the Interior, which administers most of the federal government's Indian programs, has given the trust doctrine a narrow interpretation. The Interior Department believes that only officially "recognized" tribes have a trust relationship with the United States.[22] Thus the more than one hundred and twenty tribes not recognized by Interior cannot participate in the department's programs.

The Supreme Court has yet to determine the extent to which the trust doctrine applies to nonrecognized tribes. Several lower federal courts, however, have rejected the Interior Department's argument that only recognized tribes can have a trust relationship with the United States. These courts have held that a trust relationship is not "all or nothing." Although a recognized tribe has a trust relationship with the United States for all purposes, a nonrecognized tribe may still enjoy that relationship for some purposes. For example, tribal members can enforce a trust obligation created by a treaty even though the Interior Department does not recognize the tribe's continued existence.[23] Similarly, a nonrecognized tribe may be eligible to participate in programs that Congress has not restricted to recognized tribes.[24]

Does the trust doctrine apply to individual Indians?

Yes. The trust doctrine extends not only to tribes but to their members.[25] Theoretically, the federal government's trust responsibility extends to all tribal members, whether they live on or off the reservation.[26] However, few of the government's Indian programs have been made available to off-reservation Indians. In 1975 the Supreme Court held that the Interior Department cannot withhold its social welfare programs from tribal members who live near their reservation and maintain close ties with the tribe.[27] The courts have not yet decided whether all federal Indian programs must be made available to off-reservation Indians. A Senate commission recently stated that the trust responsibility extends to off-reservation Indians and criticized the government for withholding Indian programs from them.[28] Of course, statutes specifically requiring federal officials to provide services to off-reservation Indians create a trust obligation to do so.[29]

Does the trust responsibility extend to off-reservation activities which affect on-reservation Indians?

Yes. For example, federal activities off the reservation that would diminish on-reservation water supplies[30] or would pollute reservation property[31] have been held to violate the trust doctrine.

Can Congress terminate a trust relationship?

Yes. Congress can terminate its trust relationship with an Indian tribe at any time, with or without the tribe's consent.[32] Over the years, Congress has terminated its trust relationship with more than a hundred tribes. In each case it accomplished this by passing a law which terminated the tribe itself. Termination laws forbid a tribe from exercising governmental powers, require distribution of the tribe's property and assets to tribal members, and end the tribe's trust relationship with the United States.[33]

Congress also has the power to terminate its trust relationship with individual Indians,[34] although the only time Congress has done this is when it has terminated their tribe. Certain Indians were made citizens of the United States in treaties with the federal government. In 1905 the Supreme Court held that these Indians had lost their trust status,[35] but a few years later the Court reversed this decision.[36] Consequently, when citizenship was extended to all Indians by statute in 1924, their trust relationships with the United States were not affected.

A trust relationship is so important to Indians and tribes that the Supreme Court has held that it cannot be terminated except by an express act of Congress. Termination of a trust relationship cannot be implied.[37] Thus federal officials cannot withhold trust services from an Indian tribe unless there is clear evidence that Congress has terminated the trust relationship.[38]

Which federal agencies have the power to terminate a trust relationship?

None of them do. Once Congress has created a trust relationship with an Indian tribe, only Congress can end it.[39] Even the tribe cannot terminate the relationship.[40] A federal agency must faithfully execute its trust obligations.[41]

Similarly, states have no power to terminate a tribe's trust relationship with the United States. Therefore, a state's decision to provide services to an Indian tribe and the tribe's decision to accept those services do not diminish the federal government's trust obligations.[42]

In what ways can a tribe benefit from having a trust relationship with the United States?

Tribes that have a trust relationship with the United States are eligible to participate in many federal Indian programs. These programs offer assistance in such areas as housing, health care, land development, education, and employment. Chapter 16 describes these programs.

Does the trust relationship ever operate to the tribe's detriment?

Yes. There is a constant clash between the federal government's trust responsibilities and the tribe's interest in self-government. The federal government has severely injured many tribes in the name of protecting them.[43]

The problem stems from the Interior Department's interpretation of the trust doctrine. In 1831 the Supreme Court compared a tribe's relationship with the United States to that of "a ward of his guardian."[44] The Department of the Interior and its subagency, the Bureau of Indian Affairs, have often applied this phrase literally to justify extensive control of Indian affairs. But Indians are entitled to federal protection, not federal control. As a recent Senate commission report states:

> The Bureau of Indian Affairs . . . has used the trust doctrine as a means to develop a paternalistic control over the day to day affairs of Indian tribes and individuals. Federal-Indian trust law, as expressed by both Congress and the courts, calls for Federal protection, not Federal domination. . . . The relationship should be thought of not only in the terms of a moral and legal duty, but also as a partnership agreement to insure that Indian tribes have available to them the tools and resources to survive as distinct political and cultural groups.[45]

Federal agencies have been reluctant to allow Indians to exercise greater control over their lives and property, choking their development. To make matters worse, federal agencies are notorious for mismanaging Indian property and Indian programs. A comprehensive investigation in 1987 by the *Arizona Republic* concluded that the Bureau of Indian Affairs (BIA) "has failed to fulfill its responsibility as trustee for Indian holdings and as the designated protector of Indian rights"[46] and that federal agencies are "costly, ineffective and unresponsive" to Indian needs.[47] The BIA "actually has thrived on the failure of Indian programs . . . [and] deterred development" of Indian self-government.[48] Specifically cited in the report were massive failures in employment, housing, and health care programs; mismanagement of tribal timber, mineral, and oil and gas resources; "terrible" Indian education; and ineffective law enforcement.[49] Even the director of the BIA conceded that we "have an intractable bureaucracy here that doesn't want to change."[50]

Has the United States been faithful to its trust responsibilities?

No. The United States "has been notoriously unfaithful in observing its commitments to the Indian tribes."[51]

The fault lies primarily with Congress. Congress has the responsibility to fulfill this nation's treaty commitments. Yet Congress has broken nearly all of its Indian treaties. Congress guaranteed most treaty tribes protection and safety. However, during the 1950s Congress abolished more than a hundred tribal governments.[52] Congress has a trust responsibility to enhance the social and economic well-being of Indian people, but Indians are the most disadvantaged and impoverished group in our society.[53] Congress is responsible for supervising the federal agencies entrusted with Indian programs; its performance has clearly been inadequate.

To be sure, Congress has passed many laws benefitting Indians, and it continues to provide Indians and tribes with numerous special programs and services. But Congress also has passed laws severely detrimental to Indians, broken Indian treaties, placed Indians on barren reservations, and failed to provide tribes with the means to meet their basic governmental, economic, and social needs. In general, Congress has not been faithful to its trust responsibilities.[54]

The Supreme Court has recognized that, in some situations, Congress cannot remain loyal to Indians to the exclusion of other interests. For example, Congress must allocate scarce water resources to federal reclamation projects as well as to Indian reservations.[55] However, it is fair to ask why Congress allowed the reclamation project to be built. In any event, Indians have the right to expect that a federal agency will at least take measures to minimize harm to Indian interests, even if some harm cannot be avoided.

Can the federal government's trust responsibilities be enforced by the courts?

It depends on whether the trust responsibility is being violated by Congress or by a federal agency. Few treaties require that Congress provide specific services, such as health care, housing, employment, or education. Therefore, Congress is not obligated to provide these services and cannot be forced to do so. With respect to Congress, then, the trust responsibility is more of a moral than a legal obligation.[56] In fact, if Congress decides to terminate its services to an Indian tribe—or even to terminate the tribe itself—a federal court has no authority to prevent it.[57] Indians, in other words, must rely on the good faith of Congress to keep the promises it made more than a century ago in exchange for Indian land.

However, even though Indians cannot enforce the trust doctrine against Congress, federal officials cannot ignore the trust responsibilities Congress has delegated to them. Congress has the authority to modify a trust relationship, but administrative agencies do not. Federal officials must faithfully execute the trust duties they have been delegated, and courts are required to carefully scrutinize their actions.[58] Indians have been successful, for example, in preventing federal officials from selling tribal lands,[59] from diverting water from their reservations,[60] from denying them access to their property,[61] and from mismanaging their resources.[62] They have also obtained money damages for injuries caused by agency mismanagement.[63] All of these successful actions have been based on the doctrine of trust responsibility. Chapter 18 explains how to file a lawsuit against federal officials who are ignoring their trust obligations.

NOTES

1. *U.S. v. Mitchell*, 463 U.S. 206, 225 (1983).
2. *Cherokee Nation v. Georgia*, 30 U.S. 1 (1831); *Worcester v. Georgia*, 31 U.S. 515 (1832).
3. Indian treaties are further discussed in ch. 4.
4. *Cherokee Nation*, note 2 above, 30 U.S. at 16–17.
5. *U.S. v. Kagama*, 118 U.S. 375, 384 (1886). *See also Seminole Nation v. U.S.*, 316 U.S. 286 (1942).
6. For a further discussion of the trust doctrine, see R. Chambers, *Judicial Enforcement of the Federal Trust Responsibility to Indians*, 27 Stan. L. Rev. 1213 (May 1975); N. Carter, *Race and Power Politics as Aspects of Federal Guardianship over American Indians: Land Related Cases, 1887–1924*, 4 Am. Indian L. Rev. 197 (1976).
7. An "agreement" is similar to a treaty in that it is negotiated between a tribe and the federal government. Agreements, however, are ratified by both houses of Congress, rather than by just the Senate. Like treaties, agreements have the same status as a law passed by Congress. *Antoine v. Washington*, 420 U.S. 194 (1975).
8. *See, e.g., Oneida Indian Nation v. County of Oneida*, 414 U.S. 661 (1974); *Squire v. Capoeman*, 351 U.S. 1, 6–7 (1956); *Mitchell*, note 1 above.
9. *Joint Tribal Council of the Passamaquoddy Tribe v. Morton*, 528 F.2d 370 (1st Cir. 1975).
10. *Menominee Tribe v. U.S.*, 391 U.S. 404, 406 (1968).
11. *Winters v. U.S.*, 207 U.S. 564 (1908).
12. *See, e.g., Manchester Band of Pomo Indians v. U.S.*, 363 F. Supp. 1238 (N.D. Cal. 1973); *Pyramid Lake Paiute Tribe v. Morton*, 354 F. Supp. 252 (D.D.C. 1972), *rev'd on other grounds*, 499 F.2d 1095 (D.C. Cir. 1974); *White v. Califano*, 581 F.2d 697 (8th Cir. 1978); *Eric v. Secretary of HUD*, 464 F. Supp. 44 (D. Alaska 1978); *McNabb v. Heckler*, 628 F. Supp. 544 (D. Mont. 1986), *aff'd*, 829 F.2d 789 (9th Cir. 1987).
13. American Indian Policy Review Commission, *Final Report* p. 130 (Washington, DC: Government Printing Office, 1977).
14. *Seminole Nation*, note 5 above, 316 U.S. at 296–97. *See also U.S. v. Mason*, 412 U.S. 391, 397 (1973); *Morton v. Mancari*, 417 U.S. 535, 551–52 (1974).
15. *Final Report*, note 13 above, p. 128.
16. 445 U.S. 535 (1980).
17. 463 U.S. 206 (1983).
18. *Nevada v. U.S.*, 463 U.S. 110, 127 (1983).

19. *Confederated Tribes of the Coos, Lower Umqua, and Suislaw Indians v. U.S.*, 16 Indian L. Rep. 3033 (D. Or. 1988).

20. *Mitchell*, note 1 above; *Jicarilla Apache Tribe v. Supron Energy Corp.*, 782 F.2d 855 (10th Cir. 1986) (en banc), *adopting in relevant part* 728 F.2d 1555, 1563–73 (10th Cir. 1984) (dissenting opinion), *cert. denied*, 107 S.Ct. 471 (1986); *Assiniboine & Sioux Tribes v. Board of Oil & Gas Exploration*, 792 F.2d 782 (9th Cir. 1986); *Pawnee v. U.S.*, 830 F.2d 187 (Fed. Cir. 1987), *cert. denied*, 486 U.S. 1032 (1988).

21. *Mitchell*, note 1 above; *Jicarilla Apache Tribe*, note 20 above; *Yankton Sioux Tribe v. U.S.*, 623 F.2d 159 (Ct. Cl. 1980).

22. The subject of recognition is discussed in ch. 15, sec. E.

23. *U.S. v. Washington*, 384 F. Supp. 312 (W.D. Wash. 1974), *aff'd*, 520 F.2d 676 (9th Cir. 1975), *cert. denied*, 423 U.S. 1086 (1976).

24. *Passamaquoddy Tribe*, note 9 above.

25. *U.S. v. Holliday*, 70 U.S. 407 (1865); *McClanahan v. Arizona State Tax Comm'n*, 411 U.S. 164 (1973); *Morton v. Ruiz*, 415 U.S. 199 (1974).

26. *Holliday*, note 25 above. *See also Final Report*, note 13 above, pp. 131–32.

27. *Ruiz*, note 25 above.

28. *Final Report*, note 13 above, pp. 131–32.

29. *Ruiz*, note 25 above; *St. Paul Intertribal Housing Bd. v. Reynolds*, 564 F. Supp. 1408 (D. Minn. 1983); *Eric v. Sec'y of HUD*, 464 F. Supp. 44 (D. Alaska 1978).

30. *Pyramid Lake*, note 12 above.

31. *Nance v. Environmental Protection Agency*, 645 F.2d 701 (9th Cir. 1981), *cert. denied*, 454 U.S. 1081 (1981).

32. *Menominee Tribe*, note 10 above; *Kagama*, note 5 above.

33. *See, e.g.*, 25 U.S.C. Secs. 564, 677, 691. The subject of termination is discussed in ch. 5, sec. B.

34. *U.S. v. Nice*, 241 U.S. 591 (1916).

35. *Matter of Heff*, 197 U.S. 488 (1905).

36. *Nice*, note 34 above.

37. *Menominee Tribe*, note 10 above; *Heckman v. U.S.*, 224 U.S. 413 (1912). *But see Rosebud Sioux Tribe v. Kneip*, 430 U.S. 584 (1977).

38. *Passamaquoddy Tribe*, note 9 above.

39. *Nice*, note 34 above.

40. *Kennerly v. District Court*, 400 U.S. 423 (1971); *Passamaquoddy Tribe*, note 9 above.

41. *See* cases cited in note 19 above.

42. *See* cases cited in note 40 above.

43. This topic has received considerable attention. *See, e.g.,* V. Deloria, Jr., *Custer Died for Your Sins* (1969); E. S. Cahn, ed., *Our Brother's Keeper: The Indian in White America* (1969); *Final Report,* note 13 above, pp. 121–38. *See also Lone Wolf v. Hitchcock,* 187 U.S. 553 (1903) (Congress dissolved a tribe in an effort to "civilize" it).

44. *Cherokee Nation,* note 2 above, 30 U.S. at 17.

45. *Final Report,* note 13 above, pp. 106, 127. *See also* authorities cited in note 43 above.

46. *Fraud in Indian Country,* Arizona Republic (Oct. 4, 1987), composite reprint, p. 6.

47. *Id.* (Oct. 10, 1987), composite reprint, p. 28.

48. *Id.,* (Oct. 9, 1987), composite reprint, p. 24.

49. *Id.* See composite reprint, pp. 1–36.

50. Ross Swimmer, quoted in *id.* (Oct. 4, 1987), composite reprint, p. 7.

51. *Final Report,* note 13 above, p. 130. *See also U.S. v. Ahtanum Irrig. Dist.,* 236 F.2d 321, 328 (9th Cir. 1956), *cert. denied,* 352 U.S. 988 (1957), and cases cited in note 12 above.

52. This subject is discussed in ch. 5, sec. B.

53. This subject is discussed in chs. 1 and 16.

54. *See Final Report,* note 13 above, pp. 125–36. *See also* Chambers, note 6 above.

55. *Nevada v. U.S.,* 463 U.S. 110 (1983).

56. *See, e.g., Tee-Hit-Ton Indians v. U.S.,* 348 U.S. 272 (1955); *Mitchell,* note 20 above. However, see discussion in ch. 5, note 17 and accompanying text.

57. *Lone Wolf,* note 43 above; *Menominee Tribe,* note 10 above.

58. *Lane v. Pueblo of Santa Rosa,* 249 U.S. 110 (1919); *Cramer v. U.S.,* 261 U.S. 219 (1923); *U.S. v. Creek Nation,* 295 U.S. 103 (1935); *Seminole Nation,* note 5 above.

59. *Lane,* note 58 above; *Cramer,* note 58 above.

60. *Pyramid Lake,* note 12 above.

61. *Creek Nation,* note 58 above.

62. *See* cases cited in note 20 above.

63. *Mitchell,* note 1 above; *Jicarilla Apache Tribe,* note 20 above; *Manchester Band,* note 12 above.

IV
Indian Treaties

A treaty is a contract between sovereign nations. The Constitution authorizes the President, with the consent of two-thirds of the Senate, to enter into a treaty on behalf of the United States.[1] The Constitution declares that treaties are "the supreme law of the land."[2] As such, they are superior to state laws and state constitutions and are equal to laws passed by Congress.[3] A treaty can be made on any subject, but it may not deprive a citizen of any right guaranteed by the U.S. Constitution.[4]

Until 1871 treaties were the accepted method by which the United States conducted its relations with Indian tribes. Nearly every tribe has at least one treaty with the United States.[5]

Is an Indian treaty a grant of rights to a tribe?
No. The Supreme Court has expressly held that an Indian treaty is "not a grant of rights to the Indians, but a grant of rights from them."[6] The purpose of an Indian treaty was not to give rights to the Indians but to remove rights they had. Thus Indians have a great many rights in addition to those described in treaties. In fact, any right not expressly extinguished by a treaty or federal statute is reserved to the tribe.[7] This fundamental principle of Indian law is known as the "reserved rights" doctrine.

Did Indian tribes enter into treaties voluntarily?
Before the War of 1812 the United States and the Indian tribes negotiated treaties as relative equals.[8] The new nation, weakened from years of war with Great Britain, would have been no match for the Indians. Consequently, the early Indian treaties were voluntary and mutually advantageous. The United States acquired land and peace from the Indians in exchange for goods and services provided by the federal government.

After the War of 1812, which ended the threat of British intervention in U.S. internal affairs, friendship with the Indians became less valuable. The United States then wanted Indian land, which it began to take by force. Indian treaties after the War of 1812 rarely were voluntary.[9]

The Creeks and Cherokees, who lived in southeastern United States, suffered some of the first losses. In 1814 the Creeks were forced to surrender twenty-three million acres of land to the federal government.[10] In 1835 President Andrew Jackson forced the Cherokees to sign the Treaty of New Echota, in which they gave up all of their land east of the Mississippi River in exchange for land in the Oklahoma Territory.[11] (After the treaty was signed the federal government ordered the Cherokees to march to Oklahoma—the Trail of Tears, during which many died.)

In the decades that followed, white settlers and prospectors moved westward by the thousands, and the U.S. Cavalry went along to protect them. One by one, the government defeated the Indian tribes, forced them to sign treaties, and placed them on reservations. These reservations were often hundreds of miles from their original homelands.[12]

What do Indian treaties contain?

Nearly every Indian treaty contains at least two provisions. First, the Indians agree to relinquish land to the United States. Second, the United States promises to create a federally protected reservation for the Indians. Some treaties also promise the Indians specific goods or services, such as medical care or food and clothing, but many do not. (As discussed previously, the purpose of an Indian treaty was to take rights away from Indians; treaties rarely listed the rights reserved to them.)

Almost every treaty assured the Indians that they could live on their reservation permanently and would not be forced to move. In 1854 Senator Sam Houston described the perpetual nature of these reservations in the following terms: " As long as water flows, or grass grows upon the earth, or the sun rises to show your pathway, or you kindle your camp fires, so long shall you be protected by this Government, and never again be removed from your present habitations."[13] Only rarely has the United States lived up to these promises.

Does the United States still make treaties with Indian tribes?

No. In 1871 Congress passed a law that prohibited the making of treaties with Indians. This law (Title 25, United States Code, Section 71) declared that Indian tribes were not sovereign nations with whom the United States could make treaties. Since 1871 Congress has regulated Indian affairs through legislation, greatly preferring this approach because laws, unlike Indian treaties, do not need the consent of the Indians.

Section 71 was passed largely because the House of Representatives disliked its exclusion from Indian policy making. Under the Constitution, treaties are made by the President and the Senate only. The House pressured the Senate into passing this law so that it could have a hand in formulating Indian policy.[14]

The passage of section 71 marked the end of an era. Tribes were no longer considered sovereign nations by the federal government. This loss in status had severe consequences. Congress no longer had to negotiate with Indians or obtain their consent in Indian matters. If Congress, for example, wanted to take land from the Indians, all it had to do was pass a law to that effect.

Did section 71 repeal the earlier Indian treaties? If not, are all of these treaties valid today?

Section 71 states that "no obligation of any treaty . . . shall be hereby invalidated or impaired." Therefore section 71 did not affect any existing Indian treaty. This does not mean, however, that every Indian treaty is still valid. To the contrary, most treaties have been abrogated, that is, broken or breached, by Congress. In 1903 the Supreme Court held in *Lone Wolf v. Hitchcock*[15] that Indian treaties have the same dignity as federal statutes, but no greater dignity. Therefore, a federal law can amend or even repeal an Indian treaty in the same way that it can amend or repeal a prior law. The *Lone Wolf* decision has been severely criticized because it permits Congress to break its treaty promises whenever it wants to,[16] a power it has used quite often.

The Supreme Court has consistently upheld the power of Congress to break Indian treaties.[17] In a recent case, for example, the Court reviewed a treaty in which Congress promised never to diminish the size of a tribe's reservation without the tribe's consent. Not long after the treaty was signed, Congress passed a law diminishing the reservation in direct violation of the treaty. The Supreme Court upheld the power of Congress to abrogate the treaty and take the land.[18]

The Fifth Amendment to the Constitution states that Congress may not deprive anyone of "private property . . . without just compensation." The Supreme Court has held that Indian treaty rights are a form of private property protected by the Just Compensation Clause.[19] Consequently, Indians must receive compensation whenever Congress abrogates their treaty rights. Realistically, however, a monetary award usually provides little compensation to people who have lost their homes or sacred lands. In a recent case, the Supreme Court awarded the Sioux more than $100 million in compensation for the loss of the Black Hills.[20] Immediately afterward, a number of Sioux filed a lawsuit demanding that the federal government keep the money and return the land. The court refused to interfere with Congress's power to take the tribe's land.[21]

How are Indian treaties interpreted?

Many disputes have arisen over the terms and provisions of Indian treaties. These disputes often involve important and valuable interests in land, water, minerals, and wildlife.[22]

The Supreme Court has developed a set of rules that govern the interpretation of Indian treaties. These rules are known as the "canons of treaty construction." There are three basic canons. First, ambiguities in treaties must be resolved in favor of the Indians.[23] Second, Indian treaties must be interpreted as the Indians would have understood them.[24] Finally, Indian treaties must be construed liberally in favor of the Indians.[25]

These canons obviously benefit the treaty tribe, as the Supreme Court intended. Tribes were at a significant disadvantage in the treaty-making process. For one thing, treaties were always negotiated and written in English and the Indians were not certain what they were signing. Also, most treaties were signed under threat of force and were fundamentally unfair. Consequently, Indians should receive the benefit of the doubt when questions arise. As the Supreme Court recently explained:

> Accordingly, it is the intention of the parties, and not solely that of the superior side, that must control any attempt to interpret the treaties. When Indians are in-

volved, the Court has long given special meaning to this rule. It has held that the United States, as the party with presumptively superior negotiating skills and superior knowledge of the language in which the treaty is recorded, has a responsibility to avoid taking advantage of the other side. The treaty must therefore be construed, not according to the technical meaning of its words to learned lawyers, but in the sense in which they would naturally be understood by the Indians.[26]

These principles of law have been extremely important to Indians.[27] Tribes in the Northwest have particularly benefited from them. All of these tribes depend on fishing for their subsistence. The treaties they signed recognize their right to fish but fail to say exactly how many fish they may catch, where they may fish, or whether and how much the state may regulate Indian fishing. The Supreme Court has liberally interpreted these treaties in favor of the Indians. The Court assumed that fishing must have been discussed when the treaty was made, because it was the Indians' livelihood. In addition, nothing in the treaties removes their fishing rights. Thus the Indians would have assumed that their fishing rights remained intact. Accordingly the treaties must be so interpreted today, with any uncertainties resolved in the Indians' favor.[28]

In short, an Indian treaty must be interpreted broadly to effectuate the purpose of the treaty. For example, a treaty that creates a permanent reservation for a tribe is presumed to reserve enough water to make the reservation livable.[29] If a treaty's purpose is to change a nomadic tribe into an agrarian one, it is presumed to reserve grazing rights to the tribe even though it says nothing about grazing.[30]

Has the United States honored its treaty commitments?
Generally, no. The United States has broken nearly every one of its Indian treaties. Most of them were broken to obtain Indian land.

The Sioux experience typifies what happened to many tribes. In 1851 the Sioux signed a treaty that guaranteed a sizable reservation as a permanent home. However, the federal government allowed hundreds of non-Indians to settle on this land in violation of the treaty. After several battles, in 1868 the Sioux were forced to sign a treaty that drastically diminished the size of their reservation. Although this treaty took most of their land, it at least left the Sioux their sacred Black Hills and promised that no additional land would be taken from them. However, gold was found in the Black Hills in 1874, and in 1877 Congress removed the Black Hills from the reservation. Even this was not the end. In 1889 Congress removed half of what remained and carved the rest into six separate reservations, dividing the Sioux among them. Resistance to this action ended quickly with the killing of scores of unarmed Sioux at Wounded Knee in 1890. Between 1904 and 1910 Congress removed additional lands from the six reservations. The Rosebud Reservation, for example, was reduced to one-fourth of its 1889 area.[31]

What standards are used to determine whether Congress has abrogated a treaty?

Lone Wolf v. Hitchcock makes it easy for Congress to break its treaty promises. However, other decisions of the Supreme Court have limited the potential damage caused by *Lone Wolf*. In 1941 the Court held that Indian treaties cannot be broken by a subsequent federal law unless Congress's intent to do so is "clear and plain."[32] Indian treaties cannot be abrogated "in a back-handed way."[33] Although Congress can abrogate an Indian treaty, it must plainly state this intention; treaty abrogation cannot be inferred.[34]

Unfortunately, the Supreme Court recently diluted this "clear showing" standard. In 1973 the Court ruled that a federal law could abrogate an Indian treaty if the "surrounding circumstances and legislative history" indicated that intent.[35] Four years later, the Court used this "implied abrogation" standard to decide that a federal law abrogated an Indian treaty even though nothing in the statute clearly stated that intent.[36] In 1986 the Court reached a similar conclusion in another case.[37]

Treaty abrogation discredits the integrity of the United States. As the Supreme Court has noted, "Indian treaty rights are too fundamental to be easily cast aside."[38] Tribes relinquished vast amounts of land in exchange for treaty promises, and they have a right to expect the United States to keep those promises. As the late Supreme Court Justice Hugo Black stated in criticizing the breaking of Indian treaties by the federal government, "Great nations, like great men, should keep their word."[39]

Can an administrative agency abrogate an Indian treaty?

No. A federal agency cannot abrogate an Indian treaty without specific congressional authority.[40] This is true even if the agency has the general authority to undertake the activity in question.[41] For example, the Army Corps of Engineers has the general authority to build dams for flood control but it cannot build a dam on land reserved by treaty to an Indian tribe without the express consent of Congress.[42]

Can a state abrogate an Indian treaty?

No. A state cannot amend or repeal Indian treaty rights,[43] even if the treaty was made before the state entered the Union.[44]

How can treaty rights be enforced?

Indian treaties have the same force and effect as federal statutes. A violation of an Indian treaty is a violation of federal law.

Indians and tribes are entitled to enforcement of their treaty rights. If state or federal officials violate these rights, a lawsuit can be filed in federal court to stop their activity.[45] Treaty rights can also be raised as a defense to a criminal prosecution by state[46] or federal[47] authorities. If the treaty protects the action one is being prosecuted for, the charges must be dismissed. For example, if state game officials arrest someone for hunting or fishing out of season, that person is not guilty of the charges if he or she was exercising a treaty right.[48] Chapter 18 explains how to file a lawsuit to protect treaty rights.

NOTES

1. U.S. Const., art. II, sec. 2, cl. 2.
2. U.S. Const. art. VI, sec. 2, provides: "This Constitution, and the laws of the United States which shall be made in Pursuance thereof; and all Treaties made, or which shall be made, under the Authority of the United States, shall be the Supreme Law of the Land; and the Judges in every State shall be bound thereby, any Thing in the Constitution or Laws of any State to the Contrary notwithstanding."

3. *Id. See Worcester v. Georgia,* 31 U.S. 515 (1832); *U.S. v. Forty-Three Gallons of Whiskey,* 93 U.S. 188 (1876).

4. *Asakura v. Seattle,* 265 U.S. 332 (1924).

5. For a comprehensive discussion of Indian treaties, see F. Cohen, *Handbook of Federal Indian Law* (1982).

6. *U.S. v. Winans,* 198 U.S. 371 (1905).

7. *Menominee Tribe v. U.S.,* 391 U.S. 404 (1968); *U.S. v. Dion,* 476 U.S. 734, 739 (1986); *Swim v. Bergland,* 696 F.2d 712 (9th Cir. 1983).

8. *Worcester,* note 3 above, 31 U.S. at 548.

9. *See generally* C. Wilkinson and J. Volkman, *Judicial Review of Indian Treaty Abrogation: "As Long As Water Flows, or Grass Grows upon the Earth"—How Long a Time Is That?,* 63 Cal. L. Rev. 601, 608–10 (1975).

10. 7 Stat. 478.

11. The Treaty of New Echota provided, however, that under certain conditions, reservations of 160 acres of land would be given to Chero-kees who chose to remain east of the Mississippi River, and many did. In later years a reservation was created for these Cherokees in North Carolina and they became officially known as the Eastern Cherokee Tribe. *See* 25 U.S. Sec. 331.

12. *See, e.g., Choctaw Nation v. Oklahoma,* 397 U.S. 620, 630–31 (1970). *See also* Wilkinson and Volkman, note 9 above, pp. 608–11.

13. Cong. Globe, 33d Cong., 1st Sess., App. 202 (1854).

14. *See Antoine v. Washington,* 420 U.S. 194, 202 (1975).

15. 187 U.S. 553 (1903).

16. *See* V. Deloria, Jr., *Custer Died for Your Sins* pp. 35–60 (New York: Avon Books, 1969); S. Steiner, *The New Indians* pp. 160–74 (New York: Dell Publishing Co., 1968). *See also* Wilkinson and Volkman, note 9 above, p. 604.

17. *See Rosebud Sioux Tribe v. Kneip,* 430 U.S. 584 (1977), and cases cited therein.

18. *Id.*

19. *Shoshone Tribe v. U.S.,* 299 U.S. 476, 497 (1937); *Menominee Tribe v. U.S.,* 391 U.S. 404, 413 (1968).

20. *U.S. v. Sioux Nation of Indians,* 448 U.S. 371 (1980).

21. *Oglala Sioux Tribe of Pine Ridge Indian Reservation v. U.S.,* 862 F.2d 275 (8th Cir.), *cert. denied,* 109 S.Ct. 2087 (1989).

22. *See, e.g., Menominee Tribe,* note 19 above (hunting and fishing rights); *Winters v. U.S.,* 207 U.S. 564 (1908) (water rights); *Choctaw and Chickasaw Nation v. Seay,* 235 F.2d 30 (10th Cir. 1956) (boundary dispute).

23. *Carpenter v. Shaw*, 280 U.S. 363, 367 (1930); *DeCoteau v. District Court*, 420 U.S. 425, 447 (1975); *Bryan v. Itasca County, Minnesota*, 426 U.S. 373, 392 (1976).

24. *Jones v. Meehan*, 175 U.S. 1, 10 (1899); *U.S. v. Shoshone Tribe*, 304 U.S. 111, 116 (1938); *Choctaw Nation v. Oklahoma*, 397 U.S. 620, 631 (1970).

25. *Tulee v. Washington*, 315 U.S. 681, 684–85 (1942); *Washington v. Washington State Commercial Passenger Fishing Vessel Ass'n*, 443 U.S. 658, 690 (1979); *County of Oneida v. Oneida Indian Nation*, 470 U.S. 226, 247 (1985).

26. *Fishing Vessel Ass'n*, note 25 above, 443 U.S. at 675–76, *citing Jones v. Meehan*, note 24 above, 175 U.S. at 10.

27. *See* Wilkinson and Volkman, note 9 above. *See also* cases cited in note 22 above.

28. *See Fishing Vessel Ass'n*, note 25 above, and cases cited therein. Indian fishing rights are discussed in detail in ch. 11.

29. *Winters v. U.S.*, note 22 above. *See also Menominee Tribe*, note 19 above, 391 U.S. at 406.

30. *Swim v. Bergland*, note 7 above. *See also U.S. v. Adair*, 723 F.2d 1394 (9th Cir. 1983), *cert. denied*, 467 U.S. 1252 (1984).

31. *See Rosebud Sioux Tribe*, note 17 above.

32. *U.S. v. Santa Fe Pacific R.R. Co.*, 314 U.S. 339, 353 (1941).

33. *Menominee Tribe*, note 19 above, 391 U.S. at 412–13. *See also Cook v. U.S.*, 288 U.S. 102, 120 (1933).

34. *See* cases cited in notes 32 and 33 above. *See also U.S. v. Winnebago Tribe of Nebraska*, 542 F.2d 1002 (8th Cir. 1976).

35. *Mattz v. Arnett*, 412 U.S. 481, 505 (1973).

36. *Rosebud Sioux Tribe*, note 17 above. *See also DeCoteau*, note 23 above. *But see Solem v. Bartlett*, 465 U.S. 463 (1984).

37. *U.S. v. Dion*, 476 U.S. 734 (1986). *See also Oregon Dep't of Fish & Wildlife v. Klamath Indian Tribe*, 473 U.S. 753, 754 (1985).

38. *Dion*, note 37 above, 476 U.S. at 739.

39. *Federal Power Commission v. Tuscarora Indian Nation*, 362 U.S. 99, 142 (1960) (Black, J., dissenting).

40. *Menominee Tribe*, note 19 above; *Oneida Indian Nation v. County of Oneida*, 414 U.S. 661, 670 (1974).

41. *Phillips Petroleum Co. v. U.S. Environmental Protection Agency*, 803 F.2d 545, 556 (10th Cir. 1986); *Donovan v. Coeur d'Alene Tribal Farm*, 751 F.2d 1113, 1116 (9th Cir. 1985).

42. *Winnebago Tribe*, note 34 above.

43. *Winters*, note 22 above; *Arizona v. California*, 373 U.S. 546 (1963).

44. *Winters*, note 22 above; *Antoine*, note 14 above.

45. *See, e.g., Puyallup Tribe v. Washington Dep't of Game,* 433 U.S. 165 (1977); *Winnebago Tribe,* note 34 above.

46. *Mattz,* note 35 above.

47. *U.S. v. Cutler,* 37 F. Supp. 724 (D. Idaho 1941); *U.S. v. White,* 508 F.2d 453 (8th Cir. 1974). *Cf. Dion,* note 37 above.

48. *Antoine,* note 14 above; *Puyallup Tribe,* note 45 above.

V

Federal Power over Indian Affairs

The United States gained its independence from Great Britain in 1787, after a long and bitter struggle. A few Indian tribes participated on each side of that struggle, but most tribes in the East, and all of the tribes in the West, were not involved. Nevertheless, soon after the Revolutionary War, the newly formed federal government claimed it had the right to control every Indian tribe. It even claimed to own all the land within the United States, land the Indians had occupied for centuries.

For obvious reasons, Indians could not accept these claims. How did the United States get power over them? How had the Indians lost their land? As one might expect, the attempt by the United States to impose its laws on Indians caused animosity and war. One by one, however, Indian tribes either voluntarily surrendered or were defeated militarily, their land was taken, and they were placed on reservations.

Many people still question the federal government's right to govern Indians and believe that Indian tribes have not lost their independence. The United States government strongly disagrees, and its courts have consistently upheld the federal government's power over Indians and its right to intervene in their affairs.[1]

For many reasons, Congress may be wrong in presuming it has the right to govern Indians. For persons interested in pursuing this subject, there are many sources that can be consulted.[2] In all probability, however, the federal government will continue to exercise its power over Indians and tribes, and this book proceeds on that assumption. The old saying of "might makes right" controls the relationship between Indians and the United States. The federal government will never permit Indians to be truly self-governing, nor will it return their land. However, the failure of this book to question the government's right to meddle in Indian affairs should not be interpreted as an acceptance of the government's position.

A. THE SOURCE AND SCOPE OF FEDERAL POWER OVER INDIANS

What is the source of federal power over Indians?

The ultimate source of the federal government's power over Indians is its military strength. The United States Constitution provides the legal justification for the use of that power. Article I, section 8, clause 3 (the Commerce Clause) provides that "Congress shall have the Power . . . to regulate Commerce with foreign Nations, and among the several States, and with the Indian Tribes." Article II, section 2, clause 2 (the Treaty Clause) gives the President and the Senate the power to make treaties, including treaties with Indian tribes. The Supreme Court has held that these two constitutional provisions provide Congress with "all that is required" for complete control over Indian affairs.[3]

The Supreme Court has given two other justifications for federal control over Indians. The first is a rule of international law which states that "discovery and conquest [gives] the conquerors sovereignty over the ownership of the lands thus obtained."[4] In other words, to the victor belongs the spoils. The Supreme Court has held that, by virtue of the "discovery" of North America by the Europeans and the "conquest" of its inhabitants, the federal government is entitled to enforce its laws over all persons and property within the United States.[5] Second, the Supreme Court has cited the doctrine of trust responsibility (discussed in chapter 3) as a source of federal power over Indians. Most Indian treaties contain a guarantee that the federal government will "protect" the treaty tribe. This promise, the Court has held, gives the federal government not only the right, but the duty, to regulate Indians for their "protection."[6]

What is the scope of federal power over Indian affairs?

The scope is virtually unlimited. Congress has "plenary power"—full and complete power—over all Indian tribes, their government, their members, and their property.[7] As the Supreme Court recently stated, "Congress has plenary authority to legislate for the Indian tribes in all matters, including their form of government."[8] "Congress has plenary authority to limit, modify or eliminate the powers of local self-government which the tribes otherwise possess."[9]

Are there any limitations on the power of Congress over Indian affairs?

Yes. The Commerce and Treaty Clauses give Congress plenary power over Indian affairs, but other provisions of the Constitution limit that power. The Supreme Court has recognized that the "power of Congress over Indian affairs may be of a plenary nature; but it is not absolute."[10]

There are two constitutional limitations on the power of Congress that are particularly important to Indians and tribes. These are the Due Process Clause and the Just Compensation Clause, both contained in the Fifth Amendment to the U.S. Constitution.[11] The Due Process Clause prohibits Congress from enforcing any law that is arbitrary, unreasonable, or invidiously discriminatory.[12] This means, among other things, that Congress cannot discriminate against Indians on account of race and that its laws must be fair and reasonable. However, many federal laws that the courts have upheld have appeared quite unfair and unreasonable to the Indians who challenged them.

The Just Compensation Clause prohibits the federal government from taking private property without fair compensation. For instance, if Congress deprives a tribe of land or vested rights, the government must compensate the tribe for its loss. The courts have required compensation for the loss of hunting or fishing rights,[13] the taking of land belonging to an Indian[14] or a tribe,[15] and the loss of a tax immunity.[16]

Another limitation on Congress, at least in theory, is the doctrine of trust responsibility. As explained in chapter 3, this doctrine obligates the federal government to remain loyal to Indians and tribes, to act in their best interests, and to fulfill the promises made to them in treaties. However, the trust responsibility has not been effective in limiting Congress. In fact, until recently courts have viewed Congress's trust responsibility as merely an unenforceable moral obligation. Only the executive branch of government (which includes the federal agencies) has enforceable legal duties, and even then, only those duties that Congress has ordered executive officials to undertake. But courts have begun to consider the government's trust responsibility in determining whether a federal Indian statute violates the Due Process Clause.[17] This new approach helps to enforce the argument that Congress must obey the trust doctrine in enacting these laws.

It must be remembered that it is Congress that has plenary power over Indians and not federal agencies. The only power that federal officials have to meddle in Indian affairs is the power that Congress has given them. It is unlawful for a federal agent to act beyond the authority granted by Congress.[18]

If the Constitution prohibits discrimination on the basis of race, why can Congress pass laws that give Indians special treatment?

Over the years, Congress has passed thousands of laws that give Indians special treatment—sometimes to their benefit, sometimes to their detriment. Federal laws, for example, provide Indians with medical, educational, loan, and housing benefits that non-Indians are not eligible to receive. Other laws, however, place restrictions on Indians, particularly in the use of their land, that non-Indians do not have.

All these laws have one thing in common. They treat Indians differently than non-Indians. Yet the Constitution prohibits Congress from differentiating on the basis of race. Why is Congress allowed to discriminate between Indians and non-Indians?

This discrimination is allowed because Indians are not only a separate racial group, but also a separate political group. The United States did not enter into treaties with Indians because of their race but because of their political status. Although Indians and non-Indians are different races, Congress may treat them differently, not for this reason, but because the Commerce and Treaty Clauses authorize Congress to do so. In addition, the federal government has a trust responsibility to undertake special programs for Indians. As the Supreme Court has explained, "classifications expressly singling out Indian tribes as subjects of legislation are expressly provided for in the Constitution and supported by the ensuing history of the federal government's relations with Indians."[19]

A case that illustrates this principle is *Morton v. Mancari*,[20] decided by the Supreme Court in 1974. In *Mancari* the Court considered the constitutionality of a federal law (the Indian

Preference Act of 1934, 25 U.S.C. Sec. 472) that requires that Indians receive a hiring preference for job vacancies within the Bureau of Indian Affairs (BIA). Non-Indians challenged this employment preference on the grounds of racial discrimination. In a unanimous decision, the Court upheld the Preference Act. The Constitution gives Congress the power to treat Indians "as a separate people with their own political institutions," the Court said.[21] The Preference Act was politically, not racially, motivated: Congress wanted to give Indians greater control over the BIA because the BIA administers most of the federal government's Indian programs. The preference policy must be upheld, the Court explained, because it is a reasonable exercise of Congress's plenary power over Indians.[22]

Thus, each federal Indian law must be examined in its historical, political, and cultural context to determine if it constitutes race discrimination. Congress is permitted to give Indians such things as special fishing and hunting rights, water rights, commercial advantages, and federal services if these things are a reasonable exercise of Congress's plenary powers over Indians.[23] Likewise, Congress can impose restrictions or disadvantages on Indians that are not imposed on non-Indians. For example, the Supreme Court has held that Congress can punish Indians under federal law for certain crimes, even if this means they will be punished more severely than non-Indians who commit the same crime under state law.[24] The Court, in fact, has not invalidated a single one of the thousands of federal Indian laws on the grounds that it constitutes race discrimination, even though most of them treat Indians differently than non-Indians.

Does Congress have the authority to discriminate among groups of Indians?

Yes. For the same reason that Congress can discriminate between Indians and non-Indians, it can discriminate among groups of Indians, even within the same tribe. For example, Congress can choose to distribute funds only to tribal members having a certain minimum amount of tribal blood.[25] Congress can also give property to a tribe that otherwise would have gone to tribal members[26] or give property to one group of Indians that otherwise would have gone to a different group of Indians.[27] Congressional discretion is extremely broad. Any legislation that can be "tied rationally to the fulfillment of Congress' unique obligation toward the Indians" is a valid exercise of congressional authority.[28]

Did the federal government lose its power to regulate Indian affairs when Congress made Indians United States citizens in 1924?

No. The Supreme Court has held that the granting of citizenship to Indians did not diminish the power of Congress to regulate their affairs.[29]

B. IMPLEMENTATION OF FEDERAL POWER

Congress has virtually unlimited authority to regulate Indian affairs. Congressional power extends to all matters of government and to all Indians and tribes within the United States. Congress has complete discretion, the Supreme Court has held, to either assist a tribal government or to destroy it. The rest of this chapter examines the many ways in which Congress has intervened in Indian affairs: administration of Indian affairs; regulating tribal governments; termination; tribal membership; Indian property (land, tribal assets, and personal property); trade and liquor regulation; and criminal jurisdiction.

1. Administration of Indian Affairs

Only Congress has the authority to formulate the federal government's Indian policies. But it obviously cannot administer these policies on a day-to-day basis. Congress has delegated this task to various federal agencies.

Virtually every aspect of Indian life falls under the supervision of some federal agency. Congress has created an Indian bureaucracy so vast that there is one government official for every nineteen Indians.[30]

In reality, these officials have a greater effect on Indian rights than Congress has because they implement the law on a daily basis. Congress does not have the time to closely supervise federal agencies to ensure correct administration of its Indian policies. These officials sometimes over or under react, sometimes they ignore their duties, and each day they make choices of when, where, and how to enforce the laws Congress has passed. As a result, the implementation of federal Indian policy "rarely resembles anything previously described" by Congress.[31]

Which federal agencies administer Indian policy?

The Constitution divides the federal government into three separate branches: the legislative, the judicial, and the executive. The legislative branch (Congress) makes the law. The judicial branch (the courts) interprets the law. The executive branch (whose chief officer is the President) administers the law. Federal administrative agencies, such as those which administer Indian programs, are part of the executive branch of government. These agencies are created by Congress but staffed with people appointed by the President or persons acting under the President's command.

The first agency Congress created to administer Indian policy was the Office of Indian Affairs. Congress established it in 1824 and placed it within the War Department. In 1849 Congress transferred this agency to the newly created Department of the Interior, where it has remained ever since. In 1947 the Office of Indian Affairs was renamed the Bureau of Indian Affairs. Most of the government's Indian programs are administered by the BIA.

The highest official in the BIA is the Commissioner of Indian Affairs, who is appointed by the President with the approval of the Senate. The Commissioner is directly responsible to the Secretary of the Interior, who is the highest official in the Department of the Interior. The Secretary is appointed by the President with the Senate's approval and is directly responsible to the President.

The Secretary of the Interior and the Commissioner of Indian Affairs hire thousands of officials to assist them in performing the tasks that Congress has delegated to their offices. Most agency decisions are made by these subordinate officials, but are usually announced in the name of the Secretary or the Commissioner.

Although the BIA administers most of the federal government's Indian programs, other agencies administer a number of programs as well. In fact, at least nine cabinet-level departments and ten independent agencies administer Indian programs, and the budget for these programs totals over one billion dollars.[32] Chapter 16 discusses these programs.

What powers have been delegated by Congress to the Secretary of the Interior?

Most of the programs that affect Indians on a daily basis are administered by the Secretary of the Interior. For example, the Secretary has the power to regulate the sale and lease of Indian land, operate social welfare programs on reservations, control the use of water on irrigated Indian lands, regulate and approve Indian wills, operate Indian schools, purchase land for Indians and tribes, and regulate federal law enforcement on reservations.[33]

What powers have been delegated by Congress to the President?

A law passed by Congress in 1834 gives the President the general power to "prescribe such regulations as he may think fit for carrying into effect the various provisions of any act relating to Indian affairs."[34] However, the President has been delegated few specific powers regarding Indians, and it is not clear what authority the President actually has. During the late nineteenth century several presidents created Indian reservations without Congress's consent. Congress was so angered that it passed a law prohibiting the creation of any additional executive order reservations.[35]

In 1887 Congress authorized the President to give parcels of tribal lands to tribal members and to sell unoccupied tribal lands to non-Indians,[36] but Congress eliminated this power in 1934.[37] At the present time, the only specific Indian affairs authority that the President has is the power to appoint the Secretary of the Interior and the Commissioner of Indian Affairs. Of course, the President's position as chief executive gives the President the opportunity to exert a tremendous influence in Indian affairs, but few presidents have chosen to use that power.

Can an officer in the executive branch of government, such as the President or the Secretary of the Interior, formulate federal Indian policy?

No. Executive officials can only administer Indian policy;

they cannot establish it. Every action taken by an executive official must be authorized by Congress.[38]

Can Congress delegate authority to Indian tribes?

Yes. Congress can delegate to Indian tribes the same powers it can delegate to executive officials.[39] In 1953 Congress authorized tribes to regulate the sale of liquor within the reservation.[40] In recent years, tribes have been authorized to administer many social service and educational programs formerly administered by federal agencies.[41]

Have federal officials done a good job in their administration of Indian affairs?

In 1977 a Senate committee reported that the federal agencies administering the government's Indian programs are inefficient, unnecessarily complex, patronizing, insensitive, and antagonistic to tribal self-government.[42] These same criticisms have been voiced by many people[43] and by the courts.[44] In 1979 the Assistant Secretary of the Interior, the officer in charge of the Bureau of Indian Affairs, described the BIA as "a public administration disaster" that must make "radical changes" in the way it treats Indians and administers Indian programs.[45] In 1987 his successor in office described the bureau in similar terms.[46]

The BIA has the "reputation in Washington as the worst-managed agency in the federal government."[47] For example, two recent federal studies indicate that the BIA has failed to collect eleven billion dollars owed to tribes from oil royalties.[48] The BIA "has a sorry record of waste, corruption and choking red tape. A recent survey of government executives ranked it the least respected of 90 federal agencies, with the Indian Health Service close behind."[49]

Given that the majority of BIA employees are Indian, one might expect better results. However, the problem goes beyond personnel. As one commentator explained, the problem is threefold. First, the BIA is a "relatively powerless bureau" and is not situated within the Department of the Interior "so as to effectively help or represent Indians." Second, the department contains other agencies, such as the Bureau of Mines and the Bureau of Land Management, whose interests conflict with the BIA's, and the BIA "typically loses in those conflicts."

Finally, the BIA's internal structure is cumbersome and resistant to change.[50] In short, the BIA's primary goal is self-preservation rather than service to its clients. Consequently, it has increased rather than decreased its bureaucratization, and it has strenuously resisted efforts to diminish its stranglehold on Indian affairs.[51]

2. Regulating Tribal Governments

As one of its principal methods of regulating Indian affairs, Congress requires various government agencies, and particularly the Department of the Interior, to review certain actions of tribal governments. For example, the 181 tribes that organized their governments under the Indian Reorganization Act of 1934 had to submit their constitution and bylaws to the Interior Department for the Secretary's approval.[52] The Secretary then required many of these IRA tribes to include in their constitutions a provision that required every tribal law to be approved by the Secretary before it could go into effect, even though this provision was not required by the IRA.[53]

In recent years there has been a tendency both in Congress and in some federal agencies to allow more tribal self-government. IRA tribes, for instance, have been allowed by the Secretary of the Interior to remove from their constitutions the previously mentioned requirement of Secretarial approval of tribal laws.[54] In addition, Congress has passed laws that give tribes substantial authority over reservation activities.[55] Moreover, the Supreme Court has recognized that Indian tribes retain inherent powers of self-government and that many of these powers can be exercised without federal approval.[56]

Even in those areas (and many still remain) where federal agencies supervise and must approve of tribal activities, the courts have placed limits on agency action. These agencies must act as a trustee to Indian tribes and must exercise their powers in the tribe's best interests.[57] Further, when interpreting tribal constitutions or statutes, an agency must give deference to the tribe's own interpretation of its laws.[58] In other words, although a federal agency has a duty to ensure that a tribe conducts its activities in compliance with federal law, once compliance is obtained, the agency should not further interfere with the tribe's governmental affairs.[59]

On occasion disputes have arisen within a tribe as to which person or group is the legitimate governing body of the tribe. The federal government usually is reluctant to attempt to resolve such internal controversies. However, in order to carry out government-to-government relations between the United States and the tribe, the Bureau of Indian Affairs must identify the tribe's governing body. In these instances the bureau has examined tribal law to determine if it has been followed and, if not, the bureau has directed the tribe to follow tribal law and to designate a legitimate governing body.[60]

3. Termination

Congress has also implemented its authority over Indian affairs through the termination of tribal governments. Congress can do nothing worse to an Indian tribe; termination, according to some authorities, is equivalent to "genocide."[61]

What is "termination"?
Termination is the process by which Congress abolishes a tribe's government and ends (terminates) the federal government's trust relationship[62] with that tribe. Between 1954 and 1966 Congress terminated over one hundred tribes, most of them in Oregon and California.[63] In each case, Congress passed a law directing the Secretary of the Interior either to distribute all the tribe's property to tribal members or, if the tribe chose to incorporate itself under state law, to distribute all of the tribe's property to the corporation. Once the tribe's property was distributed, the Secretary was directed to place a notice in the Federal Register that the tribe was terminated. As soon as this notice appeared, the tribe lost its powers of self-government, the tribe and its members became ineligible for government services generally provided to Indians and tribes, and tribal members became subject to state law.[64]

Nothing else that Congress can do causes tribal members to lose more of their rights than termination. Termination is the ultimate weapon of Congress and the ultimate fear of tribes. Despite its drastic effect, the Supreme Court has held that Congress has the power under the Commerce Clause to terminate a tribe.[65]

Why has the federal government terminated Indian tribes?

A number of explanations have been offered for the government's termination policy. Some people claim that termination serves the best interests of the Indians. Termination, they say, will help Indians integrate into white society and eventually reduce Indian poverty. On the other hand, many Indians believe that Congress did not design termination to help them. They believe that Congress terminates tribes so that non-Indians can obtain Indian land and the federal government can save money by eliminating its treaty promises and trust responsibilities. "The Congressional policy of termination . . . [is] a new weapon in the ancient battle for Indian land. . . . In practice, termination is used as a weapon against Indian people in a modern war of conquest."[66]

What have been the consequences of the termination policy?

Termination has had disastrous effects.[67] Termination abolishes tribal government and eliminates all tribal landholdings. It forces Indians to make sudden and drastic changes in their way of life. Termination goes far beyond offering the Indian an opportunity to integrate into white society, an opportunity that many Indians find unappealing anyway. Termination eliminates most of the tribe's social, cultural, and governmental systems.

Has Congress halted its termination policy?

Yes, but the threat of termination is never far away. A bill introduced in Congress in 1977 called for the termination of every Indian tribe, but the bill did not pass. Congress has not terminated a tribe since 1966, and in 1973 and 1977 it even restored to federal status several tribes it previously terminated.[68] In 1970 President Nixon explained why the federal government had abandoned its termination policy.

This policy of forced termination is wrong, in my judgment, for a number of reasons. First, the premises on which it rests are wrong. Termination implies that the Federal Government has taken on a trusteeship responsibility for Indian communities as an act of generosity toward a disadvantaged people and that it can therefore discontinue this responsibility on a unilateral basis whenever it sees fit. But the unique status of Indian tribes does not rest on any premise such as this. The special relationship between Indians and the Federal Government is the result instead of solemn obligations which have been entered into by the United States Government. Down through the years, through written treaties and through formal and informal agreements, our Government has made specific commitments to the Indian people. For their part, the Indians have often surrendered claims to vast tracts of land and have accepted life on government reservations. In exchange, the Government has agreed to provide community services such as health, education, and public safety, services which would presumably allow Indian communities to enjoy a standard of living comparable to that of other Americans.

This goal, of course, has never been achieved. But the special relationship between the Indian tribes and the Federal Government which arises from these agreements continues to carry immense moral and legal force. To terminate this relationship would be no more appropriate than to terminate the citizenship rights of any other American.

The second reason for rejecting forced termination is that the practical results have been clearly harmful in the few instances in which termination actually has been tried. The removal of Federal trusteeship responsibility has produced considerable disorientation among the affected Indians and has left them unable to relate to a myriad of Federal, State, and local assistance efforts. Their economic and social condition has often been worse after termination than it was before.

The third argument I would make against forced termination concerns the effect it has had upon the overwhelming majority of the tribes which still enjoy a special relationship with the Federal Government. The very threat that this relationship may someday be ended has created a great deal of apprehension among Indian groups and this apprehension, in turn, has had a blighting effect on tribal progress. Any step which might result in great social, economic, or political autonomy is regarded with suspicion by many Indians who fear that it will only bring them closer to the day when the Federal Government will disavow its responsibility and cut them adrift.[69]

Have the courts established any protective rules regarding termination?

Yes. Because of the harmful effects of termination, courts have created several protective rules governing its application. The Supreme Court has held that, although a court cannot prevent Congress from terminating a tribe, it can refuse to recognize a termination unless the evidence shows "a clear and unequivocal intention of Congress to terminate its relationship with a tribe."[70] In addition, the Court has held that vested rights survive termination unless Congress expressly extinguishes them in the termination act. In *Menominee Tribe v. United States* (1968),[71] the Court held that the Menominee Indians could continue to exercise their treaty rights to hunt and fish, even though their tribe had been terminated, because the Menominee Termination Act had not expressly extinguished those rights.

Finally, courts have held that termination must comply with the Just Compensation and Due Process Clauses of the Constitution.[72] Therefore, Congress must provide monetary compensation for any land or other vested interests that are lost through termination.[73] In addition, if federal officials fail to comply with all of the requirements of a termination law, a federal court can "unterminate" the tribe.[74]

4. Tribal Membership

Who controls tribal membership, the tribe or the federal government?

Actually, both do. A tribe has the right to determine tribal membership for tribal purposes.[75] The federal government has the right to determine tribal membership for federal purposes.[76]

Each time Congress creates an Indian program, it decides which Indians can participate in it. Congress has used different standards for different programs. Most federal programs are available to everyone listed on a tribe's membership roll. Other programs require a certain amount of tribal blood, such as one-quarter or one-half. Consequently, a tribal member can qualify for some federal programs and not qualify for others. Similarly, persons ineligible for tribal membership may qualify for certain federal programs if they have the requisite amount of Indian blood.[77]

Another situation in which Congress must determine tribal membership arises when the government takes property from a tribe. When it does, compensation must be paid to the tribe's members and Congress must decide who they are. Congress can adopt the tribe's standard or use a different standard. The Supreme Court has held that Congress can use any reasonable method to determine tribal membership for federal purposes.[78] Once Congress determines the standard, the Secretary of the Interior is then instructed to prepare a final roll of tribal members using that standard.

Is the Secretary's decision reviewable by the courts?

To some extent, yes. If an individual's name does not appear on the Secretary's final roll, there are two types of challenges she or he can make. An argument can be made that the federal standard is so arbitrary and unreasonable it violates the Due Process Clause of the Fifth Amendment, discussed earlier. However, in most situations, this argument will fail because Congress has wide discretion in determining tribal membership for federal purposes.[79]

If an individual agrees with the federal standard but feels it was misapplied in her or his case, the individual can argue that the omission occurred due to mistake or fraud or because the Secretary failed to follow proper procedures for determining eligibility. If the court agrees, it can order the Secretary to add the individual's name to the roll.[80]

5. Regulating Indian Land

The extensive taking of Indian land, and the extensive regulation of what remains, clearly shows how Congress has implemented its Indian policies over the years.[81] Indians have very little land left and what they do have is heavily regulated by Congress. Congress justifies its paternalistic regulation of Indian land on the grounds that Indians need protection from market forces and from improvident disposal of their property.[82]

Indian land is either trust land or non-trust land. Trust land is owned by the federal government but has been set aside for the exclusive use of an Indian or tribe. Non-trust land is owned outright by an Indian or tribe. With few exceptions, every Indian reservation created by the federal government originally consisted entirely of trust land. At one time these landholdings were very large, but the government continually reduced the size of reservations. Today, only fifty million acres remain in tribal hands, and most of it is still in trust status.[83] The Supreme Court has held that all Indian land is subject to the control of Congress.[84] Congress has placed many restrictions on the use and sale of Indian land.

What restrictions have been placed on the sale of Indian land, both trust and non-trust?

The federal government controls the sale of trust land because the federal government owns it. Indians and tribes only have a "beneficial interest" in trust land—the right to use it. The federal government holds the title to all trust land.[85]

As explained in chapter 1, from 1887 until 1934 many Indians were allotted parcels of trust land. Later, some of these Indian allottees were given deeds to these parcels. Any Indian whose allotment still remains in trust status can request the Secretary of the Interior to issue a "fee patent" (a deed) to the land.[86] If the Secretary issues the patent, the Indian becomes the owner of the land and can sell it whenever he or she wishes.

In order to obtain this patent, the Indian must prove that he or she "is competent and capable of managing his or her affairs."[87] Once the applicant proves competency, the Secretary must issue the patent.[88] Determinations of competency are left by law to the Secretary's discretion and courts generally will not overrule the Secretary's decision.[89] At one time the Secretary routinely issued fee patents to Indians who had not applied for them, but courts looked so unfavorably on these "forced" patents that the Secretary has given up this practice.[90]

Many Indians feel that they should be able to sell their trust land whenever they want to. Unfortunately, the continued sale of trust land is harmful to tribal government because most of it is sold to non-Indians. In order to protect tribes, the Secretary usually gives them a first option of buying trust land whenever its sale would adversely affect their interests.[91] However, if the tribe refuses to purchase the land, the Secretary must issue a fee patent to the Indian allottee even if the tribe requests that the application be denied.[92]

Non-trust land receives different treatment. Congress does not regulate the sale of non-trust land owned by an individual Indian. Indians who own land can sell it in the same way that non-Indians can. Tribal property, however, has more restrictions. A federal statute enacted in 1790 prohibits tribes from selling their land, whether trust or non-trust, without the approval of the federal government.[93] Any sale of tribal land without the government's consent is void, and the tribe can bring a lawsuit (even many years later) to recover the land.[94]

How does the federal government regulate the leasing of trust land?

In virtually every way. Indian trust land can be leased to Indians or non-Indians, but only in accordance with federal law. Any lease that does not comply with federal law is invalid.[95]

A separate federal statute governs each kind of trust lease, including farming and grazing leases, mining leases, oil and gas exploration leases, and leases for public, religious, educational, recreational, residential, or business purposes.[96] The Secretary of the Interior must approve each of these leases before it becomes valid. The Secretary has established a large number of regulations that govern the terms and conditions of these various leases.[97]

The government's leasing laws and the Secretary's regulations are too numerous and extensive to be individually examined here. Each type of lease has its own requirements. For instance, a lease for grazing purposes cannot exceed a term of ten years, while a lease for residential purposes may be made for twenty-five years. Oil and gas leases, in particular, are closely scrutinized (at least in theory).[98]

If you are involved in the leasing of Indian trust land, you will need to pay close attention to the laws and regulations governing your type of lease. Even after a lease is approved, the Secretary can cancel it if it violates federal law or if its terms and conditions are not being met.[99] In such cases, the parties to the lease are entitled to a hearing before the cancellation takes effect, and the Secretary's decision can be reversed by a court if it was improper.[100]

As a general rule, Indian trust land cannot be leased unless the Indian owner consents.[101] (Although the federal government, and not the Indian, owns trust land, the Indian beneficiary is often referred to as the "owner.") However, trust land that is owned by more than one Indian (a situation that may occur when trust land is inherited by more than one heir) can be leased at the Secretary's discretion if the owners cannot agree on whether to lease the land. As with all other exercises of Secretarial discretion, the terms of such a lease must be in the Indians' best interests.[102]

On most Indian reservations the Realty Office of the Bureau of Indian Affairs handles the leasing of Indian land, under the direction of the Secretary of the Interior. Those persons who lease Indian land (the "lessees") pay their rent to the Realty Office. The Realty Office then gives this money to the Indian beneficiary (the "lessor").

The Secretary of the Interior has the same broad power to regulate a tribe's trust land as an Indian's trust land.[103] However, the Secretary usually approves a tribe's leasing decision unless there is evidence of mistake, fraud or undue influence.[104]

Does the federal government regulate the inheritance of Indian land?

This depends on whether it is trust land or non-trust land. Congress has decided not to regulate the inheritance of non-trust land. Therefore, tribal law controls the inheritance of this property if it is located within the reservation and state law controls if it is located outside the reservation.

On the other hand, Congress heavily regulates the inheritance of trust land, virtually preempting the tribe's authority. For instance, Congress has determined that (1) if an Indian dies without a will, the Indian's trust land will be inherited according to state law rather than tribal law; (2) if an Indian dies with a will, the will is invalid unless it previously had been approved by the Secretary of the Interior; (3) if an Indian dies without a will and without legal heirs, the Indian's trust land will go to the tribe; and (4) trust land cannot be inherited by any person who is not a tribal member or who is not a legal heir of the deceased,[105] although this does mean that a non-Indian spouse or relative can inherit an Indian trust allotment (and a fee patent will then be issued).[106] The Supreme Court has upheld the authority of Congress to regulate Indian inheritance.[107] However, Congress does not have absolute authority. In 1987 the Court invalidated a federal statute that required an Indian's inherited interest in trust land to "escheat" (be returned to) the tribe if it constituted less than 2 percent of the total acreage of the property. The Court held that the statute constituted a taking of property without just compensation in violation of the Just Compensation Clause in the U.S. Constitution.[108]

Congress has directed the Secretary of the Interior to administer the federal laws governing the inheritance of trust land. The Secretary, in turn, has issued extensive regulations.[109] These regulations include the previously mentioned authority to approve wills.[110] However, the Supreme Court has held that the Secretary may not disapprove a will unless there is evidence of fraud or duress or lack of mental competency on the part of the Indian who made it.[111] The Secretary's decision regarding the distribution of property, moreover, can be challenged in court if it is arbitrary and capricious.[112]

Are there other ways in which Congress regulates trust land?

Yes. Besides controlling the sale, lease, and inheritance of trust land, the federal government also controls easements and rights of way on trust land. The Secretary of the Interior must consent to any highway, powerline, or oil and gas pipeline across trust land,[113] although the tribe must also consent in most cases.[114] The Secretary also manages the forestry on and irrigation of trust land.[115] In addition, by federal statute (Title 25 United States Code, Section 81) no contract or agreement can be made with Indian tribes "relative to their lands" unless it is approved by the Secretary of the Interior. This statute is so broad that even a contract for a bingo hall on tribal land was found to require federal approval.[116] An Indian who wishes to mortgage a trust allotment (which is permitted in certain situations) must obtain prior Secretarial approval.[117]

Tribes and individual Indians can acquire additional trust land by two methods, both of which require Secretarial approval. First, the Secretary can purchase non-trust land and convert it into trust land for an Indian or tribe.[118] However, this authority is discretionary, and the Secretary cannot be forced to purchase land. However, the Secretary must follow the Interior Department's written guidelines in making these decisions.[119] Applicants do not have to prove that they are "needy" or "landless" to qualify.[120] Unfortunately, though, Congress has appropriated very little money for these land purchases.[121]

Second, an Indian or tribe can purchase non-trust land and request that the Secretary convert it into, or exchange it for, trust land.[122] As explained later in this book, there are a number of tax and other advantages to having land in trust status. In 1988, for example, the Secretary placed in trust status land owned by a tribe so that the tribe could conduct a bingo operation on it free from state regulation.

Can Congress diminish the size of, or abolish, an Indian reservation?

Yes. Congress has diminished the size of many reservations and abolished many others. The Supreme Court has upheld the right of Congress to do this providing the government compensates the tribe for any land that is lost.[123]

As explained earlier, Congress terminated over one hundred tribes between 1950 and 1965, thereby abolishing their reservations. Many other reservations were abolished prior to 1950, especially between 1820 and 1870, when tribes on eastern reservations were relocated to the Oklahoma Indian Territory or to other western lands. In addition, Congress frequently has decreased the size of Indian reservations.

There are, in fact, four methods that the government has used to reduce or eliminate Indian reservations. Termination is the first and most drastic, completely abolishing the reservation. The reservation simply ceases to exist. The second method is to sever a portion of land from the reservation, remove the Indians from this area, eliminate the trust land located there, and declare this portion of the reservation "terminated" or "restored to the public domain."[124] This allows the land to be purchased by non-Indians and, at the same time, extinguishes the tribe's control over the region. The third method is to sever a portion of land from the reservation, while allowing individual allotments of trust land to remain in it, but still declare the area terminated and restored to the public domain.[125] This extinguishes the tribe's control over the area except for the remaining trust land, which is still considered "Indian country."

("Indian country" and its legal implications are discussed in chapter 2.) The fourth method is to "open" the reservation to settlement by non-Indians, allowing them to purchase unoccupied ("surplus") land within the reservation.[126] This does not diminish the size of the reservation or change exterior boundaries. However, it creates a "checkerboard" pattern within the reservation in which non-Indian land adjoins Indian trust land.

This fourth method has spawned considerable litigation. It often is difficult to determine what Congress intended long ago when it first allowed non-Indians to purchase land on a particular reservation. Was Congress merely opening the reservation to non-Indian settlement or was Congress removing ("disestablishing") this area from the reservation? The Supreme Court has held that if a reasonable doubt exists as to what Congress intended, it will be presumed that Congress did not disestablish the opened area from the reservation.[127]

Are there any limitations on the federal government's control over Indian land?

The major limitation is the Just Compensation Clause,[128] but it is not very effective. It does not stop Congress from taking Indian land; it only guarantees that Congress will pay compensation for any land that is taken. In 1984, for example, the Supreme Court held that Congress can authorize federal and state officials to build dams or other public work projects on tribal land even without the tribe's consent, although the tribe is entitled to compensation.[129] Compensation must be paid not only for the value of the land but also for the value of such things as timber and minerals, as well as interest from the day the land was taken.[130]

6. Regulating Tribal Assets

What control does Congress have over tribal assets?

The power of Congress to regulate tribal assets—such as tribal funds, land, and other property—is "one of the most fundamental expressions, if not the major expression, of the constitutional power of Congress over Indian affairs."[131] Congressional power over tribal assets is virtually absolute.[132] This power is so extensive that Congress can order a tribe to distribute all of its assets and to disband as a government—a power that Congress exercised with disastrous results during the termination era of the 1950s.

Federal statutes give the Secretary of the Interior ongoing authority to administer most tribal assets. The Secretary has extensive control over tribal land, as already explained. The Secretary also has the authority to take tribal funds and use them to pay for Indian education, road construction, hospitals, medical supplies, and tribal insurance.[133] However, as in all other areas, the Secretary has no independent authority to manage tribal assets and can only do what Congress has authorized.

7. Regulating Individual Property

Does Congress regulate the private property of Indians?

Some property, yes; other property, no. In theory, Congress has the power to regulate all private property of Indians, such as wages earned from private employment, goods, livestock, loans, and crops, but it has not chosen to do so. As a general rule, the only private property of Indians that the federal government regulates is trust land and the proceeds derived from trust land. For example, money received from the lease of trust land, or from the sale of timber from trust land, is deposited in an Individual Indian Money (IIM) account under the control of the Secretary of the Interior. Federal law requires that any money deposited in an IIM account must be used for the "benefit" of the Indian "in the discretion of the Secretary of the Interior."[134] In addition, money received directly from the federal government, such as money derived from the sale of tribal lands, usually is ordered by Congress to be placed in these IIM accounts. However, it is also clear that the Secretary is not permitted to control any Indian assets not placed under the Secretary's authority by Congress.[135]

A great deal of controversy surrounds these IIM accounts. In order for Indians to withdraw their money from them, they must convince some government official that it will be used solely for their "benefit." Some government officials make it difficult for Indians to withdraw these funds by imposing their own standards of propriety on the Indians. These officials seem to forget whose money it is. Moreover, in a recent case it was discovered that the Secretary had allowed an Indian's creditor to withdraw funds from the Indian's IIM account without notice to the Indian. A court held that this was unconstitutional.[136]

Indian children can have IIM accounts also, which hold income that they have received or inherited from trust properties. The Secretary must manage these accounts in the best interest of the children. This means that even a child's parents cannot receive funds from these accounts unless they show that the funds will be used for the minor's benefit.[137]

8. Trade and Liquor Regulation

Does Congress have the power to regulate trade with the Indians?

Yes. The Constitution gives Congress the express power to regulate commerce with the Indian tribes. The Supreme Court has described this power as being "plenary"—full and complete.[138]

There is almost no aspect of Indian trade that is not regulated by the federal government. As early as 1790 Congress passed a comprehensive law "to regulate trade and intercourse with the Indian tribes," and most of its provisions are still in effect.[139] This law requires all persons, except Indians "of the full blood," who trade on an Indian reservation to obtain a federal license and to obey certain restrictions on the type of goods and services being offered and the manner of their sale. Violators are subject to the forfeiture of their goods and a five hundred dollar fine.[140]

Congress has delegated to the Commissioner of Indian Affairs the authority to regulate Indian trade.[141] Only the Commissioner can issue a trading license, and no license will be issued unless the Commissioner is satisfied that the applicant is "a proper person to engage in such trade."[142] The Commissioner has enacted regulations describing in detail how trade with Indians must be conducted, such as the time and place of sales, the price and quality of goods and services, credit transactions, taxation of sales, and the rental of buildings.[143]

An individual who discovers that someone is violating any of these federal regulations is authorized by federal law to file a lawsuit against that person in the name of the United States.[144] If the court finds a violation, the trader's goods must be confiscated by the federal government and sold, and the person filing the suit is entitled to half the proceeds.[145] If federal officials are not fulfilling their duty to regulate reservation traders, a person can file suit to require them to enforce the law.[146]

Congress has also decided that federal employees who work in the area of Indian affairs may not trade with Indians except on behalf of the United States.[147] This law ensures that government employees cannot profit from their private relationship with Indians. In addition, Congress has made it a crime to negotiate with an Indian tribe for the sale or lease of tribal land without the federal government's consent.[148] Although this law limits the ability of tribes to manage their own affairs, when it was first passed in 1790 it protected tribes from being swindled by non-Indians who were trying to take their land.

Does the government's power to regulate trade include the power to regulate liquor?

Yes, and Congress has made extensive use of this power.[149] Congress first passed a law prohibiting all sales of liquor to Indians, both on and off the reservation. Later, this prohibition applied only to sales on or near Indian reservations. Still later, Congress amended the law again so that it applied only to on-reservation sales. Finally, Congress authorized each tribe to decide for itself what types of liquor regulations to establish and to issue liquor licenses under its own rules.[150] In a recent case the Supreme Court upheld the right of a tribe to refuse to license a non-Indian who wanted to sell liquor on the reservation.[151]

9. Criminal Jurisdiction

Indian tribes had systems of criminal justice long before non-Indians came to this continent. Until 1885 the federal government did not interfere with these traditional tribal systems. The punishment of crimes committed by one reservation Indian against another was left solely in tribal hands.

In 1885 Congress passed the Major Crimes Act,[152] which authorized federal officials to prosecute reservation Indians who committed certain crimes. This act was passed in response to a highly publicized trial that occurred in the Dakota Territory in 1883, in which an Indian by the name of Crow Dog was convicted of murdering the Chief of the Brule Sioux, Spotted

Tail. Crow Dog appealed his conviction to the Supreme Court arguing that federal officials had no right to prosecute him for something that occurred on an Indian reservation between two Indians. The Supreme Court agreed with Crow Dog.[153]

That situation quickly changed. Believing that Indians would become "civilized a great deal sooner"[154] if federal officials had criminal jurisdiction over them, Congress authorized the federal government to prosecute seven crimes when committed by one Indian against another within Indian country: murder, manslaughter, rape, assault with intent to kill, arson, burglary, and larceny. Since then, more crimes have been added to the list.[155]

The government's decision to extend its criminal laws into Indian country marked a major departure in policy and greatly expanded its control over Indians. The effect of this extension has been to diminish tribal self-government. A full discussion of the federal government's criminal jurisdiction is contained in chapter 8.

NOTES

1. *Worcester v. Georgia*, 31 U.S. 515 (1832); *Menominee Tribe v. U.S.*, 391 U.S. 404 (1968); *Antoine v. Washington*, 420 U.S. 194 (1975).
2. V. Deloria, Jr., *Custer Died for Your Sins* (1969); V. Deloria, Jr., *Behind the Trail of Broken Treaties* (1974); A. Josephy, *Red Power* (1971); J. Green and S. Work, *Inherent Indian Sovereignty*, 4 Am. Indian L. Rev. 311; F. Prucha, *The Great Father* (1984).
3. *Worcester*, note 1 above, 31 U.S. at 559. *See also U.S. v. Kagama*, 118 U.S. 375 (1886). In 1871, however, Congress passed a law, 25 U.S.C. Sec.71, prohibiting the federal government from making any more treaties with Indian tribes.
4. *Tee-Hit-Ton Indians v. U.S.*, 348 U.S. 272, 279 (1955).
5. *Johnson v. McIntosh*, 21 U.S. 542 (1823).
6. *Kagama*, note 3 above, 118 U.S. at 382–83.
7. *U.S. v. Sandoval*, 231 U.S. 28 (1913); *Morton v. Mancari*, 417 U.S. 535 (1974).
8. *U.S. v. Wheeler*, 435 U.S. 313, 319 (1978).
9. *Santa Clara Pueblo v. Martinez*, 436 U.S. 49, 56 (1978).
10. *Delaware Tribal Business Committee v. Weeks*, 430 U.S. 73, 84 (1977), citing *U.S. v. Tillamooks*, 329 U.S. 40, 54 (1946).

11. The Fifth Amendment provides: "No person shall be . . . deprived of life, liberty, or property, without due process of law; nor shall private property be taken for public use, without just compensation."

12. *Bolling v. Sharpe*, 347 U.S. 497 (1954); *U.S. v. Antelope*, 430 U.S. 641 (1977); *Hodel v. Irving*, 481 U.S. 704 (1987).

13. *Menominee Tribe*, note 1 above.

14. *Antoine v. U.S.*, 710 F.2d 477 (8th Cir. 1983).

15. *Shoshone Tribe of Indians v. U.S.*, 299 U.S. 476 (1937); *U.S. v. Sioux Nation of Indians*, 448 U.S. 371 (1980). The amount of compensation that must be paid is the value of the land at the time it was taken, plus interest. *U.S. v. Creek Nation*, 295 U.S. 183 (1935).

16. *Choate v. Trapp*, 224 U.S. 665 (1911). *But see Tiger v. Western Investment Co.*, 221 U.S. 286 (1911).

17. *See Littlewolf v. Lujan*, 877 F.2d 1058 (D.C. Cir. 1989), *cert. denied*, 110 S.Ct. 837 (1990).

18. *Morton v. Ruiz*, 415 U.S. 199 (1974), *U.S. v. Winnebago Tribe of Nebraska*, 542 F.2d 1002 (8th Cir. 1976); *Northern Arapaho Tribe v. Hodel*, 808 F.2d 741, 748 (10th Cir. 1987).

19. *Antelope*, note 12 above, 420 U.S. at 645. *See also Ruiz*, note 18 above; *Washington v. Confederated Bands and Tribes of the Yakima Indian Nation*, 439 U.S. 463, 500–501 (1979).

20. 417 U.S. 535 (1974).

21. *Id.*, 417 U.S. at 553 n.24.

22. *See also Preston v. Heckler*, 734 F.2d 1359 (9th Cir. 1984).

23. *See, e.g., Washington v. Passenger Fishing Vessel Ass'n*, 443 U.S. 658 (1979) (fishing); *Winters v. U.S.*, 207 U.S. 564 (1908) (water); *Alaska Chap., Assoc. Gen'l Contractors v. Pierce*, 694 F.2d 1162 (9th Cir. 1982) (commercial).

24. *Antelope*, note 12 above.

25. *Tiger*, note 16 above; *Simmons v. Eagle Seelatsee*, 244 F. Supp. 808 (E.D. Wash. 1965), *aff'd mem.*, 384 U.S. 209 (1966); *Weeks*, note 10 above.

26. *U.S. v. Jim*, 409 U.S. 80 (1972).

27. *Northern Cheyenne Tribe v. Hollowbreast*, 425 U.S. 649 (1976).

28. *Mancari*, note 7 above, 417 U.S., at 555. *See also Yakima Indian Nation*, note 19 above.

29. *U.S. v. Nice*, 241 U.S. 591 (1916).

30. American Indian Policy Review Commission, *Final Report* p. 232 (Washington, D.C.: Government Printing Office, 1977).

31. V. Deloria, Jr., (ed.), *American Indian Policy in the Twentieth Century* p. 6 (1985).

32. *Final Report*, note 30 above, p. 247.

33. *See respectively,* 25 U.S.C. Secs. 391–415(d), 13, 381, 371–80, 271–304(b), 463–65, 174–202.

34. 25 U.S.C. Sec. 9.

35. 25 U.S.C. Sec. 398(d).

36. 25 U.S.C. Sec. 331.

37. 25 U.S.C. Sec. 461.

38. *U.S. v. George,* 228 U.S. 14 (1913); *Organized Village of Kake v. Egan,* 369 U.S. 60 (1962).

39. *See U.S. v. Mazurie,* 419 U.S. 544 (1975).

40. 18 U.S.C. Sec. 1611. *See Mazurie, id.*

41. These programs are described in ch. 16.

42. *Final Report,* note 30 above, pp. 231–99.

43. *See, e.g.,* the sources cited in note 2 above, and *Our Brother's Keeper: The Indian in White America* (E. Cohn ed. 1969).

44. *See, e.g., Cheyenne River Sioux Tribe v. Kleppe,* 424 F. Supp. 448 (D.S.D. 1977), *rev'd on other grounds,* 566 F.2d 1085 (8th Cir. 1977), *cert. denied,* 439 U.S. 820 (1978); *City of Tacoma, Washington v. Andrus,* 457 F. Supp. 342 (D.D.C. 1978); *McClanahan v. Hodel,* 14 Indian L. Rep. 3113 (D.N.M. 1987).

45. Statement of Forrest Gerard before the National Congress of American Indians, Washington, DC, Jan. 18, 1979.

46. Statement of Ross Swimmer quoted in The Arizona Republic (Oct. 4, 1987), pp. 9–11.

47. Arizona Republic, *id.,* p. 8.

48. *Id.,* p. 3. *See also McClanahan v. Hodel,* note 44 above, 14 Indian L. Rep. at 3117.

49. "This Land is Their Land," Time Magazine (Jan. 14, 1991), 6.

50. M. G. Lacy, "The United States and American Indians: Political Relations," in V. Deloria, note 31 above, pp. 98–99 (citations omitted).

51. R. Nelson and J. Sheley, "Bureau of Indian Affairs Influence on Indian Self-Determination," in V. Deloria, note 31 above, pp. 177–82.

52. 25 U.S.C. Sec. 476.

53. *See Kerr-McGee Corp. v. U.S.,* 471 U.S. 195, 198 (1985).

54. *Id.; Ft. McDermitt Paiute Shoshone Tribe v. Acting Phoenix Area Director,* 17 IBIA 144 [16 Indian L. Rep. 7047] (1989).

55. *See* ch. 1, Sec. H.

56. *Kerr-McGee,* note 53 above.

57. *See* cases cited in note 18 above, and ch. 4.

58. *See Menominee Tribal Enterprises v. Minneapolis Area Director,* 15 IBIA 263 [14 Indian L. Rep. 7053] (1987) and cases cited therein.

59. *Rogers v. Acting Deputy Ass't Secretary,* 15 IBIA 13 [13 Indian L.

Rep. 7082] (1986); *Benally v. Navajo Area Director*, 9 IBIA 284 [9 Indian L. Rep. 6043] (1982).

60. *See Goodface v. Grassrope*, 708 F.2d 335 (8th Cir. 1983); *Milam v. U.S. Dep't of Interior*, 10 Indian L. Rep. 3013 (D.D.C. 1982); *Crooks v. Area Director*, 14 IBIA 181 [13 Indian L. Rep. 7038] (1986); *Frease v. Sacramento Area Director, BIA*, 17 IBIA 241 [16 Indian L. Rep. 7093] (1989).

61. *See, e.g.*, R. Strickland, *Genocide-At-Law: An Historic and Contemporary View of the Native American Experience*, 34 Kan. L. Rev. 713 (1986).

62. Ch. 3 explains a trust relationship.

63. *Final Report*, note 30 above, pp. 447–53.

64. *See, e.g.*, Menominee Termination Act, 25 U.S.C. Secs. 985 *et seq.*; Klamath Termination Act, 25 U.S.C. Secs. 564 *et seq. See* discussion, *South Carolina v. Catawba Indian Tribe*, 476 U.S. 498 (1986).

65. *Menominee Tribe*, note 1 above.

66. V. Deloria, Jr., *Custer Died for Your Sins* pp. 60, 81 (1969). *See also* W. Brophy and S. Aberle, *The Indians, America's Unfinished Business* (1966); F. Prucha, *The Great Father* pp. 1046–59 (1984).

67. *Final Report*, note 30 above, p. 457.

68. *See, e.g.*, 25 U.S.C. Sec. 903 (Menominee tribe); 25 U.S.C. Secs. 861–61c (Wyandotte, Peoria, and Ottawa tribes); 25 U.S.C. Sec. 761 (Paiute tribe).

69. President Nixon's Message to Congress, July 8, 1970, H.R. Doc. No. 91–363, 91st Cong., 2d Sess.

70. *Nice*, note 29 above, 241 U.S. at 599.

71. 391 U.S. 404 (1968).

72. These constitutional provisions are quoted in note 11 above.

73. *Cherokee Nation v. So. Kansas R.R. Co.*, 135 U.S. 641 (1890); *Klamath and Modoc Tribes v. U.S.* 436 F.2d 1008 (Ct. Cl. 1971).

74. *Smith v. U.S.*, 515 F. Supp. 56 (N.D. Cal. 1978); *Hardwick v. U.S.*, No. C–79–1710SW (N.D. Cal. 1979).

75. *Santa Clara Pueblo v. Martinez*, 436 U.S. 49 (1978).

76. *Cherokee Nation v. Hitchcock*, 187 U.S. 294 (1902); *Eagle Seelatsee*, note 25 above.

77. *Cf. Santa Clara Pueblo*, note 75 above.

78. *Tiger*, note 16 above; *Eagle Seelatsee*, note 25 above. *See* 25 U.S.C. Sec. 163.

79. *See* cases cited in note 76 above; *Ruff v. Hodel*, 770 F.2d 839 (9th Cir. 1985).

80. *U.S. ex rel. West v. Hitchcock*, 205 U.S. 80 (1907); *Garfield v. U.S. ex rel. Goldsby*, 211 U.S. 249 (1908). *See also Underwood v. Deputy*

Ass't Secretary, 14 IBIA 3 [13 Indian L. Rep. 7013] (1986) (Secretary's criteria to determine blood quantum must be published in the Federal Register).

81. For a summary of these policies see ch. 1. *See also* K. Kickingbird and K. Ducheneaux, *One Hundred Million Acres* (1973).

82. *See* F. Cohen, *Handbook of Indian Law* pp. 508–9 (1982).

83. Ch. 1 discusses the methods used by the federal government to obtain Indian land.

84. *Poafpybitty v. Skelly Oil Co.*, 390 U.S. 365 (1968); *Sandoval*, note 7 above.

85. *See* 25 U.S.C. Secs. 348, 372, and 483.

86. 25 U.S.C. Sec. 349. The application process is set forth in 25 C.F.R. Part 152 (1990).

87. 25 U.S.C. Sec. 349.

88. *Oglala Sioux Tribe v. Hallett*, 708 F.2d 326 (8th Cir. 1983); *Oglala Sioux Tribe v. Commissioner of Indian Affairs*, IBIA 79–11-A [6 Indian L. Rep. I–30] (1979).

89. 25 U.S.C. Sec. 349. *See West v. Hitchcock*, note 80 above.

90. *See Hallett*, note 88 above; *U.S. v. Arenas*, 158 F.2d 730 (9th Cir. 1946), *cert. denied*, 331 U.S. 842 (1947).

91. 25 C.F.R. 152.27 (1990).

92. *See* cases cited in note 88 above.

93. 25 U.S.C. Sec. 177.

94. *Sandoval*, note 7 above; *Joint Tribal Council of the Passamaquoddy Tribe v. Morton*, 528 F.2d 370 (1st Cir. 1975).

95. *Bunch v. Cole*, 263 U.S. 250 (1923); *Lawrence v. U.S.*, 381 F.2d 989 (9th Cir. 1967).

96. 25 U.S.C. Secs. 393, 396, 398, and 415, respectively.

97. 25 C.F.R. Part 162 (1990).

98. The BIA has been notoriously inept in regulating oil and gas leases of Indian trust land. *See* notes 48–49 above and accompanying text. *See also Jicarilla Apache Tribe v. Supron Energy Corp.*, 782 F.2d 855 (10th Cir. 1986) (en banc), *adopting in relevant part* 728 F.2d 1555 (10th Cir. 1984) (dissenting opinion), *cert. denied*, 479 U.S. 970 (1986).

99. *Bunch*, note 95 above; *U.S. v. So. Pacific Transp. Co.*, 543 F.2d 676 (9th Cir. 1976).

100. *Pence v. Kleppe*, 529 F.2d 135 (9th Cir. 1976); *Coomes v. Atkinson*, 414 F. Supp. 975 (D.S.D. 1976); *Danks v. Fields*, 696 F.2d 572 (8th Cir. 1982).

101. *See, e.g.*, 25 U.S.C. Sec. 395; *Coast Indian Community v. U.S.*, 550 F.2d 639, 650 n.25 (Ct. Cl. 1977).

102. 25 U.S.C. Sec. 380. *See Kenai Oil and Gas, Inc. v. Dep't of Interior*, 671 F.2d 383 (10th Cir. 1982).
103. *Sunderland v. U.S.*, 266 U.S. 226 (1924). *But see Coomes*, note 100 above (the Secretary must distribute lease income in timely fashion).
104. *See* Memo Sol. I.D. May 22, 1937.
105. 25 U.S.C. Secs. 348, 373, and 373(a) respectively. *See Cultee v. U.S.*, 713 F.2d 1455 (9th Cir. 1983), *cert. denied*, 466 U.S. 950 (1984).
106. 25 U.S.C. Sec. 464. *See Sheppard v. Sheppard*, 655 P.2d 895 (Idaho 1982); *Estate of Barnes*, 17 IBIA 72 [16 Indian L. Rep. 7011] (1989). Non-Indians cannot inherit individual trust property where the tribe is organized under the Indian Reorganization Act. *Estate of Cladoosby*, 15 IBIA 203 [14 Indian L. Rep. 7038] (1987).
107. *U.S. v. Bowling*, 256 U.S. 484 (1921); *Blanset v. Cardin*, 256 U.S. 319 (1921).
108. *Hodel v. Irving*, 481 U.S. 704 (1987).
109. 43 C.F.R. subp. D (1990).
110. 25 U.S.C. Sec. 373. *Cf. Dull Knife v. Morton*, 394 F. Supp. 1299 (D.S.D. 1974) (the Secretary must probate Indian estate within a reasonable time).
111. *Tooahneppah (Goombi) v. Hickel*, 397 U.S. 598 (1970).
112. *Kicking Woman v. Hodel*, 878 F.2d 1203 (10th Cir. 1989).
113. 25 U.S.C. Secs. 311–18.
114. *Blackfeet Indian Tribe v. Montana Power Co.*, 838 F.2d 1055 (9th Cir.), *cert. denied*, 488 U.S. 828 (1988); *McClanahan v. Hodel*, note 44 above.
115. 25 U.S.C. Secs. 466 and 381, respectively.
116. *Barona Group of Capitan Mission Indians v. American Management & Amusement, Inc.*, 824 F.2d 710 (9th Cir. 1987).
117. 25 U.S.C. Sec. 483a. *See Northwest So. Dak. PCA v. Smith*, 784 F.2d 323 (8th Cir. 1986).
118. 25 U.S.C. Sec. 465. *See Chase v. McMasters*, 573 F.2d 1011 (8th Cir. 1978).
119. *Donahue v. Butz*, 363 F. Supp. 1316 (N.D. Cal. 1973); *Eades v. Muskogee Area Director*, 17 IBIA 198 [16 Indian L. Rep. 7073] (1989).
120. *City of Tacoma*, note 44 above; *Florida v. U.S. Dep't of the Interior*, 768 F.2d 1248 (11th Cir. 1985), *cert. denied*, 475 U.S. 1011 (1986).
121. In 1989, the Secretary claimed that he had no money at all for these purchases. *See Confederated Tribes of the Coos, Lower Umqua & Suislaw Indians v. U.S.*, 16 Indian L. Rep. 3087 (D. Or. 1989).
122. 25 U.S.C. Sec. 463(e). *See Stevens v. Comm'r*, 452 F.2d 741 (9th Cir. 1971).

123. *See* cases cited in note 15 above.
124. *See, e.g.*, 17 Stat. 633 (1873), restoring a portion of a reservation to the public domain. *Cf. Russ v. Wilkins*, 624 F.2d 914 (9th Cir. 1980).
125. *See DeCoteau v. District County Court*, 420 U.S. 425 (1975); *Rosebud Sioux Tribe v. Kneip*, 430 U.S. 584 (1976).
126. *See* cases cited in note 125 above.
127. *Id. See also Solem v. Bartlett*, 465 U.S. 463 (1984); *Mattz v. Arnett*, 412 U.S. 481 (1973); *Ute Indian Tribe v. Utah*, 773 F.2d 1087 (10th Cir. 1985) (en banc), *cert. denied*, 479 U.S. 994 (1986).
128. *See* note 11 above and accompanying text.
129. *Escondido Mutual Water Co. v. La Jolla Band of Mission Indians*, 466 U.S. 765 (1984).
130. *Sioux Nation*, note 15 above; *U.S. v. Shoshone Tribe*, 304 U.S. 111 (1938); *Menominee Tribe*, note 1 above.
131. *Weeks*, note 10 above, 430 U.S. at 86 (citation omitted).
132. *Id. See also Sizemore v. Brady*, 235 U.S. 441 (1914); *Hollowbreast*, note 27 above.
133. 25 U.S.C. Secs. 123 and 123a.
134. *See, e.g.*, 25 U.S.C. Secs. 403 and 405.
135. *Choteau v. Comm'r*, 38 F.2d 976 (10th Cir. 1930), *aff'd sub nom. Choteau v. Burnett*, 283 U.S. 691 (1931); *U.S. v. Overlie*, 730 F.2d 1159 (8th Cir. 1984).
136. *Kennedy v. U.S.*, 721 F.2d 1252 (9th Cir. 1983).
137. *Rogers v. Acting Deputy Ass't Secretary*, IBIA 85–15–A [12 Indian L. Rep. 7037] (1985).
138. *Worcester*, note 1 above.
139. 1 Stat. 137, now codified as 25 U.S.C. Secs. 177, 261–64.
140. 25 U.S.C. Sec. 264. *Cf. Rockbridge v. Lincoln*, 449 F.2d 567 (9th Cir. 1971).
141. 25 U.S.C. Sec. 261.
142. 25 U.S.C. Sec. 262.
143. 25 C.F.R. Part 140 (1990).
144. 25 U.S.C. Sec. 264.
145. 25 U.S.C. Sec. 201. *See, e.g., U.S. ex rel. Hornell v. One 1976 Chevrolet Station Wagon*, 585 F.2d 978 (10th Cir. 1978).
146. *Rockbridge*, note 140 above; *Rosebud Sioux Tribe v. U.S.*, 714 F. Supp. 1546 (D.S.D. 1989).
147. 25 U.S.C. Sec. 68. *See, e.g., Moffer v. Watt*, 690 F.2d 1037 (D.C. Cir. 1982).
148. 25 U.S.C. Sec. 177.
149. *See U.S. v. Forty-Three Gallons of Whiskey*, 93 U.S. 188 (1876); *Perrin v. U.S.*, 232 U.S. 478 (1914).

150. 18 U.S.C. Sec. 1161.
151. *Mazurie*, note 39 above.
152. Now codified as 18 U.S.C. Sec. 1153. The Major Crimes Act is reproduced in appendix D.
153. *Ex parte Crow Dog*, 109 U.S. 556 (1883).
154. 16 Cong. Rec. 936 (1865) (remarks of Rep. Cutcheon), cited in *Keeble v. U.S.*, 412 U.S. 205, 211–12 (1973).
155. *See* note 152 above.

VI

Tribal Self-Government

Indian tribes have the inherent right to govern themselves. They had this right centuries before their first contact with outsiders, and they still have it today.

The Supreme Court first recognized the inherent right of tribal sovereignty in an 1832 case, *Worcester v. Georgia.*[1] *Worcester* decided the question of whether the state of Georgia could impose its laws on the Cherokee Indian Reservation, a reservation located within the state's borders. In holding that Georgia could not extend its laws within the reservation, the Court stated:

> Indian nations [are] distinct political communities, having territorial boundaries, within which their authority is exclusive, and having a right to all the lands within those boundaries, which is not only acknowledged, but guaranteed by the United States. . . . Indian nations had always been considered as distinct, independent political communities, retaining their original rights, as the undisputed possessors of the soil from time immemorial. . . . The Cherokee nation, then, is a distinct community, occupying its own territory, with boundaries accurately described, in which the laws of Georgia can have no force, and the citizens of Georgia, have no right to enter, but with the assent of the Cherokees themselves, or in conformity with treaties, and with the acts of Congress.[2]

The *Worcester* doctrine of inherent tribal sovereignty has undergone some changes over the years, but its basic premise remains the same. An Indian tribe is a distinct political community. Congress has the authority to limit or even abolish tribal powers, and thus tribes are "limited" sovereignties. But absent Congressional action, a tribe retains its inherent right of self-government, and no state may impose its laws on the reservation. The Court reaffirmed this principle in 1991: "Indian tribes are 'domestic dependent nations,' which exercise inherent sovereign authority over their members and territories."[3] Moreover, in recent years Congress has made a determined effort to strengthen tribal self-government. As the Supreme Court remarked in 1983, Congress appears "firmly committed to the goal of promoting tribal self-government, a goal embodied in numerous federal statutes."[4]

A. THE SOURCE AND LIMITS OF TRIBAL POWER

What is the source of tribal power?

The source of a tribe's power is its people. Tribes have had the inherent right to govern themselves "from time immemorial."[5] Thus the United States did not delegate to tribes the right to be self-governing. Although Congress has the ability to limit tribal powers, it did not create them. As the Supreme Court has recognized: "That Congress has in certain ways regulated the manner and extent of the tribal power of self-government does not mean that Congress is the source of that power."[6]

What are the limits of tribal power?

When the Supreme Court stated in 1978 that tribal powers are "inherent powers of a limited sovereignty which has never been extinguished," the Court reiterated two long-standing principles of federal Indian law: tribes have inherent powers, but Congress may extinguish these powers. This is a principle of law, but more than that, it is a political reality. The federal government has the raw physical power to limit the activities of Indian tribes and to abolish their governments. Over the years, Congress has abolished many tribal governments, and it has limited the authority of the rest. Needless to say, the exercise of this power, and its legal and moral validity, has been extensively criticized.[7]

Indian tribes have two types of limitations on their tribal powers: explicit and implicit. Congress has expressly prohibited tribes from doing certain things, such as selling tribal land without the federal government's permission. These express limitations on tribal powers are discussed in chapter 5. In addition, Indian tribes have implicitly lost certain powers, the Supreme Court has held, "by virtue of their dependent status."[8] For instance, Indian tribes can no longer enter into treaties with foreign governments; they have impliedly lost that power due to their subordinate position as "conquered" nations.[9] Yet despite these restrictions, Indian tribes retain an enormous amount of power.

Tribal governments have a unique position in our society. The Supreme Court has described them as "quasi-sovereign" and "semi-independent."[10] Although Indian tribes are no longer fully sovereign, they possess "attributes of sovereignty over both their members and their territory."[11] During the past two hundred years, however, most tribes have been economically, culturally, and govermentally devastated by their association with the United States. As a result, few tribes have the ability to exercise all of their powers. Even those that do, use their powers cautiously. Thirty-five years ago, during the termination era, Congress "rewarded" some of the more self-sufficient tribes by terminating their federal assistance, with disastrous results.[12] Twenty years ago, the assertion of hunting, fishing, and water rights by certain tribes created such an intense "Indian backlash" that Congress was urged by thousands of non-Indians to eliminate these rights. Although Congress did not do this, tribes have learned that they may suffer retaliation if they exercise certain powers or become financially successful.

Are tribal powers limited by the U.S. Constitution?

No. A century ago, the Supreme Court held that the Constitution does not apply to the exercise of tribal authority.[13] The Constitution was intended to limit the powers of federal and state governments, not tribal governments. As explained in chapter 5, the Constitution places Indian tribes under the authority of Congress but not under the dictates of the Constitution itself. Therefore, the Constitution does not limit tribal powers. This means that tribal governments can even enact laws that, if enacted by the federal or state governments, would violate the U.S. Constitution.[14]

B. THE SCOPE OF TRIBAL POWERS

Tribal governments have the same powers as the federal and state governments to regulate their internal affairs, with a few exceptions. The remainder of this chapter examines the nine most important areas of tribal authority: (1) forming a government; (2) determining tribal membership; (3) regulating tribal property; (4) regulating individual property; (5) the right to tax; (6) the right to maintain law and order; (7) the right to exclude nonmembers from tribal territory; (8) the right to regulate domestic relations; (9) and the right to regulate commerce and trade.

1. Forming a Government

Does an Indian tribe have the right to form a government?
Yes. The right to form a government is the first element of sovereignty, the most basic right of any political community. Indian tribes have always had the right to form governments.[15] Long before Europeans arrived on this continent, each tribe had a government, and some tribes had written constitutions; in fact, the U.S. Constitution was patterned after the Constitution of the Iroquois Confederacy.[16]

The right to form a government includes the right to establish the qualifications for tribal office, to determine how tribal officials are chosen, and to define their powers. For example, a tribe can require that candidates for tribal office be enrolled in the tribe and speak the tribe's language,[17] and the tribe can disqualify for office persons with felony convictions or a record of misconduct during a prior term in office.[18] Each tribe also has the power to determine eligibility to vote in tribal elections.[19]

What types of governments do Indian tribes have?
Tribal governments vary considerably. There are over four hundred Indian tribes in the United States and probably no two tribal governments are the same. A few tribes, for example, are theocracies (religious leaders control the government). Some tribes determine their leaders by heredity, but most tribal officials are elected. Most tribes have adopted written constitutions and tribal codes and enforce their laws in their own courts, while some tribes depend on state or federal agencies to maintain law and order on the reservation. Some tribes have a centralized government while others are decentralized. The Hopi tribe, for example, is a union of nine self-governing

villages, and each village decides for itself how it shall be organized.[20]

More than a hundred tribes chose to restructure their governments under the Indian Reorganization Act of 1934[21] and are known as IRA tribes. The IRA was intended to help tribes "modernize" their governments. Many tribes were ill-equipped to manage the type of governmental affairs associated with reservation life, such as the need to enter into business contracts, operate federal programs, manage private property, collect taxes, and borrow money.

The IRA allowed each tribe to draft a new constitution giving the tribe specific powers, subject to the approval of the Secretary of the Interior. The Secretary was directed to approve constitutions that created a tribal council with the authority to negotiate contracts with federal, state, and local governments, employ legal counsel, and prevent the disposition of tribal property without the tribe's permission.[22] The Secretary encouraged tribes, in addition, to give their councils the power to borrow money and pledge tribal property as security for the loan; to levy and collect taxes and impose licenses; to establish a tribal court system and enact a law-and-order code; to remove from the reservation nonmembers whose presence is injurious to the tribe; and to create subordinate tribal organizations for economic, educational, or other purposes.[23]

The main drawback of the IRA was that the tribe's constitution had to meet the approval of the Secretary of the Interior,[24] and the Secretary required many constitutions to include a provision that subjected every tribal law to Secretarial review and approval.[25] Because of this requirement, many tribes decided not to restructure their government under the IRA. Some non-IRA tribes, such as the Navajo tribe, have created governments similar to those approved under the IRA but which have more autonomy because they are not subject to the Secretary's constant review.[26] However, these tribes are not eligible to receive certain federal loans that the act makes available to IRA tribes.[27]

Today, most tribal governments have the same three branches as the federal and state governments: legislative, executive, and judicial. On most reservations, these branches of government are the tribal council, the tribal chairperson, and the tribal court. But tribal governments are not required to have this "separation of powers,"[28] and many do not.

Are tribal elections subject to federal review?

Generally, no. "The right to conduct an election without federal interference is essential to the exercise of the [tribe's] right to self-government."[29]

Most tribal election procedures and decisions, such as who may run for office and who may vote, are not subject to review by federal officials or by federal courts.[30] However, there are two situations in which federal officials have some control in these matters. First, as mentioned above, some IRA tribal constitutions provide for Secretarial review of all tribal laws, including election laws. However, in exercising this authority, the Secretary must give deference to the tribe's right of self-government, and only those tribal laws that clearly violate the tribal constitution or federal law can be disapproved by the Secretary.[31]

Second, when a tribal decision threatens a federal interest, federal officials may intervene to the extent necessary to protect that interest. For example, occasionally two rival groups will each claim to be a tribe's legitimate government. The federal government must then decide, for federal purposes, who has the authority to act on the tribe's behalf. In these situations, discussed more fully in chapter 5, section B(2), federal officials may refuse to recognize the results of an election that was not conducted in accordance with tribal law. However, federal officials may not then decide the election's outcome. Rather, they can only give temporary recognition to a governing body so as to permit government-to-government relations to continue. The tribe is then permitted to choose its governing body in compliance with tribal law.[32]

Is there a crisis in tribal government?

Many tribes now have a government very different from their traditional form of government. Traditionally, leadership status went to individuals who excelled in certain skills, possessed great wisdom, practiced generosity, displayed great courage, or had great spiritual powers. Today, tribal leaders are chosen by new methods, often for different reasons than before, and govern under a different set of rules than did their ancestors. Moreover, some Indians have learned how to use these new governmental systems to their personal advantage.

These rapid changes in tribal government have produced "a peculiar kind of conflict that is not easily resolved."[33] Deep factionalism has developed on some reservations between "traditionals" and "moderns," as well as along economic, religious, or political lines. "In recent years American Indian protests against their own tribal officials have seemingly become commonplace."[34]

However, Indian tribes have the inherent right to form their own government. This means, among other things, that they have the right to experiment with different governmental structures and to fashion one that best suits their needs and goals.

2. Determining Tribal Membership

Does a tribe have the right to determine tribal membership?
Definitely. Indian tribes have the inherent authority to determine who can join the tribe. If tribes lost this power, they could not control their future. As the Supreme Court has noted, "A tribe's right to define its own membership for tribal purposes has long been recognized as central to its existence as an independent political community."[35] Tribal authority over membership includes the power to take membership away from a person.[36] It also includes the right to adopt persons into the tribe and to determine which benefits of membership these people can participate in, such as whether they can use tribal property.[37] Congress has the power to limit a tribe's authority to determine membership, but in the absence of such a limitation the tribe enjoys the exclusive right to determine who belongs to the tribe for tribal purposes.[38]

What restrictions has Congress placed on tribal membership?
Few tribes have been limited by Congress in their enrollment decisions.[39] The vast majority of tribes have no federal restrictions regarding membership. Federal courts are not permitted to resolve disputes arising out of tribal enrollment policies unless expressly authorized by Congress to do so.[40]

What are the qualifications for tribal membership?

Most tribes determine eligibility for membership by blood fraction ("blood quantum"). In most tribes any person who has at least one-fourth degree of tribal blood qualifies for membership, although some tribes enroll persons having a blood quantum of one-thirty-second.

A few tribes have other qualifications. Some tribes require residence on the reservation for a certain length of time or residence at the time of application. Some require the filing of an enrollment application within a few years after the applicant's birth. Several tribes in New Mexico allow children to become members only if their father is a member; in a recent case, a tribe refused to enroll children whose mother was a full-blooded tribal member but whose father had no tribal blood.[41]

Can a person become a member of two Indian tribes?

Yes. If a person's parents are members of different tribes, that person may qualify for membership in both of them, depending on their membership rules. Many tribes, though, will not enroll someone already enrolled in another tribe unless that person first has his or her name removed from the other tribe's membership list.

3. Regulating Tribal Property

What kinds of property can tribes own?

Indian tribes can own the same kinds of property non-Indians can own, both real and personal. Real property consists of land and items attached to or found within the land, such as buildings, timber, and minerals. Personal property consists of all other kinds of property, such as cattle, bank accounts, automobiles, furniture, clothing, and other movable property.

In addition, Indian tribes can have two property interests in land which non-Indians cannot have: tribal "trust" land and "Indian title" land. Tribal trust land is land that has been set aside for the exclusive use of a tribe but is owned by the United States. Having land in trust status permits the tribe to use, lease, mortgage, or even sell this land provided that the federal government, which owns it, consents.[42]

Indian title land is land that has always been a part of a tribe's ancestral homesite. A tribe has the right to continue living on this land until Congress removes its right to do so. This right of continued occupancy is known as Indian title. The concept of Indian title and its legal implications are explained in chapter 2, section D.

How have Indian tribes obtained their interests in land?

There are six ways in which Indian tribes have obtained interests in land: treaty, federal statute, executive action, purchase, action of a foreign nation, and aboriginal possession.

Treaty: Almost every Indian tribe has a treaty with the United States in which it relinquished (under threat of force) its claim to ancestral homelands and agreed to live on a reservation. Although these treaties took a great deal of land from the Indians, they also gave them vested legal rights to control a particular area of land.[43]

Statutes: In 1871 Congress ended the practice of making treaties with Indian tribes.[44] Thereafter, whenever Congress wanted to create an Indian reservation, it passed a statute setting aside land for the tribe. Congress also used this method to reduce the size of an Indian reservation or abolish it altogether. Thus, statutes have both created and diminished many reservations.

Executive action: Some tribes have obtained interests in land by executive action, that is, by an act of the President of the United States. A number of presidents took it upon themselves to create Indian reservations from lands owned by the federal government. These Executive Order reservations are as valid as those created by Congress.[45] However, Congress passed a law in 1927 prohibiting the President from creating any additional Indian reservations.[46]

Purchase: Tribes have also acquired land by purchase. Some tribes, such as the Eastern Band of Cherokee Indians of North Carolina, have acquired a sizable reservation by purchasing private land. In 1934 Congress authorized the Secretary of the Interior to purchase land for tribes in order to increase the size of their reservations.[47] Almost a million acres have been purchased under this program.

Foreign grants: Before the United States became a nation, several Indian tribes received land grants from the foreign countries occupying North America: Spain, Mexico, France,

Great Britain, and Russia.[48] It has been the policy of the United States to respect these grants. The Pueblos of New Mexico hold the most significant grants, which they received from Spain and Mexico. Certain tribes in Florida received land grants from Great Britain.

Aboriginal possession: Finally, a number of Indian tribes have an interest in land because of aboriginal possession. This "Indian title" interest allows a tribe to continue living on its ancestral homelands until such time as Congress decides to terminate the tribe's right of continued occupancy. This interest is discussed in chapter 2, section D.

To what extent can an Indian tribe protect its property by regulating on-reservation activities?

Congress may limit the right, but until it does, a tribe has the same general authority to protect and regulate its property that other governments have.[49] The Supreme Court recognized the inherent right of a tribe to regulate on-reservation activities in one of its earliest decisions.[50] The Court recently reaffirmed that right in *Merrion v. Jicarilla Apache Tribe* (1982).[51] In *Merrion* the Court addressed the issue of whether an Indian tribe could tax the value of oil and gas taken from tribal lands by a non-Indian company operating under a tribal lease. The Court began its analysis by noting that Indian tribes have the inherent right "to tribal self-government and territorial management." The Court then upheld the tribal tax because regulating economic activity is "an essential instrument" of both of those rights. The power to regulate and tax reservation development constitutes "a fundamental attribute of sovereignty" that "derives from the tribe's general authority, as sovereign, to control economic activity within its jurisdiction."[52]

Merrion is an extremely important case. Almost two dozen non-Indian businesses, including several major oil companies, filed briefs with the Supreme Court urging it to rule against the tribe. The Court's decision firmly supports the right of Indian tribes to be independent and self-governing and to control their land and resources.

Similar decisions have been made in other contexts. Courts have held, for example, that Indian tribes have the right to regulate hunting and fishing on the reservation,[53] control the introduction of alcoholic beverages on the reservation,[54] eject trespassers from tribal lands,[55] tax Indians and non-Indians who use tribal lands for farming, grazing, or other purposes,[56] regulate commercial activities on the reservation that involve tribal interests,[57] take private land for tribal use provided that adequate compensation is paid to the owner,[58] and require non-Indians who wish to practice certain professions within the reservation to purchase a tribal license.[59] Moreover, even in those situations in which federal agencies have some authority to regulate tribal property, they may not take any action themselves, or permit others to take any action, without the tribe's consent or congressional authorization. "Determination of the use of its own land is peculiarly the province of the tribe involved."[60]

Are there any limits on the tribe's power to regulate reservation activities?

Yes. The Supreme Court recognized in *Merrion* that Indian tribes have the inherent right to regulate reservation property "unless divested of it by federal law or necessary implication of their dependent status."[61] These are the explicit and implicit limitations on tribal authority discussed earlier in this chapter.

Congress has placed a number of explicit limitations on a tribe's power to use or sell tribal trust land and other trust property, including income derived from the use of trust land. These restrictions, discussed in chapter 5, section B(5), reduce the tribe's ability to govern, and they have been criticized for that reason.[62] However, Congress has placed few limits on the general authority of tribes to regulate reservation activities, especially in such vital areas as taxation, zoning, domestic relations, commerce, and hunting and fishing. In addition, Congress has helped tribes protect their rights by authorizing them to file suit in federal court whenever their federally protected interests in land or other property are being threatened or violated.[63]

However, as explained earlier, in addition to the explicit limitations on tribal powers, implicit restrictions also exist. The Supreme Court has held that, due to the tribes' subordinate and dependent status under the federal government, tribes have lost the right to regulate certain "external relations."[64]

Supreme Court decisions have not clearly defined the difference between an internal and external relation. In *Oliphant v.*

Suquamish Indian Tribe (1978),[65] the Court held that Indian tribes may not prosecute non-Indians who commit crimes on the reservation because of the dependent status of Indian tribes. Using the same logic, the Court ruled in *Montana v. United States* (1981)[66] that tribes lack the general power to regulate hunting and fishing by non-Indians on non-Indian owned land within the reservation. Similarly, the Court ruled in *Brendale v. Confederated Tribes and Bands of the Yakima Indian Nation* (1989)[67] that Indian tribes lack the general authority to zone non-Indian owned land in any portion of the reservation where the overall population and character of that area is non-Indian. (The portion of the reservation at issue in *Brendale* had been opened by Congress for settlement by non-Indians and is now 80 percent non-Indian-owned.)

These decisions create significant exceptions to *Merrion*'s general rule of inherent tribal sovereignty over reservation activities. The *Brendale* decision is particularly troubling because four of the nine Justices stated that, in their view, tribes have no authority to zone *any* non-Indian owned ("fee") land on the reservation.[68] Clearly, support for inherent tribal sovereignty is eroding with respect to tribal jurisdiction over *non-Indians*. (This topic is discussed more fully later in this chapter.) However, the Supreme Court consistently has upheld the exercise of most tribal powers over Indians and over non-Indians on *Indian* land. In *Brendale*, although the Court ruled that the tribe could not zone non-Indian fee land in an area of the reservation where the population was predominantly non-Indian, the Court also ruled that the tribe could zone non-Indian fee land within the predominantly Indian portion of the reservation. Moreover, in both *Montana* and *Brendale* the Court held that the tribe could regulate non-Indian activities if these activities threatened the tribe's political integrity, economic security, or health and welfare.[69]

Thus, the general principle remains true that Indian tribes, as the Court said in *Merrion*, have the inherent right "to tribal self-government and territorial management."[70] This right remains secure, as it should, with respect to all activities that imperil the health, safety, and welfare of the tribe, its citizens, and their resources, whether these activities are engaged in by Indians or by non-Indians.

What are the advantages and disadvantages of having tribal land in trust status?

The disadvantage of having tribal land in trust status is that the tribe lacks full control over it because it is owned by the federal government. Everything a tribe may want to do with trust property—sell, lease, mortgage or develop it—requires federal approval, a constant source of aggravation to many tribes.[71]

However, having property in trust status provides certain advantages. States are not permitted to tax property owned by the federal government, and therefore they cannot tax Indian trust property.[72] For the same reason, state zoning laws do not apply to trust property,[73] the state cannot take it under the power of eminent domain,[74] and it cannot be lost through adverse possession.[75] These advantages are so great that, when a tribe purchases private land, it usually has the Secretary of the Interior transfer it into trust status, as Congress has authorized the Secretary to do.[76]

If a tribe sells, leases, or otherwise conveys an interest in tribal land in violation of federal restrictions, is the transfer valid?

No. Any transfer of tribal land—whether trust or non-trust—in violation of federal law is invalid and may be rescinded at any time by the United States,[77] by the tribe,[78] or by any Indian whose interests are affected.[79]

The critical law in this area is the Indian Nonintercourse Act,[80] passed by Congress in 1790. This law requires the federal government to approve all transfers of tribal land. Without that approval, the transfer is void and the land must be returned to the tribe. In one case an interest in tribal land that a railroad purchased a century earlier was rescinded because Congress had not consented to the transfer.[81]

The Nonintercourse Act was passed to protect Indian tribes from unscrupulous land-grabbers as well as to give the federal government control over the sale of Indian land.[82] The act has received much attention in recent years because it appears that portions of Maine, Massachusetts, Connecticut, Rhode Island, and New York were purchased from Indian tribes without the federal government's consent and must either be returned to the tribes or purchased again.[83] In 1980, for example, Congress appropriated $81.5 million to settle lawsuits brought by tribes in Maine seeking to recover land sold in violation of the Nonintercourse Act. This amount included funds for the purchase of 305,000 acres of land for the tribes.[84]

What is communal property?

The importance of a land base to Indian tribes cannot be overemphasized. It provides not only a home and a livelihood, but on most reservations, it is a unifying force and has religious significance as well.

Few Indian tribes believed in the private ownership of land. Any land controlled by the tribe belonged to the entire community, and each member had the same right to use it as every other member. This concept of land ownership, known as communal property, was a guiding principle of Indian life and culture: land could not be privately owned, which meant that members of the community had to work together to harvest or gather what they could from the land. Anglo-American values, on the other hand, tend to glorify private ownership of property and individual wealth.

During the late nineteenth century the federal government wanted to devise a plan that would compel Indians to assimilate into white society. The heart of this plan was the destruction of Indian communal property. The government wanted Indians to become individual farm families and abandon their communal life. The government felt that after Indians learned how to support themselves as private landholders, they would no longer need tribal governments, and their reservations could be eliminated. With these goals in mind, Congress passed the General Allotment Act of 1887,[85] which authorized federal officials to divide communal lands into lots and to assign a lot to each adult Indian.

The General Allotment Act had a disastrous effect on tribes. Congress finally repealed the act in 1934, but by then two-thirds of all communal lands had passed from tribal ownership.[86] The concept of communal property remains intact on many reservations where tribal lands still exist. However, the presence of so many individually owned parcels of land within the reservation has undermined the concept of communal property, a change many Indians deeply regret.

4. Regulating Individually Owned Property

Does the tribe have the right to regulate private property within the reservation?

Every sovereign nation must place certain restrictions on the use of private property in order to protect the safety and welfare of its citizens and resources. Indian tribes retain the inherent right to exercise these powers unless Congress has limited that right or tribes have lost it due to their dependent status.[87]

Indian tribes have broad authority to regulate private property. Congress has placed few restrictions on this authority, and the courts have rejected claims that tribes have lost this power by implication. For example, courts have upheld the right of tribes to zone land, including land owned by a non-Indian;[88] to regulate the sale of liquor, even from land owned by a non-Indian;[89] to determine who may inherit private property belonging to a deceased tribal member;[90] to take private land for public use (the power of eminent domain);[91] and to impose health, safety, and employment regulations on businesses within the reservation, including those owned by non-Indians.[92]

The general rule that tribes can regulate private property located within the reservation has two important exceptions. Both exceptions concern land privately owned (fee land) by nonmembers, and both were discussed earlier in this chapter. In *Montana v. United States*[93] the Supreme Court held that, while a tribe can regulate non-Indian hunting and fishing on Indian land, it generally cannot do so on non-Indian fee land. In *Brendale v. Confederated Tribes and Bands of the Yakima Indian Nation*,[94] the Supreme Court held that, while a tribe can zone non-Indian fee land located in predominantly Indian areas of the reservation, it generally cannot do so in predominantly non-Indian areas.

As important as these exceptions are—and as damaging to tribal sovereignty—they remain exceptions. In most circumstances, tribes can regulate private land within the reservation.

5. The Right to Tax

The right to tax is an essential instrument of government. Only by collecting taxes can a government acquire enough money to manage its affairs and provide services to its citizens. Indian tribes must be allowed the same authority to tax that state governments have in order to become truly self-governing, reduce their dependence on federal aid, and provide a full range of municipal services to their members.

Do Indian tribes have the right to levy and collect taxes?

Yes. Indian tribes have the inherent right to tax. This power stems from their right of self-government and the right to manage their land and other resources. As the Supreme Court has stated: "The power to tax is an essential attribute of Indian sovereignty because it is a necessary instrument of self-government and territorial management. This power . . . derives from the tribe's general authority, as sovereign, to control economic activity within its jurisdiction."[95]

The right of a tribe to tax its own members has never been seriously questioned. On the other hand, tribal taxation of non-Indians has been vigorously challenged. However, courts recognized very early that Indian tribes have the same inherent right to tax non-Indians as they do Indians. In 1904, for example, the Supreme Court upheld the right of a tribe to impose a personal property tax on the value of cattle owned by a non-Indian that were grazing within the reservation.[96] In 1905 a federal court allowed a tribe to collect a business license tax from a non-Indian engaged in trade on the reservation.[97] In 1956 another federal court ruled that non-Indians who lease tribal lands can be taxed by the tribe on the value of the lease.[98]

The Supreme Court reaffirmed those early decisions in *Merrion v. Jicarilla Apache Tribe* (1982)[99] and resolved most arguments concerning tribal taxation of non-Indians. As previously noted, *Merrion* upheld the right of a tribe to tax oil and gas extracted by a non-Indian within the reservation. The Court held that such taxes are essential instruments of government that tribes may impose as an attribute of their sovereign powers. (Chapter 10 addresses this subject in more detail.)

6. The Right to Maintain Law and Order

What was said about the power to tax can be said about the power to maintain law and order: no government can long survive without this power. Every nation, as an attribute of its sovereignty, has the inherent right to make its own criminal laws and enforce them. Similar to the debate regarding tribal taxation, no one questions the right of a tribe to enforce its criminal laws against tribal members, but the prosecution of non-Indians has created tremendous controversy.

Does a tribe have the right to prosecute tribal members?

Yes. Indian tribes, as an attribute of their sovereignty, have the inherent right to maintain law and order among tribal members. This includes the power to enact criminal laws, hire and train a police force, establish tribal courts and jails, and punish tribal members who violate tribal law.[100] As the Supreme Court stated in 1978:

> It is undisputed that Indian tribes have the power to en-force their criminal laws against tribe members. Although physically within the territory of the United States and subject to ultimate federal control, they nonetheless re-main a separate people, with the power of regulating their internal and social relations. Their right of internal self-government includes the right to prescribe laws applicable to tribe members and to enforce those laws by criminal sanctions.[101]

The right to maintain law and order also includes the right to regulate noncriminal (civil) matters, such as contracts, personal injury claims, and other disputes between citizens, and to determine how such disputes should be resolved. Indian tribes have the inherent right to regulate civil matters as part of their inherent right to maintain law and order.[102]

Does a tribe have the right to prosecute non-Indians?

No. In *Oliphant v. Suquamish Indian Tribe* (1978),[103] the Supreme Court held that an Indian tribe may not prosecute a non-Indian who violates tribal law unless Congress has ex-pressly conferred that power on the tribe (and Congress has not given any tribe this power, it appears). According to the Court, Indian tribes implicitly lost this power when they be-came subordinate to the federal government. This limitation also applies to criminal behavior by nonmember Indians. The Supreme Court ruled in *Duro v. Reina* (1990),[104] that a tribe may not prosecute an Indian who is not a member of the tribe.

(Chapter 8 discusses the difficulties this lack of authority causes Indian tribes.)

What restrictions has Congress placed on tribal law enforcement?

As in all other areas of tribal power, Congress may limit the right of tribes to engage in law enforcement,[105] and Congress has done so in several respects. First, Congress has given federal officials the authority to prosecute Indians who commit certain major crimes within Indian country.[106] The Supreme Court has yet to decide whether the federal government has exclusive jurisdiction over these crimes, thereby preventing tribes from also prosecuting these offenses. If tribal prosecution is prohibited, the tribe's inherent right to make and enforce its own laws will be seriously diminished. Even as things stand, the federal government's ability to enter the reservation and prosecute Indians who commit these crimes interferes with tribal self-government.[107]

Second, many tribal constitutions require approval of tribal laws by the Secretary of the Interior, and this gives the Secretary certain powers over tribal law enforcement. In a recent case, the Secretary refused to approve a tribal law that would have legalized prostitution within that tribe's reservation.[108]

Perhaps the most far-reaching limitation on tribal law enforcement is contained in the Indian Civil Rights Act of 1968.[109] This law limits the penalties that tribal courts can impose in criminal cases to one year's imprisonment and a five thousand dollar fine. In addition, it requires tribal courts to extend almost all of the rights to criminal defendants that state and federal courts must provide. (This act and the rights that it confers are the subject of chapter 14.)

What types of court systems do tribes have?

Indian tribes had their own systems of law and order long before Europeans arrived in North America. These differed greatly from the ones brought over by the Europeans. In particular, tribes handled misbehavior primarily through public scorn, the loss of tribal privileges, or the payment of restitution to an injured party, rather than by imprisonment. Tribes did not have police officers. In the more extreme cases, banishment from the tribe might occur, although in some tribes an Indian family might avenge the death or injury of one of its members. It is doubtful that any tribal government ever executed anyone for a crime, a form of punishment more popular in the so-called civilized societies.[110]

The federal government did not want Indians to retain their traditional systems of law and order. By the end of the nineteenth century Congress had established a Court of Indian Offenses on most reservations. By 1890 the tribes themselves administered the majority of these courts, although always under the control of federal agents. The Secretary of the Interior published in the Code of Federal Regulations a standard set of rules governing these courts, and these courts became known as *CFR courts*. CFR courts tended to be informal and combined Indian custom with western law. Their main function was to provide Indians with a way to prosecute crimes that was acceptable to federal officials.

When Congress passed the Indian Reorganization Act of 1934,[111] it authorized Indian tribes to establish their own courts and adopt their own law and order codes, subject to the approval of the Secretary of the Interior. The courts created in this fashion are known as *tribal courts*, and most non-IRA tribes have created similar tribal courts as well. Today less than thirty CFR courts remain. About twenty tribes still have traditional courts, which rely primarily on the tribe's traditional methods of resolving disputes and enforcing tribal law.[112]

Most tribal courts closely resemble their Anglo counterparts, the state and federal courts. Tribal courts are quickly learning to apply a set of laws and procedures unknown to them until recently. Except for some of the Pueblo tribes in New Mexico which rely heavily on traditional procedures, "tradition plays a small part in modern-day Indian courts."[113] Although tribal courts operate on various levels of what some people might call "professionalism," they are effective and comprehensive. The constitution of the Blackfeet tribe of Montana, for example, creates a small claims court, a traffic court, a juvenile court, a court of general civil and criminal jurisdiction, and an appellate court containing five judges.[114] The Navajo tribe probably has the most sophisticated judicial system; its courts process over forty-five thousand cases a year and publish their decisions in an official reporter. Every month tribal court decisions from around the country are reported in the *Indian Law Reporter*.[115]

The structure of, and procedure in, tribal court varies from one reservation to the next, responding to the needs and desires of the community. Tribes have flexibility in establishing their court systems except to the extent demanded by the Indian Civil Rights Act. For the most part, tribes are free to create their own structures and procedures for accepting and resolving disputes in tribal court.[116] Tribal methods of dispute resolution often differ from those used in state and federal courts. As one tribal court recently noted: "Tribal courts, in both their present form and their 'traditional' predecessors, however, have been centrally concerned with the overall concept of *justice* and have oftentimes managed to be free of the obsession with technicalities that has so often plagued non-tribal court systems."[117]

Each tribe is also free to adopt its own qualifications for the position of tribal judge, and these qualifications vary from tribe to tribe. Some tribes require that judges be tribal members. Some tribes require that judges be state-licensed attorneys. Some tribes elect their judges, but most appoint them. Each tribe also decides who is eligible to appear as an attorney or counselor in tribal court.[118] The Navajo tribe, for example, has its own bar examination. Indian courts in general are evolving institutions that will require breathing room and tolerance until their role in Indian life and culture can become firmly established.

Must a tribe have an appellate court?

No. Most tribes have an appellate court, but there is nothing that requires a tribe to create one. On some reservations the tribal council serves as the appellate court, but most tribes have created a separate court of appeals consisting of three to five judges. Some tribes have joined together to create an intertribal court of appeals.

7. Jurisdiction over Non-Indians

Can Indian tribes regulate the activities of non-Indians on the reservation?

Initially, most reservations were reserved exclusively for Indians. However, Congress subsequently passed laws that opened most reservations to settlement by non-Indians. In addition, many non-Indians conduct government or business relations on reservations, and many non-Indians travel to or through Indian reservations. Thus the extent to which tribes have jurisdiction over non-Indians has important consequences.

As indicated earlier, Indian tribes may not exercise criminal jurisdiction over non-Indians, although tribes can exercise most aspects of their civil jurisdiction over non-Indians. Indian tribes may assert civil powers over non-Indians when (1) Congress has specifically delegated this power to the tribe,[119] (2) non-Indians enter into a consensual relationship with Indians or the tribe, such as a joint business venture,[120] or (3) non-Indians are engaging in an activity that threatens the tribe's political integrity, economic security, or health and welfare.[121] These factors are so broad that, as a result, reservation non-Indians and their property are subject to most forms of tribal civil jurisdiction, including the tribe's powers to tax, to zone, and to regulate hunting, fishing, and commercial activities within the reservation. Indeed, even if a non-Indian traveling through a reservation gets into a car accident with an Indian, the tribe can assert its jurisdiction and subject the non-Indian to a lawsuit in tribal court. (The tribe's full range of civil jurisdiction over non-Indians is explained in chapter 9.)

Indian tribes also have another important power, one that helps to compensate for their lack of criminal jurisdiction over non-Indians: the power to exclude. Indian tribes have the inherent right to determine who can enter their reservation and under what conditions they can remain. The Supreme Court recognized this right in one of its earliest cases[122] and recently reaffirmed it. In 1983 the Court ruled unanimously that "[a] tribe's power to exclude nonmembers entirely or to condition their presence on the reservation is . . . well established."[123] Thus, tribes may at least remove non-Indian lawbreakers from the reservation even though they cannot prosecute or imprison them.

Although tribes have the inherent power to exclude, they have been cautious about using it because Congress has the authority to limit that right. It would not be wise, for example, for a tribe to suddenly remove all non-Indians from its reservation because this probably would prompt Congress to limit the exclusion power. Congress, however, added some teeth to the tribe's exclusion power when it made it a federal crime for any person to hunt, fish, or trap on tribal land without tribal or federal permission.[124] Moreover, the Supreme Court has recognized that an Indian tribe can sue a non-Indian who trespasses on Indian land in the same way that any other landowner can.[125]

8. The Right to Regulate Domestic Relations

Does a tribe have the right to regulate the domestic relations of its members?

Domestic relations include marriage, divorce, adoptions, and similar matters relating to home and private life. Regulation of domestic relations is an integral aspect of sovereignty. The inherent right of an Indian tribe to regulate the domestic relations of its members is well recognized. As the Supreme Court stated in 1978, "unless limited by treaty or statute, a tribe has the power . . . to regulate domestic relations among tribe members."[126]

Congress has the ability to limit these tribal powers, but unless it does, a tribe possesses not only the inherent authority but the exclusive authority to regulate the domestic relations of its members within the reservation. *Fisher v. District Court*,[127] decided by the Supreme Court in 1976, illustrates this principle. In that case, a reservation Indian couple who had been given custody of a foster Indian child by a tribal court filed a petition in state court seeking to adopt the child. The child's mother opposed the petition, but the state court granted the adoption. The Supreme Court reversed. The tribe had a vital interest in this matter because all parties to the adoption—the child, the mother, and the foster parents—were reservation Indians, and the tribe had authorized its own tribal courts to hear these types of cases. Therefore, the Supreme Court said, the tribe's authority over this dispute must be exclusive. It would seriously interfere with tribal government if states were allowed "to subject a dispute arising on the reservation among reservation Indians to a forum other than the one they have established for themselves."[128] Even when a tribal court places an Indian child in a non-Indian foster home outside the reservation, the tribal court retains exclusive jurisdiction over the child, and a state court cannot consider an adoption request by the foster parents.[129]

Do Indian tribes still rely on Indian custom to determine the validity of marriages, divorces, and adoptions?

Some do and some do not. Indian custom remains important on most reservations, particularly in the area of domestic relations. The central role of the family, the respect given to elders, the assistance that extended family members give to raising the children of relatives, and the overall importance of kinship have unique significance in Indian life.[130]

Nevertheless, many Indian customs have changed over the years, as customs have in all cultures, especially when one culture is suddenly surrounded by another. For example, some tribes require their members to comply with state laws concerning marriage, divorce, and adoption, such as obtaining a state marriage license. Other tribes issue their own marriage licenses, and their tribal courts issue divorce decrees. A few tribes have passed laws forbidding marriage, divorce, or adoption by Indian custom, while other tribes continue to recognize them.[131]

If an Indian couple is married under state law, can they be divorced in a tribal court?

Yes. Any court can divorce parties who were married elsewhere, provided that the legislature has given the court this power. People married in Colorado, for example, can obtain a divorce in Nevada if they meet Nevada's requirements for divorce. Similarly, Indians married under state law can be divorced in a tribal court if they meet the tribe's requirements. For that matter, Indians married under state law can be divorced according to tribal custom, provided that the tribe recognizes the continued validity of such divorces.[132]

Which court—tribal, state, or federal—determines the custody of Indian children?

It depends on the situation. As explained earlier, in *Fisher v. District Court*, the Supreme Court held that only a tribal court can decide the adoptive custody of an Indian child when all parties to the proceeding are reservation Indians. However, numerous other combinations can occur, such as when one party lives off the reservation or is a non-Indian. The Indian Child Welfare Act of 1978 addresses most of these situations. This act is the subject of chapter 17.

9. The Right to Regulate Commerce and Trade

Does an Indian tribe have the right to regulate commerce and trade within the reservation?

Yes. An Indian tribe has the same essential authority as any sovereign government to regulate economic activity within its territory.[133] This includes the authority, previously discussed, to tax business activities, zone land, and regulate the use of property within the reservation, whether owned by an Indian or a non-Indian, except as limited by *United States v. Montana* and *Brendale*.

As with all other tribal powers, Congress may limit the tribe's right to regulate commerce and trade. Congress has given federal officials considerable regulatory authority in this area, including the right to require every person other than a full-blooded Indian to obtain a federal license to trade on the reservation.[134] However, these regulatory powers generally do not limit tribal powers. Rather, they impose federal regulations in addition to those that the tribe may impose. Although tribes may not pass any laws that conflict with federal regulations, they are not prevented from regulating the same activity. For example, people who extract oil from tribal lands can be required to pay both federal and tribal taxes on it.[135] A tribe has full authority to regulate business activities within the reservation except where Congress has restricted that power, and Congress has placed few restrictions on tribal authority in this area.

Congress has recognized and supported the inherent right of tribes to control reservation commerce. For example, Congress specifically exempted Indian tribes from coverage under the Civil Rights Act of 1964, thus allowing tribes to give Indians an employment preference.[136] The Age Discrimination Act, although not expressly exempting tribes, has been interpreted by the courts to be inapplicable to tribal government activity.[137] In a recent case, the Navajo Supreme Court upheld a tribal civil rights law as applied to a non-Indian company on the reservation, stating: "The Navajo Nation has the power to enact legislation to regulate labor and employment, including provisions to protect the civil rights of workers."[138]

Do Indian tribes have the right to engage in commerce and trade?

Certainly. An Indian tribe has the inherent right to engage

in business activities[139] as well as to create and license business corporations distinct from the tribe.[140] Many tribes own businesses, including craft industries; mining, fishing, and gambling operations; ski resorts, motels, and restaurants.

Congress has passed a number of laws to assist tribes in their economic development. Tribes that incorporated themselves under the Indian Reorganization Act can receive federal loans for economic purposes.[141] The Buy-Indian Act[142] requires the Bureau of Indian Affairs to employ Indian labor and purchase Indian products whenever possible in fulfilling BIA contracts. The Indian Self-Determination and Education Assistance Act of 1975[143] authorizes Indian tribes to take over the operation of many programs operated by federal agencies, using the same federal funds these agencies are spending. The Indian Mineral Development Act of 1982[144] provides federal assistance to Indian tribes in developing and marketing mineral resources. Of considerable financial importance to many tribes is the Indian Gaming Regulatory Act of 1988,[145] which establishes a comprehensive scheme for gaming, including high-stakes bingo, on Indian lands. These laws and federal programs for tribal development are discussed in chapter 16.

Most Indian reservations are located far from urban and industrial centers. Thus they often find it difficult to attract industry, and poverty is rampant. On many reservations, unemployment exceeds 70 percent. Given these problems, it is vitally important that the federal government make a strenuous effort to improve economic conditions on the reservation. Alternatives include giving tax incentives to businesses willing to locate on an Indian reservation and assisting in the marketing of Indian products. The federal government has spent billions of dollars subsidizing farmers, tobacco growers, the dairy and airline industries, and a host of other special interests. It seems only fair that the government should also assist tribes in making their reservations economically viable.[146]

10. Other Rights of Indian Tribes

Indian tribes have numerous other rights besides those discussed in this chapter. These rights are discussed elsewhere in this book. For instance, chapter 4 discusses Indian treaty rights. Tribal rights under the doctrine of trust responsibility are discussed in chapter 3. Chapter 11 discusses hunting, fishing, trapping, and gathering rights, and chapter 12 discusses water rights. Federal Indian programs, and the benefits and services provided by them, are discussed in chapter 16. Last, but not least, the right of tribes to file lawsuits to protect their rights is discussed in chapter 18.

NOTES

1. 31 U.S. 515 (1832).
2. *Id.*, 31 U.S. at 557, 558, 560.
3. *Oklahoma Tax Comm'n v. Citizen Band Potawatomi Indian Tribe*, 111 S.Ct. 905 (1991) (citation omitted). *See also U.S. v. Wheeler*, 435 U.S. 313, 323 (1978); *Merrion v. Jicarilla Apache Tribe*, 455 U.S. 103 (1982).
4. *New Mexico v. Mescalero Apache Tribe*, 462 U.S. 324, 335 (1983).
5. *Worcester v. Georgia*, 31 U.S. 515, 558 (1832). *See also McClanahan v. Arizona Tax Comm'n*, 411 U.S. 164, 168–73 (1973).
6. *Wheeler*, note 3 above, 435 U.S. at 328.
7. *See* ch. 5, note 2 and accompanying text.
8. *Wheeler*, note 3 above, 435 U.S. at 326.
9. *Worcester*, note 5 above, 31 U.S. at 559; *Washington v. Confederated Tribes of the Colville Indian Reservation*, 447 U.S. 134, 152–54 (1980).
10. *U.S. v. Kagama*, 118 U.S. 375, 381 (1886).
11. *U.S. v. Mazurie*, 419 U.S. 544, 557 (1975).
12. *See* ch. 5, sec. B(3).
13. *Talton v. Mayes*, 163 U.S. 379 (1896).
14. *Santa Clara Pueblo v. Martinez*, 436 U.S. 49 (1978); *Native American Church v. Navajo Tribal Council*, 272 F.2d 131 (10th Cir. 1959).
15. *Martinez*, note 14 above; *Pueblo of Santa Clara Rosa v. Fall*, 273 U.S. 315 (1927).
16. F. Cohen, *Handbook of Federal Indian Law* p. 128 (1942).
17. *See respectively Shortbull v. Looking Elk*, 677 F.2d 645 (8th Cir.), *cert. denied*, 459 U.S. 907 (1982); and *Day v. Hopi Election Board*, 16 Indian L. Rep. 6057 (Hopi Tr. Ct.) (1988).
18. *See respectively Means v. Oglala Sioux Tribal Council*, 11 Indian L. Rep. 6013 (Og. Sx. Tr. Ct.) (1984); and *Runs After v. U.S.*, 766 F.2d 347 (8th Cir. 1985).
19. *Wounded Head v. Tribal Council of Oglala Sioux Tribe*, 507 F.2d 1079 (8th Cir. 1975).

20. *See Kavena v. Hopi Indian Tribal Court*, 16 Indian L. Rep. 6063 (Hopi Tr. App. Ct.) (1989).
21. 25 U.S.C. Secs. 461 *et seq.*
22. 25 U.S.C. Sec. 476.
23. *See, e.g.*, Constitution of the Rosebud Sioux Tribe of South Dakota and the Constitution of the White Mountain Apache Tribe of Arizona.
24. 25 U.S.C. sec. 476. *Cf. Merrion*, note 3 above.
25. *See Kerr-McGee Corp. v. Navajo Tribe*, 471 U.S. 195 (1985). This subject is discussed in ch. 5, sec. B(2).
26. The Secretary of the Interior rarely disapproves a tribal law, but this does occur. *See, e.g., Cheyenne River Sioux Tribe v. Andrus*, 566 F.2d 1085 (8th Cir. 1977). For a discussion of the pros and cons of the IRA, see L. Tyler, *A History of Indian Policy* pp. 131–36 (1973).
27. 25 U.S.C. Sec. 477.
28. *Talton*, note 13 above; *Santa Clara Rosa*, note 15 above.
29. *Wheeler v. Swimmer*, 835 F.2d 259 (10th Cir. 1987).
30. *Wheeler v. U.S. Dep't of Interior*, 811 F.2d 549 (10th Cir. 1987); *Means v. Oglala Sioux Tribal Council*, 11 Indian L. Rep. 3024 (D.S.D. 1984); *Committee to Save Our Constitution v. U.S.*, 11 Indian L. Rep. 3035 (D.S.D. 1984).
31. *Thompson v. Area Director*, 17 IBIA 40 [16 Indian L. Rep. 7017] (1989); *Menominee Tribal Enterprises v. Minneapolis Area Director*, 15 IBIA 263, 266 [14 Indian L. Rep. 7053] (1987). *See also Wounded Head*, note 19 above.
32. *Goodface v. Grassrope*, 708 F.2d 335 (8th Cir. 1983); *Milam v. Dep't of the Interior*, 10 Indian L. Rep. 3013 (D.D.C. 1982). *Cf. Harjo v. Kleppe*, 420 F.2d 1110 (D.C. Cir. 1978).
33. V. Deloria, Jr. (ed.), *American Indian Policy in the Twentieth Century* p. 11 (1985).
34. T. Holm, "The Crisis in Tribal Government," in Deloria, note 33 above, p. 135.
35. *Martinez*, note 14 above, 436 U.S. at 72 n.36. *See also Chapoose v. Clark*, 607 F. Supp. 1027 (D. Utah 1985), *aff'd*, 831 F.2d 931 (10th Cir. 1987).
36. *Roff v. Burney*, 168 U.S. 218 (1897). *See Estate of Antoine (Ke Nape) Hill*, IBIA 78–15 [7 Indian L. Rep. 5075] (1980).
37. *Cherokee Intermarriage Cases*, 203 U.S. 76 (1906).
38. Congress, however, has the exclusive right to determine tribal membership for federal purposes. *See ch. 2, sec. A. See also Chapoose*, note 35 above.
39. *Cf. Stephens v. Cherokee Nation*, 174 U.S. 445 (1899); *Chapoose*, note 35 above.
40. *Martinez*, note 14 above.

41. *Id.*
42. The federal government's control over Indian trust land is discussed in ch. 5, sec. B(5).
43. Ch. 4 discusses Indian treaties.
44. 25 U.S.C. Sec. 71. Ch. 4 explains why this law was passed.
45. *Spalding v. Chandler*, 160 U.S. 394 (1896); *Merrion v. Jicarilla Apache Tribe*, 455 U.S. 130, 133 n.1 (1982).
46. 25 U.S.C. Sec. 398d.
47. 25 U.S.C. Sec. 465.
48. *See Mitchell v. U.S.*, 33 U.S. 307 (1835); *Worcester*, note 5 above, 31 U.S. at 545–49.
49. *Worcester*, note 5 above; *Marsh v. Brooks*, 49 U.S. 223 (1850); *Pueblo of Isleta v. Universal Constructors, Inc.*, 570 F.2d 300 (10th Cir. 1978).
50. *Worcester*, note 5 above.
51. 455 U.S. 130 (1982).
52. *Id.* at 137.
53. This subject is discussed in ch. 11.
54. *Mazurie*, note 11 above.
55. *Marsh*, note 49 above; *Ortiz-Barraza v. U.S.*, 6 (9th Cir. 1975). *See also Merrion*, note 45 above.
56. *Morris v. Hitchcock*, 194 U.S. 384 (1904).
57. *Merrion*, note 45 above; *So. Pacific Transp. Co. v. Watt*, 700 F.2d 550 (9th Cir.), *cert. denied*, 464 U.S. 960 (1983); *United Nuclear Corp. v. Clark*, 584 F. Supp. 107 (D.D.C. 1984).
58. *Boardman v. Oklahoma City Housing Auth.*, 445 P.2d 412 (Okla. 1968); *Seneca Constitutional Rights Organization v. George*, 348 F. Supp. 51 (W.D.N.Y. 1972). *Cf.* 25 U.S.C. Sec. 1302(5).
59. *Maxey v. Wright*, 54 S.W. 807 (Ct. App. Ind. T.), *aff'd*, 105 F.1003 (8th Cir. 1900).
60. *Hawley Lake Homeowners' Ass'n v . Deputy Ass't Sec'y—Indian Affairs*, 13 IBIA 276 [12 Indian L. Rep. 7043, 7049] (1985). *See* discussion ch. 5 , sec. B(5).
61. *Merrion*, note 45 above, 455 U.S. at 137.
62. *See, e.g.*, V. Deloria, Jr., *Custer Died for Your Sins* pp. 128–47 (1969); American Indian Policy Review Commission, *Final Report* pp. 128–32, 247–99 (Washington, DC: Government Printing Office, 1977).
63. 28 U.S.C. Sec. 1362. This law is discussed in ch. 18.
64. *U.S. v. Wheeler*, note 3 above, 435 U.S. at 326.
65. 435 U.S. 191 (1978).
66. 450 U.S. 544 (1981).
67. 492 U.S. 408 (1989).

68. *Id.* at 2996 (Opinion of White, Rehnquist, Scalia, and Kennedy).
69. *Montana*, 450 U.S. at 566; *Brendale*, 492 U.S. at 431.
70. *Merrion*, note 45 above, 455 U.S. at 136. *See also Knight v. Shoshone and Arapaho Indian Tribes*, 670 F.2d 900 (10th Cir. 1982).
71. *See* note 62 above and accompanying text.
72. This subject is discussed in ch. 10.
73. *Santa Rosa Band of Indians v. Kings County*, 532 F.2d 655 (9th Cir. 1975), *cert. denied*, 429 U.S. 1038 (1977).
74. *Minnesota v. U.S.*, 305 U.S. 382 (1939).
75. "Adverse possession" is a doctrine of law that allows a nonowner to acquire a possessory interest in land as a result of that person's continued use or occupation of that land. In simple terms, adverse possession means that, if you stay long enough, the land becomes yours. However, adverse possession does not apply to federal property. Therefore it does not apply to trust land. *Joint Tribal Council of the Passamaquoddy Tribe v. Morton*, 528 F.2d 370 (1st Cir. 1975).
76. 25 U.S.C. Sec. 463e.
77. *Board of Commissioners v. U.S.*, 308 U.S. 343 (1939); *Bunch v. Cole*, 263 U.S. 250 (1923).
78. *Passamaquoddy Tribe*, note 75 above.
79. *Ewert v. Bluejacket*, 259 U.S. 129 (1922).
80. 25 U.S.C. Sec. 177.
81. *U.S. v. Southern Pacific Transportation Co.*, 543 F.2d 676 (9th Cir. 1976).
82. *See FPC v. Tuscarora Indian Nation*, 362 U.S. 99, 119 (1960).
83. *See, e.g., Passamaquoddy Tribe*, note 75 above; *Mashpee Tribe v. New Seabury Corp.*, 427 F. Supp. 899 (D. Mass. 1977), *aff'd*, 592 F.2d 575 (1st Cir.), *cert. denied*, 444 U.S. 866 (1979); *Schaghtricoke Tribe of Indians v. Kent School Corp.*, 423 F. Supp. 780 (D. Conn. 1976); *Narragansett Tribe of Indians v. Southern Rhode Island Land Development Corp.*, 418 F. Supp. 798 (D.R.I. 1976).
84. 25 U.S.C. Secs. 1721–35.
85. 25 U.S.C. Secs. 331–58.
86. This subject is discussed in ch. 1, Sec. D.
87. *Sizemore v. Brady*, 235 U.S. 441 (1914); *Montana v. U.S.*, 450 U.S. 544 (1981); *Merrion*, note 45 above.
88. *Knight*, note 70 above. *But see Brendale*, note 67 above and accompanying text.
89. *Mazurie*, note 11 above.
90. *Jones v. Meehan*, 175 U.S. 1 (1899). *Cf. Wheeler*, note 3 above, 435 U.S. at 322 n.18.
91. *Seneca*, note 58 above.

92. *Cardin v. De La Cruz,* 671 F.2d 363 (9th Cir.), *cert. denied,* 459 U.S. 967 (1982); *Arizona Public Service Co. v. Office of Navajo Labor Relations,* 17 Indian L. Rep. 6105 (Nav. Sup. Ct. 1990).

93. 450 U.S. 544 (1981).

94. 492 U.S. 408 (1989).

95. *Merrion,* note 45 above, 455 U.S. at 130. *See also Crow Creek Sioux Tribe v. Buum,* 10 Indian L. Rep. 6031 (Intertr. Ct. App.) (1983), and *Thompson v. Cheyenne River Sioux Tribe,* 13 Indian L. Rep. 6005 (Chy. R. Sx. Tr.) (1986).

96. *Morris v. Hitchcock,* 194 U.S. 384 (1904).

97. *Buster v. Wright,* 135 F. 947 (8th Cir. 1905).

98. *Iron Crow v. Oglala Sioux Tribe,* 231 F.2d 89 (8th Cir. 1956).

99. 455 U.S. 130 (1982).

100. *Wheeler,* note 3 above; *Oliphant v. Suquamish Indian Tribe,* 435 U.S. 191 (1978); *Ortiz-Barraza,* note 55 above.

101. *Wheeler,* note 3 above, 435 U.S. at 322 (citations omitted).

102. *See Wheeler,* note 3 above. *Cf. Schantz v. White Lightning,* 231 N.W.2d 812 (N.D. 1975).

103. 435 U.S. 191 (1978).

104. 110 S.Ct. 2053 (1990).

105. *See* cases cited in note 100 above.

106. 18 U.S.C. Sec. 1153. This statute is reprinted in appendix D of this book.

107. Ch. 8 further discusses this subject.

108. *Moapa Band of Paiute Indians v. U.S. Dep't of Interior,* 747 F.2d 563 (9th Cir. 1984).

109. 25 U.S.C. Secs. 1301 *et seq.*

110. *Cf. Ex parte Crow Dog,* 109 U.S. 556 (1883).

111. 25 U.S.C. Secs. 461 *et seq.*

112. For a more detailed look at Indian courts, see National American Indian Court Judges Association, *Indian Courts and the Future,* (1978); F. Pommersheim, *The Contextual Legitimacy of Adjudication in Tribal Courts,* 18 N.M. L. Rev. 51 (1988); M. Taylor, *Modern Practice in Tribal Courts,* 10 U. Puget Sound L. Rev. 231 (1987).

113. *Indian Courts and the Future,* note 112 above, p. 43.

114. *See Duckhead v. Anderson,* 555 P.2d 1334 (Wash. 1976).

115. The *Indian Law Reporter* is published by the American Indian Lawyer Training Program, Inc., 319 MacArthur Blvd., Oakland, CA 94610.

116. *Smith v. Confed. Tribes of Warm Springs,* 783 F.2d 1409 (9th Cir. 1986), *cert. denied,* 479 U.S. 964 (1987). *See also In re D.P.,* 11 Indian L. Rep. 6023 (Nav. D. Crownpoint) (1982); *U.S. v. Jones,* 11 Indian L. Rep. 6010 (Hoopa Ct. App.) (1984).

117. *Sage v. Lodge Grass Sch. Dist. No. 27,* 13 Indian L. Rep. 6035, 6040 (Crow Ct. App.) (1986).

118. *See, e.g., LaFloe v. Smith,* 12 Indian L. Rep. 6007 (Ft. Peck Ct. App.) (1984); *In re Bowman: Navajo Nation v. McDonald,* 16 Indian L. Rep. 6085 (Nav. Sup. Ct.) (1989).

119. *Mazurie,* note 11 above (delegation of authority over liquor); *Nance v. EPA,* 645 F.2d 701, 714–15 (9th Cir. 1981) (delegation of authority over air quality).

120. *Colville,* note 9 above, 447 U.S. at 152; *Williams v. Lee,* 358 U.S. 217 (1959); *Snow v. Quinault Indian Nation,* 709 F.2d 1319 (9th Cir. 1983), *cert. denied,* 467 U.S. 1214 (1984).

121. *See* note 69 above and accompanying text.

122. *Worcester,* note 5 above, 31 U.S. at 560.

123. *Mescalero Apache Tribe,* note 4 above, 426 U.S. at 333. *See also Merrion,* note 45 above, 455 U.S. at 144–45; *Hardin v. White Mountain Apache Tribe,* 779 F.2d 476 (9th Cir. 1985).

124. 18 U.S.C. Sec. 1165.

125. *Oneida Indian Nation v. County of Oneida,* 414 U.S. 661 (1974).

126. *Wheeler,* note 3 above, 435 U.S. at 324 n.15. *See also Morris v. Sockey,* 170 F.2d 599 (10th Cir. 1948); *Begay v. Miller,* 222 P.2d 624 (Ariz. 1950); *Native Village of Venetie IRA Council v. Alaska,* 918 F.2d 797 (9th Cir. 1990).

127. 424 U.S. 382 (1976).

128. *Id.,* at 387–88.

129. *Wakefield v. Little Light,* 347 A.2d 228 (Md. 1975); *Wisconsin Potowatomies v. Houston,* 393 F. Supp. 719 (W.D. Mich. 1973).

130. For a discussion of tribal customs in domestic relations matters, see *The World of the American Indian,* National Geographic Society (1974).

131. *See respectively Estate of Matthew Cook,* IBIA 80–28 [8 Indian L. Rep. 5052] (1981), and *Navajo Nation v. Murphy,* 15 Indian L. Rep. 6035 (Nav. Sup. Ct.) (1988).

132. *Estate of John Ignace,* IBIA No. 76–6 (1976).

133. *Merrion,* note 3 above; *Colville,* note 9 above. *See also Arizona Public Service,* note 92 above.

134. 25 U.S.C. Secs. 261–64. The federal government's regulation of Indian trade is discussed in ch. 5, sec. B(8).

135. *Merrion,* note 3 above.

136. 42 U.S.C. Sec. 2000e(b), 2000e–2002(i).

137. *Equal Employment Opportunity Comm'n v. Cherokee Nation,* 871 F.2d 937 (10th Cir. 1989).

138. *Arizona Public Service,* note 92 above, 17 Indian L. Rep. at 6106.

139. *Mescalero Apache Tribe v. Jones,* 411 U.S. 145 ((173); *White Moun-*

     tain Apache Tribe v. Shelley, 480 P.2d 654 (Ariz. 1971); *Turner v. U.S.,* 248 U.S. 354 (1919).

140. *Namekagon Development Co., Inc. v. Bois Fort Reservation Housing Authority,* 395 F. Supp. 23 (D. Minn. 1974), *aff'd,* 517 F.2d 508 (8th Cir. 1975); *Navajo Tribe v. Bank of New Mexico,* 700 F.2d 1285 (10th Cir. 1983).

141. 25 U.S.C. Secs. 477, 482.

142. 25 U.S.C. Sec. 47.

143. 25 U.S.C. Secs. 450 *et seq.*

144. 25 U.S.C. Secs. 2101–8.

145. 25 U.S.C. Secs. 2701 *et seq. See U.S. v. Sisseton-Wahpeton Sioux Tribe,* 897 F.2d 358 (8th Cir. 1990); *Lac Du Flambeau Band of Lake Superior Chippewa Indians v. Wisconsin,* 713 F. Supp. 645 (W.D. Wis. 1990); *United Keetoowah Band of Cherokee Indians v. Oklahoma,* 927 F.2d 1170 (10th Cir. 1991).

146. For more information on this subject, see D. Vinje, "Cultural Values and Economic Development on Reservation," in V. Deloria, note 33 above, pp. 155–75.

VII

State Power over Indian Affairs

Every Indian reservation is located within the boundaries of a state. This is a fact many state and tribal officials would like to forget.

States have the right to regulate all persons and activities within their borders, with one major exception. The U.S. Constitution gives Congress exclusive authority over certain subjects, and one of these subjects is Indian affairs.[1] Therefore, as a general rule, unless Congress has authorized a state to apply its laws within an Indian reservation, it may not do so.[2] Congress has given the states very little authority to regulate reservation Indians. As the Supreme Court has noted, "the policy of leaving Indians free from state jurisdiction and control is deeply rooted in the Nation's history."[3]

States and tribes are not the best of friends. States resent the fact that reservation Indians are not normally subject to state taxation and regulation, and Indians resent the states' constant attempts to tax and regulate them. The state-Indian conflict has been a long and bitter one. More than a century ago the Supreme Court noted that there was so much local ill-feeling against Indians that "the people of the states where they are found are often their deadliest enemies."[4] Many states and tribes, for their mutual benefit, have worked hard to improve their relations with one another. Hopefully, the future will see continued efforts in this direction.

A. STATE JURISDICTION OVER RESERVATION INDIANS

Do states have the right to regulate the activities of reservation Indians?

As a general rule, no.

In 1832 the Supreme Court held that state laws "can have no force" within an Indian reservation unless Congress has authorized the state to apply them there.[5] The Court has since departed from this absolute view.[6] Today, as the Court recently stated, "there is no rigid rule by which to resolve the question whether a particular state law may be applied to an Indian reservation or to tribal members."[7] A state law authorized by Congress is valid, but some state laws can be applied within Indian country even if not expressly authorized by Congress. ("Indian country" is defined in chapter 2.) However, almost every law the states have attempted to enforce within Indian country has been invalidated by the courts, except for those which Congress has expressly authorized.

Can Congress give rights to Indians without the state's consent?

Yes. The power of Congress over Indian affairs is supreme. Federal Indian treaties and statutes do not need state approval before becoming the supreme law of the land.[8] Even if a state did not exist when the treaty or law went into effect, the state still must obey it. For example, any hunting, fishing, or water rights given by the federal government to Indians before a territory became a state, must be honored by the state.[9]

B. CONGRESSIONAL AUTHORIZATION OF STATE JURISDICTION

State laws are powerless in Indian country, as a general rule, unless authorized by Congress. Knowing this, states often pressure Congress for permission to regulate reservation activities. Congress rarely has bowed to this pressure. There have been, however, three federal laws which have significantly increased state jurisdiction over reservation life.

1. The General Allotment Act of 1887

How did the General Allotment Act increase state jurisdiction in Indian country?

The General Allotment Act of 1887 has been discussed in earlier chapters.[10] This act was extremely harmful to Indians. By the time it was repealed in 1934, tribes had lost almost two-thirds of the lands they held in 1887, and reservation life was seriously altered.

Basically, the Allotment Act authorized federal officials to decide whether an Indian reservation contained any "surplus" land. If it did, this land could be sold to non-Indian settlers. Much tribal land was sold in this manner. In addition, the act authorized federal officials to allot parcels of tribal land to tribal members and, after twenty-five years, to give them a deed to their parcel. Once the deed was issued, the land could be sold. Many of these parcels of land were then sold to non-Indians.

The effect of the General Allotment Act was the drastic reduction in tribal landholdings and the large numbers of non-Indians who came to live on the reservation. The act also opened the door to state regulation of reservation life. First, the act authorizes the state to tax all of the land taken out of trust status in which a deed has been issued, even the privately owned land, the Supreme Court held in 1992, owned by Indians.[11] Second, on some reservations, there are now areas that are owned predominantly by non-Indians. The state has the power to zone the non-Indian land within these "opened" portions of the reservation.[12] Within these areas, the Supreme Court recently said, the tribe can enforce its zoning laws on non-Indian landowners only if the landowners are engaging in an activity that imperils the tribe's political integrity, economic security, or health and welfare. (In fact, the Court nearly held that the state can zone all non-Indian-owned land within the reservation. However, the Court voted five to four that the tribe retained the power to zone non-Indian land located within the predominantly Indian portion of the reservation.) Thus, the Allotment Act (1) took land from tribes, (2) allowed the state to tax land within the reservation, and (3) zone certain reservation land.

2. Public Law 83–280

The years between 1953 and 1968 are known as the "termination era" in federal Indian history. During this period, Congress tried to destroy certain Indian tribes, force Indians to assimilate into white culture, and reduce the government's assistance to Indians.

Public Law 83–280[13] (often written as "P. L. 280" or "Pub. L. 280") is a product of the termination era. Enacted on August 15, 1953, it is the only federal law that extends state jurisdiction to Indian reservations generally.

Public Law 83–280, according to the congressional report

that accompanied the act, was designed merely to help tribes control reservation crime.[14] However, the act is so broad that Congress clearly had other motives for passing it. In addition to the stated purpose of the act, Congress wanted to reduce federal expenditures to Indians and foster the assimilation of Indians by giving the state greater power on Indian reservations. "Without question," the Supreme Court said in 1979, P.L. 280 reflects "the general assimilationist policy followed by Congress from the early 1950s through the late 1960s."[15]

How did P.L. 280 increase state jurisdiction in Indian country?

Public Law 280 is complicated. (A copy is reprinted in appendix B.) First, the act gives to five states complete criminal and some civil jurisdiction over Indian reservations located within the state.[16] These five states had no choice but to accept this jurisdiction and are therefore known as the "mandatory" states. The five mandatory states are California, Minnesota, Nebraska, Oregon, and Wisconsin. In 1958 Alaska was added by Congress as a sixth mandatory state.[17]

P.L. 280 authorized the other forty-four states, at their option, to assume the same jurisdiction the mandatory states had received.[18] These states are known as the "option" states.

P.L. 280 divided the option states into two groups. The first group consisted of those states that had a "disclaimer clause" in their constitutions, disclaiming state jurisdiction in Indian country. (After 1889 Congress required each state admitted into the Union to disclaim jurisdiction over Indian lands.) The second group consisted of those states that did not have a disclaimer clause in their constitutions. (These states had been admitted prior to 1889.)

Public Law 83–280 authorizes the disclaimer states to amend their constitutions and remove the disclaimer.[19] States that did not have a disclaimer clause could assume P.L. 280 jurisdiction in Indian country "at such time and in such manner as the people of the State shall, by an affirmative legislative action, obligate and bind the State to assumption thereof."[20] Of the forty-four option states, only ten took steps to assume any jurisdiction under P.L. 280. The jurisdiction these states opted to accept is shown in the second table on pages 116–117.

As mentioned, P.L. 280 required the mandatory states to assume complete criminal and some civil jurisdiction over Indian reservations. The exact extent of this jurisdiction is explained in chapters 8 and 9, respectively. Briefly stated, the mandatory states were required to apply all of their criminal laws on the reservation, thereby making Indians subject to the same laws as non-Indians elsewhere in the state. The option states could choose to assume the same jurisdiction, but only a few did.

With respect to civil jurisdiction, P.L. 280 did little to change the status of the law. P.L. 280 contains no general grant of civil jurisdiction, as it does for criminal jurisdiction. In a series of recent cases, discussed in chapter 9, the Supreme Court has made it clear that states obtained little civil jurisdiction over reservation Indians as a result of P.L. 280.

What is "partial" jurisdiction?

Public Law 280 does not expressly authorize an option state to assume anything less than the jurisdiction given to the mandatory states. However, most option states that assumed any jurisdiction, assumed only partial jurisdiction. These states limited their jurisdiction to (1) less than all the Indian reservations in the state, (2) less than all the geographic areas within an Indian reservation, or (3) less than all subject matters of the law. For instance, Montana only assumed criminal jurisdiction on the Flathead Indian Reservation, one of several reservations in the state. Arizona assumed jurisdiction only with respect to the control of air and water pollution. Idaho and Washington assumed jurisdiction only with respect to eight subject areas (listed in the second table below). In 1979 the Supreme Court held that it was legal under P.L. 280 for an option state to assume only partial jurisdiction, even though this created a "checkerboard" situation in which some portions of the reservation and not others, and some crimes and not others, were subject to state jurisdiction.[21]

Which reservations within the six mandatory states are under P.L. 280 state jurisdiction?

Within the six mandatory states, all Indian reservations except for three are under P.L. 280 jurisdiction, as shown in the table below.[22]

State	Extent of Jurisdiction
Alaska	All Indian country within the state
California	All Indian country within the state
Minnesota	All Indian country within the state, except the Red Lake Reservation
Nebraska	All Indian country within the state
Oregon	All Indian country within the state, except the Warm Springs Reservation
Wisconsin	All Indian country within the state, except the Menominee Reservation

Which reservations within the option states are under P.L. 280 state jurisdiction?

Ten option states accepted jurisdiction under P.L. 280. Only Florida accepted the full jurisdiction given the mandatory states. The other nine undertook only partial jurisdiction. The pattern of state jurisdiction within the option states follows.

State	Extent of Jurisdiction
Arizona	All Indian country within the state, limited to enforcement of the state's air and water pollution control laws.[23]
Florida	All Indian country within the state.[24]
Idaho	All Indian country within the state, limited to the following subject matters: compulsory school attendance; juvenile delinquency and youth rehabilitation; dependent, neglected, and abused children; mental illness; domestic relations; operation of motor vehicles on public roads.[25]
Iowa	Only over the Sac and Fox Indian community in Tama County, limited to civil and some criminal jurisdiction.[26]
Montana	Over the Flathead Reservation, limited to criminal jurisdiction and later, by tribal consent, to certain domestic relations issues.[27]

Nevada	Over the Ely Indian Colony and any other reservation that may subsequently consent.[28]
North Dakota	Limited to civil jurisdiction over any reservation that gives its consent.[29] No tribe has consented.
South Dakota	A federal court invalidated the jurisdiction assumed by the state and therefore no P.L. 280 jurisdiction exists.[30]
Utah	All Indian country within the state with tribal consent.[21] No tribe has consented.
Washington	All fee patent (deeded) land within Indian country. Jurisdiction on trust land is limited to the following subjects unless the tribe requests full jurisdiction: compulsory school attendance; public assistance; domestic relations; mental illness; juvenile delinquency; adoptions; dependent children; operation of motor vehicles on public roads. The following tribes have requested and are now under full state jurisdiction: Chehalis, Colville, Muckleshoot, Nisqually, Quileute, Skokomish, Squaxin, Swinomish and Tulalip.[32]

Did Congress amend Public Law 83–280?

Most Indian tribes strongly opposed P.L. 280 at the time of its passage. Afterward, tribes continued to worry because option states could increase their jurisdiction whenever they wanted. In response to these concerns, Congress amended P.L. 280 in two significant respects in 1968.[33] First, Congress placed a tribal consent requirement in the law. A state can no longer obtain any P.L. 280 jurisdiction over a tribe unless a majority of the tribe's members, voting in a special election called for this purpose, gives its consent.[34] Second, the 1968 amendments authorize the United States to accept a "retrocession" (a return) of any jurisdiction previously acquired by a state under P.L. 280.[35] The United States, however, is not required to accept a state's offer to retrocede. Moreover, a tribe cannot force a retrocession. The tribe also cannot prevent a retrocession from occurring if it opposes it, although the federal government has a policy of not accepting a retrocession unless the tribe approves.

Have any states retroceded jurisdiction to the United States?

Yes, several have. Nebraska retroceded its jurisdiction over the Omaha tribe in 1970 except for traffic violations on public roads. Washington retroceded its jurisdiction over the Quinault Reservation in 1969, the Suquamish Port Madison Reservation in 1972, and the Colville Reservation in 1987. Minnesota retroceded its jurisdiction over the Nett Lake Reservation in 1975. Nevada retroceded jurisdiction over all but one of its tribes (the Ely Indian Colony) in 1975. In 1976, when Congress restored the Menominee tribe to federal status after terminating the tribe in 1961, Wisconsin retroceded the jurisdiction it had acquired by the termination.[36] In 1981 Oregon retroceded its criminal jurisdiction over the Umatilla Reservation.[37]

When Nebraska retroceded its jurisdiction over the Omaha tribe, it also offered to retrocede its jurisdiction over the Winnebago tribe. The Winnebagos opposed the retrocession, and the Secretary of the Interior refused to accept the Winnebago retrocession. A federal court later upheld the right of the Secretary to make that choice.[38] In 1986 Nebraska again offered to retrocede criminal jurisdiction on the Winnebago Reservation, and this time the tribe and the federal government accepted it.

3. Termination Laws

In addition to the General Allotment Act of 1887 and Public Law 83–280, Congress has used one other means to significantly increase state jurisdiction over Indians. This third method, termination, is the most devastating to Indian interests of the three.

The process of termination and its effects are explained in earlier chapters of this book.[39] Between 1950 and 1968 Congress passed laws that terminated more than one hundred tribes. Basically, each of these laws required the affected tribe to distribute all of its property to its members and to disband its government. The tribe ceased to exist as a governmental body, and its members became fully subject to state law. As a result of these termination laws, thousands of Indians and millions of acres of Indian land came under state jurisdiction for the first time.

4. Other Congressional Authorizations of State Jurisdiction

Congress has passed several laws that confer state jurisdiction over particular tribes. Oklahoma and New York, for example, have been given extensive jurisdiction over the Indian tribes in those states. This jurisdiction is explained in chapter 15.

Congress also has conferred state jurisdiction over particular subjects. For example, Congress has authorized the Secretary of the Interior to allow state officials to inspect reservation health conditions and enforce the state's sanitation and quarantine regulations on Indian reservations.[40] In addition, Congress has aut!.orized the state to seize by eminent domain (that is, to take for a public purpose) any federal land allotted to an Indian, provided that the Indian is paid fair compensation.[41] States have also been authorized to tax oil, gas, and other minerals produced from certain Indian lands[42] and to regulate reservation liquor transactions.[43]

Thus, every state has some jurisdiction on Indian reservations. Few states, however, have much authority. This is particularly true in the critical areas of domestic relations (marriage, divorce, adoptions, child custody, etc.), commercial transactions, taxation, and zoning. On the whole, Congress has kept tribes free from state jurisdiction.[44] This is somewhat surprising given that states have pressured Congress intensely to increase their jurisdiction over Indians. Despite two hundred years of this pressure, Congress has passed only one law, Public Law 83–280, that increases the state's criminal jurisdiction on Indian reservations generally and no similar law with respect to civil jurisdiction.

C. STATE JURISDICTION WITHOUT CONGRESSIONAL AUTHORIZATION

From the earliest days of the republic, states have attempted to extend their laws into Indian reservations. In 1832 the Supreme Court held that state laws "can have no force" in Indian country without the approval of Congress.[45] This did not stop the states. In every way imaginable, using every conceivable argument, states have attempted to control reservation activities even without congressional approval.

Occasionally, states have gotten away with it. In 1881, for instance, the Supreme Court held that a state could prosecute a non-Indian for killing another non-Indian on an Indian reservation.[46] In 1885 the Court held that a state could tax the personal property of a non-Indian that was located on an Indian reservation.[47] These cases admitted for the first time that a state could regulate certain reservation activities without the consent of Congress. It was no longer true, in other words, that state laws could have no force within Indian country.

The Supreme Court has now developed a two-part test to determine which state laws can be enforced in Indian country without congressional consent: the federal preemption test and the infringement test. A state law must pass both tests in order to be valid. Moreover, state laws affecting reservation activities must be viewed against a "backdrop" of tribal sovereignty, the *inherent* right of an Indian tribe to be self-governing. As the Court explained in 1980, "the two barriers are independent because either, standing alone, can be a sufficient basis for holding state law inapplicable to activity undertaken on the reservation." Moreover, "traditional notions of Indian self-government are so deeply ingrained in our jurisprudence that they have provided an important 'backdrop' against which" the state law must be viewed.[48] Thus, a state's claim that it can regulate reservation Indians without congressional approval is inherently suspicious given Congress's "overriding goal . . . of encouraging tribal self-sufficiency and economic development."[49]

Which state laws violate the federal preemption test?

Simply stated, a state law that is inconsistent with federal law violates the preemption test.[50] Federal law is supreme, and it must be obeyed. For example, if a federal law prohibits states from taxing Indian land, a state tax on that land violates the preemption test. Usually, however, the issue is more cloudy than this. States rarely pass laws that clearly violate federal law. In most cases, a state law will impact tribal or federal interests but is not obviously invalid. When this occurs a court must decide, the Supreme Court has said, whether the state law interferes with overriding federal and tribal interests. A state law that regulates a matter already heavily regulated by the federal government is preempted. "No room remains for state laws imposing additional burdens" on these activities.[51] Once Congress takes a matter "fully in hand," the state is not permitted to "disturb or disarrange" the federal plan.[52] State laws that interfere with tribal self-government are also preempted unless the state's interest in enforcing them is very compelling. Congress is committed to fostering tribal sovereignty. Therefore, state laws that unduly inhibit tribal self-government violate the preemption test.[53]

The leading case on this point is *Warren Trading Post Co. v. Arizona Tax Commission*,[54] decided by the Supreme Court in 1965. The issue was whether Arizona could impose a "gross proceeds" tax (similar to an income tax) on a non-Indian company engaged in trade on the Navajo reservation. The state tax did not expressly violate a federal law. However, virtually every aspect of Indian trade is regulated by the federal government. These regulations, the Court held, left no room for additional burdens, and, because the tax would disrupt the federal scheme, it was preempted by federal law.

In *McClanahan v. Arizona Tax Commission* (1973),[55] the Court held that Arizona could not require a Navajo Indian to pay state income taxes on income earned from reservation employment. The Court reviewed federal treaties in which the government assured the Navajos of relative independence from state jurisdiction. This federal purpose, especially when viewed against the backdrop of tribal sovereignty, preempted the state tax. Reservation employment by tribal members is an activity, the Court held, "totally within the sphere which the relevant treaties and statutes leave for the Federal Government and for the Indians themselves."[56]

The Supreme Court reached a similar conclusion in *White Mountain Apache Tribe v. Bracker* (1980).[57] In that case, the White Mountain Apache tribe of Arizona contracted with a non-Indian company to cut, haul, and sell tribal timber, with the tribe sharing in the profits. Arizona, however, imposed a tax on the fuel needed by the company to haul the timber and also taxed the company's sale of the timber. The non-Indian company challenged the taxes and won. The federal government already regulated virtually every aspect of tribal timber production. The tribe, moreover, had a strong interest in keeping its timber production free from state regulation. The combination of these factors compelled the conclusion, the Court said, that the state's taxes were preempted by federal law.

In similar fashion, the Supreme Court has ruled that (1) a state is preempted from taxing the money that a non-Indian company receives from a tribe for constructing an Indian school on a reservation because federal regulation of Indian education is "comprehensive and pervasive,"[58] (2) a state cannot require non-Indians who hunt or fish on tribal land to comply with state game laws because state regulation would disrupt overall federal and tribal wildlife management,[59] and (3) a state (even a P.L. 280 state) may not enforce its gambling laws within an Indian reservation because this would undermine the federal policy of encouraging tribal independence and economic development.[60] Using the same analysis, other courts have held that federal law preempts states from regulating hazardous waste activities[61] or billboards[62] on Indian reservations.

The outer reach of the preemption test is perhaps best illustrated in *Central Machinery Co. v. Arizona State Tax Commission* (1980).[63] In *Central Machinery*, a non-Indian company sold farm equipment to a tribal corporation. As in *Warren Trading Post*, the sale took place on the reservation, and payment and delivery were made there. However, the company was located off the reservation, and it had failed to obtain a federal trader's license as required by federal law. Following the sale, Arizona imposed the same gross proceeds tax it attempted to impose in *Warren Trading Post*. The Supreme Court held that even this single reservation sale by an unlicensed company located outside the reservation was beyond state control. Reservation trade was too heavily regulated by the federal government to allow any additional state burdens.

There are limits to the preemption doctrine, however. In *Rice v. Rehner* (1983),[64] the Supreme Court allowed a state to apply its liquor licensing law to a non-Indian business on the reservation. In reaching this decision, though, the Court relied on the fact that Congress had authorized some state jurisdiction in this area, that the state law did not burden a federal plan, and that the tribe had no tradition of regulating liquor sales.

Rice v. Rehner does not mean that a state can regulate a reservation activity whenever the tribe has no tradition of doing so. If this were the case, states could frustrate tribal progress and development. In *California v. Cabazon Band of Mission Indians* (1987),[65] for example, the Supreme Court held that a state could not regulate a tribal bingo operation, even though this was a new tribal activity, because state regulation would disturb a federal plan aimed at tribal self-sufficiency. Thus, the critical difference between these two decisions appears to be that Congress has consented to certain forms of state regulation of tribal liquor sales but not of tribal gaming operations, and the lack of a tribal tradition in one as opposed to the other has little practical relevance.

More troubling than *Rice v. Rehner* is the Supreme Court's 1989 decision in *Cotton Petroleum Corp. v. New Mexico*.[66] This case certainly represents a retreat from the broad principles of the preemption doctrine. The issue in *Cotton Petroleum* was whether New Mexico could impose a severance tax on oil and gas produced by a non-Indian company on tribal land. In 1982 the Court ruled that the tribe could impose its own tax on this production;[67] the issue here was whether New Mexico could impose a similar ("double") tax.

The Court upheld the tax on a vote of six to three. The Court acknowledged that the state tax might discourage oil and gas producers from leasing tribal lands, thereby reducing the tribe's income. The Court also acknowledged that New Mexico would collect millions of dollars more in revenue from this tax than it spends on reservation services and that the federal government already was regulating in this area. Nevertheless, the Court allowed the tax. There was no proof, the Court said, that the tax would make the tribe's oil and gas unmarketable; a state is not required to spend on a taxpayer as much money as it collects from the taxpayer; and the federal government's regulation of oil and gas was not comprehensive or direct enough to preempt New Mexico's tax. The Justices who dissented in *Cotton Petroleum* wrote that the majority's decision "distorts" the preemption test. "Under the majority's approach, there is no pre-emption unless the states are *entirely* excluded from a sphere of activity and provide *no* services to the Indians or to the lessees they seek to tax."[68] The majority decision clearly departs from the Court's prior preemption cases, but hopefully it does not extend as far as the dissent suggests it might.

Which state laws violate the infringement test?

In 1959 the Supreme Court held in *Williams v. Lee* that a state may not infringe "on the right of reservation Indians to make their own laws and be ruled by them."[69] This principle has become known as the infringement test. It protects the inherent right of Indian tribes to be self-governing.

In *Williams,* a non-Indian who owned a store on the Navajo reservation sued a member of the tribe in state court, seeking to collect a business debt. A tribal court was available to hear this case, but the storeowner filed suit in state court anyway. The state court ruled in favor of the non-Indian. However, the U.S. Supreme Court held that the state court had no right to decide this controversy. The storeowner had to use the tribal court because "to allow the exercise of state jurisdiction here would undermine the authority of the tribal courts over Reservation affairs and hence would infringe on the right of the Indians to govern themselves."[70]

The Court reached a similar conclusion in *Fisher v. District Court* (1976).[71] The issue in *Fisher* was whether a state court could determine the custody of an Indian child where all parties to the controversy were reservation Indians. Applying the infringement test, the Court held that the state court lacked jurisdiction. Permitting state jurisdiction "plainly would interfere with the powers of self-government" by subjecting a dispute arising on the reservation among reservation Indians "to a forum other than the one they have established for themselves." [72]

It is now accepted "that the tribal court is generally the exclusive forum for the adjudication of disputes affecting the interests of both Indians and non-Indians which arise on the reservation."[73] Some additional comments on this subject are contained in chapter 9.

Is the combination of the preemption and infringement tests equal in scope to the *Worcester* rule?

Not quite. The *Worcester* rule prohibited all state laws from being enforced in Indian country without congressional consent. This rule has been replaced by the preemption and infringement tests. The combination of these tests is nearly as strong as the *Worcester* rule, especially with respect to state laws that affect only reservation Indians. Indeed thus far every effort by the states to regulate an activity involving only reservation Indians has failed either the preemption or infringement test unless it was authorized by Congress.

States have succeeded only when they have regulated non-Indian activities, because tribal interests often are not as significant in these situations. Yet even here, few state laws have survived the preemption and infringement tests, as the cases of *Warren Trading Post*, *Bracker*, and *Central Machinery* illustrate.

D. STATE JURISDICTION OVER OFF-RESERVATION INDIANS

What powers do the states have over off-reservation Indians?

Indians who leave the reservation, even briefly, become subject to the same state laws as everyone else unless a federal law or treaty grants an immunity. As the Supreme Court stated in 1973, "absent express federal law to the contrary, Indians going beyond reservation boundaries have generally been held subject to nondiscriminatory State law otherwise applicable to all citizens of the State."[74] For example, an Indian who commits a crime off the reservation can be prosecuted by the state in the same manner as anyone else.[75] However, off-reservation Indians who are engaging in a federally protected activity, such as hunting under a federal treaty, are immune from state law.[76]

A question exists, however, whether an Indian tribe or tribal corporation can be sued in state court when it engages in a business activity outside the reservation. Individual tribal members are subject to state jurisdiction in these situations. However, as explained in chapter 18, tribes and tribal corporations normally enjoy an immunity from being sued without their consent, as do their state and federal counterparts. Some courts have held that tribes and tribal businesses may not be sued for off-reservation activities without their consent, while other courts have held to the contrary.[77] Eventually, the U.S. Supreme Court will need to resolve this dispute.

NOTES

1. U.S. Const., art. I, sec. 8, cl. 3. The federal government's authority over Indian affairs is the subject of ch. 5.

2. *Williams v. Lee*, 358 U.S. 217 (1959); *McClanahan v. Arizona State Tax Comm'n*, 411 U.S. 164 (1973); *Bryan v. Itasca County, Minnesota*, 426 U.S. 373 (1976).

3. *McClanahan*, note 2 above, 411 U.S. at 168, citing *Rice v. Olson*, 324 U.S. 786, 789 (1945).

4. *U.S. v. Kagama*, 118 U.S. 375, 384 (1886).

5. *Worcester v. Georgia*, 31 U.S. 515, 561 (1832).

6. *See Moe v. Salish and Kootenai Tribes*, 425 U.S. 463 (1976), and cases cited at 481–83.

7. *White Mountain Apache Tribe v. Bracker*, 448 U.S. 136, 142 (1980).

8. *Dick v. U.S.*, 208 U.S. 340 (1908); *Winters v. U.S.*, 207 U.S. 564 (1908).

9. *See* cases cited in note 8 above. *See also Puyallup Tribe v. Dep't of Game*, 391 U.S. 392 (1968).

10. See ch. 1, sec. D, and ch. 6, sec. B.

11. *County of Yakima v. Yakima Indian Nation*, 112 S.Ct. 683 (1992).

12. *Brendale v. Confederated Yakima Tribes*, 492 U.S. 408 (1989).

13. 18 U.S.C. Sec. 1162, 28 U.S.C. Sec. 1360.

14. *See* H.R. Rep. No. 848, 83d Cong., 1st Sess. 1–6 (1953). *See also Bryan*, note 2 above; *Three Affiliated Tribes v. Wold Engineering*, 476 U.S. 877 (1986).

15. *Washington v. Confederated Yakima Tribes*, 439 U.S. 463, 488 (1979).

16. 18 U.S.C. Sec. 1162(a) (criminal jurisdiction), 28 U.S.C. Sec. 1360(a) (civil jurisdiction).

17. Pub. L. No. 85–615, Sec. 1, 72 Stat. 545. Codified in the provisions cited in note 16 above.

18. Pub. L. No. 83–280, Secs. 6, 7.

19. *Id.*, Sec. 6.

20. *Id.*, Sec. 7.

21. *Confederated Yakima Tribes*, note 15 above.

22. *See* 18 U.S.C. Sec. 1162(a) (criminal jurisdiction) and 28 U.S.C. Sec. 1306(a) (civil jurisdiction). Originally Alaska was not given jurisdiction over the Metlakatla Indian Community but a 1970 amendment to P.L. 280 placed it under the state's criminal jurisdiction.

23. Ariz. Rev. Stat. Ann. Sec. 49–561 (1990).

24. Fla. Stat. Ann. Sec. 285.16 (1975).

25. Idaho Code Secs. 67–5101–3 (1989).

26. Iowa Code Ann. 1.12-.14 (1985). See *Youngbear v. Brewer*, 415 F. Supp. 807 (N.D. Iowa 1976), *aff'd*, 549 F.2d 74 (8th Cir. 1977) for a

discussion of the state's criminal jurisdiction, and *Iowa ex rel. Dep't of Human Services v. Whitebreast*, 409 N.W.2d 460 (Iowa 1987) (civil jurisdiction).

27. Mont. Rev. Code Ann. Secs. 2–1–301 *et. seq.* (1989). *See Liberty v. Jones*, 782 P.2d 369 (Mont. 1989).

28. Nev. Rev. Stat. Sec. 41.430 (1986).

29. N.D. Cent. Code Chap. 27–19 (1989).

30. South Dakota Compiled Laws 1–1–12 through 1–1–21 (1985). *See Rosebud Sioux Tribe v. South Dakota*, 900 F.2d 1164 (8th Cir. 1990), *cert. denied*, 59 L.W. 3767 (1991).

31. Utah Code Ann. 63–36–9 through 63–36–21 (1989).

32. Wash. Rev. Code Secs. 37.12.010–.150 (1990).

33. 25 U.S.C. Secs. 1321–26.

34. 25 U.S.C. Secs. 1322, 1326. A state cannot accept jurisdiction unless this election procedure is followed. *Kennerly v. District Court*, 400 U.S. 423 (1971).

35. 25 U.S.C. Sec. 1323(a).

36. *See Omaha Tribe of Nebraska v. Village of Walthill*, 334 F. Supp. 823, 833–35 (D. Neb. 1971), *aff'd per curiam*, 460 F.2d 1327 (8th Cir. 1972).

37. 46 Fed. Reg. 2195 (1981).

38. *Omaha Tribe*, note 36 above. *See also U.S. v. Brown*, 334 F. Supp. 536 (D. Neb. 1971).

39. *See* ch. 1, and ch. 5, sec. B.

40. 25 U.S.C. Sec. 231. *See Northern v. Kings County*, 694 P.2d 40 (Wash. App. 1985).

41. 25 U.S.C. Sec. 357. *See Nebraska Pub. Power Dist. v. 100.95 Acres of Land*, 719 F.2d 956 (8th Cir. 1983); *So. California Edison Co. v. Rice*, 685 F.2d 354 (9th Cir. 1982). The statute is limited to allotted land; tribal land cannot be condemned by the state under Sec. 357. *U.S. v. City of McAlester*, 604 F.2d 42 (10th Cir. 1977).

42. *See, e.g.*, 25 U.S.C. Secs. 398, 398c, 401.

43. 25 U.S.C. Sec. 1165. *See Rice v. Rehner*, 463 U.S. 713 (1983).

44. *See Bracker*, note 7 above, 448 U.S. at 141–45.

45. *Worcester*, note 5 above, 31 U.S. at 561.

46. *U.S. v. McBratney*, 104 U.S. 621 (1881).

47. *Utah and No. Ry. v. Fisher*, 116 U.S. 28 (1885).

48. *Bracker*, note 7 above, 448 U.S. at 143.

49. *California v. Cabazon Band of Mission Indians*, 480 U.S. 202, 216 (1987).

50. *Warren Trading Post Co. v. Arizona Tax Comm'n*, 380 U.S. 685 (1965); *Bracker*, note 7 above.

51. *Warren Trading Post*, note 50 above, 380 U.S. at 690.

52. *Bracker*, note 7 above, 448 U.S. at 144.
53. *New Mexico v. Mescalero Apache Tribe*, 462 U.S. 324 (1983).
54. 380 U.S. 685 (1965).
55. 411 U.S. 164 (1973).
56. *Id.* at 179–80.
57. 448 U.S. 136 (1980).
58. *Ramah Navajo School Board v. Bureau of Revenue*, 458 U.S. 832, 839 (1982).
59. *Mescalero Apache Tribe*, note 53 above.
60. *Cabazon Band*, note 49 above.
61. *Washington Dep't of Ecology v. EPA*, 752 F.2d 1465 (9th Cir. 1985).
62. *California v. Naegle Outdoor Adv. Co.*, 698 P.2d 150 (Cal. 1985), *cert. denied*, 475 U.S. 1045 (1986).
63. 448 U.S. 160 (1980).
64. 463 U.S. 713 (1983).
65. 480 U.S. 202 (1987).
66. 490 U.S. 163 (1989).
67. *Merrion v. Jicarilla Apache Tribe*, 455 U.S. 103 (1982).
68. *Cotton Petroleum Corp. v. New Mexico*, 490 U.S. 163, 204 (1989) (Blackmun, Brennan, Marshall, JJ., dissenting).
69. *Williams v. Lee*, 358 U.S. 217, 220 (1958).
70. *Id.* at 223.
71. 424 U.S. 382 (1976).
72. *Id.* at 387–88.
73. *Geiger v. Pierce*, 758 P.2d 279, 281 (Mont. 1988), quoting *Milbank Mut. Ins. Co. v. Eagleman*, 705 P.2d 1117, 1119 (Mont. 1985). *See also Crow Tribe of Indians v. Montana*, 819 F.2d 895, 902–3 (9th Cir. 1987), *aff'd*, 484 U.S. 997 (1988).
74. *Mescalero Apache Tribe v. Jones*, 411 U.S. 145, 148–49 (1973).
75. *Ward v. Race Horse*, 163 U.S. 504 (1896).
76. *Antoine v. Washington*, 420 U.S. 194 (1975); *Washington v. Washington State Commercial Passenger Fishing Vessel Ass'n*, 443 U.S. 658 (1979).
77. *See* cases cited in *Pueblo of Acoma v. Padilla*, 490 U.S. 1029 (1989) (White, J., dissenting from denial of certiorari).

VIII

Criminal Jurisdiction in Indian Country

What is "criminal jurisdiction"?

Every government has the power to prohibit certain behavior within the territory it controls. This power is known as its criminal jurisdiction. A government exercises this power by enacting criminal laws and by punishing those persons who violate them.

As a general rule, a government can exercise its criminal jurisdiction everywhere within its borders. Therefore, three governments could in theory exercise criminal jurisdiction on an Indian reservation: the tribe, the state, and the United States. However, Indian reservations are an exception to this general rule. There is not a single Indian reservation in the country in which all three governments can simultaneously exercise their full criminal jurisdiction.

Criminal jurisdiction in Indian country (Indian country is defined in chapter 2) is complex and difficult to explain. Its governing principles are contained in hundreds of statutes and court decisions that have been issued randomly during the past two hundred years. Thus criminal jurisdiction is one of the most confusing areas of federal Indian law. Four principles and three federal laws form its foundation. These principles and laws answer most questions about criminal jurisdiction in Indian country.

What are the four principles governing criminal jurisdiction in Indian country?

1. An Indian tribe has the inherent right to exercise criminal jurisdiction over its members. This right is derived from the tribe's status as a sovereign nation. As the Supreme Court has noted, "an Indian tribe's power to punish tribal offenders is part of its own retained sovereignty."[1]

2. Congress can limit or abolish all tribal powers, including the tribe's criminal jurisdiction. As explained in Chapter 5, section A, the U.S. Constitution gives Congress complete authority over Indian affairs. Therefore, although the tribe's crim-

inal jurisdiction is inherent, it can be restricted by Congress.

3. An Indian tribe lacks criminal jurisdiction over non-Indians unless Congress has expressly given it that power. The Supreme Court announced this principle in *Oliphant v. Suquamish Indian Tribe* (1978).[2]

4. A state does not have jurisdiction over crimes committed by tribal members on the reservation unless Congress has expressly given it that power. The principle that a state has no jurisdiction, criminal or otherwise, over Indian tribes without congressional approval is "deeply rooted in the Nation's history."[3]

These four principles may be summarized as follows: Congress has the ultimate authority to decide which government can exercise criminal jurisdiction in Indian country. Unless Congress has decided otherwise, a tribe can prosecute tribal members but not nonmembers, and a state has no criminal jurisdiction over tribal members in Indian country.

What are the three most important statutes regarding criminal jurisdiction in Indian country?

In 1832 in *Worcester v. Georgia*,[4] the Supreme Court held that state criminal laws could not be applied in Indian country without the consent of Congress. Indian tribes, in other words, had exclusive criminal jurisdiction in Indian country until Congress decided otherwise.

Since then, Congress has enacted several laws which have altered criminal jurisdiction in Indian country. These laws allow the state or the federal government to exercise criminal jurisdiction in certain situations. The three most important laws are Public Law 83–280,[5] the General Crimes Act[6] and the Major Crimes Act.[7] As a result of these laws, every Indian reservation is now subject to state or federal criminal jurisdiction to some extent.

Public Law 83–280: P.L. 280, as it is commonly known, was passed by Congress in 1953. This law required six states to exercise full criminal jurisdiction in Indian country. The other forty-four states were permitted to accept such jurisdiction at their option, and a few did. The tables in chapter 7 list the states that acquired criminal jurisdiction in Indian country under P.L. 280. Within these states, Indians are generally subject to the same criminal laws that apply to everyone else and they can be prosecuted in state court for crimes committed on the reservation.

Given the *Worcester* rule, Indian reservations within a non-P.L. 280 state are not subject to that state's criminal jurisdiction. However, Congress has given the federal government certain criminal powers on all of these reservations by the General Crimes Act of 1834 (also known as the Indian Country Crimes Act) and the Major Crimes Act of 1885. These statutes, however, do not give the federal government the full criminal jurisdiction that P.L. 280 gives to its designated states.

General Crimes Act: The General Crimes Act authorizes the federal government to extend all of its criminal laws into Indian country except for crimes committed by one Indian against the person or property of another Indian. Thus an Indian who robs a non-Indian on the reservation can be prosecuted by the federal government under the General Crimes Act, but if the same Indian robbed a fellow Indian, the General Crimes Act would not apply. In other words, the General Crimes Act did not change the rule that Indian tribes had exclusive jurisdiction over crimes committed by one reservation Indian against another. (Note: In 1990, the Supreme Court held that nonmember Indians, that is, Indians from one tribe who are on another tribe's reservation, have the same status as non-Indians for purposes of criminal jurisdiction and thus, unless authorized by Congress, tribes lack criminal jurisdiction over them. Soon after, Congress passed a law expressly authorizing tribes to extend criminal jurisdiction over nonmember Indians.[8] Therefore, the word "Indian" as used in this chapter should be interpreted to mean both member and nonmember Indians unless the contrary is clearly indicated.)

Major Crimes Act: The Major Crimes Act of 1885 greatly modified the exception contained in the General Crimes Act and extended the federal government's criminal jurisdiction in Indian country. The Major Crimes Act was passed by Congress in response to *Ex parte Crow Dog*,[9] a case decided by the Supreme Court two years earlier. In *Crow Dog*, the Court ordered federal officials to release an Indian who had murdered another Indian because the government did not have jurisdiction over reservation crimes committed by one Indian against another. Congress was so upset by the *Crow Dog* decision that it passed the Major Crimes Act, which gave the federal government jurisdiction over seven major crimes when committed by an Indian against the person or property of any other person within Indian country. The Major Crimes Act has been amended several times and now covers more than a dozen crimes.[10] Thus, as to these crimes, exclusive jurisdiction no longer rests with the tribe.

The tables below illustrate the pattern of criminal jurisdiction in Indian country in non-P.L. 280 states. The first table shows the pattern of jurisdiction when the crime committed is one of the crimes covered by the Major Crimes Act. The second table shows the jurisdictional pattern for all other crimes.

When the crime committed is a "major" crime

Persons Involved	Jurisdiction
Indian accused, Indian victim	Federal government (Major Crimes Act) and tribal government (inherent sovereignty)
Indian accused, non-Indian victim	Federal government (Major Crimes Act) and tribal government (inherent sovereignty)
Non-Indian accused, Indian victim	Federal government only (General Crimes Act)
Non-Indian accused, non-Indian victim	State government only

When the crime committed is not a "major" crime

Persons Involved	Jurisdiction
Indian accused, Indian victim	Tribal government only (inherent sovereignty
Indian accused, non-Indian victim	Federal government (General Crimes Act) and tribal government (inherent sovereignty)
Non-Indian accused, Indian victim	Federal government only (General Crimes Act)
Non-Indian accused, non-Indian victim	State government only

These tables will be discussed in the remainder of this chapter. However, one subject should be emphasized at the outset. It is bad enough that criminal jurisdiction in Indian country is so confusing. However, what is worse is that the federal government has exhibited a frightening incompetence in handling its responsibility to prosecute serious crimes on the reservation.

Recent studies have shown, for example, that violent crimes occur twice as frequently per capita on Indian reservations than elsewhere, and rape in particular occurs four times as frequently. Yet the conviction rate is much lower than it is elsewhere. Of 802 reported felonies on the Navajo reservation during 1982 and 1983, the Bureau of Indian Affairs reported only 18 convictions.[11] The problem exists in large part because the federal government has not committed sufficient law enforcement resources.[12] The FBI, which must investigate these federal crimes, gives reservation crime a low priority.[13] As a U.S. Justice Department report recently stated, "law enforcement on Indian reservations is in serious trouble."[14]

Thus, although we can learn how things are supposed to operate, in reality a vacuum exists concerning reservation law enforcement. Congress has made it nearly impossible for tribes to deal effectively with serious crimes, both by failing to adequately finance tribal law enforcement and by limiting the punishments that tribal courts may impose. (This subject is discussed in chapter 6, section B[6]). Therefore, on most non-P.L. 280 Indian reservations, federal officials have the primary law enforcement responsibility, and they are not honoring it. If federal officials continue to ignore this responsibility, tribes may decide to exercise their option, explained in chapter 7, of conferring criminal jurisdiction on the state.[15] Few tribes, though, want to increase the state's powers in Indian country. Most tribes would prefer either to have their law enforcement capabilities restored by Congress or have federal officials fulfill their responsibilities.

A. CRIMES BY INDIANS AGAINST INDIANS IN NON-PUBLIC LAW 280 STATES

What jurisdiction does the tribe have over a reservation crime committed by one Indian against another?

Indian tribes have the inherent right to enforce their criminal laws against tribal members who commit crimes against other tribal members.[16] In fact, the tribe has exclusive jurisdiction over these crimes unless Congress has authorized the state or the federal government to also prosecute these offenses.[17]

What jurisdiction does the state have over these crimes?

None, unless the state has been given this jurisdiction by Congress, as some states have. Without this authority, a state cannot prosecute Indians for crimes committed in Indian country.[18]

As explained in the last chapter, state laws can apply in Indian country in some situations even without congressional consent. However, such jurisdiction is not permitted if it would seriously interfere with the ability of the tribe to govern itself. State prosecution of reservation crimes by tribal members clearly would undermine tribal government. "As a practical matter," the Supreme Court recently explained, "this has meant that criminal offenses by or against Indians have been subject only to federal or tribal laws, except where Congress . . . has expressly provided that State laws shall apply."[19]

Therefore, only those states authorized by Congress to prosecute reservation crimes by Indians can do so. These include the P.L. 280 states and a few others, as discussed later in this chapter. Unfortunately, the absence of congressional authorization has not prevented some states from attempting to prosecute reservation Indians anyway.[20]

What jurisdiction does the federal government have over these crimes?

As explained earlier, the Supreme Court held in *Ex parte Crow Dog* that the federal government lacks jurisdiction to prosecute Indians for crimes against other Indians in Indian country unless Congress has expressly conferred that power. Congress has only passed one law, the Major Crimes Act (MCA),[21] that covers these crimes. Therefore, the federal government's jurisdiction should extend only to the crimes enumerated in that act.

However, lower federal courts have created two exceptions to this rule, although the Supreme Court has yet to approve of them. First, some courts have held that Congress intended federal jurisdiction over some crimes regardless of where they are committed. These ("wherever committed") crimes include assaulting a federal officer, counterfeiting, and tampering with the mail. Courts have held that the federal government can prosecute Indians who commit these offenses even though the Major Crimes Act does not include them.[22] Second, courts have held that an Indian can be prosecuted for a non-Major Crimes Act offense if the Indian is being prosecuted for an "underlying" Crimes Act offense. For example, an Indian who kills another Indian with a firearm can be prosecuted for the MCA offense of murder and also for the non-MCA offense of using a firearm in relation to a crime of violence.[23]

In summary, the MCA gives the federal government criminal jurisdiction over more than a dozen major crimes committed by one reservation Indian against another. Tribal courts, however, retain exclusive jurisdiction over all crimes committed by one Indian against another that are not subject to federal prosecution.[24]

Does a tribe still have jurisdiction over the "major" crimes?
Maybe. When Congress passed the Major Crimes Act in 1885, it intended to do one of two things. It either wanted to give the federal government exclusive jurisdiction over the major crimes or it wanted the government to share concurrent jurisdiction with the tribe. The act itself does not address this subject.

There is little in the legislative history of the act that indicates congressional intent on this issue.[25] Given this fact, the MCA should not be interpreted as limiting the tribe's inherent powers. It is a well-established rule of Indian law that tribal powers remain intact unless Congress limits them in clear and explicit terms.[26] Therefore, this uncertainty should be resolved in favor of the tribe.

The Supreme Court has noted the controversy in this area but has not yet resolved it.[27] However, most tribes have stopped prosecuting Indians for the crimes covered by the MCA. Consequently, the Court may never have to decide whether the act eliminated tribal jurisdiction over these offenses.

If a tribe prosecutes an Indian, can the federal government later prosecute that person for the same offense?
The Fifth Amendment to the U.S. Constitution contains the

Double Jeopardy Clause. This clause guarantees that no person shall be "subject for the same offense to be twice put in jeopardy of life or limb." The term "same offense" as used in the Double Jeopardy Clause applies to "lesser included" offenses.[28] A lesser included offense is a crime necessarily committed whenever a greater offense occurs. For example, the crime of assault is always committed whenever a murder is committed; therefore, assault is a lesser included offense of murder. A person convicted of assault cannot later be prosecuted for murder arising out of the same incident against the same victim. Similarly, a conviction for murder precludes a prosecution for assault.

The Supreme Court has held, however, that the Double Jeopardy Clause applies only to successive prosecutions by the same government and does not apply to successive prosecutions by different governments.[00] In other words, if a person's conduct simultaneously violates both state and federal law, both the state and federal government can prosecute that person.

In *United States v. Wheeler*,[30] the Court had to decide whether the federal government could prosecute an Indian for statutory rape after a tribal court had convicted him of contributing to the delinquency of a minor, a lesser included offense. The defendant claimed that the Double Jeopardy Clause prevented a second prosecution. He argued that a tribal government is merely an arm of the federal government and, therefore, a second prosecution would constitute double jeopardy. The Supreme Court disagreed. In a decision of far-reaching significance, the Court recognized that Indian tribes are distinct governments existing independently from the federal government, even though Congress may regulate them. Consequently, the Double Jeopardy Clause did not apply to successive prosecutions by the tribal and federal governments and the defendant could be prosecuted in federal court under the MCA after being prosecuted in tribal court for the same (or a lesser included) offense.

The Major Crimes Act uses the term "Indian" without defining it. Is this constitutional and, if so, who is an "Indian" for the purposes of the act?

The Major Crimes Act applies only to Indians. Therefore, in all prosecutions under the act, the government must prove that the defendant is an Indian. This has created some problems for the government because the MCA does not define the term "Indian."

Indians prosecuted under the MCA have argued that the act is unconstitutionally vague because the term "Indian" is undefined. The lack of a definition, they contend, fails to give adequate warning to persons who may be subject to the act and gives federal prosecutors too much discretion in enforcing it.

The courts that have heard these arguments have unanimously rejected them.[31] These courts have held that the Major Crimes Act does not have to define the term "Indian" because this term is adequately defined in other statutes and in court decisions. Although the Supreme Court has not specifically addressed this question, given that the Court has upheld convictions under the act,[32] it probably would uphold its constitutionality on this issue.

However, the lack of a definition continues to cause some difficulties. Courts have disagreed, for example, on whether a person having Indian blood but not enrolled in a tribe is an "Indian" for purposes of the MCA.[33] The Supreme Court has discussed this issue but has not decided it.[34] A similar controversy exists regarding Indians whose tribes have been terminated by Congress. Most courts have held that a "terminated" Indian is not an Indian for purposes of the MCA, but other courts disagree.[35] Courts have also split as to whether an Indian who commits a crime on another tribe's reservation is an "Indian" for purposes of the Major Crimes Act.[36]

The MCA clearly applies, though, to crimes committed by enrolled Indians on their own reservation. In this situation, the federal government need only prove that (1) the defendant's name is listed on the tribe's official membership roll, or (2) the defendant has tribal blood and is considered to be an Indian by the Indian community. Either of these will satisfy the government's burden of proof that the defendant is an Indian under the MCA.[37]

Is the Major Crimes Act unconstitutional because Indians are treated differently than non-Indians in some situations?

An Indian who murders someone on the reservation can be punished under the Major Crimes Act because murder is one of the "major" crimes. A non-Indian who murders another non-Indian on the reservation can only be punished under state law.[38] If the MCA happens to punish murder more severely than the state does, an Indian who commits the same offense as a non-Indian will suffer discrimination.

In *United States v. Antelope*,[39] the Supreme Court held that the Major Crimes Act is not unconstitutional even though it may subject an Indian to a harsher penalty than a non-Indian who commits the same crime. Congress has the right to treat Indians as a separate group because they have a unique status under the Constitution. Therefore, any benefits or detriments the MCA imposes on Indians are within the power of Congress to legislate. Chapter 5, section A, discusses this subject in more detail.

In a jury trial under the Major Crimes Act, is the Indian defendant entitled to a "lesser included offense" instruction?

In criminal cases a defendant often will request the judge to give the jury a "lesser included offense" instruction. This instructs the jury that they may find the defendant guilty of a less severe but included offense if they believe that the facts do not warrant conviction of the offense charged. This instruction often works to the advantage of the accused because, without it, the jury might find the defendant guilty of the more serious offense rather than let the defendant go free. In a prosecution for murder, for example, the defendant will often request an instruction on manslaughter, and in a prosecution for aggravated assault, the defendant will often seek an instruction on simple assault.

Until 1973 federal courts refused to give lesser included offense instructions in prosecutions under the Major Crimes Act. They felt that unless the lesser offense was listed in the act, a jury could not find the defendant guilty of that offense because the government could not have originally prosecuted the defendant for that crime.

In 1973 in *Keeble v. United States*,[40] the Supreme Court held that the Constitution requires a lesser included offense instruction in an MCA case if it would have otherwise been available. This means, of course, that the jury then has the power to convict the defendant of the lesser offense.[41] Courts also have held that the government can request a lesser included offense instruction even if the defendant refuses to ask for one. This is the rule in non-MCA prosecutions as well.[42]

B. CRIMES BY INDIANS AGAINST NON-INDIANS IN NON-PUBLIC LAW 280 STATES

Jurisdiction over crimes committed by Indians against non-Indians in Indian country follows the same pattern as the Indian-against-Indian crimes, with one significant difference. For reasons explained below, the federal government has greater jurisdiction over these offenses.

What jurisdiction does the tribe have over crimes committed by an Indian against a non-Indian in Indian country?

An Indian tribe has the inherent right to enforce its criminal laws against tribal members. [43] Therefore, the tribe may exercise its criminal jurisdiction whenever an Indian violates tribal law, regardless of the race of the victim.

As previously noted, the Major Crimes Act [44] probably does not eliminate the tribe's jurisdiction over the major crimes, although the Supreme Court has not yet decided this issue. Assuming the act does not have this effect, each tribe continues to have full criminal jurisdiction over tribal members.

What jurisdiction does the state have over these crimes?

None, unless Congress has authorized the state to prosecute the Indians who commit them. [45] Most non-P.L. 280 states have not been given this authority. The tables in chapter 7 list the states that have such authority.

What jurisdiction does the federal government have over these crimes?

The federal government exercises considerable jurisdiction over these crimes due to three laws that Congress has passed. The combined effect of these laws is to give the federal government jurisdiction to prosecute every kind of crime committed by an Indian against a non-Indian in Indian country.

The most far-reaching law is the General Crimes Act. [46] This law authorizes the federal government to prosecute any Indian who violates a federal "enclave law" on the reservation against a non-Indian. Enclave laws were enacted by Congress to govern activities on federal enclaves, such as national parks, post offices, and military installations. These laws are quite comprehensive. Most activities that are crimes under state laws are crimes under enclave laws.

The second law is the Assimilative Crimes Act (ACA).[47] The ACA makes it a federal crime to engage in any conduct on a federal enclave that is a crime in the state where the enclave is located unless enclave law already applies. In other words, the ACA transforms all state crimes into federal crimes if they were not federal crimes already.[48] Thus, the combined effect of the General Crimes Act and the Assimilative Crimes Act makes Indians subject to all federal enclave crimes as well as to any additional state crimes, whenever the victim of the crime is a non-Indian.

The third basis for federal jurisdiction is the Major Crimes Act. As previously explained, the MCA authorizes the federal government to prosecute more than a dozen major crimes in Indian country whenever committed by an Indian, regardless of the race of the victim. Indians who commit any of these crimes can be prosecuted in federal court.

Most of the MCA crimes are also listed as crimes under federal enclave law. Therefore, when an Indian commits any of these crimes against a non-Indian, both the Major Crimes Act and the General Crimes Act apply. The courts have held, though, that because the MCA is the more specific statute, Indians must be prosecuted under that one whenever the two overlap.[49] These laws overlap only when an Indian commits a crime against a non-Indian that is both a major crime and a federal enclave crime. The laws do not overlap when the crime is not a major crime or when the victim is an Indian; only the General Crimes Act applies in the first situation and only the Major Crimes Act applies in the second.

When an Indian commits a crime against a non-Indian, can he or she be tried in tribal court as well as in federal court for the same offense?

As explained earlier, the Supreme Court has held that it does not violate the Double Jeopardy Clause to prosecute an Indian in tribal court and in federal court for the same offense.[50] However, the General Crimes Act contains a clause that prohibits prosecution by the federal government if an Indian "has been punished by the local law of the tribe." There are few court cases interpreting this provision, but it would appear that the federal government is precluded from prosecuting an Indian under the General Crimes Act if he or she has already been prosecuted for the same offense in tribal court.[51]

C. CRIMES BY NON-INDIANS AGAINST INDIANS IN NON-PUBLIC LAW 280 STATES

The jurisdictional pattern governing crimes by non-Indians against Indians in non-P.L. 280 states is simple: only the federal government has jurisdiction. The tribe has no jurisdiction over these offenses. In *Oliphant v. Suquamish Indian Tribe* (1978),[52] the Supreme Court held that Indian tribes cannot prosecute non-Indians without the express consent of Congress, and Congress has not consented to this type of tribal jurisdiction.

The federal government, on the other hand, does have this authority. As previously mentioned, the General Crimes Act authorizes the federal government to prosecute non-Indians who commit crimes against Indians in violation of a federal enclave law. In addition, the Assimilative Crimes Act makes all state criminal laws applicable to Indian country that are not already federal crimes. The combination of these two laws gives the federal government full criminal jurisdiction over crimes committed by a non-Indian against an Indian in Indian country.[53]

As for state jurisdiction, it has long been presumed that the General Crimes Act eliminates the state's power to prosecute non-Indians for crimes committed against Indians in Indian country, although the act itself says nothing about this subject. The Supreme Court has never expressly held that the General Crimes Act gives the federal government exclusive jurisdiction over these crimes, but several of its decisions reflect this view.[54] Virtually every state court to consider the question has held that the state lacks jurisdiction over these crimes. As the South Dakota Supreme Court stated in 1990, "The prevailing rule has always been that federal courts have exclusive jurisdiction over an offense committed in Indian country by an non-Indian against the person or property of an Indian."[55]

D. CRIMES BY NON-INDIANS AGAINST NON-INDIANS

In the 1832 case of *Worcester v. Georgia*,[56] the Supreme Court held that a state has no criminal jurisdiction in Indian country without congressional consent, even over crimes committed by non-Indians. The Court later amended this decision, however. In *United States v. McBratney* (1881),[57] the Court held that a state could prosecute a non-Indian who murdered another non-Indian in Indian country. Since then, the Supreme Court has consistently upheld the rule that states can prosecute non-Indians for crimes against other non-Indians in Indian country.[58]

The tribe has no jurisdiction over these crimes. As explained earlier, the Supreme Court held in *Oliphant v. Suquamish Indian Tribe* (1978) that Indian tribes lack criminal jurisdiction over non-Indians. The federal government does not have jurisdiction, either, unless the crime is a federal crime wherever committed, such as assaulting a federal officer. Thus the state has exclusive jurisdiction over these offenses. This means that unless the state exercises its jurisdiction, non-Indians can commit state crimes on the reservation without fear of prosecution. A non-Indian, for example, can drive a car above the speed limit and even rob or murder another non-Indian and not be arrested unless the state decides to act. Unfortunately, on some reservations, state law enforcement officers have been slow to investigate and prosecute these offenses. To some extent, this predicament can be alleviated by cross-deputizing tribal police officers, thereby vesting them with the power to arrest non-Indians for violations of state law and to transport them off the reservation into the custody of state officials.

E. CRIMINAL JURISDICTION IN PUBLIC LAW 280 STATES

As explained above, it has long been the rule that state criminal laws do not apply in Indian country unless Congress has authorized the state to enforce them there. The one exception to this rule (the *McBratney* exception) is that a state can prosecute offenses committed by one non-Indian against another non-Indian. Until fairly recently, this was the extent of the state's jurisdiction. However, in 1953 Congress enacted Public Law 280,[59] which substantially altered this situation.

What is the effect of Public Law 280?

Chapter 7 discusses Public Law 280 at length. Essentially, this law requires six states to enforce their criminal laws in Indian country to the same extent that they enforce them elsewhere within the state. These six states (Alaska, California, Minnesota, Nebraska, Oregon, and Wisconsin) are known as the "mandatory" states because they had no choice but to accept criminal jurisdiction in Indian country.

In addition, P.L. 280 allowed all other states the option of assuming the same criminal jurisdiction the mandatory states had received. Several of these "option" states accepted some amount of criminal jurisdiction in Indian country.

The tables in chapter 7 illustrate the extent to which the mandatory and option states have criminal jurisdiction in Indian country today. To the extent they do, reservation Indians in those states can be arrested by state police officers and tried in state courts like other citizens of the state.

It is interesting to note that most option states assumed partial but not complete criminal jurisdiction in Indian country. Therefore, in these areas, the state will prosecute some crimes and the federal government will prosecute others (under the federal laws discussed earlier). In some narrow circumstances, a single activity can give rise to both a federal and a state prosecution.[60]

Are there any limits to the state's criminal jurisdiction under P.L. 280?

Yes. Public Law 280 contains a "saving" clause which expressly exempts three subject areas from state jurisdiction. First, the state may not tax, encumber, or alienate Indian trust property. Second, it cannot regulate the use of Indian trust property in a manner inconsistent with federal law. Third, the state may not deprive any Indian or tribe of federally guaranteed hunting, fishing, or trapping rights and the right to license, control, and regulate the same.[61]

These limitations are very important. Reservation Indians, even in the mandatory states, need not comply with state laws on zoning, hunting, fishing, or trapping nor pay property taxes on their trust lands, and the state may not impose criminal penalties for their failure to do so.[62] Thus, P.L. 280 states cannot apply all of their criminal laws in Indian country.

Did P.L. 280 abolish the tribe's criminal jurisdiction?

Probably not, although the Supreme Court has yet to resolve this issue. The courts that have considered this question have held that P.L. 280 did not limit the tribe's criminal jurisdiction.[63] Tribes located in P.L. 280 states have the right to prosecute tribal members under tribal law, and the state has the concurrent power to prosecute them under state law, even for the same offense.[64]

Have any other states received criminal jurisdiction in Indian country besides the P.L. 280 states?

Yes, at least five states have. Specific acts of Congress have given Iowa, Kansas, Maine, New York, and Oklahoma some criminal jurisdiction in Indian country. The jurisdiction of New York and Oklahoma is discussed is chapter 15.[65]

F. JURISDICTION OVER VICTIMLESS CRIMES IN INDIAN COUNTRY

What is a "victimless" crime?

Certain activities have been made crimes even though they cause no identifiable harm to anyone or anything. These activities are prohibited because they are said to place people and property in danger of being harmed or to violate society's standards of morality. Adultery, prostitution, gambling, and possession of marijuana are examples of victimless crimes. Most traffic offenses are also victimless crimes, such as driving with a faulty taillight, speeding, or failure to possess a valid driver's license.

When an Indian commits a victimless crime in Indian country, which government has jurisdiction over it: the tribe, the state, or the federal government?

The scope of tribal and state jurisdiction over such a crime is straightforward: the tribe has jurisdiction and the state does not. As discussed earlier in this chapter, a tribe has the inherent right to impose all of its criminal laws on tribal members, while a state can never do so without express permission from Congress, such as that found in P.L. 280.

A more difficult question is the extent of federal jurisdiction over victimless crimes in Indian country. The Major Crimes Act and the General Crimes Act authorize the federal government to enforce many criminal laws in Indian territory, but neither act appears to include victimless crimes. The MCA authorizes the federal government to prosecute certain major crimes, none of them victimless. Therefore, if the federal government has any authority over victimless crimes, that authority can be found only in the General Crimes Act.

Yet the General Crimes Act contains an express exception. It withholds jurisdiction from the federal government over any crime committed by one Indian against another.[66] This would seem to preclude jurisdiction over victimless crimes because these crimes are considered crimes against the community. In other words, a victimless crime on an Indian reservation must be viewed as a crime against other Indians, and this places it within the exception contained in the General Crimes Act.

Courts have reached differing conclusions on this matter. In 1916 the Supreme Court held in *United States v. Quiver*[67] that the federal government could not prosecute an Indian for committing adultery with another Indian because of the exception contained in the General Crimes Act. In recent years, however, at least three federal courts have allowed the federal government to prosecute reservation Indians for gambling, distributing marijuana, and selling fireworks, all of which are victimless crimes.[68] These crimes probably should have been viewed as crimes against the Indian community and the charges dismissed under the *Quiver* rationale. Two of these courts did not even mention *Quiver* and the third limited *Quiver* to "internal and social" matters, such as the crime of adultery.[69] The Supreme Court obviously needs to address this issue again.

Which government has jurisdiction when a non-Indian commits a victimless crime in Indian country?

Both the state and federal governments may have the authority to prosecute a non-Indian who commits a victimless crime in Indian country, but one thing is clear: the tribe cannot. As indicated, in *Oliphant* the Supreme Court held that Indian tribes have no criminal jurisdiction over non-Indians.

The U.S. Department of Justice has taken the position that the state, and not the federal government, has jurisdiction over non-Indian victimless crimes.[70] The department relies on *United States v. McBratney*,[71] in which the Supreme Court held that the state has jurisdiction over a crime committed by a non-Indian against a non-Indian in Indian country. The Justice Department believes that the *McBratney* rule controls this situation because non-Indian victimless crimes should generally be viewed as crimes against the non-Indian community. According to the department, only where such crimes directly threaten Indians, Indian property, or tribal interests, would federal prosecution be justified under the General Crimes Act. Several courts have agreed with this view.[70] This is another area of Indian law requiring the Supreme Court's clarification.

G. PROBLEMS RELATING TO EXTRADITION

It often happens that a person will commit a crime in one state and flee to another state to escape prosecution. Extradition provides the means by which the victim state can arrest and obtain custody of this person. The U.S. Constitution provides that if one state is asked by the governor of another state to "deliver up" a person accused of crime, it must comply with that request.[73]

Tribal governments can become involved with extradition procedures in three situations: when an Indian commits a crime on the reservation and flees elsewhere, when an Indian commits a crime off the reservation and flees to the reservation, and when a non-Indian commits a crime off the reservation and flees to the reservation. Indian tribes, then, sometimes seek extradition and sometimes are asked to extradite.

Does the clause in the Constitution regarding extradition apply to tribal governments?

Probably not. Almost a century ago the Supreme Court held that the provisions of the Constitution do not apply to tribal governments unless Congress has expressly made them applicable.[74] Congress has not made the extradition clause applicable to Indian tribes; accordingly, courts have held that it is inapplicable.[75] The issue has yet to reach the Supreme Court. As it now stands, tribes need not return a person who has fled to the reservation and states need not return an Indian who has fled from the reservation. The constitutional provision regarding extradition applies only when two states are involved. At least one court has held, however, that state officials are permitted to arrest and extradite an Indian under a tribal warrant, even though they are not required to.[76]

In order to avoid the appearance of harboring criminals and to assist each other in prosecuting lawbreakers, many tribes and their surrounding states have entered into extradition agreements. This type of mutual effort should be encouraged.

Are state officers allowed to enter the reservation and arrest an Indian who has committed a crime in state territory?

Not unless Congress has authorized state criminal jurisdiction on the reservation, as in Public Law 280. Without congressional authority, state officers may not arrest Indians in Indian country even for crimes committed off the reservation.[77] At least one state court has disagreed with this position. The Montana Supreme Court has held that state officials can arrest Indians on the reservation if the tribe does not have a procedure allowing for extradition.[78] The validity of this decision is questionable. Indeed, a federal court recently held that state law enforcement officers do not have the authority to search an Indian home on the reservation, even when the items that are seized are turned over to federal authorities for prosecution.[79]

Are state officers allowed to enter the reservation and arrest a non-Indian who has committed a crime in state territory?

Probably. Under the *McBratney* rule, the state has jurisdiction over crimes committed by non-Indians against other non-Indians within the reservation. Given that the state can enter the reservation to arrest these offenders, it probably can also enter the reservation to arrest non-Indians who have committed crimes off the reservation.[80]

What remedy is available to an Indian who has been illegally arrested on the reservation by state officials? Is release from custody required?

The courts have split on this question. The South Dakota Supreme Court has held that Indians illegally arrested on the reservation by state police officers are not automatically entitled to be released from state custody: "It is no defense in a criminal prosecution that defendants were illegally brought before the court."[81] Other courts have taken the opposite view.[82] The latter view seems correct. State officials should obey the law. Allowing them to prosecute people they arrest illegally encourages them to violate the law. It also provides no protection for the civil rights of the people arrested. The best way to prevent illegal kidnapping from the reservation is to release the victims as soon as their arrest is determined illegal. Another alternative is to allow these persons to sue their arresting officers for damages.[83]

Which government has jurisdiction over off-reservation crimes committed by Indians?

An Indian who engages in an activity outside the reservation that is a crime under state law can be punished in the same fashion as a non-Indian who commits that crime,[84] unless the Indian has a federal exemption. For example, Indians exercising federal treaty rights need not comply with state laws that would restrict the exercise of those rights.[85] Chapters 4 and 11 discuss this subject in further detail. Consistent with this principle, if an area outside the reservation has been set aside for the exercise of Indian treaty rights, and an Indian commits a crime on that site, the tribe or federal government rather than the state has jurisdiction over the offense.[86]

NOTES

1. *U.S. v. Wheeler*, 435 U.S. 313, 328 (1978). *See also Oliphant v. Suquamish Indian Tribe*, 435 U.S. 191 (1978). This subject is discussed in ch. 6, sec. B(6).
2. 435 U.S. 191 (1978).
3. *McClanahan v. Arizona State Tax Comm'n*, 411 U.S. 164, 168 (1973), quoting *Rice v. Olson*, 324 U.S. 786, 789 (1945).
4. 31 U.S. 515 (1832).
5. 18 U.S.C. Sec. 1162, 28 U.S.C. Sec. 1360. P.L. 280 is reproduced in appendix B.

6. 18 U.S.C. Sec. 1152. The General Crimes Act is reproduced in appendix C.
7. 18 U.S.C. Sec. 1153. The Major Crimes Act is reproduced in appendix D.
8. The decision in *Duro v. Reina*, 110 S.Ct. 2053 (1990) was legislatively overruled by Congress by the passage in 1990 of Pub. L. 102-137, 105 Stat. 646.
9. 109 U.S. 556 (1883).
10. The Major Crimes Act is reproduced in appendix D.
11. The Denver Post, Sept. 8, 1985, at 15A.
12. *See Fraud in Indian Country,* The Arizona Republic, reprint of Oct. 4–11, 1987 series of articles, at 20–22.
13. The Denver Post, Sept. 8, 1985, at 14A, citing FBI Director William H. Webster.
14. Unidentified U.S. Dep't of Justice report, cited in The Arizona Republic, note 12 above, at 20.
15. *See* ch. 7, note 34 and accompanying text. *See also Langley v. Ryder,* 602 F. Supp. 335, 346 (W.D. La.), *aff'd,* 778 F.2d 1092 (5th Cir. 1985).
16. *Oliphant,* note 1 above; *Wheeler,* note 1 above. *See also Washington v. Yakima Indian Nation,* 439 U.S. 463 (1979).
17. *See* cases cited in note 16 above.
18. *U.S. v. John,* 437 U.S. 634 (1978); *Worcester v. Georgia,* 31 U.S. 515 (1832).
19. *Yakima,* note 16 above, 439 U.S. at 470–71 (citations omitted). *See also U.S. v. John,* note 18 above.
20. *See, e.g., County of Vilas v. Chapman,* 361 N.W.2d 699 (Wis. 1985); *Vermont v. St. Francis,* 563 A.2d 249 (Vt. 1989).
21. 18 U.S.C. Sec. 1153. The act is reproduced in appendix D. A year after the act was passed, the Supreme Court upheld its constitutionality in *U.S. v. Kagama,* 118 U.S. 375 (1886).
22. *See, e.g., Walks on Top v. U.S.,* 372 F.2d 422 (9th Cir.), *cert. denied,* 389 U.S. 879 (1967); *U.S. v. Cowboy,* 694 F.2d 1228 (10th Cir. 1982); *U.S. v. Blue,* 722 F.2d 383 (8th Cir. 1983).
23. *U.S. v. Laughing,* 855 F.2d 659 (9th Cir. 1988); *U.S. v. Goodface,* 835 F.2d 1233 (8th Cir. 1987).
24. *U.S. v. Antelope,* 430 U.S. 641, 643 n.2 (1977); *U.S. v. Jackson,* 600 F.2d 1283 (9th Cir. 1979); *U.S. v. Johnson,* 637 F.2d 1224, 1231 (9th Cir. 1980); *U.S. v. Barquin,* 799 F.2d 619 (10th Cir. 1986).
25. *See Oliphant,* note 1 above, 435 U.S. at 203 n.14.
26. This subject is discussed in ch. 4, notes 23–26 and accompanying text.
27. *Oliphant,* note 1 above, 435 U.S. at 203 n.14. *See Felicia v. U.S.,* 495

F.2d 353 (8th Cir.), *cert. denied*, 419 U.S. 849 (1974) (holding that the Major Crimes Act is exclusive).

28. *Brown v. Ohio*, 432 U.S. 161 (1977).

29. *Bartkus v. Illinois*, 359 U.S. 121 (1959).

30. 435 U.S. 313 (1978).

31. *U.S. v. Broncheau*, 597 F.2d 1260 (9th Cir. 1979); *U.S. v. Heath*, 509 F.2d 16 (9th Cir. 1974). *See also U.S. v. Mazurie*, 419 U.S. 544, 553 (1975).

32. *See, e.g., Keeble v. U.S.*, 412 U.S. 205 (1973); *Wheeler*, note 1 above; *Kagama*, note 10 above.

33. *Compare Heath*, note 31 above (unenrolled Indian is not an "Indian" for purposes of the Major Crimes Act) *with Ex parte Pero*, 99 F.2d 28 (7th Cir. 1938) (*contra*).

34. *Antelope*, note 24 above, 430 U.S., at 646 n.7.

35. *Compare Heath*, note 31 above, *and St. Cloud v. U.S.*, 702 F. Supp. 1456 (D.S.D. 1988) *with Cook v. State*, 215 N.W. 2d 832 (S.D. 1974).

36. *Compare State v. Attebery*, 519 P.2d 53 (Ariz. 1974), *and People ex rel. Schuyler v. Livingston*, 205 N.Y.S. 888 (Sup. Ct. 1924), *with Idaho v. Allan*, 607 P.2d 426 (Idaho 1980).

37. *U.S. v. Dodge*, 538 F.2d 770 (8th Cir. 1976), *cert. denied*, 429 U.S. 1099 (1977); *U.S. v. Lossiah*, 537 F.2d 1250 (4th Cir. 1976). *But see St. Francis*, note 20 above (defendant seeking to avoid state prosecution has burden of proving he is an Indian).

38. *U.S. v. McBratney*, 104 U.S. 621 (1882).

39. 430 U.S. 641 (1977). *See also U.S. v. Broncheau*, note 31 above.

40. 412 U.S. 205 (1973).

41. *See, e.g., Felicia v. U.S.*, note 27 above; *U.S. v. Pino*, 606 F.2d 908 (10th Cir. 1979); *U.S. v. Bowman*, 679 F.2d 798 (9th Cir. 1982).

42. *U.S. v. Thompson*, 492 F.2d 359, 362 (8th Cir. 1974). For criticism of this holding see Vollman, *Criminal Jurisdiction in Indian Country*, 22 U. Kan. L. Rev. 387 (1974). In *Keeble v. U.S.*, 412 U.S. 205, 214 n.4 (1973), the Court questions whether the government should be able to request a lesser included offense instruction.

43. *See* cases cited in note 1 above and accompanying text.

44. 18 U.S.C. Sec. 1153. The Major Crimes Act is reproduced in appendix D.

45. *See* cases cited in notes 18 and 19 above and accompanying text. *See also Williams v. U.S.*, 327 U.S. 711 (1946); *State v. Greenwalt*, 663 P.2d 1178 (Mont. 1983).

46. 18 U.S.C. Sec. 1152. The General Crimes Act is reproduced in appendix C.

47. 18 U.S.C. Sec. 13. The Supreme Court has upheld the validity of this law as applied to reservation Indians. *Williams*, note 45 above.

48. *U.S. v. Sharpnack*, 355 U.S. 286 (1958); *U.S. v. Marcyes*, 557 F.2d 1361 (9th Cir. 1977). Normally, unless an enclave law precisely covers the crime at issue, the state law is used pursuant to the Assimilated Crimes Act. *U.S. v. Kaufman*, 862 F.2d 236 (9th Cir. 1988); *U.S. v. Renville*, 779 F.2d 430 (8th Cir. 1985). *But see Hall v. State*, 539 So. 2d 1338 (Miss. 1989).

49. *See, e.g., U.S. v. John*, 587 F.2d 683 (5th Cir.), *cert. denied*, 441 U.S. 925 (1979). For a further discussion of this subject, see F. Cohen, *Handbook of Federal Indian Law* pp. 288–97 (1982).

50. *Wheeler*, note 1 above. For a discussion of this subject, see notes 28–30 and accompanying text.

51. Perhaps the only reported case on this subject is *U.S. v. La Plant*, 156 F. Supp. 660 (D. Mont. 1957), which dismissed federal charges against an Indian convicted of the same offense in tribal court.

52. 435 U.S. 191 (1978).

53. *Donnelly v. U.S.*, 228 U.S. 243 (1939); *U.S. v. Chavez*, 290 U.S. 357 (1933).

54. *Williams v. U.S.*, 327 U.S. 711, 714 (1946); *Williams v. Lee*, 358 U.S. 217, 220 (1958). *See also U.S. v. Big Crow*, 523 F.2d 955 (8th Cir. 1975), *cert. denied*, 424 U.S. 920 (1976).

55. *South Dakota v. Larson*, 455 N.W.2d 600 (S.D. 1990). *See also State v. Flint*, 756 P.2d 324 (Ariz. Ct. App. 1988), *cert. denied*, 109 S.Ct. 3228 (1989); *Greenwalt*, note 45 above; *St. Cloud v. U.S.*, 702 F. Supp. 1456, 1458 (D.S.D. 1988).

56. 31 U.S. 515 (1832).

57. 104 U.S. 621 (1881).

58. *Wheeler*, note 1 above, 435 U.S. at 324 n.21; *Antelope*, note 24 above, 430 U.S. at 643 n.2. *See also Ryder v. New Mexico*, 648 P.2d 774 (N.M. 1982).

59. 18 U.S.C. Sec. 1162, 28 U.S.C. Sec. 1360, as amended by 25 U.S.C. Secs. 1321–26.

60. *See Idaho v. Marek*, 736 P.2d 1314 (Idaho 1987); *Idaho v. Major*, 725 P.2d 115 (Idaho 1986).

61. 18 U.S.C. Sec. 1162(b) (mandatory states); 25 U.S.C. Sec. 1321(b) (option states).

62. This rule is discussed in chs. 7 and 9. The one exception to this rule is that Indians and tribes are required to comply with certain state conservation laws. This exception is explained in ch. 11.

63. *See, e.g., Santa Rosa Band of Indians v. Kings County*, 532 F.2d 655 (9th Cir. 1975), *cert. denied*, 429 U.S. 1038 (1977); *Walker v. Rushing*, 898 F.2d 672 (8th Cir. 1990).

64. *Wheeler*, note 1 above.

65. *See* 25 U.S.C. Secs. 1721–35 (Maine); *Iowa Tribe of Indians of Ne-*

braska v. Kansas, 787 F.2d 1434 (10th Cir. 1986) and *Negonsott v. Samuels*, 696 F. Supp. 561 (D. Kan. 1988) (Kansas); *Youngbear v. Brewer*, 415 F. Supp. 807 (N.D. Iowa 1976), *aff'd*, 549 F.2d 74 (8th Cir. 1977) (Iowa).

66. 18 U.S.C. Sec. 1152. Congress deliberately placed this exception in the act in order to allow tribes to continue to regulate purely internal matters in their own way. *See* Cohen, note 49 above, pp. 291–93.

67. 241 U.S. 602 (1916).

68. *U.S. v. Sosseur*, 181 F.2d 873 (7th Cir. 1950), *U.S. v. Blue*, 722 F.2d 383 (8th Cir. 1983), and *Marcyes*, note 48 above, respectively. *Cf. In re Mayfield*, 141 U.S. 107 (1891) (the General Crimes Act does not authorize the prosecution of an Indian for adultery with a non-Indian).

69. *U.S. v. Blue*, note 68 above, 722 F.2d at 386.

70. U.S. Dep't of Justice, Office of Legal Counsel, *Memorandum to Benjamin R. Civiletti: Jurisdiction over Victimless Crimes Committed by Non-Indians in Indian Country*, reprinted in Indian L. Rep. K-I (Aug. 1979).

71. 104 U.S. 621 (1881).

72. *State v. Warner*, 379 P.2d 66 (N.M. 1963); *State v. Burrola*, 669 P.2d 614 (Ariz. Ct. App. 1983); *State v. Thomas*, 760 P.2d 96 (Mont. 1988).

73. U.S. Const., art. IV, sec. 2. The process of extradition is explained in *Pacileo v. Walker*, 449 U.S. 86 (1980).

74. *Talton v. Mayes*, 163 U.S. 379 (1896).

75. *See, e.g., State of Arizona ex rel. Merrill v. Turtle*, 413 F.2d 683 (9th Cir. 1969); *Schauer v. Burleigh County*, 17 Indian L. Rep. 3132, 3136 (D.N.D. 1987). *See also Northern Cheyenne Tribe v. Crow Tribe*, 11 Indian L. Rep. 6006 (Crow Ct. App. 1983) (lack of extradition agreement between two tribes precludes one tribe from honoring extradition request from other tribe).

76. *Schauer*, note 75 above.

77. *Bennally v. Marcum*, 553 P.2d 1270 (N.M. 1976); *Turtle*, note 75 above; *State v. Spotted Horse*, 462 N.W.2d 463 (S.D. 1990).

78. *State ex rel. Old Elk v. District Court*, 552 P.2d 1394 (Mont. 1976), *cert. dismissed*, 429 U.S. 1030 (1976). *See also Fournier v. Roed*, 161 N.W.2d 458, 459–67 (N.D. 1968).

79. *U.S. v. Baker*, 914 F.2d 208 (10th Cir. 1990).

80. *See State v. Herber*, 598 P.2d 1033 (Ariz. Ct. App. 1979).

81. *State v. Winckler*, 260 N.W.2d 356, 358 (S.D. 1977). *See also Frisbie v. Collins*, 342 U.S. 519 (1952); *Davis v. Mueller*, 643 F.2d 521 (8th Cir.), *cert. denied*, 454 U.S. 892 (1981).

82. *Cf. U.S. v. Toscanino*, 500 F.2d 267 (2d Cir. 1974); *Benally*, note 77 above.

83. *See* discussion in *Schauer*, note 75 above.

84. *Ward v. Race Horse,* 163 U.S. 504 (1896); *DeCoteau v. District County Court,* 420 U.S. 425, 427 n.2 (1975).
85. *See Mattz v. Arnett,* 412 U.S. 481, 505 (1973).
86. *U.S. v. Sohappy,* 770 F.2d 816 (9th Cir. 1985), *cert. denied,* 477 U.S. 906 (1986); *U.S. v. Burnett,* 777 F.2d 593 (10th Cir. 1985), *cert. denied,* 476 U.S. 1106 (1986); *U.S. v. Azure,* 801 F.2d 336 (8th Cir. 1986).

IX

Civil Jurisdiction in Indian Country

What is "civil jurisdiction"?

Every government has two broad powers: criminal jurisdiction and civil jurisdiction. Criminal jurisdiction maintains law and order. Civil jurisdiction maintains everything else, particularly a society's culture and values. Most family matters, such as marriage, divorce, child custody, and adoptions, and most property matters, such as the sale of goods and services, taxation, zoning, and inheritance, are regulated through the government's civil jurisdiction. A government that loses its right to regulate civil matters eventually loses its identity.

A. TRIBAL JURISDICTION

Does an Indian tribe have the right to exercise civil jurisdiction?

Yes. An Indian tribe has the inherent right to exercise civil jurisdiction within the territory it controls.[1] This right is vital to its survival.

No one questions the fact that an Indian tribe may exercise the full range of its civil jurisdiction over tribal members within the reservation. Tribal members, for example, who wish to marry, divorce, adopt children, develop their real estate, or engage in a commercial enterprise on the reservation can do so only if they comply with tribal law.[2] With regard to non-Indians, the rule is somewhat similar but there are a few exceptions to the tribe's jurisdiction.

In 1978 the Supreme Court held that an Indian tribe cannot exercise criminal jurisdiction over a non-Indian unless Congress has expressly given the tribe that power.[3] In other words, it is presumed that tribes have no criminal jurisdiction over non-Indians. Regarding civil jurisdiction, the presumption is just the opposite, at least, that is, with respect to activities of non-Indians that affect the tribe's political integrity, economic security, or health and welfare. Indian tribes have the inherent right to regulate these activities. As the Supreme Court stated in 1980, Indian tribes may exercise "a broad range of civil jurisdiction over the activities of non-Indians on Indian reservation lands in which the tribes have a significant interest."[4] "Tribal authority over the activities of non-Indians on reservation lands is an important part of tribal sovereignty."[5]

Courts have upheld the tribe's civil jurisdiction over non-Indians in a wide range of situations. As early as 1904 the Supreme Court held that a tribe can tax the personal property owned by an non-Indian located on the reservation.[6] A tribe also can tax the income received by a non-Indian company from its reservation business.[7] A non-Indian who wishes to sell liquor[8] or conduct a commercial transaction[9] on the reservation must comply with tribal law. A tribe can regulate hunting and fishing by non-Indians on Indian land.[10] A tribe also can enforce its health and building requirements[11] and its clean air and water[12] regulations on non-Indians within the reservation. Non-Indians who buy goods on the reservation can be charged a tribal sales tax.[13] Moreover, if an Indian buys something off the reservation from a non-Indian, the non-Indian cannot attempt to repossess it on the reservation without complying with tribal law.[14] Even tribes located in the "mandatory" Public Law 83–280 states (discussed in chapter 7) retain these inherent powers; P.L. 280 gives certain powers to the states, but "nothing in the wording of Public Law 280 or its legislative history precludes concurrent jurisdiction " by the tribe.[15]

However, when a non-Indian's conduct does not affect tribal interests, the tribe lacks jurisdiction. If two non-Indians, for example, are in a traffic accident on the reservation, a lawsuit by one driver against the other has to be brought in state and not in tribal court. The same is true if two reservation non-Indians seek a divorce. In both of these examples, the tribe's interests are not sufficiently implicated to confer jurisdiction on the tribal court. On the other hand, even if only one spouse in a divorce action[16] or one party involved in a traffic accident[17] or a commercial contract[18] is a tribal member, the interest of the tribe in regulating the activities of tribal members and resolving disputes over Indian property is sufficient to confer jurisdiction on the tribal court.

Thus virtually every activity by a non-Indian on the reservation that involves Indians or Indian property is subject to the tribe's civil jurisdiction. The Supreme Court has held, however, that Indian tribes cannot regulate hunting and fishing by non-Indians on non-Indian-owned land,[19] and tribes cannot zone non-Indian-owned land located within an area of the reservation that is owned predominantly by non-Indians.[20] (These two exceptions are discussed in more detail in chapter 6.)[21] However, even in these situations a tribe may assert its authority if the non-Indian activity threatens or has a direct effect on the political integrity, economic security, or health and welfare of the tribe or if the activity is the result of a consensual agreement, such as a business contract, with the tribe.[22]

Can non-Indians be sued in tribal court?

Yes. Tribal courts, like state and federal courts, enforce the government's civil jurisdiction. Normally, whenever a tribe has the right to regulate a non-Indian activity, the non-Indian can be sued in tribal court concerning that activity.[23] For example, non-Indians who can be taxed by a tribe can be sued in tribal court for failure to pay the tax. Of course, a tribal court can hear the case only if the tribal legislature has authorized it to do so, but most tribal courts have been given broad jurisdiction. Thus on most reservations, Indians and non-Indians can sue one another in tribal court.[24]

Can a non-Indian who is being sued in tribal court challenge the court's jurisdiction?

Yes. As previously explained, a tribe cannot exercise its civil jurisdiction over non-Indians in certain situations. As a result, non-Indians who are being sued in tribal court can challenge the court's jurisdiction. In *National Farmers Union Insurance Co. v. Crow Tribe of Indians* (1985),[25] the Supreme Court held that the question of whether a tribe has exceeded its lawful jurisdiction is a "federal question" that federal courts are authorized to decide.[26] However, *National Farmers Union* also held that non-Indians who challenge the tribe's jurisdiction must first raise the issue in the tribal court proceeding and exhaust tribal appellate procedures before raising the issue in a federal court. Federal courts have the final word regarding the scope of a tribe's jurisdiction, but federal courts should not address this question until after the tribal courts have done so. "Congress is committed to a policy of supporting tribal self-government and self-determination," the Supreme Court noted, and imposing an exhaustion requirement is consistent with this federal policy.[27]

Non-Indians do not have to exhaust tribal remedies if the tribe does not have a court system, if tribal jurisdiction is clearly lacking, or if exhausting tribal remedies would be futile or unreasonably slow.[28] However, these are limited exceptions. Exhaustion is required even if the tribal court is alleged to be biased or incompetent and even if the lawsuit otherwise qualifies for federal court jurisdiction.[29] Moreover, when a federal court reviews a tribal court's decision regarding the scope of its jurisdiction, all findings of fact made by the tribal court must be accepted as conclusive by the federal court. In other words, a person cannot relitigate factual issues in federal court that she or he lost in tribal court.[30] These rules apply regardless of whether a non-Indian is suing an Indian or an Indian is suing a non-Indian.[31]

In short, with regard to the reservation activities of non-Indians, civil jurisdiction "presumptively lies in the tribal courts unless affirmatively limited by a specific treaty provision or federal statute."[32] Thus, non-Indians who engage in activities involving Indians or Indian property should presume that their actions are subject to the tribe's civil jurisdiction, including the authority of the tribal courts.

B. STATE JURISDICTION

Does the state have the right to exercise civil jurisdiction in Indian country?

Immediately after the United States became a nation, state governments tried to extend their laws into Indian territory in a deliberate effort to change Indian culture and control Indian life. They would have succeeded far more than they did had it not been for the U.S. Supreme Court. But the Supreme Court has not always been a friend to the Indians. At times, the Court has been notoriously anti-Indian, and a few of the Court's recent decisions have shifted in this direction. However, tribes would have little civil jurisdiction today—and the states would have much more than they do—if the Supreme Court had not protected the rights of tribes so vigorously.

As early as 1832, in *Worcester v. Georgia*,[33] the Supreme Court established the rule that state officials can exercise only that authority within Indian country which Congress has expressly given them. Indian tribes have the inherent right to regulate their internal affairs, the Court said, and state officials can intervene in these affairs only with congressional approval.

Even today, civil jurisdiction in Indian country remains almost entirely a tribal matter. This is because (1) Congress has authorized relatively few extensions of state laws into Indian country, and (2) the Supreme Court has defended the right of Indian tribes to remain free of state jurisdiction in the absence of this authorization.

The Supreme Court has since modified the *Worcester* rule, and state governments may now extend certain laws into Indian country without Congress's consent. As explained in chapter 7, section C, the Supreme Court has replaced the *Worcester* rule with two tests: the infringement test and the federal preemption test. If a state law passes these two tests, it can be enforced in Indian country even though Congress has not given its approval.

The infringement and federal preemption tests are very difficult tests to pass, however. In practice, they create a barrier nearly as formidable as the *Worcester* rule. The Supreme Court has decided many cases in which it has used these two tests and, in almost every case, the state was prevented from exercising its civil jurisdiction in Indian country. The Court has held, for instance, that the states have no authority to tax such things as the income Indians earn from reservation employment;[34] Indian personal property located on the reservation;[35] sales of goods to Indians within the reservation;[36] profits made by a non-Indian company from the sale of equipment to a tribal business;[37] the fuel used by a non-Indian company hauling tribal timber under a tribal contract;[38] the profits made by a non-Indian construction company when it builds a reservation Indian school under a tribal contract;[39] or the income that a tribe receives (royalty interests) when it leases land for mineral development.[40]

In addition to invalidating these state taxes, the Supreme Court also has held that, without express authority from Congress, state courts may not resolve reservation contract disputes between Indians and non-Indians;[41] state courts may not decide adoption cases involving reservation Indian children and their parents;[42] states cannot require non-Indians who hunt on tribal lands to comply with state hunting and licensing laws;[43] and states cannot impose regulations on tribal gambling operations within the reservation.[44] Based upon these Supreme Court decisions, other courts have held that a state has no authority to regulate billboards[45] or hazardous waste[46] located on the reservation. In addition, a state cannot enforce its child support laws on reservation Indians[47] or its rent control laws on reservation trust land.[48]

Naturally, in those situations in which the state is not permitted to enforce its laws against Indians in Indian country, state courts cannot resolve reservation controversies. For example, unless Congress has given its express consent, state courts may not evict an Indian tenant who rents property on the reservation;[49] may not hear negligence claims arising out of a reservation dispute between an Indian and a non-Indian;[50] may not garnishee the wages of an Indian employed on the reservation[51] or attach Indian property located there;[52] may not resolve reservation commercial disputes even if one of the parties is a non-Indian[53] nor disputes involving Indian trust land;[54] may not consider divorce actions involving reservation Indians, even if one spouse is a non-Indian;[55] and they have no authority to involuntarily commit a reservation Indian to a state mental hospital.[56]

Admittedly, in most of these situations, the state has an interest at stake. However, the state's interest is secondary to the tribe's interest in self-government. A state is only allowed to protect its interest, the Supreme Court has held, "up to the point where tribal self-government would be affected," unless Congress has expressly authorized the state to act.[57] If state courts were permitted, for example, to resolve disputes over Indian property, their decisions might be inconsistent with tribal court decisions, and this would interfere with the tribe's ability to enforce tribal law. By definition, this exercise of state jurisdiction would violate the infringement test.[58]

Every exercise of state jurisdiction on an Indian reservation interferes with tribal self-government. Consequently, most of these exercises fail the infringement test. However, the Supreme Court has allowed states to regulate certain activities of reservation *non*-Indians, even where this regulation creates some burdens for the tribe or its members. For example, the

Court has permitted states to require Indian merchants to collect a state sales tax from their non-Indian customers even though this may discourage non-Indians from purchasing goods on the reservation.[59] The state can also require Indian merchants to keep records of their sales to non-Indians for state taxation purposes.[60] Likewise, a non-Indian who wishes to sell liquor on the reservation can be required to obtain both a tribal and a state liquor license,[61] and any personal property a non-Indian owns on the reservation can be taxed by the state as well as the tribe.[62] In two recent and highly controversial cases, discussed in chapter 7, section C, the Court permitted a state to impose its zoning laws on non-Indians who own land in "opened" portions of the reservation[63] and to impose a severance tax on oil and gas produced by a non-Indian company on leased tribal land.[64]

Although these recent extensions of state jurisdiction apply to non-Indians, they clearly inhibit a tribe's ability to develop a comprehensive management and zoning plan and attract non-Indian businesses to the reservation. Thus the exercise of this jurisdiction affects interests upon which the vitality of some reservations may depend. In reaching these decisions, the Supreme Court narrowed the protections afforded by the infringement and preemption tests, a distressing development for Indians and tribes concerned about state encroachment.

What civil jurisdiction has Congress authorized the states to apply in Indian country?

Congress rarely has authorized a state to extend its civil jurisdiction into Indian country.[65] The few notable exceptions are discussed in chapter 7.

In the preceding chapter it was explained that a number of states have been authorized by Public Law 83–280[66] to enforce all of their criminal laws in Indian country. P.L. 280 also addresses the subject of civil jurisdiction. Section 1360(a) of that law allows the "mandatory" states to assume civil jurisdiction in Indian country "to the same extent that such State has jurisdiction over other civil causes of action, and those civil laws of such State that are of a general application to private persons or private property shall have the same force and effect within such Indian country as they have elsewhere in the State." Although this language is unclear, it can be argued that it authorizes considerable state powers in Indian country. This interpretation, however, was rejected by the Supreme Court in 1976 in *Bryan v. Itasca County*.[67] In a unanimous decision *Bryan* found nothing in Section 1360(a) "remotely resembling an intention [by Congress] to confer general state regulatory control over Indian reservations."[68] The Court applied a rule of construction it had developed a century earlier to interpret Indian treaties: ambiguities must be resolved in favor of the Indians; the treaty must be liberally interpreted in favor of the Indians; and a congressional intention to deprive Indians of their rights will not be implied.[69]

Using that rule of construction, the Court held that section 1360(a) did nothing more than authorize reservation Indians to resolve their disputes in state courts should they want to. Section 1360(a) "in its entirety may be read as simply a reaffirmation of the existing reservation Indian-Federal Government relationship in all respects save the conferral of state court jurisdiction to adjudicate private civil [disputes] involving Indians."[70] In fact, although an Indian in a P.L. 280 state can sue a non-Indian in state court concerning a reservation dispute, the non-Indian's only option is to file suit in tribal court. P.L. 280 allows Indians but not non-Indians to adjudicate their claims in state court.[71]

It is now settled that a P.L. 280 state has no more right to impose its civil laws in Indian country than a non-P.L. 280 state. It may not tax reservation Indians,[72] zone Indian land,[73] determine the ownership of Indian trust property,[74] or regulate reservation bingo operations[75] merely because it has acquired jurisdiction under Public Law 83–280. The only difference between a P.L. 280 state and a non-P.L. 280 state is that courts of the former are permitted to resolve private disputes brought to it by reservation Indians. A state court in a non-P.L. 280 state has no jurisdiction over such a dispute, even if all the parties ask the court to resolve it.[76]

For jurisdictional purposes, is a state-chartered corporation owned by Indians considered Indian or non-Indian?

Corporations that are licensed under state law usually are considered non-Indian for jurisdictional purposes even if they are Indian-owned. Thus, for example, a dispute between that corporation and one owned by non-Indians concerning a contract performed on the reservation must be filed in state court rather than tribal court.[77]

On the other hand, an Indian-owned corporation that is licensed under tribal or federal law, and not state law, is considered Indian for jurisdictional purposes. In that situation, the corporation could not be sued in state court regarding a reservation contract dispute.[78]

Can a situation arise in which neither a tribal court nor a state court has jurisdiction over a reservation dispute?

Yes. As with the federal and state governments, tribal governments are not required to authorize tribal courts to hear every type of controversy. This means that sometimes an aggrieved party lacks an avenue for judicial relief.

For example, in *Schantz v. White Lightning*[79] a non-Indian named Schantz and an Indian named White Lightning, both North Dakota residents, were involved in an automobile accident on the Standing Rock Reservation in North Dakota. Schantz filed a civil suit for damages against White Lightning in tribal court, but the tribe allows non-Indians to use its courts only when they reside on the reservation or do business there, and Schantz did neither. The tribal court therefore dismissed his suit. Schantz then filed the same suit in state court, which had to dismiss it because state courts lack jurisdiction over accidents occurring on the reservation involving a tribal member.[80] Schantz then filed his suit in federal court, which dismissed the case for essentially the same reason.[81] Schantz was thus unable to file his lawsuit anywhere.[82]

May a state "serve process" on an Indian on the reservation for an activity that occurred off the reservation?

Probably. As chapter 7 explains, Indians who leave the reservation are subject to state jurisdiction unless they are engaging in an activity that is protected by federal statute or treaty. A reservation Indian, for example, who causes an automobile accident while off the reservation can be sued for damages in state court.

No lawsuit can begin, however, until the plaintiff files with the court a summons and complaint, and the defendant is personally served with a copy of them. This latter procedure is called "service of process."

Most courts to consider the question have held that Indians may be served with process on the reservation for their off-reservation activities.[83] However, a tribal officer or private process server, rather than a state officer, may need to perform the service.[84] The Supreme Court has not addressed this question directly, but in a recent case it permitted a state lawsuit to proceed where the Indians who were being sued had been served with process on the reservation.[85] The Court apparently saw nothing wrong with this procedure.

May a state court enforce a judgment against an Indian by seizing reservation property owned by that person?

When a person is sued for money and loses, the court issues a "judgment" ordering that person (the "judgment debtor") to pay the amount awarded. If the money is not paid, the court can order court officials to seize and sell property belonging to the judgment debtor so as to satisfy the judgment.

As a general rule, a court may not seize property located outside its jurisdiction.[86] Accordingly, a state court should not be able to seize Indian property within a reservation. However, the few courts that have addressed this question have reached differing conclusions.[87] A noted authority has criticized state court seizures of reservation Indian property because "tribal authority over Indian property on a reservation [is] exclusive of state jurisdiction" under the infringement test.[88] Control over reservation Indian property is a substantial tribal concern. Therefore, the state should not be allowed to enter the reservation and seize Indian property without obtaining an appropriate decree from the tribal court, as explained below.

Must state and tribal governments give "full faith and credit" to each other's laws and court decrees?

The U.S. Constitution expressly requires each state to give "full faith and credit" to the laws and court decisions of another state.[89] If this were not done, there would be chaos. For example, one state could refuse to recognize a marriage that was performed in another state, and the same would be true for divorces and adoptions.

There is nothing in the Constitution that expressly requires a state and a tribe to give full faith and credit to each other's laws and court decisions. However, to avoid a similar chaos, courts have held that states and tribes must voluntarily extend full faith and credit (or "comity") to one another.[90] Some states and tribes have passed laws that require their courts do so.[91]

For example, if two Indians are married according to tribal custom, leave the reservation, and later seek a divorce in state court, the state court should recognize the validity of the marriage.[92] Similarly, if a reservation Indian borrows money from a bank off the reservation, and the bank obtains a judgment in state court to enforce repayment, a tribal court should issue an order allowing the state decree to be enforced on the reservation.

If states and tribes do not extend comity to one another, this can cause bitterness and tremendous personal loss. For instance, reservation Indians will have difficulty purchasing goods on credit or borrowing money outside the reservation if businesses and lenders are unable to enforce state court decrees in tribal court. It is in everyone's best interest for tribes and states to extend full faith and credit to each other's laws and court decrees. Federal courts, as well, should enforce valid tribal court orders whenever applicable.[93]

C. FEDERAL JURISDICTION

Which civil laws has the federal government been authorized to apply in Indian country?

Federal civil laws, like state civil laws, cannot be applied in Indian county without the approval of Congress.[94] Congress has given such authorization in a few subject areas. For example, as explained in chapter 5, federal officials have authority to regulate reservation trade with Indians, control the sale, use, and inheritance of Indian trust land, and control the sale and use of reservation resources, such as timber, oil, gas, and other minerals. The tribe is permitted to regulate in these areas as well, provided that its laws do not conflict with federal laws.[95]

Apart from these areas, Congress has allowed Indian tribes to remain relatively free from the federal government's civil powers. The same is true for the state's civil jurisdiction, as explained earlier. As a consequence, civil jurisdiction on the reservation is almost entirely tribal.

NOTES

1. *Williams v. Lee*, 358 U.S. 217 (1959); *Fisher v. District Court*, 424 U.S. 382 (1976); *Merrion v. Jicarilla Apache Tribe*, 455 U.S. 103 (1982); *Iowa Mutual Ins. Co. v. LaPlante*, 480 U.S. 9 (1987).
2. *See, e.g.*, *Fisher*, note 1 above; *Santa Clara Pueblo v. Martinez*, 436 U.S. 49 (1978).
3. *Oliphant v. Suquamish Indian Tribe*, 435 U.S. 191 (1978).
4. *Washington v. Confederated Tribes of the Colville Indian Reservation*, 447 U.S. 134, 152–53 (1980).
5. *Iowa Mutual*, note 1 above, 480 U.S. at 17.
6. *Morris v. Hitchcock*, 194 U.S. 384 (1904).
7. *Merrion v. Jicarilla Apache Tribe*, 455 U.S. 103 (1982). *See also Kerr-McGee Corp. v. Navajo Tribe*, 471 U.S. 195 (1985).
8. *U.S. v. Mazurie*, 419 U.S. 544 (1975).
9. *Ashcroft v. U.S.*, 679 F.2d 196 (9th Cir.), *cert. denied*, 459 U.S. 1201 (1983).
10. *New Mexico v. Mescalero Apache Tribe*, 462 U.S. 324, 333 (1983).
11. *Cardin v. De La Cruz*, 671 F.2d 363 (9th Cir.), *cert. denied*, 459 U.S. 967 (1982).
12. *Nance v. EPA*, 645 F.2d 701 (9th Cir. 1981) (air); *Confederated Salish and Kootenai Tribes v. Namen*, 665 F.2d 951 (9th Cir.), *cert. denied*, 459 U.S. 977 (1982) (water).
13. *Washington v. Confederated Tribes*, note 4 above.
14. *Babbitt Ford, Inc. v. Navajo Tribe* , 710 F.2d 587 (9th Cir. 1983), *cert. denied*, 466 U.S. 926 (1984); *Amigo Chevrolet, Inc. v. Lee*, 15 Indian L. Rep. 6047 (Nev. Sup. Ct. 1988).
15. *Walker v. Rushing*, 898 F.2d 672, 675 (8th Cir. 1990). *See also Native Village of Venetie IRA Council v. Alaska* , 918 F.2d 797 (9th Cir. 1990).
16. *Sanders v. Robinson*, 864 F.2d 630 (9th Cir. 1988), *cert. denied*, 109 S.Ct. 3165 (1989); *Hunt v. Hunt*, 16 Indian L. Rep. 6039 (Ft. McDermitt Tr. Ct. 1988).
17. *Milbank Mut. Ins. Co. v. Eagleman*, 705 P.2d 1117 (Mont. 1985); *Sage v. Lodge Grass School Dist.*, 13 Indian L. Rep. 6035 (Crow Ct. App. 1986).
18. *Williams v. Lee*, note 1 above; *Wellman v. Chevron U.S.A., Inc.*, 815 F.2d 577 (9th Cir. 1987).
19. *Montana v. U.S.*, 450 U.S. 544 (1981).
20. *Brendale v. Confederated Yakima Tribes*, 492 U.S. 408 (1989).
21. *See* ch. 6, notes 66–67 and 93–94 and accompanying text.

22. *Montana v. U.S.*, 450 U.S. 544, 565 (1981); *Fisher*, note 1 above, 424 U.S. at 386; *Brendale*, note 20 above, 492 U.S. at 431.
23. See *Iowa Mutual*, note 1 above, 480 U.S. at 18.
24. *See, e.g., Rosebud Housing Auth. v. La Creek Elec. Coop.*, 13 Indian L. Rep. 6030 (Rbd. Sx. Tr. Ct. 1986); *Ft. Peck Housing Auth. v. Home Savings & Loan Ass'n*, 16 Indian L. Rep. 6083 (Ft. Peck Tr. Ct. 1989); *McDonald v. Harlan Racine & Guar. Nat. Ins. Co.*, 15 Indian L. Rep. 6003 (C.S.&K. Tr. Ct. 1988).
25. 471 U.S. 845 (1985).
26. *National Farmers Union Ins. Co. v. Crow Tribe of Indians*, 471 U.S. 845 (1985). *See also Native Village of Tyonek v. Puckett*, 890 F.2d 1054 (9th Cir. 1989), *cert. denied*, 110 S.Ct. 1812 (1990).
27. *Id.* at 856.
28. *National Farmers Union*, note 26 above. *Cf. Brown v. U.S.*, 486 F.2d 658 (8th Cir. 1973); *Necklace v. Tribal Court*, 554 F 2d 845 (8th Cir. 1977).
29. *Iowa Mutual Ins. Co. v. LaPlante*, 480 U.S. 9 (1987).
30. *Id.* at 18.
31. *See, e.g., National Farmers Union*, note 26 above and *Stock West, Inc. v. Confederated Tribes of the Colville Reservation*, 873 F.2d 122 (9th Cir. 1989) (suit by Indian against non-Indian initiated in tribal court); *Wellman*, note 18 above (suit by Indian against non-Indian initiated in federal court); *Brown Constr. Co. v. Washoe Housing Auth.*, 835 F.2d 1327 (10th Cir. 1988) and *Weeks Constr. Inc. v. Oglala Sioux Housing Auth.*, 797 F.2d 668 (8th Cir. 1986) (suit by non-Indian against Indian initiated in federal court).
32. *Iowa Mutual*, note 29 above, 480 U.S. at 18.
33. 31 U.S. 515 (1832).
34. *McClanahan v. Arizona Tax Commission*, 411 U.S. 164 (1973).
35. *Bryan v. Itasca County*, 426 U.S. 373 (1976).
36. *Moe v. Confederated Salish and Kootenai Tribes*, 425 U.S. 463 (1976).
37. *Central Machinery Co. v. Arizona Tax Comm'n*, 448 U.S. 160 (1980).
38. *White Mountain Apache Tribe v. Bracker*, 448 U.S. 136 (1980).
39. *Ramah Navajo School Board, Inc. v. Bureau of Revenue*, 458 U.S. 832 (1982).
40. *Montana v. Blackfeet Tribe*, 471 U.S. 759 (1985).
41. *Williams v. Lee*, note 1 above. However, some states have been authorized by Congress to resolve civil actions in state courts when commenced by reservation Indians. *See Three Affiliated Tribes v. Wold Engineering*, 476 U.S. 877 (1986).
42. *Fisher*, note 1 above. The subject of child custody is discussed at length in ch. 17.
43. *New Mexico v. Mescalero Apache Tribe*, 462 U.S. 324 (1983).

44. *California v. Cabazon Band of Mission Indians*, 480 U.S. 202 (1987).
45. *California v. Naegle Outdoor Adv. Co.*, 698 P.2d 150 (Cal. 1985), *cert. denied*, 475 U.S. 1045 (1986).
46. *Washington Dep't of Ecology v. EPA*, 752 F.2d 1465 (9th Cir. 1985).
47. *Flammond v. Flammond*, 621 P.2d 471 (Mont. 1980); *Jackson County v. Swayney*, 352 S.E.2d 413 (N.C. Ct. App. 1987), *cert. denied*, 484 U.S. 826 (1987). *But see State ex rel. Dep't of Human Services v. Jojola*, 660 P.2d 590 (N.M. 1983), *cert. denied*, 464 U.S. 803 (1983).
48. *Segundo v. City of Rancho Mirage*, 813 F.2d 1387 (9th Cir. 1987).
49. *Chino v. Chino*, 561 P.2d 476 (N.M. 1977).
50. *Milbank*, note 17 above; *Wyoming ex rel. Peterson v. District Court*, 617 P.2d 1056 (Wyo. 1980).
51. *Joe v. Marcum*, 621 F.2d 358 (10th Cir. 1980). *Contra, Little Horn State Bank v. Stops*, 555 P.2d 211 (Mont. 1976), *cert. denied*, 431 U.S. 924 (1977).
52. *Annis v. Dewey County Bank*, 335 F. Supp. 133 (D.S.D. 1971).
53. *Geiger v. Pierce*, 758 P.2d 279 (Mont. 1988).
54. *O'Connell v. Hamm*, 267 N.W.2d 839 (S.D. 1978); *Matter of Guardianship of Sasse*, 363 N.W.2d 209 (S.D. 1985); *Conroy v. Conroy*, 575 F.2d 175 (8th Cir. 1978). *But see Lonewolf v. Lonewolf*, 657 P.2d 627 (N.M. 1982); *Smith Plumbing Co., Inc. v. Aetna Cas. & Surety Co.*, 720 P.2d 499 (Ariz. 1984), *cert. denied*, 479 U.S. 987 (1986).
55. *In re Marriage of Limpy*, 636 P.2d 266 (Mont. 1981).
56. *White v. Califano*, 437 F. Supp. 543 (D.S.D. 1977), *aff'd*, 581 F.2d 697 (8th Cir. 1978).
57. *McClanahan*, note 34 above, 411 U.S. at 179.
58. *See Williams v. Lee*, note 1 above.
59. *Moe*, note 36 above; *Oklahoma Tax Comm'n v. Citizen Band Potawatomi Indian Tribe*, 111 S.Ct. 905 (1991). *See also Fort Mojave Tribe v. County of San Bernardino*, 543 F.2d 1253 (9th Cir. 1976), *cert. denied*, 430 U.S. 983 (1977).
60. *Confederated Tribes*, note 4 above.
61. *Mazurie*, note 8 above; *Berry v. Arapaho and Shoshone Tribes*, 470 F. Supp. 934 (D. Wyo. 1976).
62. *Barta v. Oglala Sioux Tribe*, 259 F.2d 553 (8th Cir. 1958).
63. *Brendale*, note 20 above. *See also Baker Elec. Coop., Inc. v. P.S.C.*, 451 N.W.2d 95 (N.D. 1990) (state can regulate electric utility company on the reservation).
64. *Cotton Petroleum Corp. v. New Mexico*, 490 U.S. 163 (1989).
65. Those tribes that have been terminated, however, have been placed completely under the state's civil jurisdiction. *See* ch. 5, sec. B.
66. 18 U.S.C. Sec. 1162; 28 U.S.C. Sec. 1360.
67. 426 U.S. 373 (1976).

68. *Id.* at 386.
69. *Id.* at 392. For a further explanation of these rules of construction, see ch. 4, notes 23–27 and accompanying text.
70. *Id.* at 390.
71. *Wold Engineering*, note 41 above.
72. *Bryan*, note 35 above.
73. *Santa Rosa Band of Indians v. Kings County*, 532 F.2d 655 (9th Cir. 1975), *cert. denied*, 429 U.S. 1038 (1977).
74. *Ollestead v. Native Village of Tyonek*, 560 P.2d 31 (Alaska), *cert. denied*, 434 U.S. 938 (1977); *In re Humboldt Fir, Inc.*, 426 F. Supp. 292 (N.D. Cal. 1977). *Contra: Fisher v. Fisher*, 656 P.2d 129 (Idaho 1982) (allowing state court to adjudicate divorce action and allocate property, including interests in trust property).
75. *Cabazon*, note 44 above.
76. See *Wold Engineering*, note 41 above; *Camenout v. Burdman*, 525 P.2d 217 (Wash. 1974). *Cf. Kennerly v. District Court*, 400 U.S. 423 (1971).
77. *Airvator, Inc. v. Turtle Mountain Mfg. Co.*, 329 N.W.2d 596 (N.D. 1983).
78. *Seneca-Cayuga Tribe v. Oklahoma*, 874 F.2d 709 (10th Cir. 1989). *Cf. Padilla v. Pueblo of Acoma*, 754 P.2d 845 (N.M. 1988), *cert. denied*, 490 U.S. 1029 (1989) (allowing suit for off-reservation activity).
79. 231 N.W.2d 812 (N.D. 1975). *Contra: Larrivee v. Morigeau*, 602 P.2d 563 (Mont. 1979), *cert. denied*, 445 U.S. 964 (1980) (allowing state court to accept jurisdiction).
80. Other courts holding similarly include *Enriquez v. Superior Court*, 565 P.2d 522 (Ariz. App. 1977); *Smith v. Temple*, 152 N.W.2d 547 (S.D. 1967).
81. *Schantz v. White Lightning*, 502 F.2d 67 (8th Cir. 1974).
82. If Schantz and White Lightning had been residents of different states, the federal court could have accepted the case under its diversity jurisdiction. See *Poitra v. Demarrias*, 502 F.2d 23 (8th Cir. 1974), *cert. denied*, 421 U.S. 934 (1975); *Palmer v. Yankton Sioux Tribe*, 15 Indian L. Rep. 3001 (D.S.D. 1987).
83. See, *e.g.*, *State Securities, Inc. v. Anderson*, 506 P.2d 786 (N.M. 1973); *Little Horn State Bank*, note 51 above. See also F. Cohen, *Handbook of Federal Indian Law* p. 361 (1982).
84. *Dixon v. Picopa Constr. Co.*, 772 P.2d 1104 (Ariz. 1989); *Wells v. Wells*, 451 N.W.2d 402 (S.D. 1990).
85. *Puyallup Tribe, Inc. v. Dep't of Game*, 433 U.S. 165 (1977).
86. 30 Am. Jur. 2d, *Executions*, Sec. 213 (1969); 6 Am. Jur. 2d, *Attachment and Garnishment*, Sec. 25 (1969).

87. *See* cases cited in note 51 above and accompanying text.

88. F. Cohen, note 83 above, p. 359.

89. U.S. Const., art. IV, sec. 1.

90. *Tom v. Sutton*, 533 F.2d 1101 (9th Cir. 1976); *Wippert v. Blackfeet Tribe*, 654 P.2d 512 (Mont. 1982); *Mexican v. Circle Bear*, 370 N.W.2d 737 (S.D. 1985); *Fredericks v. Eide-Kirschmann Ford*, 462 N.W.2d 164 (N.D. 1990).

91. *See, e.g., Airvator, Inc.*, note 77 above.

92. *See Mexican v. Circle Bear*, note 90 above; *Sheppard v. Sheppard*, 655 P.2d 895 (Idaho 1985).

93. *Smith v. Confederated Tribes of the Warm Springs Reservation*, 783 F.2d 1409, 1411 (9th Cir. 1986); *Santa Clara Pueblo v. Martinez*, 436 U.S. 49, 66 n.21 (1978); *Sanders v. Robinson*, note 16 above.

94. *Northwest South Dakota Prod. Credit Ass'n v. Smith*, 784 F.2d 323, 326–27 (8th Cir. 1986); *U.S. v. Winnebago Tribe of Nebraska*, 542 F.2d 1002 (8th Cir. 1976); *Administrative Appeal of the Morongo Band of Mission Indians*, 7 Indian L. Rep. 5002 [IBIA 79–18-A (1980)].

95. *See, e.g., U.S. v. Wheeler*, 435 U.S. 313 (1978); 55 Interior Dec. 14 (1934) (Powers of Indian Tribes).

X
Taxation

Taxes are the lifeblood of government. Governments need money to hire employees, provide services, and conduct their affairs. The principal means of raising this money is taxation. Those who live or work on an Indian reservation may find themselves being taxed by three governments—tribal, state, and federal. Below is an explanation of which taxes these persons must pay.

Throughout this chapter, terms are used that need to be defined, including "trust" and "fee" land, "allotted" and "unallotted" land, and "competent" and "noncompetent" Indian. Trust land is land owned by the federal government that has been set aside for the exclusive use of an Indian or tribe. The Indian or tribe assigned this land is called the beneficial owner. Fee land is owned by a party outright. It is also called deeded or patented land because someone holds a deed or patent to it. Indians and tribes can obtain fee land by purchasing, inheriting, or receiving it as a gift, just as everyone else can.

Allotted land is land that has been assigned by the federal government to an Indian. (This assignment is called an allotment.) Unallotted land is land that has been assigned by the government to a tribe. Indian trust land, in other words, is either allotted or unallotted, depending on whether the beneficial owner is an Indian or a tribe.

A noncompetent (or "incompetent") Indian is an Indian who holds an allotment of trust land. Being trust land, it is owned by the federal government and the Indian is not competent to sell it without the government's permission. If the government should later give the Indian a patent to this land, the owner becomes a competent Indian, competent to sell the land at any time. The term "noncompetent" has nothing to do with an Indian's mental competency.

Most of these terms originated with the General Allotment Act of 1887.[1] Under that act, tribal trust land was divided into parcels by the federal government and allotted to tribal members. (Why Congress did this, and the disaster it caused, is discussed elsewhere in this book.)[2] In 1934 Congress ended the practice of forcing Indians to take allotments of land, but thousands of allotments had already been issued,[3] and special tax rules apply to this land.

A. FEDERAL TAXATION

Can the federal government tax Indians?

Yes. In *Squire v. Capoeman* (1956),[4] the Supreme Court held that Indians must pay federal income taxes unless a treaty or statute gives them an exemption: "We agree with the Government that Indians are citizens and that in ordinary affairs of life, not governed by treaty or remedial legislation, they are subject to the payment of income taxes as are other citizens."[5] It is now well settled that Indians must pay the same federal taxes other citizens pay unless a federal treaty or statute provides an express exemption. This principle is contrary to the one that exists in most other areas of federal Indian law. Generally, a federal law does not apply to reservation Indians unless Congress expressly says it does.[6] A federal tax law, in contrast, applies to reservation Indians unless Congress expressly says it does not. Courts have held that Indians must pay federal taxes on income they earn from reservation employment,[7] even if they are tribal officials and their salary is paid from tribal funds.[8] Income earned from a federally protected fishing operation[9] or wildlife industry[10] is subject to federal income taxation. The federal government can also tax income Indians are distributed from the rental of tribal lands[11] and from tribal investments.[12] In each of these cases, the Indian taxpayer had no express immunity from the federal tax and was therefore required to pay it.

What about the provision in the Constitution that refers to "Indians not taxed"? Does this provide a general exemption from federal taxation?

No. The clause "Indians not taxed" appears in the section of the Constitution that describes how representatives are elected to Congress.[13] The Constitution requires each state, when it counts its citizens for purposes of congressional apportionment, to exclude "Indians not taxed." This is because, at the time the Constitution was written, Indians were not U.S. citizens, and they were not taxed. This clause does not confer a tax immunity;

rather it simply records the fact that Indians were not taxed at that time.[14] Today, Indians are citizens, the federal government taxes them, and Indians are counted for purposes of congressional apportionment.[15] The clause "Indians not taxed" no longer has any practical relevance. In any event, it does not provide an exemption from federal taxation because it was not meant to.

Has Congress given Indians any exemptions from federal taxation?

Yes, two major exemptions. First, Congress has exempted from taxation any federal money received by an Indian as compensation for the taking of property.[16] The Just Compensation Clause of the Fifth Amendment requires the federal government to pay compensation whenever it takes private property, such as Indian treaty land, for government use.[17] A federal law exempts these "judgment funds" or "judgment proceeds" from federal taxation.

Second, Congress has exempted from federal taxation all income earned directly from an Indian's trust allotment. As mentioned earlier, the Supreme Court held in *Squire v. Capoeman* that Indians must pay federal taxes unless they have an express exemption. However, there were two issues in *Squire*, a broad issue and a narrow one. The broad issue was whether Indians had to pay federal taxes; the Court held that they do, unless they have an express immunity. The narrow issue was whether the General Allotment Act of 1887[18] conferred an immunity from the particular tax at issue in that case.

In *Squire*, the federal government was attempting to tax income earned by an Indian from the sale of timber harvested from his trust allotment. The taxpayer claimed that the General Allotment Act, under which this land had been allotted to him, conferred an immunity from this tax. The Court concluded that the main purpose of that act was to enable Indians to become economically self-sufficient. This purpose would be frustrated, the Court said, if the federal government could tax income earned from selling the allotment's timber. The government in essence would be taking away with one hand what it had given with the other. Besides, the act provided that if the Indian received a deed to the allotment, this would remove "all restrictions as to . . . taxation."[19] This clause implied that Congress did not want the land, or income earned from the land, to be taxed while it remained in trust status. Reading the General Allotment Act liberally, as courts must do whenever they interpret a federal Indian law,[20] the Supreme Court held in favor of the Indian.

Under the *Squire* rule, Indians who farm or ranch on their allotments[21] or who sell timber, oil, or minerals from them[22] do not have to pay federal income taxes on the money they earn. Similarly, Indians are exempt from paying inheritance (estate) taxes when they inherit an allotment.[23] They also are exempt from taxation on income earned from an allotment they received as a gift or by exchanging other land for it.[24]

Does *Squire v. Capoeman* exempt from federal taxation all income earned from the use of trust land?

Squire v. Capoeman can be interpreted broadly or narrowly. Broadly, it exempts Indians from paying taxes on any income earned from the use of trust land. However, most federal courts and the Internal Revenue Service have given *Squire* a very narrow interpretation. First, they have held that *Squire* only exempts income earned from the taxpayer's *own* trust allotment. Second, they have held that *Squire* only exempts income earned *directly* from the allotment and not indirectly through any improvements made to it or on it. Thus, courts have held that income earned by an Indian from using someone else's trust land is subject to federal taxation.[25] The purpose of the General Allotment Act, these courts have held, was to provide Indians with an allotment from which they could earn a living, and not to make available other allotments for this purpose. Therefore, income earned from the taxpayer's own allotment is exempt from taxation, but income earned from another allotment or from tribal trust land is not.

Second, the *Squire* exemption also does not apply to income earned from investing allotment proceeds, that is, to "reinvestment" income.[26] Thus, income earned from an Indian's allotment is not taxable under *Squire,* but if the taxpayer takes that income and reinvests it, those proceeds are taxable. To illustrate, if the taxpayer in *Squire* took the income he earned from his timber business and deposited it in a bank account, the interest he earned on that account would be taxable.

Similarly, courts have held that income earned by changing

or improving a trust allotment is taxable. As previously explained, under *Squire* income earned by an Indian from farming, logging, or mining his or her trust allotment is not taxable.
However, if the same Indian builds a store[27] or a motel[28] on
that allotment, the income earned from the business is taxable.
The Supreme Court has not yet addressed this issue. However,
it certainly can be argued that the distinction some courts have
made between income earned from existing resources (such as
timber) and income earned from improvements to the land
(such as a motel), strips *Squire* of much of its meaning and
defeats the purpose of the General Allotment Act.

To summarize, Indians normally must pay the same federal
taxes that everyone else must pay, including income taxes.
However, Indians are not taxed on their judgment proceeds,
they are not taxed on income earned directly from their own
trust allotments or on the value of trust land they inherit.

To what extent are Indian tribes taxed by the federal government?

Congress has passed laws that provide to the states and
to their political subdivisions an immunity from most federal
taxes.[29] These statutes do not mention Indian tribes expressly.
However, it was assumed until recently that tribes enjoy the
same immunities that states do. Indeed, the Internal Revenue
Service had ruled that tribes were exempt from federal income
taxes,[30] even though no statute expressly conferred that exemption.

However, in 1982 a federal appellate court ruled that Indian
tribes were not exempt from federal taxation because no such
immunity had been expressly conferred by Congress.[31] In response to this decision, Congress enacted the Indian Tribal
Governmental Tax Status Act.[32] This act expressly exempts
tribes from having to pay certain federal taxes. However, several taxes that states are exempt from paying are not listed in
the act, including unemployment and insurance contribution
taxes. At least one court has ruled that Indian tribes must pay
all federal taxes not listed in the act, unless some other federal
statute or treaty provides a tribe with an express immunity.[33]

Indian tribes should enjoy the same immunity from federal
taxation that Congress has given the states. It appears that some

additional legislation is necessary from Congress in order to ensure that tribes have this immunity.

Can Congress abolish an Indian tax exemption?

Yes. Congress can abolish a tax immunity previously given to Indians, even one conferred by a treaty.[34] However, the extinguishment of a tax immunity is a "taking" of property under the Just Compensation Clause for which compensation must be paid.[35] Given its importance, the Supreme Court has held that a tax immunity will remain in effect until Congress expresses a clear intention to abolish it.[36]

B. STATE TAXATION

Chapter 7 explains that a state is, in general, not permitted to enforce its laws on an Indian reservation without congressional consent. The Constitution gives Congress exclusive authority to regulate tribal affairs. A state law that interferes with this congressional power is said to be "preempted" by federal law. This preemption doctrine draws support from the fact that an Indian tribe has the inherent right to be self-governing and to regulate its own internal matters unless limited by Congress.

This doctrine applies especially to state tax laws. The Supreme Court has decided at least ten cases involving state taxation without congressional authorization of reservation Indians, tribes, or Indian activities.[37] In every case but one, the Court invalidated the state tax. (The one exception, discussed later, involved a state tax on tribal sales to *non*-Indians.) As the Supreme Court noted in 1985, "Indian tribes and individuals generally are exempt from state taxation within their own territory."[38]

1. State Taxation of Reservation Indians

Do reservation Indians have to pay state income taxes?

No. The Supreme Court ruled nine to zero that Indians do not have to pay state income taxes on income they earn within the reservation.[39]

Do reservation Indians have to pay state personal property taxes?

No. The Supreme Court also ruled unanimously that personal property on the reservation owned by a tribal member is exempt from state taxation.[40] This is true even if the state has accepted jurisdiction under Public Law 83–280,[41] as explained more fully in chapter 7.

Consequently, states may not require Indians to pay personal property taxes on such things as automobiles, mobile homes, furnishings, or equipment. Indians who register their automobiles or mobile homes with the state can only be charged a registration fee and need not pay any portion of the license fee that is a personal property tax.[42] Similarly, a state may not tax the personal property of an Indian-owned business within the reservation.[43] If an Indian marries a non-Indian the personal property they own on the reservation is not taxable by the state even though part of it may be said to belong to the non-Indian spouse.[44]

Do reservation Indians have to pay state sales taxes on purchases made within the reservation?

No. Indians who purchase goods or services on their reservation cannot be charged a state sales tax. This is true whether the seller is an Indian,[45] a non-Indian,[46] or a tribe,[47] and even if the item is to be used off the reservation.[48]

Can a state impose a real estate tax on Indian or tribal trust land?

No. A state may not tax trust land, whether the beneficial owner is an Indian or a tribe,[49] even if the land is located off the reservation.[50] Public Law 83–280 did nothing to change this rule; to the contrary, that law expressly prohibits states from taxing Indian trust land.[51]

Permanent attachments to land, such as a house, a fence, or a well, are considered to be part of the land. Therefore, these improvements cannot be taxed when they are attached to trust land.[52]

Can a state impose an inheritance tax on the estate of a reservation Indian?

Not without congressional consent, and the only state that

appears to have been given this consent is Oklahoma. Courts have prohibited states from taxing the estates of Indians, regardless of whether the property being inherited is in trust status[53] or in fee, although there remains some dispute concerning the latter.[54]

What other state taxes have been invalidated as applied to reservation Indians? What state taxes do Indians have to pay?

Only rarely has Congress authorized a state to tax reservation Indians. Consequently, there are few state taxes that reservation Indians must pay. In addition to the taxes already mentioned, a state may not impose a vendor's license fee[55] nor a gross receipts tax[56] on a reservation Indian business, an excise tax on cigarettes sold to reservation Indians,[57] nor a tax on motor fuel purchased on the reservation by an Indian,[58] unless Congress has given its consent.

Congress's consent to tax reservation Indians must be expressed in clear terms. Such consent cannot be inferred, and ambiguities in federal statutes must be resolved in favor of the Indians.[59] A federal law will not be interpreted as having eliminated an Indian tax immunity unless "Congress has made its intention to do so unmistakably clear."[60]

Accordingly, even when Congress consents to a state tax in general, the state may not impose that tax on reservation Indians unless Congress has expressly conferred that particular authority. For example, a law passed by Congress in 1940 authorizes states to impose income, sales, and use taxes in any "Federal area."[61] In 1965 the Supreme Court held that nothing in this law consents to such taxation of reservation Indians.[62] A 1936 federal law authorizes states to tax the sale of gasoline sold "on United States military or other reservations."[63] This law, too, was held inapplicable to Indian reservations, at least with respect to activities involving substantial tribal or federal interests.[64] Similarly, laws passed in 1924 and 1938 authorize states to tax the production of oil and gas on federal lands.[65] However, states cannot tax such production by Indian tribes because of the absence of clear congressional consent.[66]

For the most part, state taxation of reservation Indians is prohibited because Congress has passed very few laws that consent to such taxation. One such law authorizes states to tax reservation sales of liquor to Indians.[67] Another law, the General Allotment Act of 1887,[68] authorizes the state to tax all privately owned land within Indian reservations where deeds to that land had been issued under the act, including, the Supreme Court recently held,[69] private land owned by Indians. Millions of dollars in property taxes are collected by states every year as a result of this law.

Indians who leave the reservation even briefly are subject to the same state taxes as non-Indians, unless a federal treaty or statute confers an immunity. Few such immunities exist. Thus, as a general rule, Indians must pay state sales taxes whenever they purchase goods off the reservation, state income taxes on income earned off the reservation, and state real estate taxes on deeded land outside the reservation.[70] In addition, if an Indian or tribe operates a business outside the reservation, its income can be taxed by the state even if the business is located on federal land.[71]

Can a state refuse to provide services to reservation Indians on the grounds that they are exempt from state taxation?

No. Indians may not be denied the full rights of state citizenship even though they are exempt from most state taxes.[72] A state, for example, cannot condition the right to vote on the payment of property taxes, thereby discriminating against Indians, who pay no taxes on their trust allotments.[73]

Indians have long enjoyed an immunity from most state taxes because of federal statutes and treaties protecting Indians and their property. This protection was given to the Indians in exchange for vast amounts of Indian land. Indians, in other words, have already paid for their tax immunities.

Non-Indians frequently claim that a state suffers financially from having an Indian reservation within its borders. This argument is misguided for two reasons. First of all, a state incurs comparatively little cost in providing Indians with social welfare programs because the federal government reimburses the state for most of its expenses. Second, Indians eventually spend the money they earn from reservation employment or receive from federal and state grants and programs outside the reservation. This not only stimulates the state and local economy but permits these governments to obtain considerable revenue through sales taxes. In fact, income is earned not only when the state taxes these sales, but also when the state taxes the revenues received by these businesses. Thus few states suffer financially, and many prosper because an Indian reservation is located within their borders.[74]

Are nonmember Indians entitled to these same tax immunities?

Indians who are on a reservation other than their own (nonmember Indians) probably are not entitled to the same tax immunities enjoyed by members of that tribe. For example, although tribal members are exempt from paying state sales taxes on goods purchased on the reservation, the Supreme Court held in 1980 that nonmember Indians do not share that immunity.[75] These nonmember Indians, the Court held, "stand on the same footing as non-Indians" with respect to state sales taxes.[76] Similarly, the Supreme Court ruled in 1990 that nonmember Indians are to be treated the same as non-Indians, rather than as Indians, in determining which government may exercise its criminal jurisdiction.[77]

2. State Taxation of Indian Tribes

It is well settled that a state may not tax the income that a tribe earns within its reservation unless Congress has given its express consent.[78] For example, states may not tax the income a tribe receives when it leases tribal land to non-Indians for oil and gas production[79] or for mineral development.[80] In addition, tribal trust property is not taxable by the state even if it is located outside the reservation.[81]

The only exception to this rule concerns certain "pass on and collect" taxes, that is, taxes that are paid exclusively by a non-Indian purchaser, and the tribe needs only to collect and remit them to the state. For example, the Supreme Court has held that a state can require a tribe to collect the state's sales tax when the tribe sells cigarettes to a non-Indian.[82] However, these cigarettes were not manufactured by the tribe nor produced with tribal resources. "Pass on and collect" laws that require tribes to collect taxes, for example, on sales of tribal timber to non-Indians[83] or on the value of leases of tribal land for mineral production[84] have been invalidated.

Tribal business activities outside of Indian country, on the other hand, can be taxed by the state. In *Mescalero Apache Tribe v. Jones*,[85] the Supreme Court upheld the right of a state to tax the income earned by a tribal ski resort located off the reservation.

In short, Indian tribes cannot be taxed by state governments except with respect to off-reservation activities. Within their own borders, Indian tribes remain free from state taxation in the absence of express authorization from Congress.

Can Indians and tribes immediately file suit in federal court to challenge the validity of a state tax?

Tribes can, but individual Indians cannot. A federal law known as the Tax Injunction Act[86] prohibits all persons from challenging state taxes in a federal court "where a plain, speedy and efficient remedy may be had in the courts of such state." Indian tribes, however, are exempt from this exhaustion requirement. A federal statute allows Indian tribes to seek relief in federal court from violations of their federal rights.[87] This law allows tribes to file suit in federal court to challenge the constitutionality of a state tax law without first exhausting state remedies.[88]

3. State Taxation of Reservation Non-Indians

Do non-Indians on the reservation have to pay state taxes?

Most taxes, yes. As explained in chapter 7, section C, a state may not enforce a law within Indian country if such enforcement would (1) violate a federal law or treaty (the preemption test) or (2) infringe on the right of the tribe to make its own laws or be ruled by them (the infringement test).

Most state taxes, when imposed on reservation non-Indians, will pass these tests. Of course, the enforcement of any state law on the reservation infringes to some extent on tribal self-government. The Supreme Court has held, however, that minimal infringements are permitted.[89] Taxes that apply exclusively to non-Indians—that is, when the burden of the tax falls entirely on non-Indian taxpayers—are allowed. State income taxes, personal property taxes, real estate taxes, gasoline taxes, cigarette taxes, and the like, when imposed on reservation non-Indians and their property, are normally upheld by the courts.[90]

However, the fact that the taxpayer is non-Indian does not necessarily mean that the tax is valid. The federal government has so heavily regulated certain subject areas that any additional state tax, even of non-Indians, violates the preemption test. For example, a non-Indian who builds a school for an Indian tribe will charge a higher price if state taxes must be paid, and thus the burden of the tax falls on the tribe. In this situation, the state tax is likely to be invalid because the federal government heavily regulates the subject of Indian education.[91] The federal government also comprehensively regulates Indian trade. Therefore, a state cannot tax non-Indian merchants on their reservation sales to Indians because, although non-Indians pay the tax, the tax burden falls on the Indian customers who must pay a higher price for the merchant's goods.[92] Indeed, in a series of cases discussed in chapter 7, the Supreme Court invalidated state taxation of non-Indians in several different contexts because the tax burden fell primarily on Indians and the federal government was already regulating that subject area.

The Supreme Court's decision in *Cotton Petroleum Corp. v. New Mexico* (1989)[93] places a limit on the reach of these cases. In *Cotton Petroleum*, the Supreme Court held that New Mexico could tax a non-Indian company on the value of oil and gas it produced from tribal lands even though part of the tax burden fell on the tribe and even though the state would be collecting millions of dollars more in these taxes than it was spending on reservation services. This decision encourages states in their efforts to tax non-Indians doing business on Indian reservations, except in those few subject areas in which the federal government has enacted a comprehensive regulatory scheme. (This subject is discussed more fully in chapter 7.) Consistent with *Cotton Petroleum*, other courts have permitted states to tax a railroad on the value of its right-of-way across tribal land,[94] to tax a non-Indian rancher on the value of livestock grazing on tribal land,[95] to impose a cigarette excise tax on reservation sales of cigarettes to non-Indians,[96] and to impose a property tax on non-Indians on the value of their leasehold interest in tribal lands.[97]

Once a state tax is determined to be valid, a tribe can be required to assist the state in collecting it, provided that its involvement is merely a mechanical one. The Supreme Court has held, for example, that Indian shopkeepers can be required to collect a state tax on their sales to non-Indians.[98] These shopkeepers can also be required to keep accurate records of such sales for state taxation purposes.[99] In reaching these decisions, the Supreme Court admitted that these requirements imposed some burden on reservation Indians, but the Court characterized this burden as being "minimal."[100] The Court also admitted that allowing the state to tax these sales could have a harmful effect on reservation trade: If an Indian business did not have to charge a state sales tax, its prices would be lower than off-reservation businesses, and this would attract customers. The Court held, however, that Indians are not entitled to such an "artificial" advantage.[101]

In summary, although the infringement and federal preemption tests protect Indians and tribes from most state taxes, they offer limited protection to reservation non-Indians. This is because state taxation of non-Indians rarely interferes substantially with tribal government (the infringement test) or violates federal laws and regulations (the preemption test). In fact, as explained below, non-Indians on the reservation not only have to pay most state taxes but also most tribal taxes.

C. TRIBAL TAXATION

Can an Indian tribe tax its members?

Yes. An Indian tribe has the inherent right, as an attribute of its sovereign powers, to tax tribal members.[102] A tribe may impose the same taxes on its citizens as the federal and state governments can impose on theirs.

In 1982 in *Merrion v. Jicarilla Apache Tribe*,[103] the Supreme Court explicitly recognized the inherent right of tribal taxation. The Court stated:

The power to tax is an essential attribute of Indian sovereignty because it is a necessary instrument of self-government and territorial management. This power enables a tribal government to raise revenues for its essential services. . . . [I]t derives from the tribe's general authority, as sovereign, to control economic activity within its jurisdiction, and to defray the cost of providing governmental services by requiring contributions from persons or enterprises engaged in economic activities within that jurisdiction.[104]

Can an Indian tribe tax nonmembers, including non-Indians, on the reservation?

Yes. As early as 1904 the Supreme Court held that an Indian tribe can tax the personal property owned by a non-Indian located on the reservation.[105] Although the Court ruled in 1978 that tribes lack *criminal* jurisdiction over non-Indians,[106] its 1982 decision in *Merrion* reaffirmed that tribes possess broad *civil* jurisdiction over non-Indians. This authority, which includes the power to tax non-Indians and even to exclude them from the reservation, "is an inherent power necessary to tribal self-government and territorial management."[107] Moreover, a tribe need not obtain the federal government's consent before it taxes non-Indians, except in those rare circumstances when Congress has required it.[108]

Thus, non-Indians who voluntarily enter the reservation and enjoy its benefits can be taxed by the tribe. Courts have held, for example, that a tribe can tax minerals extracted from reservation lands by a non-Indian company;[109] it can tax sales made by non-Indian shopkeepers on the reservation;[110] it can require non-Indians to purchase a tribal license to conduct business on the reservation[111] and pay a license tax;[112] and it can tax non-Indians on the value of their leasehold interest in tribal lands.[113]

Non-Indians sometimes argue that tribal taxes constitute "taxation without representation" because they cannot vote in tribal elections. However, federal and state governments tax people who cannot vote in their elections. Aliens cannot vote in federal or state elections but they must pay federal and state income taxes. Residents of one state who purchase goods in a second state pay state sales taxes but cannot vote in that state's elections. The fact that non-Indians cannot become members of a tribe or vote in tribal elections does not deprive the tribe of the right to tax them. In this respect, Indian tribes are no different than any other government.

NOTES

1. 25 U.S.C. Secs. 331–58.
2. *See* ch. 1, sec. D; ch. 5, sec. B; and ch. 7, sec. B.
3. The General Allotment Act was repealed by the Indian Reorganization Act, 25 U.S.C. Secs. 461 *et seq.*

4. 351 U.S. 1 (1956).

5. *Id.* at 5–6.

6. *See, e.g., U.S. v. Winnebago Tribe of Nebraska,* 542 F.2d 1003 (8th Cir. 1976). *See also Carpenter v. Shaw,* 280 U.S. 363 (1930). *But see FPC v. Tuscarora Indian Nation,* 362 U.S. 99, 120 (1960).

7. *Jourdain v. Commissioner,* 617 F.2d 507 (8th Cir. 1980).

8. *Hoptowit v. Commissioner,* 709 F.2d 564 (9th Cir. 1983).

9. *Satiacum v. Commissioner,* T.C. Memo 1986–356 (13 Indian L. Rep. 7067); *Strom v. Commissioner,* 6 T.C. 621 (1946), *aff'd,* 158 F.2d 520 (9th Cir. 1947).

10. *Karmun v. Commissioner,* 749 F.2d 567 (9th Cir. 1984), *cert. denied,* 474 U.S. 819 (1985).

11. *Anderson v. U.S.,* 845 F.2d 206 (9th Cir.), *cert. denied,* 488 U.S. 966 (1988).

12. *Choteau v. Burnet,* 283 U.S. 691 (1931).

13. U.S. Const., art. I, sec. 2, cl. 3.

14. *Jourdain,* note 7 above.

15. *See Ely v. Klahr,* 403 U.S. 108, 118–19 (1971) (Douglas, J., concurring), *on remand, Klahr v. Williams,* 339 F. Supp. 922, 926–28 (D. Ariz. 1972) (three-judge court).

16. 25 U.S.C. Sec 1407.

17. *See* ch. 5, notes 13–15 and accompanying text.

18. 25 U.S.C. Secs. 331–58.

19. 25 U.S.C. Sec. 349.

20. *Squire v. Capoeman,* 351 U.S. 1, 5–7 (1956).

21. *Stevens v. Commissioner,* 452 F.2d 741 (9th Cir. 1971).

22. *Squire,* note 20 above (timber); *U.S. v. Daney,* 371 (10th Cir. 1966) (oil); *Hayes Big Eagle v. U.S.,* 300 F.2d 765 (Ct. Cl. 1962) (minerals).

23. *Asenap v. U.S.,* 283 F. Supp. 566 (W.D. Okla. 1968); *Landman v. U.S.,* 71 F. Supp. 640 (Ct. Cl.), *cert. denied,* 332 U.S. 815 (1947).

24. *Stevens,* note 21 above. *See also Kirkwood v. Arenas,* 243 F.2d 863 (9th Cir. 1957); *Kirschling v. U.S.,* 746 F.2d 512 (9th Cir. 1984). With respect to exchanges of land, see 25 U.S.C. Sec. 463(e).

25. *Holt v. Commissioner,* 364 F.2d 38 (8th Cir. 1966), *cert. denied,* 386 U.S. 931 (1967); *U.S. v. Anderson,* 625 F.2d 910 (9th Cir. 1980).

26. *Superintendent of Five Civilized Tribes v. Commissioner,* 295 U.S. 418 (1935).

27. *Dillon v. U.S.,* 792 F.2d 849 (9th Cir. 1986), *cert. denied sub nom. Cross v. U.S.,* 480 U.S. 930 (1987).

28. *Critzer v. U.S.,* 597 F.2d 708 (Ct. Cl. 1979) (en banc), *cert. denied,* 444 U.S. 92 (1979); *Hale v. U.S.,* 579 F. Supp. 646 (E.D. Wash. 1984).

29. *See, e.g.,* 26 U.S.C. Secs. 3121(b)(7), 3306(c)(7), exempting states

and their political subdivisions from paying taxes under the Federal Insurance Contribution Act and the Federal Unemployment Tax Act.

30. *See* Rev. Rul. 67–284 and Rev. Rul. 81–291. *See also* Cohen, *Handbook of Federal Indian Law* pp. 399–401 (1982).

31. *Confederated Tribes v. Kurtz,* 691 F.2d 878 (9th Cir. 1982), *cert. denied,* 460 U.S. 1040 (1983).

32. 26 U.S.C. Sec. 7871.

33. *Cabazon Indian Casino v. IRS,* 13 Indian L. Rep. 7021 (BAP 9th Cir. 1986).

34. *Lone Wolf v. Hitchcock,* 187 U.S. 553 (1903).

35. *Choate v. Trapp,* 224 U.S. 665 (1912).

36. *Board of County Commissioners v. Seber,* 318 U.S. 705 (1943).

37. *McClanahan v. Arizona Tax Commission,* 411 U.S. 164 (1973); *Moe v. Confederated Salish and Kootenai Tribes,* 425 U.S. 463 (1976); *Bryan v. Itasca County,* 426 U.S. 373 (1976); *White Mountain Apache Tribe v. Bracker,* 448 U.S. 136 (1980); *Central Machinery Co. v. Arizona State Tax Commission,* 448 U.S. 160 (1980); *Ramah Navajo School Board, Inc. v. Bureau of Revenue,* 458 U.S. 832 (1982); *Montana v. Blackfeet Tribe,* 471 U.S. 759 (1985); *California State Board of Equalization v. Chemehuevi Indian Tribe,* 474 U.S. 9 (1985); *California v. Cabazon Band of Mission Indians,* 480 U.S. 202 (1987); *Crow Tribe of Indians v. Montana,* 819 F.2d 895 (9th Cir. 1987), *aff'd,* 484 U.S. 997 (1988).

38. *Montana v. Blackfeet Tribe,* 471 U.S. 759, 764 (1985).

39. *McClanahan,* note 37 above. *See also Eastern Band of Cherokee Indians v. Lynch,* 632 F.2d 373 (4th Cir. 1980).

40. *Moe,* note 37 above.

41. *Bryan,* note 37 above.

42. *Valandra v. Viedt,* 259 N.W.2d 510 (S.D. 1977).

43. *Sohol v. Clark,* 479 P.2d 925 (Wash. 1971).

44. *Makah Indian Tribe v. Callam County,* 440 P.2d 442 (Wash. 1968).

45. *Moe,* note 37 above.

46. *Washington State Dep't of Revenue v. Wofford,* 622 P.2d 1278 (Wash. Ct. App.), *cert. denied,* 454 U.S. 965 (1981).

47. *Washington v. Confederated Colville Tribes,* 447 U.S. 134 (1980).

48. *Wofford,* note 46 above. *But see Colville,* note 47 above (state may be able to impose a motor vehicle tax proportionate to the amount of off-reservation use).

49. *The Kansas Indians,* 72 U.S. 737 (1867); *McCurdy v. U.S.,* 264 U.S. 484 (1924); *Brooks v. Nez Perce Co., Idaho,* 670 F.2d 835 (9th Cir. 1982).

50. *Mescalero Apache Tribe v. Jones,* 411 U.S. 145 (1973).

51. 28 U.S.C. Sec. 1360(b).
52. *U.S. v. Rickert,* 188 U.S. 432 (1903).
53. *See Oklahoma Tax Comm'n v. U.S.,* 319 U.S. 598 (1942); *West v. Oklahoma Tax Comm'n,* 334 U.S. 717 (1947).
54. *Kirkwood,* note 24 above; *Arenas v. U.S.,* 140 F. Supp. 606 (C.D. Cal. 1956); *Rickert,* note 52 above; *Dewey County v. U.S.,* 26 F.2d 434 (8th Cir.), *cert. denied,* 278 U.S. 649 (1928).
55. *Moe,* note 37 above.
56. *Eastern Navajo Industries, Inc. v. Bureau of Revenue,* 552 P.2d 805 (N.M. Ct. App. 1976). *Cf. Warren Trading Post v. Arizona Tax Comm'n,* 380 U.S. 685 (1965).
57. *Moe,* note 37 above.
58. *Marty Indian School Board, Inc. v. South Dakota,* 824 F.2d 684 (8th Cir. 1987).
59. *See Bryan,* note 37 above, 426 U.S. at 392 and cases cited therein.
60. *Montana v. Blackfeet Tribe,* 471 U.S. 759, 764 (1985).
61. 4 U.S.C. Secs. 105–10.
62. *Warren Trading Post,* note 56 above, 380 U.S. at 691 n.18.
63. 4 U.S.C. Sec. 104.
64. *Bracker,* note 37 above.
65. 28 U.S.C. Secs. 396a, 398.
66. *Montana v. Blackfeet Tribe,* note 60 above.
67. 18 U.S.C. Sec. 1161. *See Rice v. Rehner,* 463 U.S. 713 (1983).
68. 25 U.S.C. Secs. 331 *et seq.*
69. *County of Yakima v. Yakima Indian Nation,* 112 S.Ct. 683 (1992).
70. *See, e.g., Leading Fighter v. County of Gregory,* 230 N.W.2d 114 (S.D.), *cert. denied,* 425 U.S. 1032 (1975) (real estate taxes).
71. *Mescalero Apache Tribe,* note 50 above.
72. This subject is discussed in ch. 13, sec. B.
73. *Prince v. Board of Education,* 543 P.2d 1176 (N.M. 1975); *Goodluck v. Apache County,* 417 F. Supp. 13 (D. Ariz. 1975), *aff'd sub nom. Apache County v. U.S.,* 429 U.S. 876 (1976).
74. For a further discussion of this topic, see American Indian Policy Review Commission, *Final Report* pp. 168–70 (Washington, DC: Government Printing Office, 1977).
75. *Confederated Colville Tribes,* note 47 above.
76. *Id.,* 447 U.S. at 154–59.
77. *Duro v. Reina,* 110 S.Ct. 2053 (1990).
78. *Cabazon Band,* note 37 above; *Indian Country, U.S.A., Inc. v. Oklahoma,* 829 F.2d 967 (10th Cir. 1987), *cert. denied,* 487 U.S. 1218 (1988). *Cf. Rice v. Rehner,* 463 U.S. 713 (1983) (state can tax tribal

liquor sales because Congress has given its express consent).

79. *Montana v. Blackfeet Tribe*, 471 U.S. 759 (1985).
80. *Crow Tribe of Indians*, note 37 above.
81. *The Kansas Indians*, 72 U.S. 737 (1867); *Mescalero Apache Tribe*, note 50 above.
82. *Chemehuevi*, note 37 above; *Oklahoma Tax Comm'n v. Citizen Band Potawatomi Indian Tribe*, 111 S.Ct. 905 (1991). *See also Rice v. Rehner*, note 78 above.
83. *Hoopa Valley Tribe v. Nevins*, 881 F.2d 657 (9th Cir. 1989), *cert. denied*, 110 S.Ct. 1523 (1990).
84. *Blackfeet Tribe*, note 79 above.
85. 422 U.S. 145 (1973).
86. 28 U.S.C. Sec. 1341.
87. 28 U.S.C. Sec. 1361.
88. *Comenout v. Washington*, 722 F.2d 574 (9th Cir. 1983). *See also Potawatomi Indian Tribe*, note 82 above; *Osceola v. Florida Dep't of Revenue*, 893 F.2d 1231 (11th Cir. 1990).
89. *Moe*, note 37 above; *Confederated Colville Tribes*, note 47 above.
90. *See, e.g., Thomas v. Gay*, 169 U.S. 264 (1898) (personal property tax); *Utah & No. Ry. v. Fisher*, 116 U.S. 28 (1885) (real estate). *See also* 25 U.S.C. Sec. 379.
91. *Ramah*, note 37 above.
92. *Warren Trading Post Co. v. Arizona Tax Comm'n*, 380 U.S. 685 (1965).
93. 490 U.S. 163 (1989). *See also Northern Border Pipeline Co. v. Montana*, 772 P.2d 829 (Mont. 1989).
94. *Maricopa & P.R.R. v. Arizona Territory*, 156 U.S. 347 (1895).
95. *Montana Catholic Missions v. Missoula County*, 200 U.S. 118 (1906).
96. *Chemehuevi* and *Moe*, note 37 above.
97. *Fort Mojave Tribe v. County of San Bernadino*, 543 F.2d 1253 (9th Cir. 1976), *cert. denied*, 430 U.S. 983 (1977).
98. *Moe*, note 37 above.
99. *Confederated Colville Tribes*, note 47 above.
100. *Moe*, note 37 above, 425 U.S. at 483.
101. *Confederated Colville Tribes*, note 47 above, 447 U.S. at 151 n.27.
102. *Merrion v. Jicarilla Apache Tribe*, 455 U.S. 130 (1982).
103. 455 U.S. 130 (1982).
104. *Id.* at 137.
105. *Morris v. Hitchcock*, 194 U.S. 384 (1904).
106. *Oliphant v. Suquamish Indian Tribe*, 435 U.S. 191 (1978).
107. *Merrion*, note 102 above, 455 U.S. at 141.

108. *Kerr-McGee Corp. v. Navajo Tribe,* 471 U.S. 195 (1985); *Southland Royalty Co. v. Navajo Tribe,* 715 F.2d 486 (10th Cir. 1983).
109. *Merrion,* note 102 above; *Southland,* note 108 above.
110. *Confederated Colville Tribes,* note 47 above.
111. *Buster v. Wright,* 135 F. 947 (8th Cir. 1905), *appeal dismissed,* 203 U.S. 599 (1906).
112. *Snow v. Quinault Indian Nation,* 709 F.2d 1319 (9th Cir. 1983), *cert. denied,* 467 U.S. 1214 (1984).
113. *Kerr-McGee,* note 108 above.

XI
Hunting, Fishing, and Gathering Rights

Hunting, fishing, and gathering have always been important to Indians. Most tribes, of course, obtained all of their food this way. Access to wildlife, the Supreme Court has noted, was "not much less necessary to the existence of the Indians than the atmosphere they breathed."[1] Many tribes were nomadic and pursued migrations of deer, elk, bison, and anadromous[2] fish. The extent to which fishing was vital to the Northwest Indians, for example, was recently explained by the Supreme Court.

One hundred and twenty-five years ago . . . anadromous fish were even more important to most of the population of western Washington than they are today. At that time, about three-fourths of the approximately 10,000 inhabitants of the area were Indians. Although in some respects the cultures of the different tribes varied . . . all of them shared a vital and unifying dependence on anadromous fish.

Religious rites were intended to insure the continual return of the salmon and the trout; the seasonal and geographic variations in the runs of the different species determined the movements of the largely nomadic tribes. Fish constituted a major part of the Indian diet, was used for commercial purposes, and indeed was traded in substantial volume. The Indians developed food-preservation techniques that enabled them to store fish throughout the year and to transport it over great distances. They used a wide variety of methods to catch fish including the precursors of all modern netting techniques. Their usual and accustomed fishing places were numerous and were scattered throughout the area, and included marine as well as freshwater areas.[3]

Indians have a right to take a considerable amount of wildlife. However, millions of non-Indians now covet these same resources, both for sport and commercial purposes. This, unfortunately, has led to conflict. Indeed, few areas of Indian law have created more conflict between Indians and non-Indians than Indian hunting, fishing, and gathering rights.

Treaties and statutes that guarantee hunting and fishing rights have been interpreted by the courts to include gathering and trapping rights for those tribes that relied on these methods for obtaining their food.[4] Throughout this chapter, references to hunting and fishing rights refer also to gathering and trapping rights unless the contrary is indicated.

Which tribes still have hunting and fishing rights?

Every Indian tribe has the inherent right to be self-governing. This means, among other things, that every tribe has the right to regulate its land and resources, including the taking of wildlife.[5] As explained in chapter 6, a tribe's governing powers can be limited by Congress, but until this occurs, an Indian tribe essentially retains all of its original rights. Obviously, one of its original rights is to hunt and fish within the territory it controlled. "The right to hunt and fish on reservation land is a long-established tribal right."[6]

The right to hunt and fish was expressly guaranteed to many tribes in their treaties with the United States. However, this right is presumed to exist even if the treaty does not mention it. As the Supreme Court explained in 1905, a treaty is not a grant of rights to the Indians but a taking of rights from them.[7] Consequently, if a treaty is silent on the subject of Indian hunting and fishing rights, then these rights are not limited by the treaty and still exist in full force.[8] Tribes whose reservations were created by a presidential executive order rather than a treaty have these same hunting and fishing rights.[9] Indeed, once a reservation is created for an Indian tribe, the tribe can exercise its hunting and fishing rights, even if the reservation does not include any of the tribe's former homelands.[10]

Federal courts have carefully protected Indian hunting and fishing rights because of their importance. Courts have held, for instance, that a treaty that creates a reservation "for Indian purposes" thereby recognizes the tribe's right to hunt and fish on it.[11] The same is true for a treaty that provides land to a tribe "for a home, to be held as Indian lands are held."[12] Similarly, when an Indian reservation is created on an island, and the island's primary food source is fish, the tribe is presumed to retain its fishing rights.[13] Also, a treaty under which Indians can fish at a certain location "until required to remove by the President" means that the Indians can continue to fish at that location until there is a justified reason for their removal.[14]

There is a presumption, then, that a tribe may hunt and fish on its reservation. However, as explained in chapter 5, Congress has the power to extinguish Indian hunting and fishing rights, but a court will not recognize an extinguishment of these vital rights unless Congress has clearly expressed its intention to eliminate them. Extinguishment cannot be inferred, and any ambiguous language in a treaty or statute will be interpreted in favor of the Indians.[15] This is one of the most important court-made rules concerning Indian rights.

This rule was applied in *Menominee Tribe v. United States* (1968).[16] In that case, the Supreme Court held that the Menominee tribe retained its hunting and fishing rights even though Congress had terminated[17] its reservation. The termination statute did not mention hunting and fishing rights. Therefore, the Court said, these rights were not affected by the termination and the Menominees could continue to hunt and fish within the terminated area. The Court reaffirmed the principle that every tribe retains its original hunting and fishing rights unless these rights have been extinguished in clear terms by Congress.

What if a navigable waterway, such as a river or tidelands, is included within the boundaries of the reservation: who owns the land underneath it?

Valuable plant and animal life live in the land underneath navigable waterways; perhaps the clearest example are clams and oysters that are found in tidelands. Although the general rule is that a tribe may hunt, fish, gather, and trap all wildlife within its borders even if the treaty that created the reservation is silent as to these rights, an exception exists for the beds of navigable water. The Supreme Court has held that there is "a strong presumption against conveyance" of this land to an Indian tribe.[18] The tribe certainly has a right to take the fish in this water. However, the submerged land and its resources do not belong to the tribe unless it is clear that Congress intended to give them to the tribe.[19]

Is the tribe entitled to compensation when Congress extinguishes its hunting and fishing rights?

Yes. The Fifth Amendment to the Constitution requires the

federal government to pay compensation whenever it takes private property. The Supreme Court has held that Indian hunting and fishing rights are "property" protected by the Fifth Amendment. Any destruction or diminishment of this property is a "taking" within the meaning of the Fifth Amendment and entitles the tribe to compensation.[20] These rights, however, must first have been formally recognized by the federal government in some treaty, statute, or agreement; the government does not have to compensate a tribe for the loss of property interests not federally recognized.[21]

Does it violate the Constitution to give Indians special hunting and fishing rights?

No. As explained in chapter 5, section A, Congress is authorized by the U.S. Constitution to treat Indians as a unique and separate political group. Congress is permitted to give Indians special rights as well as special burdens, and this includes access to wildlife that is denied to non-Indians.[22]

Do hunting and fishing rights belong to the tribe or to the tribe's members as individuals?

In most situations, it makes no difference whether the right to hunt and fish is classified as a tribal right or as an individual right. If a state law, for instance, is interfering with a tribe's treaty rights, both the tribe and its members can file suit.[23] Their rights are identical in that situation. It is sometimes necessary, however, to determine which rights are superior, the tribe's or the members'. For example, only if the tribe's rights are superior can the tribe regulate the hunting and fishing activities of its members.

Indian hunting and fishing rights ultimately belong to the tribe. Tribal members can hunt and fish only to the extent allowed by the tribe.[24] Likewise, if Congress takes away these rights and must then pay compensation, the money goes to the tribe.[25]

Are treaties between the United States and another country that regulate hunting and fishing applicable automatically to Indian activities?

No. International treaties do not limit Indian hunting and fishing rights unless they expressly say so. As explained earlier, while Congress has the power to extinguish these rights, it must do so in clear terms. Indian tribes in the Northwest, for instance, whose fishing rights are protected by a treaty with the United States can continue to use certain nets even though the United States and Canada subsequently entered into a treaty that prohibited the use of this gear.[26]

Can Indian tribes use hunting and fishing methods that did not exist when their treaties were signed?

Yes. The right to hunt and fish carries with it the right to use modern techniques for obtaining wildlife. A tribe that fished from the shore when its treaty was written can today use motorized boats for that purpose.[27]

The right to hunt and fish also includes the right to take wildlife that was not readily available when the reservation was created. A tribe that once hunted bison (with a bow and arrow) is entitled to hunt deer (with a rifle) in exercising its treaty rights.[28] Moreover, when a state creates a hatchery fish program—to replace natural fish taken by non-Indians or depleted due to non-Indian industry—these hatchery fish are to be regarded no differently than natural fish with respect to the tribe's treaty rights.[29]

In addition, the right to hunt and fish includes the right to take wildlife for traditional uses. Indian tribes that used to capture enough fish for commercial purposes can continue to do so,[30] even if the fish are caught on the reservation and sold off the reservation.[31] Tribes also can continue to take fish for their religious needs and ceremonies.[32]

In exercising its hunting and fishing rights, a tribe is limited only by two external rules. First, it cannot take so much wildlife that it endangers continuation ("propagation") of the species in violation of state or federal conservation laws. Second, it cannot take any wildlife that Congress has expressly prohibited it from taking. (These limitations are discussed later in this chapter.) Apart from this, no limits apply except those the tribe imposes on itself.

A. ON-RESERVATION HUNTING AND FISHING

Many Indian reservations are located in unpopulated areas of the United States where fish and game are plentiful. This wildlife provides food for tribal members and also offers an opportunity for commercial and sport activity.

Most tribes that have wildlife on their reservations have created licensing and conservation programs and actively manage their resources. Many tribes have found it profitable to develop a fish and game industry and sell licenses to non-Indians. In 1966, for instance, the Mescalero Apache Tribe in New Mexico had only 13 elk on its reservation. The National Park Service donated 162 elk to the tribe. By 1983, the tribe had increased its herd to 1200 and began issuing hunting licenses to nonmembers. The tribe has had similar financial success with a hatchery fish program.[33]

There are three groups of people who may want to hunt or fish on an Indian reservation: tribal members, nonmembers who live on the reservation, and nonmembers who live off the reservation. There also are three governments that conceivably could exercise some authority over hunting and fishing on an Indian reservation: the tribe, the state, and the United States. The jurisdiction that each government has over these three groups is discussed below.

To what extent can the tribe regulate on-reservation hunting and fishing?

The Supreme Court has recognized that Indian tribes have "the power to manage the use of their territory and resources."[34] This includes the power to regulate hunting and fishing by members[35] and nonmembers[36] on tribal lands and to prohibit all such activity if the tribe wants to. Only Congress has the authority to restrict these tribal powers, and it rarely has done so.

Hunting and fishing is taken very seriously on most reservations because it is directly related to the economic, cultural, and religious heritage of the tribe. Many tribal members depend upon wildlife for food. In addition, some tribes obtain a large portion of their revenue through the sale of hunting and fishing licenses and from the resulting tourism.[37] Accordingly, most tribes strictly regulate the time, place, and manner of hunting and fishing, and they enforce these rules through the tribal courts.[38] Congress has ratified the tribe's power by making it a federal crime to hunt or fish on tribal land without the tribe's permission. Moreover, courts have allowed Indian tribes to protect their wildlife by halting both on-reservation and off-reservation activities that threaten tribal resources.[39]

Thus, as a general rule, Indian tribes can regulate all hunting and fishing within the reservation. In *Montana v. United States* (1981),[40] however, the Supreme Court created a significant exception to this rule. Tribes have limited powers, the Court held, to regulate non-Indian hunting and fishing on *non-Indian-owned* land within the reservation. In these situations, the Court said, the tribe can impose its laws only when the activity threatens or directly affects the tribe's political integrity, economic security, or health and welfare. Thus, for example, if non-Indian fishing imperils subsistence food for tribal members, the tribe can regulate this activity. Whenever such tribal interests are not affected, state law rather than tribal law governs non-Indian hunting and fishing on non-Indian land.

To what extent can the state regulate on-reservation hunting and fishing?

As explained in chapter 7, a state cannot enforce its laws on an Indian reservation if that enforcement is preempted by federal law or would interfere with the ability of the tribe to govern itself, unless Congress has given its consent. Congress has not consented to the application of state game laws on Indian reservations. Even Public Law 83–280, which extended state jurisdiction over crimes committed on the reservation, expressly withheld state jurisdiction over Indian hunting and fishing.[41]

State regulation of reservation Indian hunting and fishing always interferes with tribal self-government. In addition, such regulation often violates Indian treaties, many of which guaranteed that the tribe would remain free of state control. Therefore, courts have uniformly held that these Indian activities cannot be regulated by the state.[42] The only exception to this rule, and it is a narrow one, was created in *Puyallup Tribe, Inc. v. Department of Game* (1968).[43] The Supreme Court held in *Puyallup* that a state can regulate reservation Indian fishing in the interest of conservation, that is, when necessary to ensure that enough fish escape to propagate the species. The measures that a state can and cannot take in the interest of conservation are discussed later in this chapter.

Subsequent court decisions have made it clear that the state has very limited jurisdiction with respect to hunting and fishing on *Indian* lands, even when non-Indians are involved. In *New Mexico v. Mescalero Apache Tribe* (1983),[44] the Supreme Court ruled unanimously that states may not exercise even concurrent jurisdiction with respect to non-Indian hunting and fishing on tribal lands. Non-Indians, therefore, who wish to hunt or fish on Indian land must comply with the tribe's game laws, but not the state's. Specifically, the Court held in that case that non-Indians who wanted to hunt on tribal lands need not purchase a state hunting license.

Moreover, even if it appears that a species is in danger of extinction, the state may not automatically act. On the contrary, it may do so only if the tribe has failed to implement its own plan for adequate conservation[45] and only if the federal government has not preempted the state's jurisdiction by enacting a conservation plan for this resource.[46]

In short, the state's authority with respect to on-reservation hunting and fishing is limited to the circumstances addressed in *Montana v. United States* and *Puyallup*. First, the state can regulate non-Indians who are hunting and fishing on their own (fee) land. Second, the state can regulate Indians when this is essential for conservation purposes.

To what extent can the federal government regulate on-reservation hunting and fishing?

Federal officials have no authority on an Indian reservation except what Congress has expressly given them. Courts have held, for example, that in the absence of express congressional consent, federal officials may not tax reservation Indian hunting and fishing[47] or take any action that violates an Indian treaty.[48] In addition, federal agencies may not build dams[49] or authorize projects[50] that interfere with the exercise of Indian hunting and fishing rights.

Federal officials, however, have been given three important enforcement functions by Congress. First, federal officials are required to assist tribes in enforcing tribal law. Congress has made it a federal crime to hunt or fish on an Indian reservation except in compliance with tribal law.[51] Congress has also made it a federal crime to "transport, sell, receive, acquire or purchase any fish or wildlife" in violation of tribal law.[52] By enforcing these federal laws, federal officials put teeth into tribal law.

This is particularly important because in 1978 the Supreme Court held that non-Indians who violate tribal law cannot be prosecuted by the tribe but can only be expelled from the reservation.[53] Now, every person who violates tribal game laws can be prosecuted by the federal government. In recent cases, federal courts convicted a tribal member[54] and a nonmember Indian[55] who were caught fishing within an Indian reservation in violation of tribal law.

Second, federal officials have been authorized by Congress to file suit on behalf of Indian tribes to protect the tribe's treaty rights to hunt and fish, and quite a few such suits have been filed.[56] Lastly, Congress has authorized federal officials to enact conservation measures, applicable both on[57] and off[58] the reservation, to preserve a treaty resource when the tribe's conservation measures have proven inadequate. Certain statutes, such as the Bald Eagle Protection Act,[59] prohibit Indians and non-Indians alike from hunting certain animals, and federal officials have enforcement powers with respect to them.[60] For the most part, however, on-reservation hunting and fishing remains almost entirely a matter of tribal regulation.

B. OFF-RESERVATION HUNTING AND FISHING

What kinds of off-reservation hunting and fishing rights do Indians have?

Many Indians have a federally protected right to hunt and fish outside the reservation. Indians have acquired these rights in two ways. On occasion, Congress has reduced the size of an Indian reservation, or even eliminated it, without removing the tribe's hunting and fishing rights on that land. Therefore, these rights remain enforceable by the tribe.[61]

On other occasions, Congress has expressly given a tribe the right to hunt or fish outside its reservation. Some tribes, for example, have a treaty right to hunt "on the unoccupied and unclaimed lands of the United States," or something similar to this.[62] Members of these tribes therefore have the right to hunt on unsettled federal lands, such as areas within a national forest where hunting is otherwise restricted or prohibited.[63]

A typical off-reservation right—and the one that has created the most controversy—is the fishing right. In treaties with the

Northwestern tribes, for example, it was a common practice for a tribe to relinquish most of its homelands and to be promised, in exchange, the right to fish "at all usual and accustomed grounds and stations," both on and off the reservation.[64] Unfortunately, none of the treaties identified the precise location of any of these sites, and Indians have had to identify them one-by-one to the satisfaction of state officials or a court. The leading case in this area is *United States v. Washington*,[65] which defined "usual and accustomed grounds and stations" as being all those locations where members of a tribe customarily fished at or before the time the treaty was signed, however distant from the tribe's usual home and regardless of whether other tribes also fished in the same waters.[66]

In order to prove the existence of a traditional fishing location, the tribe must show where its members fished generations ago. Needless to say, gathering this evidence is not easy because it is almost entirely word-of-mouth.[67] However, many locations have now been identified, and treaty tribes today are exercising their fishing rights at these locations.[68] Some locations are far from the tribe's reservation. One tribe, for example, proved that it customarily fished forty miles from the shore, which was quite a feat given the equipment that was available.[69]

There are many reasons, of course, why non-Indians usually oppose the designation of an area as a traditional Indian fishing ground. For one thing, if privately owned land now surrounds this location, Indians have a right to cross this land in order to reach their protected area.[70] Likewise, if the traditional site is a river bank that is now privately owned by a non-Indian, tribal members retain their right to fish there whether the owner consents or not.[71]

Money is another factor. The fishing industry in the Northwest is a multimillion-dollar business, and Indians compete with non-Indians for the profits. The more federally protected locations Indians have, the more fish to which they have access.

However, tribes have every reason to assert their treaty rights. Tribes relinquished a large amount of land in exchange for these rights, and the United States should keep its end of the bargain. Maintaining these off-reservation sites was of primary concern to the treaty tribes. As the Supreme Court has stated about the Northwest treaties:

All of the treaties were negotiated by Isaac Stevens, the first Governor and first Superintendent of Indian Affairs of the Washington Territory, and a small group of advisors. Contemporaneous documents make it clear that these people recognized the vital importance of the fisheries to the Indians and wanted to protect them from the risk that non-Indian settlers might seek to monopolize their fisheries. There is no evidence of the precise understanding the Indians had of any of the specific English terms and phrases in the treaty. It is perfectly clear, however, that the Indians were vitally interested in protecting their right to take fish at usual and accustomed places, whether on or off the reservations, and that they were invited by the white negotiators to rely and in fact did rely heavily on the good faith of the United States to protect that right.[72]

As the Court indicated, the government agents who wrote these treaties wished to protect Indian fisheries, but their promise was easy to make at the time because few non-Indians lived in that area of the country, and the fish supply seemed inexhaustible.[73] Today the demand for fish has greatly outstripped its supply, and non-Indians deeply resent Indian treaty rights. Indians frequently have had to rely on federal courts to enforce these rights. Indeed, state officials, pressured by local citizens, have ignored even federal court decisions. This prompted the Supreme Court to warn these officials that it is "prepared to uphold the use of stern measures to require respect for federal court orders."[74] There even have been court battles between two tribes, each claiming that a location is its exclusive fishing ground.[75]

To what extent may the tribe regulate Indian hunting and fishing outside the reservation?
As explained in chapter 7, section D, tribal law usually does not apply outside the reservation; state law does. However, if a tribe has the right to engage in an off-reservation activity, the tribe can regulate participation in that activity by tribal members. For instance, if a tribe has a federal right to fish outside the reservation, the tribe can decide which members can exercise that right and under what circumstances. Members who violate these regulations can be prosecuted by the

tribe.[76] In short, tribes are presumed to have the authority to regulate their off-reservation rights.

To what extent can the state regulate Indian hunting and fishing outside the reservation?

Each state, like each tribe, has the right to regulate hunting and fishing within its borders.[77] Therefore, as a general rule, Indians who hunt or fish outside the reservation must comply with state law.

Some Indians, though, have off-reservation hunting and fishing rights based on federal treaties or statutes. By virtue of the Supremacy Clause in the U.S. Constitution, a federal right is superior to a state right when the two conflict.[78] Therefore, a state may not exercise its usual regulatory powers if doing so would interfere with a federal right, including an Indian treaty right.[79]

Yet even here, the state has some control. There are two narrow but important exceptions to the rule that a state may not regulate off-reservation Indian treaty rights. These exceptions are best illustrated by the court decisions interpreting the Northwest Indian treaties.

Almost all the treaties with Northwest tribes contain the same two clauses, one of which already has been discussed. These treaties guarantee the Indians "the right of taking fish at all usual and accustomed grounds and stations . . . in common with all citizens of the Territory." As previously explained, the "grounds and stations" clause guarantees that the tribe may fish at all of its traditional locations, free from state interference. However, the "in common with" clause, the courts have held, gives the state some regulatory authority over these off-reservation rights.

The treaties do not explain what this clause means. Indians can fish "in common with" everyone else, but how many fish can they take? Can the Indians, for example, take more than 5 percent of the fish if they represent only 5 percent of the population? For that matter, is there a limit to the amount of fish that Indians can take in exercising these treaty rights? The Supreme Court has defined the "in common with" clause to mean that Indians have a right to take a certain portion of the fish and not just a right to cast a fishing line along with the tens of thousands of non-Indians who now fish in the area. The treaties did not simply guarantee Indians an opportunity to fish. They reserved to them a certain percentage of the catch. As a result, the state must prevent non-Indians from taking too many fish.[80]

The state, in fact, has a dual regulatory function as a result of the "in common with" clause: the state must prevent both the non-Indians and the Indians from taking too many fish. The "in common with" language not only gives Indians a right to a certain amount of fish, the Supreme Court said, but it gives non-Indians a claim to the remainder. "Both sides have a right, secured by treaty, to take a fair share of the available fish. That, we think, is what the parties to the treaties intended when they secured to the Indians the right of taking fish in common with other citizens."[81]

In *Washington v. Washington State Commercial Passenger Fishing Vessel Association* (1979),[82] the Supreme Court interpreted in specific terms the "in common with" clause. Indian tribes that have the right to fish "in common with other citizens of the Territory" may take up to 50 percent of the available fish, unless a lesser amount would provide the Indians with "a moderate living." The Court stated:

> It bears repeating, however, that the 50% figure imposes a maximum but not a minimum allocation. . . . Indian treaty rights to a natural resource that once was thoroughly and exclusively exploited by the Indians secures so much as, but no more than, is necessary to provide the Indians with a livelihood—that is to say, a moderate living. Accordingly, while the maximum possible allocation to the Indians is fixed at 50%, the minimum is not; the latter will, upon proper submissions to the District Court, be modified in response to changing circumstances. If, for example, a tribe should dwindle to just a few members, or if it should find other sources of support that lead it to abandon its fisheries, a 45% or 50% allocation of an entire run that passes through its customary fishing grounds would be manifestly inappropriate because the livelihood of the tribe under those circumstances could not reasonably require an allotment of a large number of fish.[83]

Using the Court's "moderate living" standard, there are four possible situations that can arise, and three have occurred. The first possibility is that the state must prevent the tribe from capturing its entire 50 percent share because otherwise the tribe's income would exceed a moderate level. There are no reported court cases in which this situation has occurred. However, as tribes improve their technological capability of catching fish—few tribes currently take their allotted share—this may become relevant.

The second possibility is that the state must prevent non-Indians from taking so many fish that Indians are prevented from catching their treaty share. This situation arises all the time.[84] The third possibility is that, even if the tribe takes its 50 percent share, this still is insufficient to provide them with a moderate living. This is the situation in northern Wisconsin.[85] Thus far, the federal courts have not permitted the tribes to take more than 50 percent of the resource even though this will not provide the Indians with a moderate living.[86]

The fourth possibility, which has occurred infrequently, is that non-Indians fail to take their 50 percent of the wildlife. In that event, Indians are permitted to take more than their treaty share rather than waste the available resource.[87]

In short, the general rule is that a state may not interfere with Indian treaty rights to hunt and fish. The first of two exceptions to this rule is the "moderate living" exception, just discussed. The second exception is that a state can limit these activities in the interest of conservation.[88] This exception was announced by the Supreme Court in a 1968 decision, and since then the Court has reaffirmed this exception several times.[89] However, the Court has given no solid justification for it, and numerous commentators have criticized this holding.[90] As one federal court recently stated, "the basis for [this] state regulation has never been explained satisfactorily"; however, the "Supreme Court has ruled definitively" that states may regulate Indian fishing activities for conservation purposes.[91]

The Supreme Court has placed substantial limits on the state's conservation authority, however. In order to be valid, a state conservation regulation must pass four tests. First, the state must show that its regulation is reasonable and necessary to perpetuate the species, and second, that the regulation is the least restrictive alternative that can achieve this goal. If alternative methods of conservation are available that are less injurious to the tribe's treaty rights, they must be utilized.[92]

Third, the regulation must not discriminate against Indians, either by placing greater burdens on them than on non-Indians or by preventing Indians from taking their treaty share of the resource.[93] Finally, the regulation must allow the tribe to take, by reasonable means, a fair and equitable share of the resource in any given area.[94] The state cannot deny Indians access to some treaty sites even if the Indians could obtain their treaty share at remaining sites.[95]

To illustrate, a state can validly require tribes to issue identification cards to their members so that state officials can identify who has treaty rights.[96] A state can also allow non-Indians to fish at a protected Indian location provided that tribal members have the opportunity to catch their treaty share of fish.[97] A state can also prohibit Indians from taking a certain species of fish near extinction provided that non-Indians have the same prohibition.[98]

On the other hand, restrictions that are unreasonable, unnecessary, or discriminatory are invalid. A state may not impose any restrictions that would prevent the tribe from taking its fair share of treaty wildlife unless absolutely necessary to preserve the species. For example, a regulation that prohibits both Indians and non-Indians from using fishing nets is neutral on its face, but if it prevents Indians from obtaining their full treaty share of fish, it discriminates against Indians and is preempted by federal law.[99] Likewise, treaty Indians are not required to obey "neutral" state licensing requirements or state regulations on the number of fish they can take, the seasons in which they can fish, or the type of gear they can use unless absolutely necessary for conservation.[100] Clearly, a state may not enforce a regulation, as one state tried to do, that allows non-Indians to keep twenty-four-inch fish but imposes a twenty-eight-inch limit on the fish that Indians can keep.[101]

To what extent can the federal government regulate off-reservation Indian hunting and fishing?

If it wanted to, Congress could regulate every aspect of Indian hunting and fishing. Congress could even extinguish these treaty rights at any time, provided that it paid compensation to the tribe.[102]

However, regulation of off-reservation hunting and fishing has been left by Congress primarily in the hands of the tribes and the states; federal officials have been given little authority to regulate them. The Secretary of the Interior has issued rules on the identification of treaty Indians and their gear and has regulated fishing activities at certain protected locations.[103] In addition, Congress has passed a comprehensive law governing all fishing on the high seas within two hundred miles of the coast,[104] but federal officials are required by its terms to enforce this law consistent with Indian treaty rights.[105] Otherwise, federal officials exert little control over Indian hunting and fishing rights.

NOTES

1. *U.S. v. Winans,* 198 U.S. 371, 381 (1905)
2. Anadromous fish are born in fresh water, migrate to the ocean where they reach maturity, and complete their life cycle by returning on one or more occasions to the place where they were born to spawn.
3. *Washington v. Washington State Commercial Passenger Fishing Vessel Ass'n,* 443 U.S. 658, 664–66 (1979) (citations omitted).
4. *U.S. v. Aanerud,* 893 F.2d 956 (8th Cir.), *cert. denied,* 111 S. Ct. 72 (1990); *People v. LeBlanc,* 248 N.W.2d 199 (Mich. 1976); *State v. Tinno,* 497 P.2d 1386 (Idaho 1972) (treaty right to "hunt" also confers right to fish).
5. *New Mexico v. Mescalero Apache Tribe,* 462 U.S. 324 (1983).
6. *U.S. v. Felter,* 752 F.2d 1505, 1509 (10th Cir. 1985).
7. *Winans,* note 1 above, 198 U.S. at 381.
8. *Menominee Tribe v. U.S.,* 391 U.S. 404 (1968); *State v. Coffee,* 556 P.2d 1185, 1189 (Idaho 1976).
9. *U.S. v. Dion,* 476 U.S. 734, 745 n.8 (1986).
10. *Alaska Pacific Fisheries v. U.S.,* 248 U.S. 78 (1918).
11. *Quechan Tribe v. Rowe,* 531 F.2d 408 (9th Cir. 1976).
12. *Menominee Tribe,* note 8 above.
13. *Alaska Pacific Fisheries,* note 10 above.
14. *Lac Courte Oreilles Band of Lake Superior Chippewa Indians v. Voight,* 700 F.2d 341 (7th Cir.), *cert. denied,* 464 U.S. 805 (1983).
15. *See, e.g., Menominee Tribe,* note 8 above; *U.S. v. Felter,* note 6 above. *But see Oregon Dep't of Fish & Wildlife v. Klamath Indian Tribe,* 473 U.S. 753 (1985). For a full discussion of treaty interpretation, see ch. 4.
16. 391 U.S. 404 (1968). However, statutory language which removes "all right, title and interest" of a tribe in certain land has been held to extinguish the tribe's hunting and fishing rights in the land. *Red Lake*

Band of Chippewa Indians v. Minnesota, 614 F.2d 1161 (8th Cir. 1980), *cert. denied,* 449 U.S. 905 (1980).

17. The subject of termination is discussed in ch. 1, and in ch. 5, sec. B.

18. *Montana v. U.S.,* 450 U.S. 544, 552 (1981).

19. *See U.S. v. Aam,* 887 F.2d 190 (9th Cir. 1989) and cases cited therein.

20. *Menominee Tribe,* note 8 above, 391 U.S. at 413; *Hynes v. Grimes Packing Co.,* 337 U.S. 86, 105 (1949). This subject is discussed in ch. 5, notes 13–16 and accompanying text.

21. *See, e.g., Tee-Hit-Ton Indians v. U.S.,* 348 U.S. 272 (1955); *Inupiat Community of the Arctic Slope v. U.S.,* 680 F.2d 122 (Ct. Cl.), *cert. denied,* 459 U.S. 969 (1982). This subject is discussed in ch. 2, sec. D.

22. This subject is discussed in ch. 5, notes 19–24 and accompanying text. *See generally, U.S. v. Aanerud,* note 4 above; *U.S. v. Michigan,* 653 F.2d 277 (6th Cir. 1981).

23. *Puyallup Tribe, Inc. v. Dep't of Game,* 433 U.S. 165 (1977) (suit by tribe); *Sohappy v. Smith,* 302 F. Supp. 899 (D. Or. 1969) (suit by tribal members).

24. *U.S. v. Washington,* 384 F. Supp. 312 (W.D. Wash. 1974), *aff'd* 520 F.2d 676 (9th Cir. 1975), *cert. denied,* 423 U.S. 1086 (1976).

25. *Whitefoot v. U.S.,* 293 F.2d 658 (Ct. Cl. 1961), *cert. denied,* 369 U.S. 818 (1962).

26. *U.S. v. Washington,* note 24 above, 520 F.2d at 689–90. *See also U.S. v. Cutler,* 37 F. Supp. 724 (D. Idaho 1941).

27. *U.S. v. Washington,* note 24 above, 384 F. Supp. at 402. *See also Peterson v. Christensen,* 455 F. Supp. 1095, 1099 (E.D. Wis. 1978).

28. *U.S. v. Finch,* 548 F.2d 822, 832 (9th Cir. 1976), *vacated on other grounds,* 433 U.S. 676 (1977); *U.S. v. Aanerud,* note 4 above; *Lac Oreilles Band of Lake Superior Chippewa Indians v. Wisconsin,* 653 F. Supp. 1420, 1426–28, 1435 (W.D. Wis. 1987).

29. *U.S. v. Washington,* 759 F.2d 1353, 1358–60 (9th Cir. 1985) (en banc), *cert. denied,* 474 U.S. 994 (1985); *Mattz v. Superior Court,* 46 Cal. 3d 355 (Cal. 1988), *cert. denied,* 489 U.S. 1078 (1989).

30. *U.S. v. Washington,* note 24 above; *Dep't of Game v. Puyallup Tribe,* 414 U.S. 44, 48 (1973); *Lac Oreilles Band,* note 28 above, 653 F. Supp. at 1435.

31. *People v. McCovey,* 36 Cal. 3d 517 (Cal.), *cert. denied,* 469 U.S. 1062 (1984).

32. *U.S. v. Washington,* note 24 above.

33. *See Mescalero Apache Tribe,* note 5 above.

34. *Id.,* 462 U.S. at 335.

35. *Id.; Puyallup Tribe,* note 23 above; *U.S. v. Williams,* 898 F.2d 727 (9th Cir. 1990).

36. *Montana v. U.S.*, 450 U.S. 544, 558 (1981); *Quechan Tribe*, note 11 above. Tribes lack the authority to prosecute nonmembers, but they do have the authority to expel them from the reservation. *Oliphant v. Suquamish Indian Tribe*, 435 U.S. 191 (1978).

37. *See Mescalero Apache Tribe*, note 5 above; *U.S. v. Washington*, note 24 above.

38. *See* Hobbs, *Indian Hunting and Fishing Rights II*, 37 Geo. Wash. L. Rev. 1251 (1969); *Muckleshoot Indian Tribe v. Moses*, 16 Indian L. Rep. 6073 (Muckleshoot Tr. Ct. App. 1989).

39. *See, e.g., Winters v. U.S.*, 207 U.S. 564 (1908); *U.S. v. Winnebago Tribe*, 542 F.2d 1002 (8th Cir. 1976); *Confederated Tribes and Bands of the Yakima Indian Nation v. F.E.R.C.*, 746 F.2d 466 (9th Cir. 1984).

40. 450 U.S. 544 (1981).

41. 18 U.S.C. Sec. 1162(b). *See Quechan Tribe*, note 11 above.

42. *See* cases cited in notes 1, 8, and 30 above. *See also Tulee v. Washington*, 315 U.S. 681 (1942).

43. 391 U.S. 392 (1968).

44. 462 U.S. 324 (1983).

45. *Lac Courte Oreilles Band of Lake Superior Chippewa Indians v. Wisconsin*, 668 F. Supp. 1233, 1241 (W.D. Wis. 1987); *U.S. v. Michigan*, note 22 above, 653 F.2d at 279.

46. *People v. McCovey*, note 31 above; *Mattz v. Superior Court*, note 29 above.

47. *Strom v. Commissioner*, 6 T.C. 621 (1946).

48. *Mason v. Sams*, 5 F.2d 255 (D. Wash. 1925). *See also Sohappy, Sr. v. Hodel*, 911 F.2d 1312 (9th Cir. 1990).

49. *Winnebago Tribe*, note 39 above; *Confederated Tribes of the Umatilla Indian Reservation v. Alexander*, 440 F. Supp. 553 (D. Or. 1977).

50. *F.E.R.C.*, note 39 above.

51. 18 U.S.C. Sec. 1165.

52. 16 U.S.C. Sec. 3372(a)(1).

53. *Oliphant*, note 36 above.

54. *U.S. v. Sohappy*, 770 F.2d 816, 819 (9th Cir. 1985), *cert. denied*, 477 U.S. 906 (1986).

55. *U.S. v. Big Eagle*, 881 F.2d 539 (8th Cir. 1989), *cert. denied*, 110 S.Ct. 1145 (1990).

56. *See, e.g., U.S. v. Washington*, note 24 above; *U.S. v. Michigan*, note 22 above.

57. *Northern Arapaho Tribe v. Hodel*, 842 F.2d 224 (10th Cir. 1988); *U.S. v. Eberhardt*, 789 F.2d 1354 (9th Cir. 1986).

58. *McCovey*, note 31 above; *Mattz*, note 29 above.

59. 16 U.S.C. Sec. 668 *et seq.*

60. *U.S. v. Dion*, 476 U.S. 734 (1986).

61. *Menominee Tribe*, note 8 above; *Kimball v. Callahan*, 590 F.2d 768 (9th Cir. 1979), *cert. denied*, 444 U.S. 826 (1980).

62. *See Ward v. Race Horse*, 163 U.S. 504 (1896); *Antoine v. Washington*, 420 U.S. 194 (1975) ("open and unclaimed land"); *Tinno*, note 4 above ("the unoccupied lands of the United States"). *See also Holcomb v. Confederated Tribes of the Umatilla Indian Reservation*, 382 F.2d 1013 (9th Cir. 1967).

63. *State v. Arthur*, 261 P.2d 135 (Idaho 1953); *Antoine*, note 62 above; *Holcomb*, note 62 above. *Cf. U.S. v. Hicks*, 587 F. Supp. 1162 (W.D. Wash. 1984).

64. *See Winans*, note 1 above; *U.S. v. Washington*, note 24 above; *Lac Courte Oreilles Band*, note 14 above.

65. Cited in note 24 above.

66. *U.S. v. Washington*, note 24 above, 384 F. Supp. at 332.

67. These difficulties are illustrated in *State v. Petit*, 558 P.2d 796 (Wash. 1977), and *U.S. v. Lummi Indian Tribe*, 841 F.2d 317 (9th Cir. 1988).

68. *U.S. v. Washington*, note 24 above, 384 F. Supp. at 332, 408.

69. *See U.S. v. Washington*, 730 F.2d 1314 (9th Cir. 1984).

70. *Winans*, note 1 above; *Seufort Bros. v. U.S.*, 249 U.S. 194 (1919).

71. *Winans*, note 1 above.

72. *Fishing Vessel Ass'n*, note 3 above, 443 U.S. at 666–67.

73. *See id.*, 443 U.S. at 666.

74. *Id.*, 443 U.S. at 696.

75. *See, e.g., U.S. v. Skokomish Indian Tribe*, 764 F.2d 670 (9th Cir. 1985).

76. *Settler v. Lameer*, 507 F.2d 231 (9th Cir. 1974); *U.S. v. Washington*, note 24 above, 384 F. Supp. at 340–42.

77. *Geer v. Connecticut*, 161 U.S. 519 (1896).

78. U.S. Const., art. VI, sec. 2. *See Missouri v. Holland*, 252 U.S. 416 (1920); *Douglas v. Seacoast Products, Inc.*, 431 U.S. 265 (1977).

79. *Mescalero Apache Tribe v. Jones*, 411 U.S. 145, 148 (1973); *Tulee*, note 42 above; *U.S. v. Washington*, note 24 above; *Puyallup Tribe*, note 23 above.

80. *See* cases cited in notes 3 and 24 above.

81. *Fishing Vessel Ass'n*, note 3 above, 443 U.S. at 684–85. *See also Puyallup Tribe*, note 23 above.

82. 443 U.S. 685 (1979).

83. *Id.*, 443 U.S. at 686–87. *See also Lac Courte Oreilles Band*, note 28 above, 653 F. Supp. at 1434, 1435.

84. *See* note 74 above and accompanying text.

85. *Lac Courte Oreilles Band of Lake Superior Chippewa Indians v. Wisconsin*, 686 F. Supp. 226 (W.D. Wis. 1988).

86. *See Lac Courte Oreilles Band of Lake Superior Chippewa Indians v. Wisconsin*, 740 F. Supp. 1400 (W.D. Wis. 1990).

87. *U.S. v. Washington*, 761 F.2d 1404 (9th Cir. 1985).

88. *Puyallup Tribe*, note 23 above.

89. *Puyallup Tribe v. Dep't of Game*, 391 U.S. 392, 398 (1968); *Puyallup*, note 23 above; *Antoine*, note 62 above, 420 U.S. at 207. *See also Lac Courte*, note 14 above, 700 F.2d at 183.

90. *See* Johnson, *The State Versus Indian Off-Reservation Fishing: United States Supreme Court Error*, 47 Wash. L. Rev. 207 (1972); Note, *State Regulation of Lake Superior Chippewa Off-Reservation Usufructory Rights*, 11 Hamline L. Rev. 153 (1988).

91. *Lac Courte*, note 86 above, 740 F. Supp. at 1421.

92. *Puyallup Tribe*, note 30 above. *See also* cases cited in note 45 above and *U.S. v. Oregon*, 769 F.2d 1410, 1416 (9th Cir. 1985).

93. *See* cases cited in note 89 above and *U.S. v. Washington*, note 24 above, 384 F. Supp. at 342, 402–4.

94. *Fishing Vessel Ass'n*, note 3 above, 443 U.S. at 679; *Washington State Charterboat Ass'n v. Baldredge*, 702 F.2d 820 (9th Cir. 1983), *cert. denied*, 464 U.S. 1053 (1984).

95. *Puyallup Tribe*, notes 23, 30, and 89 above; *Sohappy v. Smith*, note 23 above, 302 F. Supp. at 907–8. *But see U.S. v. Oregon*, 718 F.2d 299 (9th Cir. 1983).

96. *U.S. v. Washington*, note 24 above, 384 F. Supp. at 341.

97. *Puyallup Tribe*, note 23 above.

98. *U.S. v. Oregon*, 657 F.2d 1009 (9th Cir. 1981).

99. *Puyallup Tribe*, note 30 above, 414 U.S. at 48.

100. *Puyallup Tribe*, notes 23 and 30 above; *Tulee*, note 42 above.

101. *U.S. v. Washington*, Civ. No. 9213-Phase I (W.D. Wash. 1981), 8 Indian L. Rep. 3031 (1981).

102. See notes 20 and 21 above and accompanying text.

103. 25 C.F.R. Parts 241–50 (1989).

104. 16 U.S.C. Secs. 1801–82, generally known as the Magnuson Act.

105. *Id.*, Sec. 1854(b). *See also Sohappy*, note 48 above.

XII
Indian Water Rights

Water is a scarce and valuable resource in most of the United States. In many parts of the West, where most Indians live, groundwater is being consumed faster than it can be replenished. In the not too distant future, many western wells will run dry; some are dry already.[1]

The Supreme Court has recognized that Indian tribes have rights to a considerable amount of water. For good reason, tribes have become very concerned about preserving and defending their water rights.

What is the *Winters* doctrine?

The most important case in Indian water law is *Winters v. United States*,[2] decided by the Supreme Court in 1908. The issue in *Winters* was whether a landowner could dam a stream on his property, thereby preventing water from reaching an Indian reservation. The reservation had been created by Congress eight years before the landowner had purchased his property. However, the federal statute that created the reservation made no mention of water rights. The landowner therefore argued that the reservation was not entitled to a specific amount of water, and he was free to divert the stream to his own use.

The Supreme Court ruled in favor of the tribe. The reservation was arid and of little value without irrigation. Congress must have intended, the Court said, to reserve to the Indians enough water to irrigate their lands and make the reservation livable and productive. The Court ruled that Congress has the power to reserve water for federal lands, and by implication it exercises this power every time it creates an Indian reservation. Therefore, a sufficient amount of water had to reach the reservation to enable the tribe to fulfill the purpose for which it was created. The Court ordered the landowner to dismantle the dam.

The *Winters* doctrine, also known as the "implied reservation of water" doctrine, has been consistently upheld by the Supreme Court. In *Arizona v. California* (1963)[3] the Court had to decide whether an Indian tribe was entitled to enough water to irrigate its entire reservation, even though part of the reservation had never been irrigated. The executive order that created the reservation was silent on the subject of water rights. Citing *Winters,* the Court said that, whenever an Indian reservation is created, there is an "implied reservation of water rights . . . necessary to make the reservation livable."[4] The tribe was entitled to an amount of water, the Court held, that would "satisfy the future as well as the present needs of the Indian reservation," that is, the amount necessary "to irrigate all the practicably irrigable acreage on the reservation."[5] In *Cappaert v. U.S.* (1976)[6] the Court reaffirmed the principle that whenever the federal government sets aside land for a particular purpose, it impliedly reserves sufficient water rights to accomplish that purpose.

The basic principles of the *Winters* doctrine are set forth in *Winters* and clarified in *Arizona v. California* and in *Cappaert.* These principles are as follows. Congress has the right to reserve water for federal lands, including Indian reservations.[7] When Congress sets aside land for a specific purpose, it reserves by implication a sufficient quantity of water to fulfill that purpose.[8] Indian reservations are created by Congress with the intention of making them habitable and productive, and whatever water is necessary to fulfill this goal is reserved by implication for the tribe's use.[9] Indian reservations created by the President through an executive order are entitled to the same water rights as those created by Congress through a treaty or statute.[10] Treaties, statutes, and executive orders that create an Indian reservation must be interpreted liberally in favor of the tribe. Therefore, even if they say nothing about water rights, the tribe is presumed to have a right to enough water to satisfy the reservation's purpose, that is, enough water to meet the tribe's present and future needs.[11]

What gives Congress the power to reserve water for Indians?

Article I, section 8, clause 3 of the Constitution gives Congress the power to regulate commerce with the Indian tribes. This gives Congress complete authority over Indian affairs,[12] including the power to grant water rights to Indians.[13]

What is the doctrine of prior appropriation, and how does it differ from the *Winters* doctrine?

As white settlers moved westward during the nineteenth century and bought homesteads, they quickly developed rules to govern the allocation of water. Without these rules they would have engaged in endless warfare over this scarce resource. The rules they developed, known as the "doctrine of prior appropriation," have been codified into law in every western state. This doctrine has four basic principles. The first principle is "first in time, first in right." That is, the earliest appropriator of water (the person with the earliest "priority date") has a continuing right to use the same amount of water as was initially diverted from the same source whenever it is available, and subsequent appropriators ("junior interests") can only use whatever remains. Second, these water rights are property rights. They belong to the individual just as the land does, and they can be sold when the land is sold, retained, or even sold or leased to someone else. Third, in times of scarcity the person with the earliest priority date may appropriate his or her entire water entitlement, even if no water remains for junior interests. Finally, appropriative rights are forfeited if unused for a significant period of time.[14]

To illustrate these principles, assume that Mr. A and Ms. B live along the same stream, and that Ms. C lives behind Mr. A. In 1860, Mr. A begins using fifty acre feet of water from the stream. The next year, Ms. B does the same thing. By making the first diversion, Mr. A has a "priority date" that is superior to Ms. B's. In times of drought, he can use his entire fifty acre feet of water even if nothing remains for Ms. B. Ten years later, if Mr. A sells his water rights to Ms. C, she acquires Mr. A's priority date (even if her property does not touch the stream), superior to Ms. B's rights. Even one hundred years later, someone can still purchase these same water rights, assuming that these rights have not been forfeited due to nonuse.

Indian water rights (*Winters* rights) are governed by federal law while appropriative rights are governed by state law.[15] *Winters* rights differ from rights under the doctrine of prior appropriation in two significant respects. First, Indian water rights are reserved. A tribe cannot lose its *Winters* rights through nonuse. Second, the amount of water a tribe is entitled to use is not determined by the tribe's initial use. On the contrary, a tribe with *Winters* rights is forever entitled to take all the water it needs to fulfill the purpose for which its reservation was created, provided that at the time it was created, this amount of water had not been appropriated by a landowner with a superior priority date.[16] In the West, Indian reservations were established before many non-Indians acquired land in the region. Therefore, Indian water rights usually have the earliest priority date, and thus they are very valuable.

The priority of Indian water rights is never later than the date on which the reservation was created, even if many years pass before the tribe begins using this water.[17] In fact, in certain situations, a tribe's priority date is earlier than when the reservation was created. For example, if a tribe has always caught fish from a particular lake, and a treaty recognizes the tribe's continuing right to do so, then the priority date for this use of water is "time immemorial." In these situations, the tribe obviously has the senior water interest. On the other hand, when water is reserved for a use that did not exist prior to the creation of the reservation, the priority date is the date the reservation was created. On some reservations, then, a tribe has two priority dates, one for a new use of water (the date the reservation was created) and one for an old use (time immemorial).[18]

Indians enjoy the best of both worlds when it comes to water rights. The appropriation doctrine protects Indians even though they are not bound by its limitations. It protects them by making sure that junior interests take none of the water Indians need. Yet Indians are exempt from its rule that current (and future) water use is limited to initial water use and that water rights can be forfeited by nonuse. By virtue of the *Winters* doctrine Indians can use whatever water is necessary to accomplish the reservation's purpose. Indians can even increase their initial water use because Congress has reserved for them a sufficient quantity of water to meet their present and their future needs.

An Indian tribe, consistent with the doctrine of prior appropriation, has no obligation to share its priority *Winters* rights with any junior water user.[19] In a time of drought, a tribe, like any other senior interest, has the right to use its full allocation of water even if non-Indians are left with an insufficient supply.[20] (If the tribe and these other users had the same priority date, and there was an insufficient water supply, the amount of water available to each user would be reduced proportionally.)[21]

Which water laws govern the use of water in the eastern states?

Water use in the eastern states is governed by a different set of rules known as the "riparian doctrine." This doctrine is more egalitarian than the appropriation doctrine. Under the riparian doctrine, prior use does not create a vested right to continued use, and in times of scarcity, the available water supply is distributed equitably among all users. There are a few exceptions to this, but for our purposes here they are not significant. In states governed by the riparian doctrine, Indian reservations presumably have the same *Winters* rights as they do in the West. However, this issue has never been litigated, probably because most eastern reservations usually have an adequate water supply.

Can a tribe exercising its *Winters* rights use groundwater as well as surface water?

Yes. *Winters* rights apply to groundwater as well as surface water, including rivers and streams, both navigable and non-navigable, that underlie, border, traverse, or are contained within the reservation. When surface and subsurface water are interrelated, Indians can protect their *Winters* rights, for example, by preventing junior interests from using off-reservation groundwater that would deplete their on-reservation surface water.[22]

How much water is an Indian reservation entitled to use?

The short answer to this question is that a tribe is entitled to use as much water as is necessary to fulfill the purpose of the reservation once senior claims, if there are any, have taken their entitlement. However, this short answer involves two complicated inquiries: (1) what is the purpose of the reservtion, and (2) precisely what quantity of water is needed to fulfill that purpose?

1. *Purpose.* The initial purpose for which all Indian reservations are created is to serve as a permanent and economically viable home for the Indians who live there. Therefore, every

reservation is at least entitled to enough water to satisfy its subsistence needs and maintain its viability.[23]

Water entitlement varies from one reservation to the next. An agricultural tribe, for instance, has a different need for water than a tribe dependent on fish and game. In order to determine the purpose of any particular reservation, at least three things must be considered: the history of the tribe for which the reservation was created (including the tribe's historical use of water); the stated and implied intentions of those who created the reservation; and the tribe's need to maintain itself under changed circumstances.[24] A case that illustrates how these factors are applied is *Colville Confederated Tribes v. Walton.*[25]

Walton was brought by a confederation of six Indian tribes, called the Colvilles, against a non-Indian named Walton who owned land within their reservation. The Colvilles had two traditional sources of food: fish caught from the Columbia River and crops. After the Columbia River was dammed by the federal government, the Colvilles constructed a lake on their reservation, supplied it with trout, and now depend on this fish for food. The Colvilles claimed Walton was using so much water there was not enough left to irrigate their crops and, in addition, his use of water was depleting their lake. In short, Walton's water usage was affecting their very livelihood.

Using the three factors listed above, the court ruled in favor of the Colvilles and restricted Walton's use of water. The reservation was created, the evidence showed, in order to give the Colvilles a viable home, to allow them to fish and to grow crops. Accordingly, when Congress created the reservation, it reserved by implication to the Colvilles enough water to continue their fishing activities and irrigate their lands. Due to changed circumstances, the Colvilles now needed enough water to maintain their lake. Walton's claim to water was not senior in time to the tribe's claim. Therefore, the court held, Walton was not permitted to interfere with the tribe's ability to irrigate its lands and maintain its lake at an appropriate level for its fishery.

Other courts have reached similar conclusions. Indians who traditionally have depended on hunting and fishing for food and are then placed on a reservation are entitled to enough water to keep their forests, streams, lakes, and other property capable of supporting the game and fish they need to prosper.[26] Reservation Indians who are agrarian are entitled to enough water to irrigate all tribal lands reasonably capable of producing crops.[27]

2. *Quantity*. The Supreme Court has repeatedly stated that Indian tribes are entitled to a sufficient quantity of water to fulfill the purpose of the reservation. The Court has also held, however, that a tribe's *Winters* rights do not extend beyond this. The *Winters* doctrine "reserves only that amount of water necessary to fulfill the purpose of the reservation, no more."[28] Moreover, in an Indian fishing rights case, the Supreme Court held that "Indian treaty rights to a natural resource . . . secures so much as, but not more than, is necessary to provide the Indians with a livelihood—that is to say, a moderate living."[29]

Assuming that the Court would apply the "moderate living" standard to this context, the *Winters* doctrine reserves to the tribe and its members enough water to make them economically self-sufficient but not enough to make them rich. Calculating the precise quantity of water that is needed to achieve this purpose is no easy task, as explained later in this chapter.

Can the tribe put water to a different use than Congress originally intended?

Yes. The only restriction on *Winters* rights is that the tribe use no more water than is necessary to satisfy the purpose of the reservation. How it uses this water is for the tribe to decide. As one court recently stated, an Indian tribe "is, of course, entitled to use its water for *any* lawful purpose."[30]

To be meaningful, Indian rights under the *Winters* doctrine must be flexible and accommodate change. If reservations are to serve as permanent homes, Indians must be allowed to shift their water use as their needs change and as technology develops. Water that Congress might have intended for agricultural use a century ago can be used for industrial development today.[31] As the court stated in *Walton*, "permitting Indians to determine how to use reserved water is consistent with the general purpose for the creation of an Indian reservation— providing a homeland for the survival and growth of the Indians and their way of life."[32] Similarly, a tribe can use technological advances that were not foreseen at the time the reservation was created, such as electric pumps to irrigate their lands, provided that the tribe uses no more water than its legal entitlement.[33]

Is water reserved for the tribe's recreational and environmental needs?

Yes. Under the *Winters* doctrine, every reserve of federal land, including an Indian reservation, is entitled to enough water to fulfill the purpose for which it was created. The purpose of every Indian reservation is to serve as a permanent and viable home for the Indians who live there. This purpose cannot be fulfilled unless the reservation offers recreational opportunities and a decent, hospitable environment. Therefore, a tribe with *Winters* rights is entitled to enough water to satisfy its recreational and environmental needs. If a tribe wishes to build a community swimming pool or if tribal members want to water their lawns, they have a right under the *Winters* doctrine to use water for these purposes.

A case that bears upon this question is *United States v. New Mexico*,[34] decided by the Supreme Court in 1978. The issue in that case was whether Congress, when it created the Rio Mimbres National Forest in New Mexico, reserved by implication enough water for recreational and environmental purposes in addition to the obvious purpose of growing timber. The Court reviewed the legislative history of this federal reservation and found that Congress only intended to protect timber when it created the Rio Mimbres. Therefore, the Court said, water needed for recreational and environmental purposes was not reserved under the *Winters* doctrine and had to be obtained under state law as any other user would obtain it, that is, under the doctrine of prior appropriation.

Nothing in *United States v. New Mexico* suggests that an Indian reservation is not entitled to use water for environmental and recreational needs. The purpose of an Indian reservation is different from that of a national forest. The latter fosters the growth of trees while the former fosters the growth of people, and people have environmental and recreational needs. As the Montana Supreme Court recently noted, "the purposes of Indian reserved rights . . . are given broader interpretation in order to further the federal goal of Indian self-sufficiency."[35]

Therefore, water for these uses is included in the *Winters* doctrine, although not every court has agreed with this principle.[36]

Are Indian tribes using the full amount of their *Winters* rights? If not, who is using the remainder?

There may not be a single tribe currently using its entire *Winters* entitlement of water. Money is the main reason. Many tribes have the right to irrigate their entire reservation but few of them can afford the irrigation systems necessary to do so. (This is beginning to change, however.)

When a tribe does not use its entire entitlement to water, this permits junior interests to use what the tribe leaves over. Legally, a tribe can sell its excess water to the highest bidder.[37]

Of course, before a tribe can sell any water, it needs to know *exactly* how much water it is entitled to obtain under the *Winters* doctrine, that is, its rights must be quantified. This means, as indicated earlier, that the purpose of the reservation must be determined, and then experts must calculate how much water is needed to fulfill that purpose. These determinations are time-consuming and expensive.

For example, the Supreme Court has held that an agrarian tribe is entitled to enough water to irrigate all the "practicably irrigable acreage" (PIA) on the reservation.[38] PIA has two components: the land must be of sufficient quality to sustain a crop, and the cost of supplying water to that crop must not be unreasonable. (In other words, a tribe normally would not be allowed to irrigate a desert.) Determining the amount of water agrarian tribes are entitled to use is not an easy task.[39] The same is true for tribes dependent on hunting and fishing: these tribes are entitled to enough water to reasonably maintain these resources but quantifying this precise amount of water, especially given seasonal fluctuations, is very difficult.[40] (Indian reservations that were created for both purposes—growing crops and taking wildlife—are entitled to water for both purposes.)

From the tribe's perspective, there are advantages and disadvantages to quantifying its water rights. The main advantage is that, once its rights are quantified, the tribe can prevent junior interests from stealing the tribe's water, and the tribe can begin to charge junior interests for using it. However, as explained earlier, tribes are permitted to increase their water usage if a change in circumstances requires it. Therefore, the disadvantage of quantification is that the tribe will be locked into a fixed entitlement that later may be inadequate. Moreover, quantification is expensive.

Likewise, there are advantages and disadvantages from the junior interests' perspective. The main advantage is that quantification removes the cloud over the tribe's water rights. This allows junior interests to plan for the future. Without quantification, the tribe's rights remain open-ended because no one knows what the tribe's future needs will be. The fact that tribes have open-ended rights has led to confusion and anger. As one court recently stated: "We recognize that open-ended water rights are a growing source of conflict and uncertainty in the West. Until their extent is determined, state-created water rights cannot be relied upon by property owners."[41]

The disadvantage, though, is that junior interests may suddenly learn, as they did in one Wyoming case, that the tribe's entitlement is so large that junior interests now must purchase water they had been taking for free, and some farms and ranches may be unable to meet the cost. Most observers, however, including the National Water Commission, recommend that the United States assist tribes in quantifying their water rights so as to eliminate the uncertainty that is now plaguing western development.[42]

Given the enormous expense of litigating water rights cases (the Wyoming lawsuit cost the litigants a total of fourteen million dollars) and the bitterness that usually results from them, a better solution to litigation is negotiation and mutual agreement. A number of tribes and their neighbors are now engaged in this process.

Under what circumstances may a tribe regulate the use of water by a non-Indian?

In the *Winters* case, a tribe restricted a non-Indian's water use off the reservation. In *Walton*, a tribe restricted a non-Indian's water use on the reservation. Thus non-Indians, both on and off the reservation, may not interfere with a tribe's senior right to reserved water. Tribes, however, cannot regulate the use of "excess" water by non-Indians on their own land, that is, water that is not needed to satisfy the tribe's *Winters* rights.[43]

Under what circumstances may state courts adjudicate Indian water rights?

Water reserved for Indians under the *Winters* doctrine is governed exclusively by federal law because Indian water rights are federal rights.[44] Unless Congress gives its consent, these federal rights cannot be adjudicated in a state court because the United States—which owns all federal water rights—cannot be sued in state court without the consent of Congress.

This consent was given in 1952 when Congress passed the McCarran Amendment.[45] This law authorizes state courts to adjudicate all federally secured rights to water, including Indian *Winters* rights, in a river or other water source that traverses the state. In fact, as the Supreme Court ruled in 1983, the McCarran Amendment allows state courts to adjudicate Indian water rights even if the state's constitution declares that the state lacks this power, provided the state's procedures for resolving these controversies are adequate to protect a tribe's *Winters* rights.[46]

When a state court adjudicates federal water rights under the McCarran Amendment, it must apply federal and not state law. That is, the court must apply the *Winters* doctrine.[47] The McCarran Amendment did nothing to change the nature of federal water rights; it only authorized state courts to adjudicate them.[48] Moreover, the Amendment did not remove the right of federal courts to hear these same claims.[49] It also did not remove the responsibility of the United States to defend the tribe's water rights in state court, or affect the tribe's right to appeal a state court decision to the U.S. Supreme Court.[50]

State courts are known for their hostility to Indian water rights, while federal courts are more protective of them. Indians and non-Indians both know this. For this reason, Indians usually file their water claims in federal court, while non-Indians file in state court. A water rights claim filed in state court can be removed to federal court in certain situations.[51] However, these cases tend to be so enormous in scope that federal courts try to avoid them. In fact, even when Indians win the race to the courthouse and file their suit in federal court, the court is likely to dismiss the case if non-Indians soon thereafter file a similar suit in state court, provided that the state court has the ability to determine each party's rights to this water.[52]

In short, the McCarran Amendment does more than consent to state court adjudication of federal water rights. It also places these rights in a forum that has a history of ignoring them.

Are Indian water rights protected by the Just Compensation Clause?

As explained in chapter 5, Indians and tribes are entitled to compensation whenever the federal government eliminates or reduces their vested property rights. This rule applies to Indian *Winters* rights, which are vested rights.[53]

May Indians transfer their *Winters* rights to non-Indians?

Maybe. In 1887 Congress passed the General Allotment Act,[54] under which many Indians received a deed from the federal government to a parcel (an "allotment") of reservation land. Once the deed was issued, the Indian allottee became the owner of the allotment and could sell it at any time, even to a non-Indian. Since 1887 many allottees have sold their land to non-Indians. In a recent case[55] one of these non-Indians claimed to have *Winters* rights. He argued that these rights attached to the land when the reservation was created, were transferred to the Indian allottee with the deed, and stayed with the allotment when the Indian sold it. The tribe argued, on the other hand, that these *Winters* rights were automatically lost either when the deed was issued or when the Indian sold the land to the non-Indian.

The court ruled primarily in favor of the non-Indian. It held that each Indian who obtains a deed to reservation land acquires a share in the reservation's *Winters* rights.[56] Moreover, these water rights can be transferred to subsequent purchasers of the land, whoever they may be. This ruling was necessary, the court said, so that the Indian allottee could obtain the economic benefit of his or her allotment. In other words, an allotment obviously is worth more with *Winters* rights than without them, and the allottee should receive these rights and be able to sell them so as to enjoy the full benefit of the allotment.

However, the court went on to hold that a non-Indian purchaser does not acquire the Indian allottee's full *Winters* rights. The allottee, like the tribe, is entitled to enough water to irrigate all the practicably irrigable acreage, that is, sufficient water to meet *future* needs. A purchaser, on the other hand, is entitled only to the water *then* being used by the allottee, plus any additional water that the purchaser puts to use "with reasonable diligence after the passage of title."[57] Thus, a purchaser's right to additional water (beyond what the allottee was using) is forfeited if it is not put to use fairly quickly. For the purchaser, it is "use it or lose it."[58] As for all subsequent purchasers or heirs of the first purchaser, they are limited to the amount of water diligently appropriated and continuously used by the initial purchaser.[59]

The U.S. Supreme Court has not yet ruled on this issue. Someday it will need to determine whether allottees receive any *Winters* rights when they obtain deeds to their lands, and if so, whether these rights can be transferred to non-Indians.[60]

Does the federal government have an obligation to protect Indian water rights?

Yes. As explained in chapter 3, the federal government has a trust responsibility to protect Indian property and interests. Treaties with Indian tribes, in which Indians exchanged their land for federal promises, impose an obligation on the federal government to keep its word. Nearly every tribe was promised a reservation where it could live in peace and prosperity. Water is essential to meeting this goal. Therefore, the federal government has an obligation, recognized in the *Winters* doctrine itself, of assuring adequate supplies of water to Indian reservations.[61]

The federal government, rather than the tribe, holds legal title to a tribe's *Winters* rights. For this reason, a tribe cannot prevent the federal government from representing the tribe's interests in court, even if the tribe distrusts the government's motives or abilities.[62] However, the government has an affirmative duty to protect and defend these rights and to manage them in the tribe's best interests.[63] Thus the government is responsible for what happens to these rights and can be sued for mismanaging them.[64]

Has the federal government made a good-faith effort to protect Indian water rights?

Not always. As the National Water Commission stated in its 1973 report to Congress:[65]

During most of this 50-year period [following the Supreme Court's decision in the *Winters* case], the United States was pursuing the policy of encouraging the settlement of the West and the creation of family-sized farms on its arid lands. In retrospect, it can be seen that this policy was pursued with little or no regard for Indian water rights and the *Winters* doctrine. With the encouragement, or at least the cooperation, of the Secretary of the Interior—the very office entrusted with protection of all Indian rights—many large irrigation projects were constructed on streams that flowed through or bordered Indian reservations, sometimes above and more often below the reservations. With few exceptions, the projects were planned and built by the federal government without any attempt to define, let alone protect, prior rights that Indian tribes might have had in the waters used for the projects. . . . In the history of the United States Government's treatment of Indian tribes, its failure to protect Indian water rights for use on the reservations it set aside for them is one of the sorrier chapters.

The federal government often has conflicts of interest when it comes to water rights. It is obligated on one hand to protect tribal rights. Yet it also has a continuing obligation to maintain national parks and national forests, promote land development, and undertake reclamation projects. Frequently, government agencies, when faced with scarce water resources, ignore Indian water rights in favor of other interests. As President Nixon admitted in 1970, "there is considerable evidence that the Indians are the losers when such situations arise."[66]

The Supreme Court has held that, simply because the federal government may have two conflicting responsibilities in a given situation, this does not mean that tribal rights have been violated. In *Nevada v. U.S.* (1983),[67] the Court held that the government's obligation to protect Indian water rights is equal to its obligation to protect other federal water interests, and tribes cannot expect in those situations to receive sole or even paramount consideration.[68] When these conflicts arise, it is in the tribe's best interests to hire its own attorney and intervene in any pending lawsuit. This is because a judgment against the United States, as trustee for the tribe's water rights, is binding upon the tribe as well.[69] In short, traditional rules of ethics and fairness do not govern the situation in which federal agents have two conflicting responsibilities, and tribes must defend their own interests as forcefully as they can.[70]

Indians and tribes are not without some protection, however. Chapter 18 describes the types of lawsuits that can be brought to enforce Indian rights, including Indian water rights. If federal officials ignore their responsibilities, Indians must take appropriate legal action to protect their rightful entitlement to water, including suits against the federal government for money damages to compensate for past injuries[71] and suits seeking to prevent further violations of the tribe's water rights.[72]

NOTES

1. For a further discussion of the water shortage in the West, see National Water Commission, *Water Policies for the Future—Final Report to the President and to the Congress of the United States* pp. 8–9 (Washington, DC: Government Printing Office, 1973); *Waters and Water Rights* (R. Clark ed. 1976).
2. 207 U.S. 564 (1908).
3. 373 U.S. 546 (1963).
4. *Id.* at 600.
5. *Id.*
6. 426 U.S. 128 (1976).
7. *Winters v. U.S.*, 207 U.S. 564 (1908); *U.S. v. New Mexico*, 438 U.S. 696, 698 (1978).
8. *New Mexico*, note 7 above, 438 U.S. at 700; *Cappaert v. U.S.*, 426 U.S. 128, 139 (1976).
9. *Winters*, note 7 above; *Arizona v. California*, 373 U.S. 546, 600 (1963). *See also* cases cited in note 8 above.
10. *Arizona v. California*, note 9 above, 373 U.S. at 598.
11. *Id. See also Alaska Pacific Fisheries v. U.S.*, 248 U.S. 78 (1918); *U.S. v. Winans*, 198 U.S. 371, 381 (1905). For a further discussion of the *Winters* doctrine, see Pelcyger, *The Winters Doctrine and the Greening of Reservations*, 4 J. Contemp. L. 19 (1977); Note, *Indian Reserve Water Rights: The Winters of our Discontent*, 88 Yale L.J. 1689 (1979).
12. This subject is discussed in ch. 5, sec. A.
13. *Winters*, note 7 above, 207 U.S. at 577; *Cappaert*, note 8 above, 426 U.S. at 138.

14. For additional information on the doctrine of prior appropriation, see W. Hutchins, *Water Rights in Nineteen Western States* ch. 6 (1972).

15. *Cappaert,* note 8 above, 426 U.S. at 145. *See also Colorado River Water Conservation Dist. v. U.S.,* 424 U.S. 800 (1976).

16. *Cappaert,* note 8 above, 426 U.S. at 139; *Winters,* note 7 above.

17. *Arizona v. California,* note 9 above, 373 U.S. at 600; *Cappaert,* note 8 above.

18. *See Arizona v. California,* note 9 above, 373 U.S. at 600; *U.S. v. Adair,* 723 F.2d 1394, 1412–15 (9th Cir. 1983), *cert. denied,* 467 U.S. 1252 (1984). *See also* R. Collins, *Indian Allotment Water Rights,* 20 Land & Water L. Rev. 421, 426 n.20 (1985).

19. *Joint Board of Control of the Flathead, Mission, and Jocko Irrigation Dist. v. U.S.,* 832 F.2d 1127, 1132 (9th Cir. 1987), *cert. denied,* 486 U.S. 1007 (1988); *Cappaert,* note 8 above, 426 U.S. at 138–39; *Arizona v. California,* note 9 above, 373 U.S. at 597.

20. *Kittitas Reclamation Dist. v. Sunnyside Valley Irrigation Dist.,* 763 F.2d 1032 (9th Cir.), *cert. denied,* 474 U.S. 1032 (1985).

21. *Colville Confederated Tribes v. Walton,* 752 F.2d 397, 405 (9th Cir. 1985), *cert. denied,* 475 U.S. 1010 (1986).

22. *Cappaert,* note 8 above, 426 U.S. at 142–43; *New Mexico v. Aamodt,* 618 F. Supp. 993, 1010 (D.N.M. 1985). *But see In re General Adjudication of All Rights to the Use of Water in the Big Horn River System,* 753 P.2d 76 (Wyo. 1988), *aff'd by equally divided Court,* 109 S.Ct. 2994 (1989) (where ground and surface water are not interrelated, *Winters* rights do not extend to ground water).

23. *The Kansas Indians,* 72 U.S. 737, 752–54 (1867); *Winans,* note 11 above, 198 U.S. at 381; *Arizona v. California,* note 9 above, 373 U.S. at 599–600.

24. *Arizona v. California,* note 9 above; *Colville Confederated Tribes v. Walton,* 647 F.2d 42 (9th Cir. 1981), *cert. denied,* 454 U.S. 1092 (1981).

25. 647 F.2d 42 (9th Cir. 1981), *cert. denied,* 454 U.S. 1092 (1981).

26. *Carson-Truckee Conservancy Dist. v. Clark,* 741 F.2d 257 (9th Cir. 1984); *U.S. v. Adair,* note 18 above; *Pyramid Lake Paiute Tribe v. Morton,* 354 F. Supp. 252 (D.D.C. 1972).

27. *Arizona v. California,* note 9 above; *U.S. v. Anderson,* 736 F.2d 1358 (9th Cir. 1984). *But see General Adjudication,* note 22 above (where tribe historically is agrarian, reservation water was not reserved for new or secondary purposes).

28. *Cappaert,* note 8 above, 426 U.S. at 141.

29. *Washington v. Fishing Vessel Ass'n,* 443 U.S. 658, 686 (1979).

30. *U.S. v. Anderson,* note 27 above, 736 F.2d at 1365.

31. *Winans,* note 11 above, 198 U.S. at 381; *Alaska Pacific Fisheries,* note 11 above. *Cf. Federal Power Comm'n v. Oregon,* 349 U.S. 435, 444 (1960); *Arizona v. California,* 439 U.S. 419, 422 (1979) (supplemental decree).

32. *Walton,* note 24 above, 647 F.2d at 49. *See also Walton,* note 21 above, 752 F.2d at 405.

33. *Arizona v. California,* note 9 above, 373 U.S. at 600–601. This is generally true under both the *Winters* doctrine and the doctrine of prior appropriation. *See Farmers Highline Canal & Reservoir Co. v. City of Golden,* 272 P.2d 629 (Colo. 1954); *Walton,* note 24 above.

34. 438 U.S. 696 (1978).

35. *Montana ex rel. Greeley v. Confederated Salish & Kootenai Tribes,* 712 P.2d 754, 767 (Mont. 1985). *See also U.S. v. Finch,* 548 F.2d 822, 832 (9th Cir. 1976), *rev'd on other grounds,* 433 U.S. 676 (1977); *Pyramid Lake,* note 26 above.

36. *See General Adjudication,* note 22 above.

37. *Walton,* note 21 above, 752 F.2d at 404.

38. *See* note 6 above and accompanying text.

39. *See, e.g., General Adjudication,* note 22 above; *Walton,* note 21 above.

40. *U.S. v. Adair,* note 18 above, 723 F.2d 1411.

41. *Walton,* note 24 above, 647 F.2d at 48.

42. For a further discussion of this subject see Getches and Wilkinson, *Federal Indian Law* pp. 651–52, 701–5 (1986).

43. *U.S. v. Anderson,* note 27 above, 736 F.2d at 1365. *Cf., Montana v. U.S.,* 450 U.S. 544 (1981).

44. *Colorado River Water Conservation Dist. v. U.S.,* 424 U.S. 800, 813 (1976).

45. 43 U.S.C. Sec. 666(a).

46. *Arizona v. San Carlos Apache Tribe,* 463 U.S. 545, 563–64 (1983).

47. *San Carlos,* note 46 above, 463 U.S. at 571.

48. *Colorado River,* note 44 above, 424 U.S. at 820.

49. 28 U.S.C. Secs. 1345, 1361. *See Cappaert,* note 8 above, 426 U.S. at 145.

50. *San Carlos,* note 46 above, at 551, 571 (1983).

51. The removal of cases from state court to federal court is governed by 28 U.S.C. Sec. 1441(a). For a discussion of how this statute applies to water claims, *see Colorado River,* note 44 above and *San Carlos,* note 46 above.

52. *See* cases cited in note 51 above and *U.S. v. Bluewater-Toltec Irrigation Dist.,* 580 F. Supp. 1434 (D.N.M. 1984).

53. *See* ch. 5, notes 13–16 and accompanying text, and *Gila River Pima-Maricopa Indian Community v. U.S.,* 684 F.2d 852 (Ct. Cl. 1982).

54. 25 U.S.C. Secs. 331 *et seq.* The General Allotment Act is discussed in ch. 1, sec. D, and ch. 7, sec. B.

55. *Walton*, note 24 above. *See also Skeem v. U.S.*, 273 F.2d 93 (9th Cir. 1921) (*Winters* rights can be leased).

56. At least one other court has ruled similarly. *See General Adjudication*, note 22 above (Indian allottees who obtain deeds to their allotment acquire *Winters* rights along with them).

57. *Walton*, note 24 above, 647 F.2d at 51.

58. *U.S. v. Anderson*, note 27 above, 736 F.2d at 1362.

59. *Walton*, note 24 above, 647 F.2d at 51; *Walton*, note 21 above, 762 F.2d at 422.

60. For a discussion of these various arguments see Getches, note 42 above, at 676–84.

61. *Pyramid Lake*, note 26 above; *Adair*, note 18 above; *Lane v. Pueblo of Santa Rosa*, 249 U.S. 110 (1919).

62. *See, e.g., U.S. v. White Mountain Apache Tribe*, note 62 above.

63. *White Mountain Apache Tribe v. Hodel*, 784 F.2d 921 (9th Cir. 1986), *cert. denied*, 479 U.S. 1006 (1987); *U.S. v. White Mountain Apache Tribe*, 784 F.2d 917 (9th Cir. 1986).

64. *Pyramid Lake*, note 26 above; *Gila River*, note 53 above; *White Mountain Apache Tribe v. U.S.*, 11 Cl. Ct. 614 (1987).

65. *Final Report*, note 1 above, pp. 474–75.

66. H.R. Doc. No. 363, 91st Cong., 2d Sess., 10, *reprinted in* 116 Cong. Rec. 23258, 23261 (1970).

67. 463 U.S. 110 (1983).

68. *Id.* at 128. *See also Arizona v. California*, 460 U.S. 605, 627–28 (1983).

69. *San Carlos*, note 46 above, 463 U.S. at 566 n.17; *White Mountain Apache Tribe v. Hodel*, note 63 above, 784 F.2d at 925.

70. *See, e.g., Pyramid Lake*, note 26 above; *U.S. v. Alpine Land & Reservoir Co.*, 887 F.2d 207 (9th Cir. 1989)

71. *See, e.g.*, cases cited in note 64 above and *Northern Paiute Nation v. U.S.*, 9 Cl. Ct. 639 (1986). *See generally U.S. v. Mitchell*, 463 U.S. 206 (1983).

72. *See* cases cited in note 70 above and *U.S. v. Winnebago Tribe*, 542 F.2d 1002 (8th Cir. 1976).

XIII

Civil Rights of Indians

What is a civil right?
A civil right creates a standard of equality or justice that is intended to protect a person against governmental abuse. In democratic countries, citizens decide what powers to give the government and what civil rights to keep for themselves.

Do Indians have the same civil rights as other citizens?
Yes. Indians are citizens of the United States[1] and of the states in which they live.[2] Indians have the same civil rights with respect to the federal and state governments as other citizens.[3] The most important civil rights are contained in the first ten amendments to the Constitution: the Bill of Rights. These rights include freedom of speech, freedom of the press, and freedom of religion.[4]

This chapter does not seek to explain the countless civil rights that all citizens share. Rather it focuses on those civil rights that are most important to Indians because of their culture, religion, or race. These rights have special meaning for Indians in their dealings with state and federal governments. (Chapter 14 discusses civil rights with respect to tribal governments.)

A. FREEDOM OF RELIGION

Which provisions of the Constitution guarantee freedom of religion?
The U.S. Constitution contains two religion clauses, and both are found in the First Amendment: the Establishment Clause and the Free Exercise Clause. They read as follows: "Congress shall make no law respecting an establishment of religion or prohibiting the free exercise thereof."

Many Europeans who first settled in what is now the United States came here to find freedom of worship. They were driven from their homelands because of their religious beliefs. In order to ensure religious freedom in this country, these clauses were placed in the Constitution.[5]

What do the Establishment and Free Exercise Clauses guarantee?

The Establishment Clause assures the separation of church and state. The federal and state governments can neither promote nor inhibit religion. Instead, they must remain entirely neutral in religious matters. The Establishment Clause guarantees that no agency of government will meddle in religious affairs or engage in a religious activity.[6]

The Free Exercise Clause guarantees individual freedom of worship, the right to believe and preach whatever religion one desires. Religion in this country is a matter of private choice. The government may not regulate religious beliefs or pressure citizens to believe in, or to oppose, any particular religion or form of worship.[7] Thus the religion clauses guarantee that each of us can believe in anything we want (the Free Exercise Clause) and that no group, including the majority, can use the government to promote or hinder religion (the Establishment Clause).

How have these clauses protected Indian worship?

Religion plays a major role in Indian culture. Therefore, the Constitution's guarantee of religious freedom and the separation of church and state have great significance for Indians. Until recently, the Free Exercise Clause was particularly important. Courts had interpreted this clause as forbidding the government to take any action that harmed religion unless the action could be justified by a "compelling state interest." For example, courts held that Indians who used peyote as a religious sacrament were exempt from state drug laws,[8] Indian prisoners who wore long hair for religious reasons were exempt from prison regulations mandating short hair,[9] and Indians could hunt out-of-season if they needed freshly killed meat for a religious ceremony.[10] In each case, the state's interest in prohibiting these practices was not sufficiently compelling to override the Indian's religious interests.

The Supreme Court, however, drastically narrowed the scope of the Free Exercise Clause in recent decisions. The clause continues to protect religious *belief*. However, it is now clear that religious *practice* can be restricted (or even destroyed) by a "neutral" and uniformly applied law. To illustrate, the Court held in *Bowen v. Roy* (1986)[11] that an Indian who, for religious reasons, refuses to obtain a social security number, can be denied social security benefits under a law that requires all applicants to possess such a number as a condition of eligibility. Similarly, Indians are free to believe that certain land is sacred. However, as the Supreme Court held in *Lyng v. Northwest Indian Cemetery Protective Association* (1988),[12] the federal government can use its land in any reasonable manner, even if this use "could have devastating effects on traditional Indian religious practices."[13] (In that case, the Court permitted the federal government to build a road through sacred Indian lands despite the fact that an alternative route was readily available.) In *Employment Division v. Smith* (1990),[14] the Supreme Court held that employees fired for using peyote during an off-duty religious ceremony can be denied state unemployment compensation benefits. The Court applied the rule that "generally applicable, religion-neutral laws that have the effect of burdening a particular religious practice" need only be reasonable to be valid.[15]

The Free Exercise Clause protects us against government compulsion. That is, it protects us from being forced to believe a certain way, either directly (by punishing us for our beliefs) or indirectly (by giving special benefits to other religions). However, under these new decisions, the clause does not protect us from government acts that are neutral and otherwise reasonable but which have an incidental harmful effect on our religious practices. Thus, stated bluntly, the government may not punish our beliefs, but it can prevent us from practicing them. Courts have allowed the federal government to construct dams that flooded sacred Indian lands,[16] prevent an Indian group from holding a religious ceremony on federal land,[17] construct a road through an Indian burial site located on federal property,[18] and permit a ski area to be built on federal land sacred to an Indian tribe.[19]

The Supreme Court exhibited a similar disregard for religious freedom in *O'Lone v. Estate of Shabazz* (1987).[20] In *O'Lone*, the Court held that prison regulations are valid if they are reasonably related to legitimate prison interests, even when the regulations destroy a religious practice. This ruling has serious implications for Indian prisoners who may wish to en-

gage in religious practices that require special exceptions, such
as pipe ceremonies, sweat lodges, and wearing long hair.
O'Lone sets such a low standard that prison officials can now
get away with banning almost any religious practice. Under
this new ruling, for example, some courts have upheld prison
regulations banning long hair based on the rather ridiculous
claim by prison officials that weapons can be concealed there.[21]
However, a few courts even after *O'Lone* have held that prisoners have a First Amendment right to engage in religious activities unless the prison has actual proof, and not just mere specu-
lation, that they pose a danger.[22]

In theory, these recent Supreme Court decisions threaten
all religions equally. However, the government is more likely
to enact a "neutral" law that in reality has a greater impact on
minority religions than on majority religions. For instance, a
prison is more likely to ban religious ceremonies on Mondays
through Saturdays—arguably, a neutral regulation—than ban
religious ceremonies on Sundays. Therefore religious minorit-
ies are justifiably concerned about these recent Supreme Court
decisions.

What is the American Indian Religious Freedom Act?

During the 1970s Congress investigated allegations that Indian religious practices were being severely disrupted, often
unintentionally, by state and federal laws and by the actions of
government officials. The House of Representatives issued a
report that substantiated these claims.[23] The report found that
Indians were often prevented from visiting their sacred sites,
denied the use of religious sacraments, and kept from performing worship services in their traditional manner. The report recommended that Congress take measures to protect
Indian religious practices from unnecessary government interference.

In 1978 Congress passed a joint resolution to this effect, the
American Indian Religious Freedom Act (AIRFA).[24] The act,
as with all joint resolutions, contains no penalty provision that
can be enforced against violators. However, AIRFA declares a
policy that Congress has pledged itself to pursue.

[H]enceforth it shall be the policy of the United States to
protect and preserve for Native Americans their inherent

right of freedom of belief, expression, and exercise of traditional religions of the American Indian . . . including but not limited to access to sites, use and possession of sacred objects, and the freedom to worship through ceremonials and traditional rites.

Sadly, AIRFA has not been very effective due to the absence of a penalty provision. In *Lyng*, discussed earlier, the Supreme Court stated that AIRFA has "no teeth in it."[25] Other courts have said that the act only requires public officials to "consider" Indian interests and not necessarily act in accordance with them.[26]

Given recent court decisions narrowing the Free Exercise Clause and AIRFA, Indians must now look to state constitutions and laws or lobby for the passage of new laws to protect their religious practices. The Supreme Court has recognized that a legislature can create an exemption to protect a religious practice.[27] Several states[28] and the federal government,[29] for example, provide special protection for sacramental peyote use. Now that the Supreme Court has stripped the Free Exercise Clause of much of its meaning, minority religions must seek legislative protection for their religious practices.

B. INDIANS AS STATE CITIZENS

What rights do Indians have as state citizens?

Indians are entitled to the same benefits and privileges other state citizens receive.[30] They are guaranteed this equality by the Equal Protection Clause of the Fourteenth Amendment, which reads: "No State shall . . . deny to any person within its jurisdiction the equal protection of the laws." The Equal Protection Clause, among other things, prohibits state officials from discriminating against any person on account of race, color, creed, or religion. Any difference in treatment based on one of these factors is unconstitutional unless the state has a compelling interest that necessitates this discrimination.[31]

Do state officials discriminate against Indians?

Yes, frequently. For example, Indians have had to go to court to secure their right to hold state public office,[32] attend public schools,[33] receive state public assistance,[34] serve as jurors in state court,[35] obtain state game licenses,[36] obtain state business licenses,[37] appear as witnesses in state courts,[38] and receive the same municipal services that other citizens receive.[39] Just recently the U.S. Indian Health Service accused Arizona of having a "long-standing history" of denying equal health care to Native Americans.[40] State officials have attempted to justify these inequities by pointing to the fact that Indians have special rights under federal treaties and laws[41] and do not pay certain state taxes.[42] These officials claim that Indians should not have all the benefits of state citizenship because they do not share all of the burdens.[43]

True, Indians have special rights and receive special benefits from the federal government. But so do many other groups, and yet no one denies them the full rights of citizenship. Moreover, it is particularly unfair to label Indians as being "special citizens" when they are the most impoverished and disadvantaged group in our society.[44] As one writer has stated on this subject:

> Any American who has been on an Indian reservation knows very well that Indians are not "equal." The highest infant mortality rate and lowest life expectancy in the country reflect massive unmet health needs. Family income is by far the lowest in the nation. Housing and education deficits are greater than in any other sector of our society.
>
> The fact that Indians have some special treaty rights is perfectly consistent with our form of government. The essence of American democracy is to provide "special benefits." We have special benefits for veterans, the elderly, the infirm, elementary and secondary school students, small businessmen, laborers, non-English speaking minorities and uncounted others. In our system, equality is achieved by a melding of many special programs which are directed toward special groups.
>
> Thus Indian treaty rights, which were paid for so dearly by the tribes, cannot fairly be isolated. It is ironic, and brutally so, that there are those who would claim that the Indians are "favored" or "more than equal."[45]

Many state officials, of course, do not discriminate against Indians. Some even discriminate in their favor. In Santa Fe, New Mexico, for example, Indian merchants have been given a monopoly on selling handcrafted jewelry on the grounds of the State Museum over the objections of non-Indian merchants.[46] Yet recent studies show that discrimination against Indians persists on many levels. The U.S. Commission on Civil Rights concluded, after an investigation in South Dakota, that Indians as a group receive longer criminal sentences from state judges than whites who commit the same crime.[47] Lawsuits indicate that Indian communities, even off the reservation, do not receive the same police and fire protection, road maintenance, and street lighting that the state provides to non-Indians.[48] A lawsuit filed in New Mexico indicates that some off-reservation hospitals refuse to treat Indians even in emergencies.[49]

Indians often discriminate against non-Indians, too. Hopefully, Indians and non-Indians will make a determined effort to eliminate these barriers to true equality.

C. THE RIGHT TO VOTE

Is the right to vote protected by federal law?

Yes. The right to vote is the most basic civil right in a democracy because it is the primary means by which all other rights can be safeguarded.[50]

The right to vote is protected by federal law. The Fifteenth Amendment to the Constitution guarantees that no citizen shall be denied the right to vote in a state or federal election on account of race. In addition, the Voting Rights Act of 1965 protects all persons from having to pay a fee or pass a literacy test in order to vote.[51] The 1975 amendments to this act prohibit discrimination against persons whose primary language is other than English.[52] Indians are expressly recognized as a language minority group under these amendments.[53]

Have Indians been subjected to discrimination in exercising their voting rights?

Unfortunately, Indians have been forced to go to court many

times to protect their right to vote. However, it is now firmly established that Indians have the same right to vote that all other citizens have.[54] Indians have the right to cast a ballot for all elected officials who administer over them.[55]

Indians cannot be denied the right to vote simply because they are exempt from paying certain state taxes.[56] Moreover, the election districts in which they vote must be apportioned under the constitutional principle of "one person, one vote."[57] Efforts by local governments to dilute the voting power of Indians violate federal law. For example, if a school board contains five members, and Indians have a statistical chance of electing an Indian to the board because they represent more than one-fifth the population, creating an at-large voting scheme that prevents this from occurring violates the Voting Rights Act.[58] In addition, the 1975 amendments to the act require that, where necessary to facilitate voting rights, state election officials must place voter registration offices in Indian communities, distribute voting information in the local Indian language, and recruit bilingual election officials to serve in Indian districts.[59]

In many areas of the country, Indians comprise a large portion of the population, and their vote can determine the outcome of an election. Unfortunately, many Indians fail to vote. As a result, Indians have much less political influence than they could have. Not only are they unable to determine who gets elected, but elected officials tend to ignore Indian concerns. Most states make no special effort to register Indian voters and refuse to distribute voting information in the Indian languages, thereby perpetrating the disenfranchisement of Indians. Indians could obtain a significant amount of power and influence if more Indians voted.

D. ELIGIBILITY FOR PUBLIC OFFICE

Do Indians have the right to hold public office?

Definitely. Prior to 1924, when Congress conferred citizenship on Indians, some federal and state statutes prohibited Indians from holding particular public offices. Today such statutes would violate the Fourteenth and Fifteenth Amendments to the Constitution. Indians cannot be denied public office on account of race, their exemption from paying certain taxes, or residence on an Indian reservation.[60] Indians have the same right as non-Indians to hold public office.[61]

E. PROTECTION AGAINST PRIVATE DISCRIMINATION

Do Indians have any protection against discrimination by private parties?

Sometimes. Congress has passed a number of civil rights laws that prohibit various forms of discrimination by one individual or group against another. Congress enacted these laws because many citizens were being denied basic necessities of life, such as housing and employment, on account of racial or other discrimination. The Equal Protection Clause (and all other civil rights conferred by the Constitution) only apply to the actions of public officials. They offer no protection against purely private discrimination.[62]

The civil rights laws passed by Congress protect all citizens, Indians and non-Indians alike. Therefore, if an Indian suffers discrimination on account of race, color, creed, religion, sex, or national origin with respect to housing,[63] employment,[64] commercial transactions,[65] or access to public accommodations,[66] in most instances he or she can file suit in federal court to halt this discrimination and recover damages for any injury suffered as a result of it.

F. PROTECTION OF BURIAL REMAINS

What is the Native American Graves Protection and Repatriation Act?

An investigation conducted during the late 1980s revealed that hundred of thousands of Indian human remains were held by federal agencies. Indeed it appeared that the federal government "had a firm policy which encouraged the acquisition and retention" of these remains.[67] After a concerted effort by Indians and Indian organizations, Congress in November 1990 enacted the Native American Graves Protection and Repatriation Act (NAGPRA).[68]

This law has been described as "the single more important

piece of human rights legislation for Indian people which has been enacted by Congress since passage of the American Indian Religious Freedom Act of 1973."[69] The NAGPRA requires four things. First, federal agencies and private museums receiving federal funds must inventory their collections of Indian human remains and associated funerary objects. The tribe of origin, if known, must then be notified and these objects must be returned if requested by the tribe. Second, the law makes clear that Indian tribes are the owners of human remains and cultural items excavated or discovered on federal or tribal land. Third, the NAGPRA prohibits the trafficking in Indian human remains and cultural items obtained in violation of the act. Finally, the legislation requires that federal agencies and private museums receiving federal funds must make an itemized list of their other Indian funerary or sacred objects and, if a tribe can prove a right of possession, the object must be returned to the tribe upon request.

NOTES

1. In 1924 Congress passed a law, 8 U.S.C. Sec. 1401(a)(2), that extended United States citizenship to all Indians born in the United States, although some Indians became citizens earlier in treaties with the United States.
2. The Fourteenth Amendment to the Constitution provides that all persons "born or naturalized in the United States . . . are citizens of the United States and of the State wherein they reside." This applies to Indians. *See Goodluck v. Apache County*, 417 F. Supp. 13 (D. Ariz. 1975), *aff'd sub nom. Apache County v. U.S.*, 429 U.S. 876 (1976).
3. This subject is discussed in sections B, C, and D of this chapter.
4. These particular rights are contained in the First Amendment, which states: "Congress shall make no law respecting an establishment of religion or prohibiting the free exercise thereof; or abridging the freedom of speech, or of the press, or the right of the people to petition the government for redress of grievances."
5. *See Engel v. Vitale*, 370 U.S. 421 (1962); *Abington School District v. Schempp*, 374 U.S. 203 (1963).
6. *See* cases cited in note 5 above. *See also Epperson v. Arkansas*, 393 U.S. 97 (1968); *McCollum v. Board of Education*, 333 U.S. 203 (1948).
7. *Wisconsin v. Yoder*, 406 U.S. 205 (1972); *Thomas v. Review Board*, 450 U.S. 707 (1981).

8. *People v. Woody,* 394 P.2d 813 (Cal. 1964); *State v. Whittingham,* 504 P.2d 950 (Ariz. App. 1973); *Whitehorn v. Oklahoma,* 561 P.2d 539 (Okla. Cr. 1977). *See also* 50 C.F.R. Sec. 22.22 (1989), permitting Indians to possess eagle feathers for religious purposes.

9. *See Teterud v. Burns,* 522 F.2d 357 (8th Cir. 1975). *But see New Rider v. Board of Education,* 480 F.2d 693 (10th Cir.), *cert. denied,* 414 U.S. 1097 (1973) (a public school can require Indian students to have short hair).

10. *Frank v. Alaska,* 604 P.2d 1068 (Alaska 1979).

11. 476 U.S. 693 (1986).

12. 485 U.S. 439 (1988).

13. *Id.* at 451.

14. 110 S.Ct. 1595 (1990).

15. *Id.* at 1604.

16. *Sequoyah v. TVA,* 620 F.2d 1159 (6th Cir.), *cert. denied,* 449 U.S. 953 (1980); *Badoni v. Higginson,* 638 F.2d 172 (10th Cir. 1980), *cert. denied,* 452 U.S. 954 (1981).

17. *U.S. v. Means,* 858 F.2d 404 (8th Cir. 1988).

18. *Lyng v. Northwest Indian Cemetery Protective Ass'n,* 485 U.S. 439 (1988); *Fools Crow v. Gullet,* 706 F.2d 856 (8th Cir.), *cert. denied,* 464 U.S. 997 (1983).

19. *Wilson v. Block,* 708 F.2d 735 (D.C. Cir. 1983), *cert. denied,* 464 U.S. 956 (1983).

20. 482 U.S. 342 (1987).

21. *See, e.g., Cole v. Flick,* 758 F.2d 124 (3d Cir. 1985), *cert. denied,* 474 U.S. 921 (1985); *Pollack v. Marshall,* 845 F.2d 656 (6th Cir.), *cert. denied,* 488 U.S. 897 (1988); and *Iron Eyes v. Henry,* 907 F.2d 810 (8th Cir. 1990) (upholding ban on long hair). *See also Allen v. Toombs,* 827 F.2d 563 (9th Cir. 1987) (ban on sweat lodge); *Standing Deer v. Carlson,* 831 F.2d 1525 (9th Cir. 1987) (ban on headgear).

22. *Swift v. Lewis,* 901 F.2d 730 (9th Cir. 1990) (prison ban on long hair must be supported by proof of disruption); *SapaNajin v. Gunter,* 857 F.2d 463 (8th Cir. 1988) (inmate cannot be restricted to one spiritual leader); *Whitney v. Brown,* 882 F.2d 1068 (6th Cir. 1989) (invalidating prison ban on attending religious service).

23. H.R. Rep. No. 1308, 95th Cong., 2d Sess., *reprinted in* 1978 U.S. Code Cong. & Admin. News 1262.

24. S.J. Res. 102, Aug. 11, 1978, Pub. L. No. 95–341, 92 Stat. 469, *codified in part* 42 U.S.C. Sec. 1996.

25. *Lyng,* note 18 above, 485 U.S. at 455.

26. *See Wilson v. Block,* note 19 above, 708 F.2d at 746; *Standing Deer,* note 21 above, 831 F.2d at 1530.

27. *See, e.g., Employment Division v. Smith,* 110 S.Ct. 1595, 1606 (1990).

28. *See, e.g.*, Ariz. Rev. Stat. Ann. Sec. 13–3402(b)(1)–(3) (1989); Colo. Rev. Stat. Sec. 12–22–317(3) (1985); N.M. Stat. Ann. Sec. 30–31–6(D) (Supp. 1989).

29. 21 C.F.R. Sec. 1307.31 (1990). *See Peyote Way Church of God, Inc. v. Thornburgh*, 922 F.2d 1210 (5th Cir. 1991).

30. *See* note 2 above.

31. *See generally Brown v. Board of Education*, 347 U.S. 483 (1954); *Loving v. Virginia*, 388 U.S. 1 (1967).

32. *Shirley v. Superior Court*, 513 P.2d 939 (Ariz. 1973), *cert. denied*, 415 U.S. 917 (1974).

33. *Piper v. Big Pine School Dist.*, 226 P.2d 926 (Cal. 1924); *Dewey County v. U.S.*, 26 F.2d 434 (8th Cir. 1928).

34. *Acosta v. San Diego County*, 272 P.2d 92 (Cal. 1954); *State Bd. of Pub. Welfare v. Board of Comm'rs*, 137 S.E.2d 801 (N.C. 1964).

35. *Denison v. State*, 268 P.2d 617 (Ariz. 1928).

36. *Begay v. Sawtelle*, 88 P.2d 999 (Ariz. 1939).

37. *Bradley v. Arizona Corp. Comm'n*, 141 P.2d 524 (Ariz. 1943).

38. *Fernandez v. State*, 144 P. 640 (Ariz. 1914).

39. *McMasters v. Chase*, 573 F.2d 1011 (8th Cir. 1978); *U.S. v. City of Oneida, N.Y.*, Civ. No. 77-Cc.V.–399 (D.N.Y. 1977), *reprinted in* 4 Indian L. Rep. K–18 (1977).

40. *Arizona v. U.S.*, 17 Indian L. Rep. 3001 (D. Ariz. 1989).

41. *See, e.g.*, ch. 11 (hunting and fishing rights), ch. 12 (water rights), and ch. 16 (federal programs).

42. This subject is discussed in ch. 10.

43. *See, e.g., Brough v. Appawora* , 553 P.2d 934 (Utah 1976), *vacated*, 431 U.S. 901 (1977); *Acosta*, note 34 above; *State Bd. of Pub. Welfare*, note 34 above.

44. *See* American Indian Policy Review Commission, *Final Report* pp. 87–94 (Washington, DC: Government Printing Office, 1977).

45. C. Wilkinson, *Several Myths Muddy Understanding of Indian Fishing Dispute*, p. 10 Oregon Journal (July 20, 1976).

46. *Livingston v. Ewing*, 601 F.2d 1110 (10th Cir.), *cert. denied*, 444 U.S. 870 (1979).

47. *Liberty and Justice for All*, U.S. Commission on Civil Rights, Report by the South Dakota Advisory Committee (Oct. 1977).

48. *See* cases cited in note 39 above.

49. *Penn v. San Juan Hospital, Inc.*, 528 F.2d 1181 (10th Cir. 1975), *on remand*, Civ. No. 74–419 (D. N.M. 1976) (consent decree), reprinted in 5 Indian L. Rep. K–1 (Feb. 1978).

50. *Wasberry v. Sanders*, 376 U.S. 1, 17 (1964); *Harper v. Virginia Board of Elections*, 383 U.S. 663 (1966).

51. 42 U.S.C. Secs. 1973 to 1973-bb–1.

52. 42 U.S.C. Secs. 1973b, 1973aa–1a to 1973aa–3, 1973dd–5.
53. *Id.*, Secs. 1973aa–1a(c).
54. *See, e.g., Goodluck,* note 2 above; *Prince v. Board of Education,* 543 P.2d 1176 (N.M. 1975); *Harrison v. Laveen,* 196 P.2d 456 (Ariz. 1948); *Montoya v. Bolack,* 372 P.2d 387 (N.M. 1972).
55. *Little Thunder v. South Dakota,* 518 F.2d 1253 (8th Cir. 1975).
56. *Goodluck,* note 2 above; *Prince,* note 54 above.
57. *Goodluck, id.*
58. *Windy Boy v. County of Big Horn,* 647 F. Supp. 1002 (D. Mont. 1986); *Buckanaga v. Sisseton Ind. Sch. Dist.,* 804 F.2d 469 (8th Cir. 1986).
59. *Cf. U.S. v. County of San Juan,* 7 Indian L. Rep. 3077 (D.N.M. 1980).
60. *See, e.g., Goodluck,* note 2 above; *Shirley v. Superior Court,* 513 P.2d 939 (Ariz. 1973).
61. *Yanito v. Barber,* 348 F. Supp. 587 (D. Utah 1972) (three-judge court).
62. *Civil Rights Cases,* 109 U.S. 3 (1883).
63. 42 U.S.C. Secs. 3601 *et seq.*
64. 42 U.S.C. Secs. 2000e *et seq.*
65. 42 U.S.C. Secs. 1981, 1982. *See, e.g., Scott v. Eversole Mortuary,* 522 F.2d 1110 (9th Cir. 1975).
66. 42 U.S.C. Sec. 2000a–a6.
67. Native American Rights Fund, *Legal Review* 2 (Winter 1990).
68. Public Law 101–601, 104 Stat. 3048 (1990).
69. Native American Rights Fund, *Legal Review* 5 (Fall 1990).

XIV

The Indian Civil Rights Act

In 1968 Congress passed the Indian Civil Rights Act (ICRA).[1] The ICRA is a highly controversial law because it authorizes federal courts to intervene in intratribal disputes, a power they never had before. Many Indians bitterly resent this development.

Essentially, the ICRA does two things. First, it confers certain rights on all persons who are subject to the jurisdiction of a tribal government. Second, it authorizes federal courts to enforce many of these rights. The ICRA is the only law ever passed by Congress that expressly limits the power of tribes to regulate their internal affairs.

Why did Congress pass the Indian Civil Rights Act?

In 1832 the Supreme Court recognized that Indian tribes are "distinct, independent political communities, retaining their original natural rights" in matters of local government.[2] The Constitution gives Congress the right to limit the tribe's powers, the Court said, but until Congress does, a tribe retains its inherent right to be self-governing.

In 1896 the Supreme Court held that the U.S. Constitution places no limits on tribal self-government. Neither the Constitution nor any federal law requires tribes to obey the Constitution. Consequently, the Court said, each Indian tribe retained the right to govern itself as its members saw fit.[3]

These Supreme Court decisions had the effect of leaving intratribal disputes entirely in the hands of the tribe. Indians who objected to their treatment by tribal officials had to resolve their complaints within the tribe; they could not look outside for help, even to the federal courts. Indian tribes enjoy the same "sovereign immunity" from suit that the state and federal governments enjoy. Consequently, courts were not permitted to hear lawsuits filed against an Indian tribe, even suits alleging what otherwise would be a violation of the Constitution.[4]

In 1962 a subcommittee of the U.S. Senate began a series of hearings concerning the administration of justice by tribal governments.[5] Many tribal members testified that tribal officials were tyrannical and biased. Some tribal members requested that Congress pass legislation protecting them from further abuse. Other tribal members, and many tribal officials, disputed the need for this sort of legislation and argued that federal intervention in tribal matters would destroy the tribes.

The senators who heard this testimony were startled to learn that the Constitution did not limit tribal powers. This meant that thousands of citizens were living under a government that did not have to respect constitutional rights. Senators were disturbed by allegations of misconduct and abuse of tribal authority. As one Senator stated on the floor of the Senate: "As the hearings developed and as the evidence and testimony were taken, I believe all of us who were students of the law were jarred and shocked by the conditions as far as constitutional rights for members of the Indian tribes were concerned. There was found to be unchecked and unlimited authority over many facets of Indian rights. . . . The Constitution simply was not applicable.[6]

The end result of these hearings was the passage of the Indian Civil Rights Act. The purpose of the act is "to ensure that the American Indian is afforded the broad Constitutional rights secured to other Americans . . . [in order to] protect individual Indians from arbitrary and unjust actions of tribal governments."[7]

The Indian Civil Rights Act (Title 25, U.S. Code, Sections 1301–41) has five parts, only one of which confers civil rights (Sections 1301–03). The other parts concern such matters as how a state can acquire or relinquish jurisdiction over an Indian reservation. (These subjects are discussed elsewhere in this book.)[8] The civil rights portion of the ICRA is often referred to as being the entire ICRA, but this is not accurate. In this chapter, though, all references to the ICRA relate to the civil rights portion of the act.

What civil rights are conferred by the ICRA?
Most of the civil rights conferred by the U.S. Constitution are conferred by the ICRA. Some senators initially suggested that every constitutional right be included in the act. It was pointed out, however, that certain provisions of the Constitution would seriously undermine, if not destroy, tribal government. For instance, if tribes had to comply with the Fifteenth

Amendment, they could not discriminate in voting on account of race.[9] This would mean that non-Indians who lived on the reservation could vote in tribal elections and hold tribal office. On some reservations more non-Indians live there than Indians,[10] and the reins of tribal government probably would change hands.

The Establishment Clause of the First Amendment presented another unique problem. That clause requires the federal and state governments to remain completely neutral in religious matters.[11] If this provision were enforced on Indian reservations, it would seriously disrupt those tribal governments that are theocratic.

As finally enacted, the ICRA confers every fundamental civil right in the Constitution except five. The ICRA does not contain an Establishment Clause, and it does not prevent a tribe from discriminating in voting on account of race. In addition, tribes are not required to convene a jury in civil trials or, in criminal cases, to issue grand jury indictments or appoint counsel for indigent defendants.[12]

The rights conferred by the ICRA are listed in Section 1302. (See appendix A of this book). Among them are the right to free speech, press, and assembly; protection against unreasonable search and seizure; the right to a speedy trial; the right to hire a lawyer in a criminal case; protection against self-incrimination; protection against cruel and inhuman punishment; and the right to equal protection of the laws and to due process of law.

Does the ICRA protect non-Indians as well as Indians?

Yes. The ICRA applies to "any person" who is subject to the jurisdiction of a tribal government.[13] The ICRA restricts tribal powers over Indians and non-Indians alike.[14]

Does the ICRA limit the punishment that criminals can receive?

Yes. The ICRA limits tribal punishment in criminal cases to a year's imprisonment and a five thousand dollar fine or both.[15] However, a person who commits two crimes could receive two one-year sentences to be served consecutively.[16]

Have tribes had to alter some of their institutions and practices because of the ICRA?

Yes. Prior to the passage of the ICRA, each Indian tribe had its own method for resolving disputes. The ICRA, however, requires all tribes to comply with certain standards. In order to meet these standards, a number of changes have been made, particularly in tribal judicial systems. Federal courts in ICRA cases, for example, have required tribes to advise criminal defendants of their right to a trial by jury,[17] to write their criminal laws in clear and certain language,[18] to honor a criminal defendant's right against self-incrimination,[19] and to prohibit the tribal judge from also being the prosecutor.[20] In addition, the ICRA requires the tribe's trial court to sufficiently record its proceedings so that an appellate court can determine exactly what occurred.[21]

Should the rights in the ICRA that were borrowed from the Constitution be interpreted as the Constitution is interpreted?

Not necessarily. The rights enumerated in the ICRA were patterned after those in the Bill of Rights and the Fourteenth Amendment to the Constitution. However, it was not the intent of Congress to make them identical in scope.

Clearly, Congress wanted to protect individuals from certain abuses. However, Congress was also concerned about the unique political, cultural, and economic needs of the tribe. This explains why Congress refused to include in the ICRA all of the civil rights contained in the Constitution.[22] The ICRA reflects a balancing of interests. Courts should balance these same interests when they enforce the act. In particular, courts should be reluctant to apply the ICRA in such a way as to "significantly impair a tribal practice or alter a custom firmly embedded in Indian culture."[23] In other words, a court should consider and give weight to tribal interests when interpreting the ICRA, especially when tribal traditions are at stake.

If you are facing criminal charges in tribal court and cannot afford a lawyer, must the tribe hire one for you?

No. The Sixth Amendment to the U.S. Constitution requires state and federal courts to appoint counsel for indigent defendants in criminal cases.[24] During the Senate hearings on the ICRA, tribal leaders testified that tribal courts could not afford to make these appointments because of the tremendous expense.[25] This testimony persuaded Congress. The ICRA only guarantees a defendant the right to counsel "at his own expense."[26] Thus far, the courts that have considered this issue have held that tribes are not required to appoint counsel in criminal cases.[27]

If a tribe violates rights protected by the ICRA, what can be done about it? Can the tribe be sued?

The ICRA contains a long list of rights, but the only remedy for their violation is contained in Section 1303 of the act. Section 1303 states: "The privilege of the writ of habeas corpus shall be available to any person, in a court of the United States, to test the legality of his detention by order of an Indian tribe." However, many of the rights listed in the ICRA cannot be enforced in this manner.

A writ of habeas corpus is a court decree that orders that a person being held in custody be brought before the court so that the court can determine the lawfulness of the detention. The writ is served upon the person's custodian, that is, the person who is detaining the petitioner. Thus if a person is being prosecuted or incarcerated by an Indian tribe in violation of the ICRA, she or he can petition a federal court for a writ of habeas corpus. In addition, at least one federal court has held that a writ of habeas corpus is available to challenge a tribal court's decision to grant child custody to one parent when the other parent previously had obtained custody of the child in state court,[28] although writs of habeas corpus are not usually available to challenge child custody determinations.[29]

Before you can obtain a writ of habeas corpus from a federal court, you must exhaust tribal remedies, including tribal court appeals. Section 1303 does not expressly require this. However, every court to consider the question has imposed an exhaustion requirement so as to maximize tribal autonomy and prevent unnecessary federal intervention in tribal affairs. Courts have refused to require exhaustion only when the effort would be futile or when the delay is likely to cause irreparable injury.[30] The subject of exhaustion of tribal remedies is discussed in chapter 9, section A.

A writ of habeas corpus is available only to challenge an unlawful detention or custody. It is therefore clear that some of the federal rights conferred by Section 1302 of the ICRA have no federal judicial remedy. To illustrate, if a tribe takes your property without compensating you in violation of Section

1302(5), or if a tribe discriminates against you in employment in violation of 1302(8), the federal courts are not allowed to intervene.

For several years after the ICRA was passed, lower federal courts were ordering tribal officials to comply with the entire act. That is, these courts held that the ICRA waived the tribe's sovereign immunity with respect to each right listed in the act, thereby authorizing federal courts to resolve all disputes arising under the ICRA.[31] In 1978, however, the Supreme Court held in *Santa Clara Pueblo v. Martinez*[32] that the writ of habeas corpus is the only remedy federal courts can grant under the ICRA. Indeed, given that such a writ is directed to the custodian of the person seeking the writ and not to the government itself, the ICRA did not waive tribal sovereign immunity at all, the Court said. Tribal officials, to be sure, are required to obey the entire ICRA, a federal law. However, federal courts may enforce the act only in narrow circumstances. In all other circumstances, those people who allege an ICRA violation must pursue their claims in tribal forums, whether it be in the tribal courts, the tribal council, or at the ballot box.

Both before *Santa Clara Pueblo* and after it, numerous lawsuits were filed in federal court under the ICRA alleging that tribal officials had stripped tribal members of the right to vote or the right to run for office, that tribal election results were fraudulent, that a tribe was impermissibly refusing to enroll someone as a member, that a tribe had wrongfully confiscated private property, and a host of other alleged abuses.[33] The federal courts, given *Santa Clara Pueblo*, can no longer consider these kinds of claims. Indeed, since *Santa Clara Pueblo*, there has been only one court that has accepted a non-habeas corpus case under the ICRA. The matter concerned a non-Indian whose rights were being violated by a tribe, and he had no recourse even within the tribe to challenge what was occurring.[34] This decision cannot be squared with *Santa Clara Pueblo*, and this court itself, in a later ruling, essentially agreed that it was wrongly decided.[35]

If the federal courts cannot hear an ICRA lawsuit, what remedies are available for an ICRA violation?

As indicated, numerous violations of the ICRA have no federal judicial remedy because, as the Supreme Court held in

Santa Clara Pueblo, the ICRA did not waive the tribe's sovereign immunity from suit in federal court. The Court apparently assumed, though, that victims of ICRA violations could obtain a remedy in a tribal forum. "Tribal forums are available," the Court said, "to vindicate rights created by the ICRA, and Section 1302 has the substantial and intended effect of changing the law which these forums are obliged to apply."[36] At least one federal court has expressly stated that "federal law requires a waiver of tribal immunity in tribal courts for actions under the ICRA."[37] However, the majority of tribal courts that have considered the question have held that the ICRA did not waive the tribe's immunity from suit in tribal court; these courts have refused to adjudicate ICRA claims.[38] A few tribal courts, reaching the opposite conclusion, have held that victims of ICRA violations can seek relief in tribal court.[39] Shortly after one of these courts, the Oglala Sioux tribal court, ruled that it could hear ICRA claims,[40] the tribal council passed a law prohibiting all ICRA lawsuits without the tribe's express consent.[41]

A few tribes have enacted laws that waive their sovereign immunity and authorize ICRA claims to be heard in tribal court.[42] However, on many reservations, if not on most, victims of ICRA violations have no judicial remedy at all.

For a few years after *Santa Clara Pueblo* was decided, it appeared that the Bureau of Indian Affairs would take an active role in enforcing the ICRA. In 1980 the BIA warned tribes that violations of the ICRA could result in the loss of federal funds or, in those instances where tribal election laws were being violated, a refusal by the federal government to recognize tribal officials as being legitimately seated.[43] However, the BIA's enforcement role has been spotty at best, and its director has admitted that the BIA now has a hands-off policy with regard to ICRA violations.[44]

Given that tribes cannot be sued for most violations of the ICRA, victims of tribal abuse have been requesting the BIA to exercise greater control over Indian tribes. The BIA has even been sued in an effort to force the bureau to exercise such control. Many tribal constitutions, for instance, allow the BIA to veto tribal laws that violate the tribe's constitution or federal law, and the BIA can exercise this authority.[45] A few federal courts have ordered the BIA, in furtherance of the bureau's trust responsibility, to refuse to certify the results of a tribal election if it was not conducted in accordance with tribal law,[46] although other federal courts have dismissed such cases due to the tribe's sovereign immunity.[47]

Should the ICRA be amended so as to authorize federal suits against tribal governments?

This is a very controversial question. As just indicated, many victims of ICRA violations have no realistic remedy, especially if their right to vote in tribal elections or their right to hold tribal office has been unjustly stripped by tribal officials. This does not mean, however, that Congress should amend the ICRA, as many people are urging, and authorize federal courts to resolve all ICRA disputes. After all, many people in the United States lack any realistic remedy when state or federal officials violate their civil rights, but no one seriously suggests that some outside government be designated to resolve these controversies.

In 1989 and again in 1990 a bill was introduced in Congress that, if passed, would have legislatively overruled *Santa Clara Pueblo* and authorized federal courts, after tribal remedies were exhausted, to hear all ICRA cases. That is, the bill would have waived tribal sovereign immunity with respect to ICRA claims. Opponents argue that the passage of such a law will dilute tribal powers and interfere with tribal autonomy and that, even if ICRA violations are occurring, tribal members should work within the tribal system to remedy them. Permitting outsiders to resolve tribal disputes, many of which concern tribal customs and traditions, severely disrupts tribal government and Indian culture.[48] Proponents of such a law argue that, especially on certain reservations, ICRA violations are so flagrant and injurious that resort to a federal court is necessary if basic civil rights are to be respected.[49] Moreover, the absence of an effective tribal remedy for these abuses is already undermining tribal government by creating disrespect for tribal law and tribal officials. Without a federal court "safety net," it is argued, reservation Indians are the only people in the United States whose fundamental civil liberties can be violated without the opportunity for court review.

A federal court has stated that "the effect, after *Santa Clara Pueblo*, of the ICRA is to create rights while withholding any meaningful remedies to enforce them . . . but it is for Congress, not the courts, to resolve this state of affairs."[50] Whether Indians lack meaningful remedies on their individual reservations, and, even if so, whether Congress should intervene, are questions very much in controversy.

NOTES

1. 25 U.S.C. Secs. 1301 *et seq.*
2. *Worcester v. Georgia,* 31 U.S. 515, 559 (1832).
3. *Talton v. Mayes,* 163 U.S. 376 (1896). *See also U.S. v. Wheeler,* 435 U.S. 313 (1978).
4. *See, e.g., Talton,* note 3 above; *Native American Church v. Navajo Tribal Council,* 272 F.2d 131 (10th Cir. 1959); *Twin Cities Chippewa Tribal Council v. Minnesota Chippewa Tribe,* 370 F.2d 529 (8th Cir. 1967). *But see Colliflower v. Garland,* 342 F.2d 369 (9th Cir. 1965).
5. The legislative history of the Indian Civil Rights Act is discussed in *Santa Clara Pueblo v. Martinez,* 436 U.S. 49 (1978). *See also* Burnett, *An Historical Analysis of the 1968 "Indian Civil Rights" Act,* 9 Harv. J. on Legis. 557 (1972).
6. 113 Cong. Rec. part 26, p. 35473, 90th Cong., 1st Sess. (Dec. 7, 1967) (statement of Sen. Hruska [R. Neb.]).
7. S. Rep. No. 841, 90th Cong., 1st Sess. 6 (1967).
8. *See, e.g.,* ch. 7, sec. B, which discusses part 3 of the ICRA (assumption and retrocession of state jurisdiction over Indian reservations).
9. The Fifteenth Amendment states in pertinent part: "The right of citizens of the United States to vote shall not be denied or abridged by the United States or by any State on account of race, color, or previous condition of servitude."
10. *See* ch. 2, note 43 and accompanying text.
11. *See* ch. 13, note 6 and accompanying text.
12. The reason why these protections were omitted from the ICRA is explained in *Santa Clara Pueblo,* note 5 above, 436 U.S. at 66–70. *See also* Burnett, note 5 above.
13. 25 U.S.C. Sec. 1302.
14. *Dodge v. Nakai,* 298 F. Supp. 17 (D. Ariz. 1968); *Dry Creek Lodge, Inc. v. U.S.,* 515 F.2d 926 (10th Cir. 1975).
15. 25 U.S.C. Sec. 1302(7).
16. *Ramos v. Pyramid Lake Tribal Court,* 13 Indian L. Rep. 3003 (D. Nev. 1985); *Tuckta v. Cruz,* 16 Indian L. Rep. 3102 (D. Or. 1988).
17. *Red Elk v. Silk,* 10 Indian L. Rep. 3109 (D. Mont. 1983). *Cf. U.S. v.*

McGahuey, 10 Indian L. Rep. 6051 (Hoopa Ct. Ind. Off. 1983) (if no imprisonment, no right to a jury trial).

18. *Big Eagle v. Andera,* 508 F. Supp. 1293 (8th Cir. 1975), *on remand,* 418 F. Supp. 126 (D.S.D. 1976).

19. *Springer v. Woods,* 12 Indian L. Rep. 3106 (D.S.D. 1984).

20. *Wounded Knee v. Andera,* 416 F. Supp. 1236 (D.S.D. 1976).

21. *Rosebud Sioux Tribe v. White Hat,* 11 Indian L. Rep. 6033 (Intertr. Ct. App. 1983).

22. *See Santa Clara Pueblo,* note 5 above, 436 U.S. at 66–70; *Tom v. Sutton,* 533 F.2d 1101, 1103–4 (9th Cir. 1976).

23. *Howlett v. Salish and Kootenai Tribes,* 529 F.2d 233, 234 (9th Cir. 1976). *See also Crowe v. Eastern Band of Cherokee Indians,* 506 F.2d 1231 (4th Cir. 1974); *Wounded Head v. Tribal Council,* 507 F.2d 1079 (8th Cir. 1975). Tribal practices of recent vintage have not been accorded the same dignity. *See Wounded Knee v. Andera,* note 20 above; *White Eagle v. One Feather,* 478 F.2d 1311 (8th Cir. 1973); *Randall v. Yakima Nation Tribal Court,* 841 F.2d 897 (9th Cir. 1988).

24. *See Argersinger v. Hamlin,* 407 U.S. 25 (1972).

25. *See* Burnett, note 5 above.

26. 25 U.S.C. Sec. 1302(6).

27. *Tom v. Sutton,* 533 F.2d 1101 (9th Cir. 1976). *See also Spotted Eagle v. Blackfeet Tribe,* 301 F. Supp. 85 (D. Mont. 1969).

28. *DeMent v. Oglala Sioux Tribal Court,* 874 F.2d 510 (8th Cir. 1989).

29. *Lehman v. Lycoming County Children's Services Agency,* 458 U.S. 502, 511 (1983); *Weatherwax on Behalf of Carlson v. Fairbanks,* 619 F. Supp. 294, 296 (D. Mont. 1985).

30. *See, e.g., Wounded Knee,* note 20 above; *DeMent,* note 28 above. *See also National Farmers Union Ins. Co. v. Crow Tribe,* 471 U.S. 845, 856 (1985) (in most instances, exhaustion of tribal remedies is a prerequisite to a federal action).

31. *See, e.g., Luxon v. Rosebud Sioux Tribe,* 455 F.2d 698 (8th Cir. 1972); *Johnson v. Lower Elwha Tribal Community,* 484 F.2d 200 (9th Cir. 1973); *Dry Creek Lodge,* note 14 above.

32. 436 U.S. 49 (1978).

33. *See* cases cited in note 31 above and *Nero v. Cherokee Nation,* 892 F.2d 1457 (10th Cir. 1989); *Shortbull v. Looking Elk,* 677 F.2d 645 (8th Cir.), *cert. denied,* 459 U.S. 907 (1982); *Wheeler v. Swimmer,* 835 F.2d 259 (10th Cir. 1987); *Crowe v. Eastern Band of Cherokee Indians,* 506 F.2d 1231 (4th Cir. 1974).

34. *Dry Creek Lodge, Inc. v. U.S.,* 623 F.2d 682 (10th Cir. 1980), *cert. denied,* 449 U.S. 1118 (1981).

35. *See White v. Pueblo of San Juan,* 728 F.2d 1307, 1313 (10th Cir. 1984).

36. *Santa Clara Pueblo v. Martinez,* 436 U.S. 49, 65 (1978).

37. *White*, note 35 above, 728 F.2d at 1312.
38. *See, e.g., Satiacum v. Sterud*, 10 Indian L. Rep. 6013 (Puyallup Tr. Ct. 1983); *Garman v. Fort Belknap Community Council*, 11 Indian L. Rep. 6017 (Ft. Belknap Tr. Ct. 1984); *Stone v. Sonday*, 10 Indian L. Rep. 6039 (Colv. Tr. Ct. 1983); *Johnson v. Navajo Nation*, 14 Indian L. Rep. 6037, 6040 (Nav. Sup. Ct. 1987).
39. *See, e.g., Dupree v. Cheyenne River Housing Auth.*, 16 Indian L. Rep. 6106 (Chy. R. Sx. Tr. Ct. App. 1988); *Miller v. Adams*, 10 Indian L. Rep. 6034 (Intertr. Ct. App. 1982); *Committee v. Better Tribal Government v. Southern Ute Election Board*, 17 Indian L. Rep. 6095 (S. Ute Tr. Ct. 1990). *See also Lawrence v. So. Puget Sound Inter-Tribal Housing Auth.*, 14 Indian L. Rep. 6011 (Suq. Tr. Ct. 1987); *Comm. for Better Tribal Government v. So. Ute Election Board*, 17 Indian L. Rep. 6145 (S. Ute. Tr. Ct. 1990).
40. *See, e.g., Red Shirt v. Personnel Board*, 16 Indian L. Rep. 6054 (Og. Sx. Tr. Ct. App. 1985).
41. Og. Sx. Tr. Council Res. No. 87–76 (July 14, 1987).
42. *See, e.g., Drags Wolf v. Tribal Business Council of the Three Affiliated Tribes*, 17 Indian L. Rep. 6051 (Ft. Bert. Tr. Ct. 1990).
43. *Interior Department/Bureau of Indian Affairs Policy Regarding Relationship with Tribal Governments*, issued June 12, 1980, discussed in 7 Indian Law Rep. 6021 (Aug. 1980). *See generally* A. Ziontz, *After Martinez: Indian Civil Rights Under Tribal Government*, 12 U.C. Davis L. Rev. 1 (1979).
44. Statement of Ross Swimmer, *Hearing on the Enforcement of the ICRA of 1968 Before the U.S. Commission on Civil Rights*, Wash. DC, Jan. 28, 1988, 13.
45. *See, e.g., Frease v. Sacramento Area Director, BIA*, 17 IBIA 241 [16 Indian L. Rep. 7093] (1989).
46. *See* cases cited in ch. 5, note 60 and accompanying text.
47. This subject is discussed in ch. 18, note 20 and accompanying text.
48. *See* Ziontz, note 43 above.
49. Many of these violations are recorded in *Hearings on the Enforcement of the ICRA of 1968 before the U.S. Commission on Civil Rights*, Rapid City, S.D., Hearings (1986), Flagstaff, Ariz. Hearings (1987), and Washington, DC Hearings (1988).
50. *Wells v. Philbrick*, 486 F. Supp. 807, 809 (D.S.C. 1980). *See* also *Shortbull v. Looking Elk*, 677 F.2d 645 (8th Cir.), *cert. denied*, 459 U.S. 907 (1982).

XV

The Special Status of Certain Indian Groups

Certain Native American groups occupy a special status under United States law. These groups include the Pueblos of New Mexico, Alaska Natives, Oklahoma Indians, New York Indians, and the nonrecognized tribes. This chapter discusses the federal government's unique relationship with each of these groups.

A. THE PUEBLOS OF NEW MEXICO

What is the historical background of the Pueblos of New Mexico?

Native communities were well established in what is now New Mexico long before the Spanish conquistadors entered the region during the 1600s. Each community had its own government, language, and culture. Today there are nineteen of these Pueblos in New Mexico, each a different tribe politically and anthropologically.

The Spaniards felt it was their duty to "civilize" the Indians. To help accomplish this, they built a church in each Pueblo. Spain then issued a land grant recognizing the Pueblo's ownership of all the land surrounding the church for one league (approximately 2.5 miles) in every direction. Spain also passed laws prohibiting non-Indians from living or trespassing within the Pueblo.

After Mexico became independent from Spain, the Mexican government reaffirmed these land grants and extended citizenship to the Pueblo Indians. However, the Mexican government did little to protect the Pueblos from being attacked by outsiders, and many Pueblos lost some land during this period.

The United States acquired the territory of New Mexico in an 1848 treaty with Mexico, the Treaty of Guadalupe Hidalgo. In the treaty the United States promised to preserve the land rights that Mexico had granted to the Pueblos. Soon afterward,

Congress passed legislation recognizing the ownership rights of each Pueblo and conferring United States citizenship on the Pueblo Indians.

The federal government did little to protect the Pueblos, and again the Pueblos were attacked by non-Indians, and land was stolen. Some government officials went to court to help the Pueblos protect their land. However, these efforts stopped in 1876 when the Supreme Court ruled that the Pueblos were not "Indian tribes" under federal laws that allowed for such protection.[1]

Fortunately, in 1913 the Supreme Court reversed its 1876 decision and ruled that the Pueblos were indeed "Indian tribes" for purposes of federal protection.[2] Soon thereafter Congress appropriated funds for the construction of schools, bridges, roads, and irrigation systems within the Pueblos and passed laws that protected Pueblo lands. The Pueblo Lands Act of 1924,[3] for example, helped the Pueblos recover their stolen lands. The act required that all former Pueblo land be returned to the Pueblo unless the purported owner could prove continuous payment of state real estate taxes from the date the land was removed from Pueblo control.

It is now well established that the United States has a trust relationship with the Pueblos. As explained in chapter 3, this means that the federal government has a duty to protect Pueblo lands, and the Pueblos Indians are entitled to the same benefits and services other federally recognized tribes receive.[4] The federal government's trust obligation is not diminished by the fact that the Pueblos own their land[5] or because the Pueblos have incorporated themselves under state law.[6]

In what respects is the relationship between the federal government and the Pueblos unique?

The Pueblos have a unique relationship with the United States. No other group of Indians has been so free of federal interference as the Pueblos. Congress rarely intrudes into Pueblo life.

It is not clear why Congress has treated the Pueblos differently than other tribes. It may be a combination of several factors. First, the Pueblos own their own land. Most other reservations are owned in large part by the United States and are therefore closely administered by federal officials.[7] Second, few tribes other than the Pueblos have obtained rights to land from foreign nations. Finally, the Pueblos have remained highly traditional and are well known for their industriousness and close church affiliation.[8]

In any event, the Pueblos have been spared much of the harm that other tribes have suffered. No Pueblo was ever forced to sign a treaty with the United States. In addition, not a single piece of Pueblo land was removed under the General Allotment Act of 1887, although few other reservations were spared. It is obvious that the Pueblos enjoy a special status with the federal government.

B. ALASKA NATIVES

What is the historical background of the native inhabitants of Alaska?

The land that is now the state of Alaska has long been inhabited by two races of indigenous people, the American Indians and the Eskimos and the Aleuts.[9] When Alaska was purchased from Russia in 1867, its native population was scattered in two hundred villages, located principally along the southern and far northwestern coasts. Hunting and fishing were the main sources of livelihood, as they are today.

Until recently, Congress dealt with the Alaska Natives in the same manner as Indian groups generally. The Citizenship Act of 1924, which extended United States citizenship to all Indians born in the United States, expressly included the Eskimos, Aleuts, and Indians of the Alaska Territory.[10] Likewise, the Indian Reorganization Act of 1934[11] included Alaska Natives among its beneficiaries (and more than seventy tribes have organized under that act).[12] Most other federal Indian laws and programs have been interpreted to apply to the Native people of Alaska,[13] and Alaska Natives have been recognized as having a trust relationship with the United States, entitling them to all the benefits of this relationship.[14]

Like the Pueblos of New Mexico, no treaties were ever signed between the United States and any of the Native groups of Alaska. This is largely because, until recently, few whites wanted to live in Alaska, and there was no conflict over land acquisition.

In 1955 the Supreme Court was asked to decide whether the Alaska Natives had recognized title (defined in chapter 2) to their ancestral homelands or whether their interest was possessory only, that is, whether compensation had to be paid to the Natives if the federal government took their land. In *Tee-Hit-Ton v. United States*,[15] the Court held that the Natives lacked recognized title and that the federal government could take Native land without paying compensation.

In what respects do the Alaska Natives have a unique relationship with the United States?

In 1971 Congress passed a comprehensive law regarding the land rights of Alaska's eighty thousand native inhabitants. Despite the Supreme Court's decision in *Tee-Hit-Ton*, Congress agreed to compensate the Natives for taking their land and also agreed to give them ownership rights to certain parcels of land. This law, the Alaska Native Claims Settlement Act (ANCSA),[16] changed the nature of the government's relationship with the Alaska Natives.

The ANCSA gives Alaska Natives $962.5 million in compensation for extinguishing all of their aboriginal land claims, and in addition, it gives them ownership rights to 40 million acres of land.[17] Of this 40 million acres, the surface estate in 22 million acres was divided among the 200 Native villages according to their population, with each village selecting the land it wanted to live on. The remaining 18 million acres and the subsurface estate of the entire 40 million acres were conveyed to twelve Native regional corporations. (Thus, the 22 million acres patented to the villages are dually owned: the surface is owned by the village while the subsurface is owned by the regional corporation.)[18] Each Alaska Native is enrolled in a region, and each region and each village within each region is organized and incorporated under state law.

All persons living on December 18, 1971, and possessing one-quarter or more Native blood were issued one hundred shares of corporate stock in their regional corporation. The ANCSA requires each regional corporation to use its land and resources for the profit of its shareholders. As originally enacted, the ANCSA prohibited shareholders from selling their shares for twenty years (until 1991), but thereafter these shares could be sold to any person, including a non-Native. Lands owned by the Native corporation were to be exempt from state and local taxation only during this 20-year period. However, in 1988 Congress amended the ANCSA and extended the restrictions on sales of stock and on state taxation indefinitely. But Congress also permitted each corporation to issue and sell new stock to non-Natives, and Congress rejected the Natives' request to allow these corporations to transfer their land to tribal governments in order to give this land further protection. Thus, the 1990s will be critical years for Alaska Natives and their villages and corporations, as Natives attempt to make their corporations profitable and prevent non-Natives from acquiring any control over them.

The Native inhabitants of Alaska have a unique relationship with the United States. For one thing, the ANCSA gives them extensive rights to land. It places forty million acres under their direct ownership and control, free from state and local taxation, and provides almost $1 billion in compensation. Alaska Natives thus own more land than all other Native groups combined. Congress also has enacted other laws aimed at assisting Alaska Natives. The Alaska National Interest Lands Conservation Act of 1980 (ANILCA)[19] gives the Native population priority rights in hunting and fishing for subsistence needs over all other uses of these natural resources. ANILCA also prohibits federal agencies from allowing anyone to use public lands in Alaska if such use would have a harmful effect on these subsistence rights. The Reindeer Industry Act[20] provides federal funds and property to the Natives of Alaska for sustaining the economic use of reindeer. In addition, Alaska Natives and their tribal organizations are entitled to receive the same federal services available to Indians elsewhere in the United States. The ANCSA did not diminish their right to participate in federal Indian programs.[21]

Unfortunately, the state of Alaska has strongly opposed Native governments and is constantly attempting to erode, or have Congress erode, their powers. Alaska has even taken the position that Native tribes and villages lack the powers of self-government enjoyed by Indian tribes generally. The U.S. Supreme Court has not decided the extent to which Native villages in Alaska may exercise the powers of self-government. However, there is no reason to deny them this power. Only Congress can strip a tribe of its inherent right of local self-government, and Congress has not done so here. This issue, though, is a complex and controversial one, and the Supreme Court eventually will need to resolve it.[22]

C. OKLAHOMA INDIANS

What is the historical background of the Oklahoma Indians?
The area that is now the state of Oklahoma was named Indian Territory during the 1830s. Originally, Indian Territory was reserved exclusively for Indians. The federal government chose this largely barren land for the relocation of many eastern tribes that were forcibly removed to the West. Today there are more than twenty-five tribes located in Oklahoma, few of them indigenous.[23]

The first tribes to be placed in Indian Territory were the Cherokees, Choctaws, Chickasaws, Creeks, and Seminoles. These tribes are often called the Five Civilized Tribes because they had an advanced governmental structure long before the nineteenth century and operated their own schools and courts. Each of the Five Civilized Tribes signed a treaty with the United States in which the tribe was assigned a reservation in Indian Territory. The treaty assured the tribe that it would not be disturbed and that its lands would never become part of a state without the tribe's consent.

The federal government honored this promise until the Civil War. At least two of the Civilized Tribes, the Choctaws and Chickasaws, owned slaves and sided with the Confederacy, and several leaders of the other tribes were sympathetic to the South. After the war, this provided a good excuse for taking tribal lands. Allegedly as a penalty for sympathizing with the Confederacy, all five tribes lost the western portion of their reservations. Their vacated lands were then assigned to some twenty other tribes, all of whom were forcibly placed in Indian Territory.

Even after the Civil War, Indian Territory remained officially closed to white settlement, but thousands of whites settled there illegally, and the federal government did little to stop them. In fact, during the 1890s Congress authorized the federal government to sell "surplus" tribal lands to non-Indians. In the ensuing years most tribal lands throughout Indian Territory were sold. By 1907 non-Indians vastly outnumbered the Indians, and the territory was admitted into the Union as the state of Oklahoma.

In what ways do the Indians living in Oklahoma have a unique relationship with the United States?

The United States has so drastically interfered in the way of life of the Oklahoma tribes that they have acquired a unique relationship with the federal government. This relationship has left the tribes with little land or other property to govern. Several laws allowing the government to sell "surplus" tribal lands were so comprehensive that they abolished entire reservations, especially in the western part of the territory, leaving some tribes landless except for a few parcels of trust land still under federal supervision.[24]

Congress has created an entire set of laws dealing exclusively with Oklahoma tribes, especially the Five Civilized Tribes and the Osage tribe.[25] Some of these laws limit tribal powers, particularly with regard to the control of tribal property. For example, Congress has placed most of the resources and income of the Osage tribe under the direct control of the Secretary of the Interior.[26]

As explained in chapter 1, Congress enacted the General Allotment Act in 1887, which authorized the President to sell "surplus" tribal lands to non-Indians. The Five Civilized Tribes were excluded from the act because their treaties with the United States gave them their land outright rather than hold it in trust status. However, Congress wanted these tribes to sell some of their land. The tribes refused to do so, which angered Congress into passing the Curtis Act in 1898.[27] This act not only forced the allotment of tribal lands, but it also abolished all tribal courts and removed certain powers of self-government from the tribes, including the right to collect taxes.

In 1934, when Congress passed the Indian Reorganization Act (discussed in chapter 1), it excluded the Oklahoma tribes from its benefits. Fortunately, in 1936 Congress had a change of heart, and the Oklahoma Indian Welfare Act (OIWA) was passed.[28] The OIWA provides to Oklahoma tribes the same basic benefits as the IRA; for example, it restores the tribe's right to establish tribal courts having both civil and criminal jurisdiction.[29] It is now generally recognized that Oklahoma tribes possess the powers of self-government, particularly if they have organized under the OIWA.[30]

Congress has dealt with the Oklahoma tribes in a haphazard way, and federal officials within the Department of the Interior and its subagency the Bureau of Indian Affairs have treated them similarly. Their attitude has been less than exemplary. As one federal court recently stated, "This attitude, which can only be characterized as bureaucratic imperialism, manifested itself in deliberate attempts to frustrate, debilitate, and generally prevent from functioning the tribal governments expressly preserved" by the OIWA.[31]

As explained in chapter 3, every tribe that has a treaty with the United States has a trust relationship with the federal government unless Congress has terminated that relationship. Oklahoma tribes are no exception to this rule. Almost all of them have at least one treaty with the United States. As the Supreme Court held in 1943 with respect to the Creeks, the federal government continues to have a trust responsibility with respect to these treaty tribes.[32]

Therefore, Oklahoma tribes have the same rights and are eligible for the same benefits as all other tribes unless Congress has declared otherwise. For the most part, Congress has not stripped the Oklahoma tribes of their governmental powers nor their right to participate in federal programs, although Congress has removed much of their land. In 1959, during the termination era (discussed in chapter 1), Congress terminated the federal status of three Oklahoma tribes—Wyandotte, Peoria, and Ottawa—but restored their federal status in 1977.[33]

Within the past ten years, a line of court decisions have recognized that Oklahoma Indian tribes continue to possess the inherent right of self-government and, therefore, that the state of Oklahoma lacks general criminal and civil jurisdiction within Indian country. (Indian country is defined in chapter 2.) The Oklahoma tribes have this power whether they own their own lands or whether their lands are held in trust status by the federal government. Even if their trust land is not part of a reservation, it remains Indian country, the Supreme Court held in 1991, and Oklahoma, for instance, cannot tax the sale of cigarettes sold by the tribe on trust land to tribal members (although Oklahoma can, as other states can, tax the sale of cigarettes sold by a tribe to non-Indians).[34] In addition, Oklahoma may not regulate or tax a tribal bingo operation located on tribal trust land or tribally owned land.[35] Likewise, the federal government—and not Oklahoma—has jurisdiction to prosecute crimes committed by or against Indians within Indian country.[36] A number of jurisdictional issues still remain, both with respect to the powers of Oklahoma tribes and the power of Oklahoma to regulate tribal activities.[37] However, recent federal cases strongly support the right of Oklahoma tribes to exercise the same powers of local self-government that other tribes possess.

D. NEW YORK INDIANS

What is the historical background of the New York Indians?

The Europeans who first settled in what is now New York were greeted by the Iroquois Confederacy, the most powerful group of Indians north of Mexico. The Confederacy consisted of the Seneca, Cayuga, Onondaga, Oneida, Mohawk, and Tuscarora tribes. The Confederacy's territory at one time extended from what is now New England to the Mississippi River and from upper Canada into North Carolina. Other tribes that were occupying this domain were either expelled, annihilated, or absorbed by the Iroquois.

The Iroquois Confederacy played an important role in the early history of the United States. The Confederacy's alliance with Great Britain during the so-called French and Indian War, which ended in 1763, helped assure a British victory against France. During the Revolutionary War, two of the six tribes— the Oneidas and Tuscaroras—sided with the United States and the others sided with Great Britain. The Oneidas, however, were the most powerful Indian tribe in the Northeast, and their assistance to the colonists was significant.[38]

The treaty that ended the war between the United States and Great Britain was signed in 1783. The next year the United States signed treaties with all six nations of the Iroquois Confederacy. These treaties established boundary lines for the territory of each tribe and recognized each tribe's right to remain free from outside interference.[39]

The United States did not honor these treaties for very long. By the 1820s Iroquois land was highly coveted by non-Indians.

The federal government "persuaded" a large number of Indians to leave New York and relocate on reservations in Wisconsin and Kansas.[40] The Indians who remained were eventually placed on reservations. Today, there are nine Indian reservations in the state.[41]

In 1790 Congress passed the Indian Nonintercourse Act (INA), discussed in chapter 6,[42] which prohibited the sale of Indian land without the federal government's approval. Both before the INA and afterwards, the state of New York purchased Indian land without federal approval. Recently, courts have ruled that these pre-act purchases are valid,[43] but the post-act purchases are not.[44] As explained in chapter 2, section D, the Supreme Court ruled in 1823 that, although the Indians lost the right to own their original homesites when they became subordinate to the United States, they retained the right to occupy these sites until Congress ordered their removal. Accordingly, when New York violated the INA and illegally purchased tribal land, the Indians were deprived of their possessory rights. Recently, courts have held that New York tribes are entitled to compensatory damages for the loss of those rights.[45] These damages are in the millions of dollars.

In what respects is the relationship between the New York Indians and the federal government unique?

New York Indians have been among the most politically active tribes in the United States. For many years there was a presumption that these tribes were under the state's general jurisdiction,[46] in contrast to most Indian tribes, which are presumed to be free of state control.[47] In 1942, however, a federal court questioned New York's right to exercise any authority on Indian reservations.[48]

In 1984 Congress passed a law that clarified the situation, at least with respect to New York's criminal jurisdiction. This law gives jurisdiction to New York over "all offenses committed by or against Indians on Indian reservations within the State of New York."[49] However, this law expressly denies New York the right to regulate any hunting or fishing rights guaranteed the Indians by federal law or to require that Indians obtain a state license to exercise these rights.

With regard to civil jurisdiction, in 1950 Congress passed a law[50] that confers authority on the courts of New York to resolve civil disputes involving Indians. This law, too, expressly denies the state the right to require Indians to purchase state licenses to engage in federally protected hunting and fishing activities and prohibits the state from taxing, levying upon, or selling reservation lands. In 1976 the U.S. Supreme Court reviewed a similar law applicable to other states and held that it did not confer general state civil jurisdiction over Indian reservations. Rather, it merely allows Indians to use a state court to resolve reservation disputes if they choose to.[51]

Therefore, New York was given extensive criminal jurisdiction but very limited civil jurisdiction over reservation Indians. Only where Congress has expressly conferred civil jurisdiction on New York may the state exercise that authority.[52] For example, courts have ruled that New York cannot tax the sale of goods to Indians on the reservation,[53] and the state cannot bring suit in state court to enforce tribal laws.[54] Of course, the fact that New York has received some amount of jurisdiction in Indian country does not diminish each tribe's inherent powers of criminal and civil jurisdiction over its own members.[55]

E. NONRECOGNIZED TRIBES

Congress has created many special programs for Indian tribes, including housing, educational assistance, social services, and medical benefits, as discussed in the next chapter. Not every tribe is eligible to participate in these programs, however. Most federal Indian programs have been limited by Congress to recognized tribes: those tribes whose existence has been officially acknowledged by the federal government. There are more than four hundred groups that claim tribal existence. Less than three hundred of them have been acknowledged by the federal government.[56] "Approximately two hundred Indian tribes do not exist as legal entities in the eyes of the federal government; they have no recognized land base and they receive few, if any, federal services."[57]

How can a tribe become recognized by the federal government?

Congress has delegated to the Secretary of the Interior the authority to recognize the tribal existence of an Indian group.

In 1978 the Secretary, through the Bureau of Indian Affairs, issued regulations that set forth the qualifications for federal acknowledgment.[58] In order to receive federal recognition, an Indian group must prove that (1) the group can be identified by historical evidence, written or oral, as being an American Indian tribe; (2) its members are descendants of an Indian tribe that inhabited a specific area, and these members continue to inhabit a specific area in a community viewed as American Indian and distinct from other populations in the area; (3) the Indian group has maintained governmental authority over its members as an autonomous entity throughout history until the present; (4) the membership of the group is composed principally of persons who are not members of any other Indian tribe; and (5) the tribe has not been the subject of congressional legislation expressly terminating their relationship with the federal government.[59]

Since 1978, more than 110 tribes have petitioned the BIA for recognition, each spending an average of $250,000 in an effort to meet the BIA's burden of proof. As of early 1990, the BIA had acted on only nineteen of these petitions and had rejected twelve of them.[60]

Many tribes are ineligible for federal recognition because of the fifth requirement listed above; more than one hundred tribes were terminated by Congress between 1953 and 1963 (as explained in chapter 1), and these tribes are thus disqualified. Other tribes have been denied federal recognition because of difficulties in proving continuous political or geographic existence,[61] a cruel basis for denying recognition given what the federal government has done to so many tribes. As one court recently stated, the requirements for recognition should be "interpreted liberally in favor of Indian groups" and, for example, a tribe should not be deemed to have ceased to exist without clear proof that the tribe "has voluntarily sought, and achieved, assimilation into non-Indian culture."[62]

Nonrecognition does not mean, of course, that an Indian group is not an Indian tribe. It means only that the group does not satisfy the BIA's qualifications for federal recognition. However, the economic and social consequences of nonrecognition can be exceedingly severe, and for this reason the government's recognition policy has been extensively criticized.[63]

What relationship does a nonrecognized tribe have with the United States?

None, according to the Department of the Interior. A department regulation states that "acknowledgement of tribal existence by the Department is a prerequisite to the protection, services and benefits from the Federal Government available to Indian tribes."[64]

It is not the Interior Department, however, that has the final word as to whether a tribe should be federally recognized or whether a nonrecognized tribe can nevertheless receive certain federal benefits. Congress does, and a court can reverse the department's decision if the department has ignored the will of Congress. A tribe first must exhaust its remedies within the Interior Department, but thereafter it may seek federal review of the department's decision to withhold recognition[65] or to deny to a nonrecognized tribe eligibility for a federal program.[66] One court has held, for example, that a tribe can enforce a treaty it has with the United States even if the tribe is not federally recognized.[67] Another court has held that nonrecognized tribes are entitled to participate in certain federal programs that Congress has not restricted to recognized tribes.[68] In limited situations, then, even nonrecognized tribes are entitled to certain federal protections, but for the most part, a decision not to acknowledge an Indian tribe is crippling.

NOTES

1. *U.S. v. Joseph,* 94 U.S. 614 (1876).
2. *U.S. v. Sandoval,* 231 U.S. 28 (1913).
3. 25 U.S.C. Sec. 331. *See generally Mountain States Telephone and Telegraph Co. v. Pueblo of Santa Ana,* 472 U.S. 237 (1985).
4. *See Sandoval,* note 2 above; *U.S. v. Chavez,* 290 U.S. 357 (1933).
5. *See U.S. v. Candelaria,* 271 U.S. 432 (1926); *State of New Mexico v. Aamodt,* 537 F.2d 1102 (10th Cir. 1976), *cert. denied,* 429 U.S. 1121 (1977); *Plains Electric G. & T. Corp., Inc. v. Pueblo of Laguna,* 542 F.2d 1375 (10th Cir. 1976).
6. *See Lane v. Pueblo of Santa Rosa,* 249 U.S. 110 (1919).
7. The degree to which the federal government regulates reservation lands is explained in ch. 5, sec. B.

8. *Joseph,* note 1 above, 99 U.S. at 616–19.
9. *See* ch. 2, notes 9 and 10 and accompanying text.
10. 8 U.S.C. Sec. 1401(a)(2).
11. 25 U.S.C. Secs. 461 *et seq.* For a discussion of this act, see ch. 1, sec. E.
12. 25 U.S.C. Sec. 479.
13. *See, e.g., Wilson v. Watt,* 703 F.2d 395 (9th Cir. 1983).
14. *See, e.g., Alaska Pacific Fisher ies v. U.S.,* 248 U.S. 78 (1918); *Pence v. Kleppe,* 529 F.2d 135 (9th Cir. 1976). *See generally* F. Cohen, *Handbook of Federal Indian Law* 739–70 (1982).
15. 348 U.S. 272 (1955).
16. Pub. L. No. 92–203, 85 Stat. 688, codified as amended at 43 U.S.C. Secs. 1601–28.
17. In 1891 Congress created a reservation for the Metlakatla Indian Community on Annette Island in the Alaska Territory. This reservation was not affected by the provisions of the ANCSA. See 43 U.S.C. Sec. 1618(a).
18. *Tyonek Native Corp. v. Cook Inlet Region, Inc.,* 853 F.2d 727 (9th Cir. 1988).
19. 16 U.S.C. Sec. 3120. *See Kenaitze Indian Tribe v. Alaska,* 860 F.2d 318 (9th Cir. 1988). *See also Amoco Production Co. v. Village of Gambell,* 480 U.S. 531 (1987) (ANILCA does not apply to any subsistence interest which natives have, if any, in the outer-continental shelf).
20. 25 U.S.C. Sec. 500.
21. The ANCSA expressly provides that the act is not a "substitute for any governmental programs otherwise available to the native people of Alaska . . ." 43 U.S.C. Sec. 1626(a). Since the enactment of the ANCSA, Congress has not excluded Alaska Natives from any programs available to other Native Americans.
22. *See Alaska v. Native Village of Venetie,* 856 F.2d 1384, 1387 (9th Cir. 1988); *Native Village of Stevens v. Alaska Management and Planning,* 757 P.2d 32 (Alaska 1988); *Native Village of Venetie IRA Council v. Alaska,* 918 F.2d 797 (9th Cir. 1990).
23. For general information about the Oklahoma tribes, see R. Strickland, *The Indians in Oklahoma* (1980); M. Wright, *A Guide to the Indians of Oklahoma* (1951); A. Debo, *A History of the Indians of the United States* pp. 97–98, 112–13 (1970).
24. *See Toosigah v. U.S.,* 186 F.2d 93 (10th Cir. 1950); *Ellis v. Page,* 351 F.2d 250 (10th Cir. 1965).
25. *See* Cohen, note 14 above, pp. 770–97.
26. The Osage Act of 1906 includes several provisions limiting tribal powers. For instance, leases of tribal lands must be approved by the

Secretary of the Interior. 34 Stat. 539, 543. For further information on this subject, see Cohen, note 14 above, pp. 780, 790.

27. Act of June 28, 1898, ch. 517, 30 Stat. 495, 504.

28. 25 U.S.C. Secs. 501–9.

29. *Muscogee (Creek) Nation v. Hodel*, 851 F.2d 1439 (D.C. Cir. 1988), *cert. denied*, 109 S.Ct. 795 (1989). *Contra Muscogee (Creek) Nation v. Acting Area Director*, IBIA 84–15-A (12 Indian L. Rep. 7017) (July 22, 1985).

30. *See Hodel*, note 29 above; *Seneca-Cayuga Tribe of Oklahoma v. Oklahoma*, 874 F.2d 709 (10th Cir. 1989); Cohen, note 14 above, pp. 782–83. *See also Oklahoma Tax Comm'n v. Citizen Band Potawatomi Indian Tribe*, 111 S.Ct. 905 (1991) (Oklahoma tribe enjoys same sovereign immunity from suit as other tribes).

31. *Harjo v. Kleppe*, 420 F. Supp. 1110, 1130 (D. D.C. 1976), *aff'd sub nom. Harjo v. Andrus*, 581 F.2d 949 (D.C. Cir. 1978).

32. *Board of County Comm'rs v. Seber*, 318 U.S. 705, 718 (1943).

33. 70 Stat. 893, 937 and 963 (1959), and 92 Stat. 246 (1977) (codified as 25 U.S.C. Secs. 861–861c, respectively).

34. *Potawatomi Indian Tribe*, note 30 above.

35. *Seneca-Cayuga*, note 30 above (trust land); *Indian Country, U.S.A., Inc. v. Oklahoma Tax Comm'n*, 829 F.2d 967 (10th Cir. 1987), *cert denied sub nom. Oklahoma Tax Comm'n v. Muscogee (Creek) Nation*, 487 U.S. 1218 (1988) (fee land). *See also Housing Auth. of Seminole Nation v. Harjo*, 790 P.2d 1098 (Okla. 1990) (state lacks jurisdiction to resolve dispute over rented property on Indian fee land within reservation).

36. *U.S. v. Burnett*, 777 F.2d 593 (10th Cir. 1985), *cert. denied*, 476 U.S. 1106 (1986); *State v. Burnett*, 671 P.2d 1165 (Okla. Crim. 1983); *State v. Klindt*, 782 P.2d 401 (Okla. Crim. 1989). *But see Eaves v. State*, 800 P.2d 251 (Okla. Crim. 1990) (Oklahoma can prosecute crime by Indian that occurred in tribal housing project).

37. *Cf. State ex rel. May v. Seneca-Cayuga Tribe*, 711 P.2d 77, 88 (Okla. 1985) (suggesting that Oklahoma has "residual" powers over the state's Indian tribes); *Eaves*, note 36 above.

38. *See* B. Graymont, *The Iroquois in the American Revolution* (1972).

39. For further information on this subject, see *Federal Indian Law* pp. 967–73 (Washington, DC: Government Printing Office, 1958), and *Oneida Indian Nation of New York v. New York*, 860 F.2d 1145 (2d Cir. 1988), *cert. denied*, 110 S.Ct. 200 (1989).

40. *Federal Indian Law*, note 39 above, pp. 973–74.

41. *Id.* at 979–85.

42. *See* ch. 6, notes 80–84 and accompanying text.

43. *Oneida Indian Nation*, note 39 above.

44. *County of Oneida v. Oneida Indian Nation*, 470 U.S. 226 (1985).
45. *Id. See also Oneida Indian Nation v. County of Oneida*, 414 U.S. 661 (1974).
46. *See Hearings on S.1686, S.1687 Before the Subcomm. on Indian Affairs of the Senate Comm. on Interior and Insular Affairs*, 80th Cong., 2d Sess. 13 (1948); Comment, *The New York Indians' Right to Self-Determination*, 22 Buffalo L. Rev. 985, 992 (1973).
47. *See* ch. 7, note 2 and accompanying text.
48. *U.S. v. Forness*, 125 F.2d 928 (2d Cir.), *cert. denied*, 316 U.S. 694 (1942).
49. 25 U.S.C. Sec. 232. *See People v. Edwards*, 432 N.Y.S.2d 567 (App. Div. 1980). The federal government, however, retains jurisdiction over federal crimes committed by Indians on New York reservations. *See U.S. v. Cook*, 922 F.2d 1026 (2d Cir. 1991), *cert. denied, Tarbell v. U.S.*, 111 S.Ct. 2235 (1991).
50. 25 U.S.C. Sec. 233.
51. *Bryan v. Itasca County*, 426 U.S. 373 (1976).
52. *See, e.g., John v. City of Salamanca*, 845 F.2d 37 (2d Cir. 1988), *cert. denied*, 488 U.S. 850 (1988).
53. *Herzog Bros. Trucking, Inc. v. State Tax Comm'n*, 508 N.E.2d 914 (N.Y. Ct. App. 1987), *vacated and remanded*, 487 U.S. 1212, *reinstated*, 533 N.E.2d 255 (N.Y. Ct. App. 1988). *See also Milhelm Attea & Bros., Inc. v. Dep't of Taxation and Finance*, 564 N.Y.S.2d 491, 164 A.D.2d 300 (1990).
54. *N.Y. ex rel. Abrams v. Anderson*, 15 Indian L. Rep. 5059 (N.Y. App. Div. 1988).
55. *See, e.g., People v. Boots*, 434 N.Y.S.2d 850, 860 (1980).
56. American Indian Policy Review Commission, *Final Report* p. 461 (Washington, DC: Government Printing Office, 1977).
57. S. O'Brien, "Federal Indian Policies and the International Protection of Human Rights," in *American Indian Policy in the Twentieth Century* p. 45 (V. Deloria, Jr., ed. 1985).
58. 25 C.F.R. Sec. 83 (1989).
59. 25 C.F.R. Sec. 83.7 (1989).
60. J. E. Echohawk, *The First Californians Are Still the Last*, L.A. Times (Mar. 12, 1990).
61. *See, e.g., Mashpee Tribe v. Watt*, 707 F.2d 23 (1st Cir.), *cert. denied*, 464 U.S. 1020 (1983).
62. *Native Village of Venetie*, note 22 above, 918 F.2d at 806. *See also Mashpee Tribe v. New Seabury Corp.*, 592 F.2d 575, 586 (1st Cir.), *cert. denied*, 444 U.S. 866 (1979).
63. *See, e.g., Final Report*, note 56 above, pp. 461–67, and Echohawk, note 60 above.

64. 25 C.F.R. Sec. 83.2 (1989).

65. *James v. U.S. Dep't of Health and Human Services,* 824 F.2d 1132 (D.C. Cir. 1987). *See also Cayuga Indian Nation of New York v. Cuomo,* 667 F. Supp. 938 (N.D.N.Y. 1987).

66. *Joint Tribal Council of Passamoquoddy Tribe v. Morton,* 528 F.2d 370 (1st Cir. 1975).

67. *U.S. v. Washington,* 384 F. Supp. 312, 406 (W.D. Wash. 1974), *aff'd,* 520 F.2d 676 (9th Cir. 1975), *cert. denied,* 423 U.S. 1086 (1976).

68. *Passamoquoddy Tribe,* note 66 above.

XVI

Government Services to Indians

Indians and tribes are eligible for a wide range of federal programs. Most of these programs are administered by the Bureau of Indian Affairs and are available only to Indians. Some are designed to fulfill treaty obligations, while others are provided for humanitarian reasons and to satisfy the government's trust responsibility[1] to Indians. In addition, Indians are eligible to participate in all federal programs available to citizens in general. As a result, Indians receive services through almost every department of government, including the Departments of Education, Agriculture, Housing and Urban Development, Commerce, Labor, and Health and Human Resources.

Indians are also eligible for the general services provided by state governments. Indians are citizens of the states in which they live,[2] and they are entitled to participate in state programs on an equal basis with all other citizens.[3] In addition, many Indians participate in programs through their tribe.

It would be difficult to describe all of the programs that are available to Indians and tribes. There are almost six hundred federal programs alone.[4] This chapter focuses on the more important of them. Several related topics are addressed in other chapters. Chapter 3 discusses the doctrine of trust responsibility, one reason why the government provides services to Indians. Chapter 4 discusses Indian treaties, some of which promised particular services to Indians. Chapter 5 explains why Congress can create programs exclusively for Indians even though these programs discriminate against non-Indians. Finally, chapters 10 and 13 explain why Indians are entitled to receive services from state governments even though Indians and tribes are exempt from most state taxes.

Nearly all government services that are now available to the general public can be terminated at any time. This is true even for such essential programs as Social Security, public schools, and health care. Nothing in the United States Constitution requires the federal or the state governments to offer these services.

Similarly, each program discussed in this chapter is subject to revocation. Even if the program was promised to a tribe in a treaty, the treaty itself can be repealed, and the program can be terminated.[5] In recent years, though, it has been the federal government's policy to increase its assistance to Indians and tribes in an effort to strengthen tribal self-government and meet the basic needs of Indians, who remain the most disadvantaged group in the country.

A. EDUCATION

What Indian education programs does the federal government administer?

As early as 1819 Congress appropriated money to teach tribes "the habits and arts of civilization."[6] Much of this money was given to religious missionary groups to finance their efforts to "educate" Indians.[7]

By the turn of the century the federal government had created scores of Indian boarding schools, one of the largest of which was the Carlisle Indian School in Carlisle, Pennsylvania. Tens of thousands of Indian children were removed from their homes and given a "proper" education in these boarding schools. Many of these schools were notoriously severe; students were forbidden to speak their native language or practice cultural and religious traditions.

Some seventy boarding schools still exist, mostly in Alaska, the Dakotas, and on the Navajo Reservation, but the federal government no longer favors their operation, and it continues to close them.[8] In 1978 Congress passed a law that guarantees the students in these schools the right to free speech and freedom of religious expression.[9] Today, however, most Indian students attend state-operated public schools in their own communities, and the federal government encourages tribes to construct and operate their own schools using federal funds.[10]

In addition to operating Indian boarding schools, the federal government, through the Department of the Interior, gives financial assistance to several tribal schools of higher education, and it directly operates Haskell Indian Junior College in Lawrence, Kansas. It also finances a number of tribal adult education centers. These centers are administered by tribes and provide a variety of programs, including vocational training and high school equivalence instruction.[11]

What Indian education programs do the states administer?

Indians are citizens of the United States and of the state in which they reside. Therefore, they are entitled to participate in all programs that the state provides to its citizens, including its public schools.[12] The vast majority of Indian students attend state public schools.

Most public schools are financed by real estate taxes on local property. Indian trust land is exempt from this form of taxation.[13] Consequently, school districts that encompass Indian reservations often lack a sufficient tax base. To alleviate this problem, the federal government has created two major programs that give financial aid to these school districts. One program was created by the Johnson-O'Malley Act of 1934[14] and the other by the Federally Impacted Areas Act of 1950.[15] The former is administered by the Bureau of Indian Affairs (BIA), an agency within the Department of the Interior, while the latter is administered by the Department of Education.

The Johnson-O'Malley Act (JOM) assists school districts that have nontaxable Indian land within their borders. The Impacted Areas Act (Impact Aid) assists school districts that have any kind of nontaxable federal land within their borders, such as military bases, national parks, and Indian reservations. Under both acts, qualifying school districts receive a certain amount of money for each student who resides on nontaxable land. For many years, JOM was the centerpiece of the federal government's program for funding Indian education, but Impact Aid has replaced JOM as the greatest single source of these funds. In theory, Impact Aid and JOM overlap. However, JOM funds are limited to providing "special needs" except in those school districts ineligible to receive Impact Aid funds.[16] These special needs include guidance counseling, teacher training, home-school coordinators, clothing, athletic equipment, and summer school programs.

Impact Aid, in contrast, meets the basic educational needs of students; it pays for such things as textbooks and teachers' salaries. Schools that receive these funds must keep accurate records to show that this money is not being spent on ineligible students or on equipment that does not meet the educational needs of Impact Aid children.[17]

Congress has created a few other programs that provide money to state public schools in particular situations. The School Facilities Construction Act of 1953,[18] also known as Public Law 81-815, authorizes the BIA to provide funds for the construction of public schools in those school districts where federal installations (such as military bases and Indian reservations) are located.

Another federal law that provides educational assistance to Indians is Title I of the Elementary and Secondary Education Act of 1965.[19] This act provides federal funds to help improve the educational performance of all students who are economically or educationally disadvantaged, Indians and non-Indians alike. Title I funds can be used by state and tribal[20] schools to provide eligible students with a wide range of educational programs, especially in the elementary grades, as well as such things as medical and dental services, food programs, and speech and hearing therapy.

A 1969 study of Indian education revealed that, even with JOM, Impact Aid, and Title I funding, the states were failing miserably to educate Indian children and to reduce an exceedingly high dropout rate.[21] Three years later, Congress responded by enacting the Indian Education Act (IEA).[22] The IEA offers funds for both urban and reservation Indian education, especially for counseling and for remedial programs in language, mathematics, and reading. It also offers scholarships for graduate studies in law, medicine, forestry, business, and engineering and for adult education classes. As with JOM funds, IEA funds are intended to be supplemental and cannot be used by school districts to meet basic education needs.

In addition to its Indian programs, the federal government provides education assistance to groups that include Indians, such as the handicapped,[23] adults who seek a primary education,[24] and students who need bilingual instruction.[25] As indicated earlier, all of these programs can be eliminated by Congress at any time or inadequately funded.[26] However, the federal agencies that administer these programs have no independent authority to make these decisions and must follow the directions of Congress.[27]

If a school has a high concentration of Indian students, is it required to offer a bilingual-bicultural education?

Maybe. Title VI of the Civil Rights Act of 1964[28] prohibits educational institutions that receive federal funds from discriminating against their students on account of race. In *Lau v. Nichols*[29] the Supreme Court interpreted Title VI to require the San Francisco public school system to provide a bilingual-bicultural education to its Chinese students, more than twenty-eight hundred of whom did not speak English, because without these programs they would be unable to obtain a basic education.

Under this principle, public schools may be required to offer a bilingual-bicultural education to Indian students who are deficient in English. A federal court has held, however, that this service is not required if the school district makes adequate alternatives available to students, such as providing tutors.[30]

Most public schools that have a high Indian enrollment would qualify for assistance under the Indian Education Act and/or the Johnson-O'Malley Act, both of which offer federal funds for bilingual and bicultural programs.[31] Therefore, these schools should make available language and cultural programs to facilitate the education of Indian students.

Who is an "Indian" for the purpose of these various programs? Are off-reservation Indians eligible for them?

That depends on the program. When Congress creates an Indian program, it usually identifies the Indians who are eligible to participate in it, but occasionally Congress leaves this task to federal agencies. The Johnson-O'Malley Act, for example, contains no definition of Indian. It says only that the Secretary of the Interior is authorized to enter into contracts for the education "of Indians." However, the BIA, which administers the JOM program, has defined Indian so as to exclude anyone having less than one-quarter Indian blood.[32] Recently, a federal court invalidated a similar restriction and held that the BIA could not deny Indian scholarship funds to an enrolled member of a federally recognized tribe who had slightly less than one-quarter Indian blood.[33] In 1974 the Supreme Court invalidated a BIA regulation that disqualified off-reservation Indians from receiving general welfare services.[34] Thus, when Congress has allowed the BIA to decide who an Indian is, the BIA often has excluded many deserving Indians from the program. Courts will overrule these exclusions if the BIA's regulations are inconsistent with the federal statute.

What Indian education programs do the tribes administer?

Many Indian tribes operate their own education programs, including elementary and secondary schools, institutions of higher education, and adult education centers. The federal government has encouraged Indian tribes to offer these programs by allowing them to obtain Indian education funds that otherwise would have gone to federal or state agencies for that purpose.

The most important law in this area is Title I of the Indian Self-Determination and Education Assistance Act of 1975 (ISDEA).[35] The ISDEA authorizes the Secretary of the Interior to contract with a tribe or tribal organization for the administration of any Indian education program now administered by the Department of the Interior, using the same funds that Congress appropriated to the federal agency for this purpose.[36] A tribe requesting this authority may not be refused unless the Secretary can prove that the tribe is incompetent to manage the program.[37] In 1978 Congress expressly directed the Secretary "to facilitate Indian control of Indian affairs in all matters relating to education."[38] The Self-Determination Act thus encourages tribes to operate the schools and education programs now operated by the BIA.

In addition, tribes may initiate their own education programs by applying for grants under the Johnson-O'Malley Act. A number of tribes and tribal organizations have used JOM grants to operate colleges and adult education centers on the reservation.[39]

Congress has passed other laws enabling tribes to initiate and operate their own education programs. For example, the Tribally Controlled Community College Assistance Act of 1978[40] allows a tribal college, if the majority of its students are Indians, to receive funds to finance educationally related activities. Funds for the construction of tribal schools is also available under the ISDEA.

Indian tribes can also participate in most of the federal government's general education programs. For instance, tribal schools can receive funds under the Elementary and Secondary

Education Act,[41] just as state schools can, to educate disadvantaged students. Tribal schools can also receive funds for advanced learning under the Higher Education Act,[42] and they qualify for the same funds that are available to the states through the Indian Education Act, discussed earlier.[43]

What control has been given to Indian parents over Indian education?

Quite a bit of control. Most federal Indian programs in state public schools give Indian parents and Indian tribes some control in developing and selecting the services to be funded. For example, Indian parents have a veto power in determining what a school will do with its JOM money.[44] Indian parents and tribes also have significant authority under the Impact Aid Act,[45] the Indian Education Act,[46] and the Elementary and Secondary Education Act.[47] Indian parents and tribes should exercise the powers they have under these laws.

B. HEALTH CARE

Indians have staggering health problems. They have the lowest health level and the highest disease rate of all major population groups in the United States. Most disturbing, Indian deaths from curable illnesses, such as tuberculosis, dysentery, and influenza, is over four hundred times the national average. Many physical illnesses suffered by Indians are directly related to malnutrition and substandard housing, while many of their psychological problems—reflected in excessive alcohol use, a rising divorce rate, and increasing violent crime—are attributable to chronic unemployment, a personal sense of displacement, and cultural conflicts.[48]

The federal government has failed to make a concerted effort to meet Indian health needs. What little the government has provided has been so substandard and inadequate that many Indians distrust government health services and refuse to use them even when they are available. Another part of the problem is that many Indians live in small, isolated communities, far from medical centers. In addition, many Indians are reluctant to seek medical care from non-Indians for a variety of cultural reasons.

The Snyder Act of 1921[49] was the first effort by Congress to improve general health care for Indians. This law authorizes the expenditure of federal funds "for the relief of distress and conservation of health of Indians." However, until 1955 most Snyder Act programs were administered by the Interior Department's Bureau of Indian Affairs, and the BIA did a notoriously poor job of obtaining funds and recruiting doctors for reservation health services. In 1955 Indian health care was transferred from the BIA to a special branch of the Public Health Service, now known as the Indian Health Service (IHS),[50] located within the Department of Health and Human Services. The IHS has had more success than the BIA in obtaining funds and doctors for Indian health care, and the quality of care has improved somewhat since 1955.[51]

Is the federal government obligated to provide health care to Indians?

A number of Indian tribes have treaties with the United States in which they were promised medical supplies and physician services. Today the federal government provides free medical services on most reservations, for the same humanitarian reasons that it provides similar services to other impoverished groups. The federal government, though, has a unique obligation to provide for the welfare of Indians, known as its "trust responsibility."[52] In 1976, when Congress passed the Indian Health Care Improvement Act (IHCIA),[53] it affirmed this responsibility in the following terms: "The Congress hereby declares that it is the policy of this Nation, in fulfillment of its special responsibilities and legal obligation to the American Indian people, to meet the national goal of providing the highest possible health status to Indians and to provide existing Indian health services with all resources necessary to effect that policy."[54] The IHCIA recognizes that the government has a trust responsibility to Indians. Perhaps more importantly, it gives Indians a legal right to certain health services, and the government can be sued if it fails to perform its legal duties.[55] As one court explained in requiring the federal government to provide a reservation Indian with emergency mental health care, "Congress in 1976 stated that the federal government had a responsibility to provide health care for Indians. Therefore, when we say that the trust responsibility requires a certain course of action, we do not refer to a relationship that exists only in the abstract but rather to a congressionally recognized duty to provide services for a particular category of human needs."[56]

What Indian health care services does the federal government provide?

Meeting the health needs of Indians, especially those who live on reservations, is a formidable task. Before major improvements can be expected, Indians must not only receive better physician care, but the underlying causes of disease—malnutrition, substandard housing, unemployment, and poverty—must be decreased substantially. Unfortunately, little is being done to improve either the medical or the social problems Indians face. The federal government's Indian health care programs are notoriously inadequate. The Indian Health Service, the primary agency responsible for providing health care to Indians, is underfunded and understaffed. As a Senate committee reported in 1977, "Even today the Indian Health Service has a severe shortage, inadequate facilities, limited funds, a backlog of unmet medical services, and a poor budget and management system."[57] As a result, many Indians do not receive needed medical care, and quite a few IHS medical centers have limited their services to emergency cases.

Rather than build new facilities or increase its staff, IHS has begun contracting with local doctors and health centers to provide medical services to Indians who live in their vicinity. This is known as "contract care," as opposed to the "direct care" provided in an IHS facility. IHS now spends about a third of its budget on contract care. Contract care allows Indians to obtain medical services in localities where IHS facilities are inadequate to meet their medical needs. However, some off-reservation hospitals have been accused of discriminating against Indians and of failing to provide proper care; lawsuits have been filed against some of them to obtain equal services.[58]

When the IHCIA was passed in 1976, it was heralded as a major step forward. The act is designed to increase the staff of the IHS, provide scholarships to Indians who wish to enter health fields, and fund the construction of new hospitals, the renovation of old hospitals, and the construction of safe water and sanitary waste disposal facilities.[59] Although the act has brought about some improvements in these areas, it has never been funded sufficiently to accomplish its overall goals.

Perhaps due to a shortage of funds, IHS has reduced its responsibilities. Of most significance, IHS has made off-reservation Indians ineligible for contract care even though the majority of Indians live off the reservation.[60] Off-reservation Indians are eligible only for direct care, which means they must travel to a reservation to receive it, often hundreds of miles away. On-reservation Indians, however, who are off the reservation temporarily, including Indian students and foster care children, can obtain contract care.[61] IHS defends these arbitrary classifications by arguing that Indians do not have a legal entitlement to medical services.[62] At least two federal courts have criticized this view.[63] One court ordered IHS to increase its services to both on- and off-reservation Indians in California, finding that IHS had ignored the responsibilities Congress had given it.[64]

Are Indians entitled to health care under the Medicare, Medicaid, and Veterans Administration programs?

Yes. Indians are eligible on the same basis as other citizens, regardless of their eligibility for IHS medical services.[65] Unfortunately, many Indians are unable to take advantage of these programs because they live in remote areas and cannot travel to facilities licensed to provide such care.[66]

What Indian health care services do the states provide?

Medicaid is the only general health program the states provide. Medicaid offers basic medical care for poor people and is funded by federal and state monies. As explained earlier, Indians are eligible for state services, such as Medicaid, to the same extent as other citizens. On the local level, many counties and cities offer free health services in certain situations, and Indians have an equal right to receive them, too.[67] Some state and local health care facilities have signed contracts with IHS, as described above, to provide health services to Indians.

When an Indian is eligible for both federal assistance under the IHCIA and for state assistance, federal assistance is considered to be the secondary source.[68] However, if a dispute arises between the state and federal governments as to which government must pay an Indian's bill, the federal government—and not the Indian—must pursue that dispute.[69]

What Indian health care services do the tribes provide?

Indian tribes have become increasingly interested in providing medical care to their members and in staffing reservation facilities with Indian professionals. Unfortunately, few tribes can afford to provide medical services, and there is a shortage of Indian health professionals.

The Indian Self-Determination and Education Assistance Act[70] and the Indian Health Care Improvement Act,[71] both enacted in 1975, offer some hope. The Self-Determination Act authorizes IHS to help tribes create their own health care programs. Thus, tribes can now receive federal funds to provide medical services to their members.

The IHCIA provides scholarships to Indian students studying in health fields. Together with the Self-Determination Act, the IHCIA will allow tribes to create their own health facilities and staff them with tribal members, assuming that Congress appropriates sufficient funds to implement these two programs.

C. PUBLIC ASSISTANCE AND SOCIAL SERVICES

What public assistance and social service programs does the federal government administer?

The federal government operates a number of programs designed to assist impoverished Indians. Each program has its own guidelines for determining eligibility. Congress authorized the BIA to provide services for the welfare of Indians when it enacted the Snyder Act in 1921.[72] However, it was not until 1944 that the BIA began to offer public assistance (welfare) to Indians.[73] The BIA now operates a number of such programs, including general assistance and aid to dependent children.[74] These programs, however, offer assistance as a last resort. Indians who apply for these funds must show that they are ineligible to receive similar assistance from state, local, or other federal welfare agencies.[75]

Until recently, the BIA allowed only on-reservation Indians to receive welfare payments. In 1974 the Supreme Court reviewed federal statutes and held that Congress intended to permit Indians who lived near their reservation and maintained close social and economic ties with the tribe to receive these same benefits.[76] Current BIA regulations incorporate this ruling.[77]

The federal government also administers, through the Department of Agriculture, a commodity food program.[78] Under this program, the federal government purchases surplus food and distributes it to needy persons, including Indians. The Department of Agriculture allows participating agencies, such as tribal organizations and state agencies, to distribute this food with financial assistance from the department.[79] Although commodity food is better than no food at all, it tends to be below average in quality, not well balanced, and high in starch content.

What public assistance and social service programs do the states administer?

Most social service and welfare programs administered by the states are funded primarily, if not entirely, by the federal government. These programs are designed to assist impoverished citizens of the state. Indians are entitled to participate in these programs to the same extent as all other citizens.[80]

The two most important social service programs administered by the states are the food-stamp program[81] and the welfare programs created by the Social Security Act of 1935: Aid to Families with Dependent Children (AFDC),[82] Supplemental Security Income to the Aged, Blind, and Disabled (SSI),[83] and Child Welfare Services.[84]

The food-stamp program is a federally funded, locally administered program designed to allow low-income households to obtain a nutritious diet. It is funded through the Department of Agriculture. Each state has the option of participating in the program. If a state chooses to participate, it must distribute food stamps in every political subdivision in the state, including Indian reservations.[85] A tribe can request permission from the department to administer the program on its reservation.[86] On those reservations in which the state operates the food-stamp program, the state is obliged by law to consult with tribal authorities.[87] Eligibility for the program is based on uniform standards established by the department and apply nationwide.[88]

The welfare programs created by the Social Security Act are funded primarily by the federal government but the states are required to pay part of the cost. Each state establishes its own eligibility standards and decides how much assistance households will receive; payment levels vary from state to state. The AFDC program provides public assistance to needy families with dependent children. SSI provides financial support to needy persons who are aged, blind, or permanently and totally disabled. The Child Welfare Services program provides financial assistance and services to adoptive and foster care families.

In addition, most states and many municipalities have their own relief programs that are not federally funded. These programs are usually limited to special needs, such as medical care. Indians are eligible for this relief assistance to the same extent as other citizens, and they cannot be forced to seek funds under a federal program before qualifying for them.[89]

What public assistance and social service programs do the tribes administer?

Until recently, few tribes had public assistance or social service programs because they could not afford them. However, tribes may now operate the federal government's programs on their reservation. For instance, tribes can obtain federal funds to operate the food-stamp[90] and commodity food programs.[91] The Self-Determination Act of 1975 authorizes the BIA to allow tribes to administer the BIA's welfare programs.[92] Indian tribes also have substantial authority regarding adoption and foster care placement of Indian children under the Indian Child Welfare Act of 1978. This subject is discussed in the next chapter.

D. HOUSING

How adequate is reservation housing?

Most Indian reservations have a severe shortage of adequate housing. A recent study by the Bureau of Indian Affairs indicates that more than half of reservation homes do not meet federal habitability standards, and a third need outright replacement. On the Pine Ridge Sioux Reservation in South Dakota, for example, 88 percent of the homes have been classified as substandard dwellings. Some 15 percent of reservation Indian families who need their own homes live with other families due to the shortage of housing.[93] The situation is getting worse rather than better. For one thing, few commercial lenders extend credit on reservations because Indian homes are usually built on trust land owned by the United States on which they cannot obtain a mortgage.[94] The federal government operates several Indian housing programs, but they are terribly underfunded. A 1977 Senate committee reported that "present production [of Indian homes] must more than double to eliminate the deficit within a reasonable time."[95]

Substandard housing conditions cause serious health problems for Indian people. Crowded living conditions, insufficient quantities of safe water, and the lack of sanitation facilities help spread disease. Significant improvement in Indian health and welfare is unlikely until Indian housing is greatly improved.

What housing programs are available to Indians and tribes?

Few state or local governments have programs that provide permanent housing for low-income people, other than those programs funded by the federal government. Virtually all of the housing programs that offer permanent Indian housing are federal programs. Two federal agencies, the BIA and the Department of Housing and Urban Development (HUD), operate housing programs for reservation Indians.

The BIA administers the Housing Improvement Program[96] from funds provided under the Snyder Act.[97] This program creates four categories of assistance: (1) repairs to substandard housing that will remain substandard even after the repairs; (2) repairs to substandard housing that will then meet standards; (3) downpayments for new homes; and (4) construction of new housing.[98] Originally, the program emphasized the construction of new houses, but since 1968 the BIA has shifted its emphasis to providing grants for housing repair. More than twenty-five thousand Indian homes have been repaired or constructed under this program.[99]

The most significant housing programs in the country are administered by HUD. HUD was created by the Housing Act of 1937[100] to remedy the acute shortage of safe dwellings for low-income families. HUD operates two major programs that benefit reservation Indians. Both programs are funded under the Housing Act of 1937 and are administered locally by an Indian Housing Authority (which can be created by tribal law or by state statute.[101])

The first program is the Mutual-Help Homeownership Opportunity Program,[102] initiated by HUD with BIA cooperation in 1964. This program allows eligible Indians to purchase houses with federal funds if they agree to contribute land, labor, cash, materials, or equipment to help build the house. Applicants must agree to maintain the house and make monthly payments based on their income.[103] Once the house is paid for, the Indian owns it. Financing for the house is arranged through the Indian Housing Authority (IHA), which receives its funds from HUD.

The second program is the Rental Housing Project.[104] Under this program an IHA can obtain funds from HUD for the planning and development of low-income housing. HUD also provides annual loans and contributions sufficient to amortize development and financing costs of the project. The IHA may purchase the property itself and hire its own contractor to build the homes (the "conventional method"), or it may purchase the housing project after it is completed (the "turnkey method"). The project, once completed, will allow the IHA to rent homes to low-income families.[105]

Indian farmers are eligible for housing assistance under several of the general programs operated by the Farmer's Home Administration. Grants and loans are available to low- and moderate-income farm families for repair and construction of dwellings.[106]

Thus, there are several housing programs available to Indians. Yet thousands of Indians live in substandard housing, and on many reservations the situation is getting worse. There are at least three reasons for this. First, Congress has not adequately funded the programs it has created. Second, some programs are administered so poorly that people are discouraged from seeking help under them. Finally, tribal housing officers often change after each tribal election, and there is a lack of expertise and consistency within many Indian Housing Authorities.[107]

As one federal court recently stated, the federal government's trust responsibility to Indians includes "the provision of social welfare benefits, including housing."[108] Providing Indians and all other citizens with decent, safe, and adequate housing should be one of this nation's highest priorities.

E. ECONOMIC DEVELOPMENT

One of the most pressing problems for Indians is economic deprivation, both on and off the reservation. Unemployment among Indians is ten times the national average, and on some reservations the unemployment rate is as high as 80 percent. The majority of Indian families have barely enough money to survive. Economic stagnation exists on most reservations because tribes lack the money to initiate their own businesses and their geographic isolation makes them unattractive to private investors. Even when private businesses have located on reservations, many have been unprofitable because of problems adjusting to the tribe's cultural and religious traditions and the particular needs of their workers.[109]

The federal government operates several economic development programs for Indians, but they are not adequately funded. To illustrate, Indian tribes in 1970 applied for $25.3 million in loans from a government fund that contained only $3.3 million.[110]

Since 1965 the Economic Development Administration (EDA) in the Department of Commerce has been authorized to give economic assistance, including low-interest, long-term loans, for industrial development in chronically depressed areas, including Indian reservations.[111] Most reservations have now received at least some assistance from EDA in the form of grants or loans for such public works as industrial parks, recreational facilities, water and sewage systems, and airports, as well as business loans.[112] The EDA is also authorized to assist tribes in hiring experts to conduct long-range economic planning.[113]

In 1972 a congressional study indicated that a billion dollars in economic financing was needed to revitalize Indian reservations.[114] However, the Indian Financing Act[115] that was passed two years later authorized only fifty million dollars for that purpose, although this has been helpful. The act authorizes the Department of the Interior to lend money to tribes and tribal members and to guarantee loans from private lenders. Money repaid on these loans is then lent to other tribes or individuals.[116] The stated purpose of this act is "to help develop and utilize Indian resources" to a point where Indians "will enjoy a standard of living from their own productive efforts comparable to that enjoyed by non-Indians in neighboring communities."[117] This goal, however, is a long way from becoming a reality.

The Indian Industrial Development Loan Program, operated by the BIA, publicizes investment opportunities on Indian reservations and assists businesses that may want to locate there. The Small Business Administration operates several loan programs that are available to non-Indians and Indians alike to help finance business ventures.[118]

Recent laws that have been very important to the economy of some tribes include the Indian Mineral Development Act of 1982,[119] which assists tribes in developing and utilizing their mineral resources, and the Indian Gaming Regulatory Act of 1988,[120] which allows tribes in certain situations to operate gaming businesses, such as bingo. The Indian Self-Determination and Education Assistance Act of 1975[121] allows Indian tribes to assume control of programs operated by government agencies. Today, due to this act, more than 50 percent of BIA programs are now being administered by tribes. Not only does this give a tribe greater control over reservation affairs, but it helps tribal employment, and a larger share of federal funds remain on the reservation.

Stimulating the tribe's economy and achieving the goal of economic self-sufficiency will take time, money, and dedication. However, economic recovery is the only hope reservation Indians have of ever attaining a decent standard of living.

F. EMPLOYMENT TRAINING AND DEVELOPMENT

Indians have an exceedingly high rate of unemployment, both on and off the reservation. Within the past thirty years the federal government has initiated several programs in an effort to improve this situation. The BIA's first major employment project was the Relocation Program (later called the Employment Assistance Program), which pays Indians to leave the reservation and accept employment in urban areas. Although this program is still in operation, it has been a dismal failure. Most relocated Indians cannot adjust to city life and resent the menial jobs they usually are required to take once they get there. The vast majority of participants soon return to the reservation.[122]

In recent years, rather than attempt to relocate Indians in urban job markets, the BIA has concentrated its efforts on attracting private businesses to the reservation. It has done this by offering to pay part of the salary of certain Indian employees for a period of time, by operating job-training programs for Indians, and by offering technical assistance to private business ventures willing to locate on a reservation.[123]

In addition, Congress has passed three laws that give Indians an employment preference, and these laws have helped to bring reservation Indians into the job market. One law, passed as part of the Indian Reorganization Act of 1934,[124] requires that Indians be given a preference for jobs within the Bureau of Indian Affairs, and most bureau employees now are Indian. A second law, the Buy Indian Act,[125] requires that, so far as practicable, Indian labor shall be employed and Indian products shall be purchased by the BIA in negotiating and fulfilling its contracts. The third law, enacted as part of the Indian Self-Determination and Education Assistance Act of 1975, requires that in fulfilling government contracts under this act (discussed earlier in this chapter) a preference shall be given to Indian-owned businesses and Indian labor.[126]

Unfortunately, Congress has abolished or curtailed several national employment programs created during the 1960s that were very important to reservation Indians, such as Operation Mainstream and Comprehensive Employment Training Act (CETA) programs. These programs hired and trained unemployed workers for a host of public service jobs. When CETA was repealed in 1982, thousands of reservation Indians lost their jobs, and many tribal services were abolished.[127]

G. RESOURCE MANAGEMENT: IRRIGATION, FARM- AND RANGELAND, TIMBER, AND MINERALS

Indian tribes own (in trust status) more than 51 million acres of land, including 44 million acres of rangeland, 2.7 million acres of cropland, and 5.3 million acres of forest.[128] Within these lands are vast, mostly undeveloped reserves of oil, gas, coal, and minerals. It was estimated in 1973 that Indian lands contain 3 percent of the nation's oil and gas reserves and 13 percent of its coal reserves.[129] These lands already supply the federal government with almost all of its uranium.[130] A number of western tribes have formed an organization called the Council of Energy Resource Tribes (CERT)[131] to help coordinate management of these valuable resources.

Various federal agencies offer technical and other assistance to tribes to help manage their resources. For more than a century, for example, the BIA has assisted reservations with irrigation projects. The BIA also supervises the construction and operation of drainage systems, pumping plants, storage and flood control dams, and power-generating plants.[132]

The BIA also offers technical assistance in the development of Indian farm- and rangeland, including help with soil conservation and moisture control and water and air pollution control.[133] The BIA also administers the leasing of Indian lands to non-Indians for farming or grazing purposes.[134] In the process, the BIA is supposed to control land management and ensure that Indian lands are not being depleted by improper farming or overgrazing, but it often ignores this responsibility. In addition, the BIA's tight control over Indian land, and the low fee it often charges non-Indians for leasing this land, have caused many Indians to resent the BIA's involvement in their leasing activities.[135]

The BIA is also authorized to manage timber on Indian lands. The BIA has initiated a conservation program designed to preserve tribal timber in a perpetually productive state. Lack of funds and BIA mismanagement have prevented the BIA from achieving this goal.[136] Since 1910 Indians and tribes have been permitted to sell timber from their trust lands, but the sale is subject to the BIA's approval, and the BIA is allowed to keep 10 percent of the proceeds as an administrative cost.[137]

The extent to which Indians may control their mineral resources has become an exceedingly controversial subject because of the vast wealth these resources represent. The federal government had no idea when it created Indian reservations that underneath these largely barren lands lay some of the richest oil, gas, and coal deposits in the world, today worth billions of dollars. Tribes are just beginning to learn about the power—and the problems—this wealth can bring them.

Indian lands are not public lands for purposes of mineral regulation.[138] This means that the federal government cannot authorize the extraction of minerals from them without the tribe's approval. However, federal law gives the Department of the Interior the power to manage the sale and lease of Indian mineral rights.[139] This allows the department to regulate the terms and conditions under which minerals are extracted from Indian lands. The department has recognized that its principal objective is to help tribes receive the maximum benefit from their mineral resources consistent with sound conservation policies.[140] Unfortunately, the federal agencies most responsible for carrying out this objective—the Bureau of Indian Affairs and the United States Geological Survey (USGS)—have been doing a scandalous job of implementing it, and tribes have good reason to distrust the government's ability to manage their resources. A 1976 study by the Comptroller General of the United States revealed that the BIA had yet to determine the amount of mineral resources on most reservations, that its technical expertise was limited, and that its development plans were inadequate. The USGS had failed to inspect or audit many mineral operations it had authorized and had failed to require timely royalty payments so that neither the Indians nor the USGS had any idea what payments were due or when they would be made. Losses are in the millions of dollars.[141]

Partly in response to these government failures, Congress enacted the Indian Mineral Development Act of 1982.[142] This act imposes specific obligations on the BIA to assist tribes in developing their mineral resources, and includes an obligation to make available independent expert advice on all phases of mineral development. However, the BIA is still vested with the authority to disapprove tribal contracts for mineral development.[143]

H. PROGRAMS SUPPORTING INDIAN GOVERNMENTS

As explained in chapter 1, during most of this country's history the federal government has tried to weaken, if not destroy, tribal government and to assimilate Indians into white society. In recent years, however, Congress has passed important legislation supporting Indian tribes and making it easier for tribes to govern themselves.

The most far-reaching of these laws is the Indian Self-Determination and Education Assistance Act of 1975,[144] which allows Indians to assume control over many of the programs administered by the Departments of the Interior, Education, and Health and Human Services. Under the act, the secretaries of these departments are required to transfer the administration of various programs, especially in the areas of education and health, to qualifying Indian tribes and to give these tribes the same amount of funds that the department would have spent on the program. The Self-Determination Act eliminates the government's monopoly over Indian services and permits tribes to plan and administer their own programs. Most of the programs covered by the act were discussed earlier in this chapter.

Another important law is the State and Local Fiscal Assistance Act of 1972[145] (the Revenue-Sharing Program). The act provides direct financial assistance to state and local governments, including Indian tribes, to provide health, transportation, recreation, and other services. In 1974 Congress passed the Native American Programs Act "to promote the goal of economic and social self-sufficiency" of Indians.[146] The act established the Office of Native American Programs (ONAP), later renamed the Administration for Native Americans (ANA). ANA is located within the Department of Health and Human Resources, and it funds a broad range of programs for Indians. ANA programs are aimed at strengthening tribal administration, providing human services, and fostering economic growth. ANA programs provide food, emergency medical services, consumer education, and recreational and economic development. In 1975 alone, more than 150 reservations received ANA grants.[147]

I. LEGAL AND JUDICIAL ASSISTANCE

As explained in chapter 6, most tribes exercise civil and criminal jurisdiction over their members, maintain a police force, and operate several levels of tribal courts. Many of these tribal law enforcement programs were created with the assistance of the federal government. The Bureau of Indian Affairs helps train tribal police, inspects tribal jail facilities, and gives general advice and assistance to tribes in their law enforcement efforts.[148] Most tribal judicial systems, however, are funded primarily from tribal sources and are operated with only limited assistance from the federal government.[149]

Tribes are eligible to receive grants from the Law Enforcement Assistance Administration (LEAA). LEAA grants may be used to establish a plan for a comprehensive law enforcement program and thereafter for recruitment, training, and education of law enforcement personnel.[150] A number of Indian tribes have received LEAA grants for these purposes.

On occasion the federal government will represent Indian tribes in legal matters as part of its trust responsibility.[151] A federal law provides, "In all States and Territories where there are reservations or allotted Indians the United States attorney shall represent them in all suits at law and in equity."[152] This law has been interpreted by the courts to be nonbinding,[153] and the federal government represents tribes in relatively few lawsuits. However, most of the major court battles over Indian rights to water, land, and wildlife have been brought by the United States on behalf of an Indian tribe.

During the 1960s the federal government created a program that provided free legal assistance to poor people. This program is now operated by the Legal Services Corporation, a separate, federally funded organization.[154] A number of Legal Services offices have been established on Indian reservations, although only a minority of reservations have one. The Reagan administration attempted to eliminate the entire program but Congress voted to continue its funding.

NOTES

1. The government's trust responsibility is discussed in ch. 3.
2. Act of June 2, 1924, codified as 8 U.S.C. Sec. 1401(a)(2). *See* ch. 13, notes 1–3 and accompanying text.
3. *See* ch. 13.
4. *See* Office of Vice-President, Nat'l Council on Indian Opportunity, *A Study of Federal Indian Domestic Assistance Programs* (1974), re-

printed in Legislation to Extend the Older Americans Act: Hearings on S. 1425, H.R. 3922, 94th Cong., 1st Sess. 828, 830 (1975).

5. This subject is discussed in ch. 4.

6. Act of Mar. 3, 1819, ch. 85, Sec. 2, 3 Stat. 516, 517.

7. *See* 8(2) *Am. St. Papers, Indian Affairs*, 16th Cong., 1st Sess. 200–201 (1980).

8. *See, e.g., Cheyenne-Arapaho Tribes v. Watt*, Civ. No. 82–1091 (10 Indian L. Rep. 3017) (D.D.C. 1983).

9. 25 U.S.C. Sec. 2017. *See* 25 C.F.R. Sec. 32.4 (1990).

10. *See Ramah Navajo School Bd. v. Bureau of Revenue*, 458 U.S. 832 (1982).

11. *See* American Indian Policy Review Commission, *Final Report* part 2, pp. 21–23, and part 4, pp. 812–14, 893–911 (Washington, DC: Government Printing Office, 1977).

12. *See* 42 U.S.C. Sec. 2000d. *Cf Goodluck v. Apache County*, 417 F. Supp. 13 (D. Ariz. 1975), *aff'd sub nom. Apache County v. U.S.*, 429 U.S. 876 (1976). *See also Piper v. Big Pine School District*, 226 P. 926 (Cal. 1924).

13. *See* ch. 10, notes 49–51 and accompanying text.

14. 25 U.S.C. Secs. 452 *et seq.*

15. 20 U.S.C. Secs. 236 *et seq.*

16. 25 C.F.R. Sec. 273.1 (1990).

17. *See Natonabah v. Bd. of Educ.*, 355 F. Supp. 716 (D.N.M. 1973).

18. 20 U.S.C. Secs. 631 *et seq. See also* 25 U.S.C. Sec. 458.

19. 20 U.S.C. Secs. 2701 *et seq.*

20. 20 U.S.C. Sec. 2711(d).

21. Special Subcomm. on Indian Education of the Comm. on Labor and Public Welfare, *Indian Education: A National Tragedy—A National Challenge,* S. Rep. No. 501, 91st Cong., 1st Sess. 163 (1969).

22. Now codified at 25 U.S.C. Secs. 2601 *et seq. See also* 34 C.F.R. Part 250 (1989).

23. *See, e.g.,* Education of the Handicapped Act, 20 U.S.C. Secs. 1401 *et seq.*

24. *See, e.g.,* Adult Education Act, 20 U.S.C. Secs. 1201 *et seq.*

25. *See, e.g.,* Title VII of the Elementary and Secondary Education Act, 20 U.S.C. Secs. 3281 *et seq.*

26. *See, e.g., Eastern Band of Cherokee Indians v. U.S.*, No. 71–87L (16 Indian L. Rep. 4017) (Ct. Cl. 1988).

27. *See Vigil v. Andrus*, 667 F.2d 931 (10th Cir. 1982).

28. 42 U.S.C. Sec. 2000d.

29. 414 U.S. 563 (1974).

30. *Guadalupe Organization, Inc. v. Tempe Elem. School Dist.*, 587 F.2d 1022 (9th Cir. 1978).

31. Funds are also available under the act listed in note 25 above.
32. 25 C.F.R. Sec. 273.12 (1990).
33. *Zarr v. Barlow*, 800 F.2d 1484 (9th Cir. 1986).
34. *Morton v. Ruiz*, 415 U.S. 199 (1974).
35. 25 U.S.C. Secs. 450, 450f–n.
36. 25 U.S.C. Sec. 450f.
37. *Id.*
38. 25 U.S.C. Sec. 2010.
39. Tribal organizations and communities can qualify for JOM grants. *See* 25 C.F.R. 271.11 (1990).
40. 25 U.S.C. Secs. 1801 *et seq.*
41. Note 19 above.
42. 20 U.S.C. Secs. 1001 *et seq.*
43. Cited in note 22 above.
44. 25 C.F.R. Sec. 273.16 (1990).
45. *See* 20 U.S.C. Sec. 240(b)(3) and 34 C.F.R. Secs. 223.20 *et seq.* (1989).
46. 25 U.S.C. Sec. 2604(b)(2)(B)(ii).
47. 25 U.S.C. Sec. 2726.
48. *See* Staff of American Indian Police Review Comm'n, 94th Cong., 2d Sess., *Report on Indian Health* pp. 51–65 (Comm. Print 1976); A. Sorkin, *American Indians and Federal Aid* pp. 52–55 (Washington, DC: The Brookings Institute, 1971); R. Strickland, *Genocide-At-Law*, 34 U. Kan. L. Rev. 713, 717 (1986).
49. 25 U.S.C. Sec. 13.
50. 42 U.S.C. Secs. 2001–5f.
51. Sorkin, note 48 above, p. 56.
52. The government's trust responsibility toward Indians is discussed in ch. 3. *See also McNabb v. Bowen*, 829 F.2d 787 (9th Cir. 1987).
53. 25 U.S.C. Secs. 1601 *et seq.* For implementing regulations, *see* 42 C.F.R. Secs. 36.301 *et seq.* (1989).
54. 25 U.S.C. Sec. 1602.
55. *See, e.g., Anderson v. U.S.*, 731 F. Supp. 391 (D.N.D. 1990).
56. *White v. Califano*, 437 F. Supp. 543, 557 (D.S.D. 1977), *aff'd*, 581 F.2d 697 (8th Cir. 1978).
57. American Indian Policy Review Comm'n, 94th Cong., 2d Sess., *Final Report* pp. 375–76 (Washington, DC: Government Printing Office, 1977).
58. *See, e.g., Penn v. San Juan Hospital, Inc.*, 528 F.2d 1181 (10th Cir. 1975). *See also U.S. v. North Dakota Hospital Ass'n*, 640 F. Supp. 1028 (D.N.D. 1986).
59. *See also* 42 U.S.C. Sec. 2004a, the Indian Sanitation Facilities Act.
60. 42 C.F.R. Secs. 36.12, 36.15 (1989).
61. 42 C.F.R. Sec. 36.10 (1989).

62. *Lewis v. Weinberger*, 415 F. Supp. 652 (D.N.M. 1976); *Bullchild v. Schweiker*, 8 Indian L. Rep. 3128 (W.D. Wash. 1981). *Cf. Morton v. Ruiz*, 415 U.S. 199, 231–36 (1974).

63. *Lewis*, note 62 above; *Rincon Band of Mission Indians v. Califano*, 464 F. Supp. 934 (N.D. Cal. 1979), *aff'd sub nom. Rincon Band of Mission Indians v. Harris*, 618 F.2d 569 (9th Cir. 1980).

64. *Rincon Band*, note 63 above.

65. Senate Committee on Interior and Insular Affairs, *Report on the Indian Health Care Improvement Act*, 93rd Cong., 2d Sess., 113 (S. Rep. No. 93–1283). *See also* note above and accompanying text.

66. *Id.* at 113–14.

67. *See generally* ch. 13.

68. 42 C.F.R. Sec. 36.12(c) (1989).

69. *McNabb*, note 52 above.

70. *See* note 35 above.

71. *See* note 53 above.

72. 25 U.S.C. Sec. 13.

73. Wolf, *Needed: A System of Income Maintenance for Indians*, 10 Ariz L. Rev. 597, 607 (1968).

74. *See* 25 C.F.R. Part 20 (1990).

75. 25 C.F.R. Secs. 20.21–.23 (1990). *See Adams v. Hodel*, 617 F. Supp. 359 (D.D.C. 1985).

76. *Morton v. Ruiz*, 415 U.S. 199 (1974).

77. 25 C.F.R. Sec. 20.20 (1990).

78. 7 U.S.C. Sec. 1431. For implementing regulations, see 7 C.F.R. Part 250 (1990).

79. *Id.*

80. *See* ch. 13, and *Morton*, note 76 above.

81. 7 U.S.C. Secs. 2011 *et seq*.

82. 42 U.S.C. Secs. 601 *et seq*.

83. 42 U.S.C. Secs. 1381 *et seq*.

84. 42 U.S.C. Secs. 620 *et seq*.

85. 7 U.S.C. Sec. 2020(d).

86. *Id.*

87. *Id.*

88. 7 U.S.C. Sec. 2014(b). *See* 7 C.F.R. Sec. 273.1 (1990).

89. *County of Blaine v. Moore*, No. 13578 (Mont. Sup. Ct., Sept. 14, 1977), *reprinted in part in* 4 Indian L. Rep. G–102 (1977).

90. 7 U.S.C. Sec. 2020(d).

91. 7 C.F.R. Sec. 253.4 (1990).

92. 25 U.S.C. Sec. 450f.

93. *See Final Report*, note 57 above, p. 387, and Strickland, note above, p. 717. For a comprehensive survey of Indian housing, see Staff of the

Senate Comm. on Interior and Insular Affairs, *Indian Housing in the United States*, 94th Cong., 1st Sess. (Comm. Print 1975) (hereinafter, *Indian Housing*).

94. *Indian Housing*, note 93 above, pp. 181–95.
95. *Final Report,* note 57 above, p. 387.
96. 25 C.F.R. Part 256 (1990).
97. 25 U.S.C. Sec. 13.
98. *See* 25 C.F.R. Sec. 256.4 (1990). For discussion, *see Sanders v. Muskogee Area Director*, IBIA 90-42-A [18 Indian L. Rep. 7055] (1991).
99. *Indian Housing,* note 93 above, p. 8.
100. 42 U.S.C. Secs. 1437 *et seq.*
101. *See* 42 U.S.C. Secs. 1437b–c; 24 C.F.R. Secs. 905.108–.109 (1989).
102. 24 C.F.R. Part 905, Subsec. D. In 1988 Congress gave this program independent status and funding. *See* 42 U.S.C. Sec. 1437(A)(A).
103. 24 C.F.R. Sec. 905.103(b) (1989).
104. 41 Fed. Reg. 10,135 (1976). *See also* 24 C.F.R. Part 905, Subp. B (1990).
105. *See* 24 C.F.R. Secs. 905.102, .209, .210. *See also* M. Ulmer, *The Legal Origin and Nature of Indian Housing Authorities and the HUD Indian Housing Programs,* 13 Am. Indian L. Rev. 109–114.
106. *See* 42 U.S.C. Secs. 1472, 1474, 1484, and 1485; 7 C.F.R. Part 1944.
107. *See generally Final Report,* note 57 above, pp. 390–93; *Indian Housing,* note 93 above, pp. 9–15.
108. *St. Paul Intertribal Housing Board v. Reynolds*, 546 F. Supp. 1408, 1411 (D. Minn. 1983). *See also Eric v. Secretary of HUD*, 464 F. Supp. 44 (D. Alaska 1978).
109. *See Final Report,* note 57 above, pp. 305–8, 347–50, and D. Vinje, "Cultural Values and Economic Development on Reservations," in *American Indian Policy in the Twentieth Century* pp. 155–76 (V. Deloria, ed. 1985).
110. Vinje, note 109 above, p. 157.
111. 42 U.S.C. Secs. 3121 *et seq.*
112. *See* Economic Development Administration, Dep't of Commerce, *Indian Development Program, reprinted in* Staff of Subcomm. on Economy in Government of the Joint Economic Comm., 91st Cong., 1st Sess., *Toward Economic Development of Native American Communities,* 2:364–66. As an example, see *New Mexico v. Mescalero Apache Tribe*, 462 U.S. 324, 327 n.3 (1983).
113. 42 U.S.C. Secs. 3151, 3151(a).
114. H.R. Rep. No. 907, 93d Cong., 2d Sess. 16 app., *reprinted in* 1974 U.S. Code Cong. & Admin. News 2873, 2882.
115. 25 U.S.C. Secs. 1451 *et seq.*

116. 25 U.S.C. Secs. 1468, 1511.

117. 25 U.S.C. Sec. 1451.

118. For an explanation of programs relating to Indian economic development, see Cohen, *Handbook of Federal Indian Law* pp. 760–66 (1982). *See also Final Report*, note 57 above, pp. 401–19.

119. 25 U.S.C. Secs. 2101 *et seq.*

120. 25 U.S.C. Secs. 2701 *et seq.*

121. 25 U.S.C. Secs. 450 *et seq.*

122. For a discussion of the relocation program, see S. Tyler, *A History of Indian Policy* pp. 153–60 (Washington, DC: Government Printing Office, 1973).

123. Cohen, note 118 above, p. 767.

124. 25 U.S.C. Sec. 472. *See Morton v. Mancari*, 417 U.S. 535 (1974). *See also* 25 U.S.C. Secs. 44–46, 25 C.F.R. Part 5.

125. 25 U.S.C. Sec. 47. However, the BIA appears to have considerable discretion under this act to choose non-Indian labor. *See Lakota Contractors Ass'n v. U.S. Dep't of Health and Human Resources*, 882 F.2d 320 (8th Cir. 1989).

126. 25 U.S.C. Sec. 450e(b). *See Berube v. Bellcourt School Dist.*, 16 Indian L. Rep. 6133 (Turt. Mt. Tr. Ct. 1989).

127. *See* Cohen, note 118 above, pp. 768–69.

128. Comptroller General, Senate Comm. on Interior and Insular Affairs, *Management of Indian Natural Resources*, 94th Cong., 2d Sess. (Comm. Print 1976), p. 9.

129. *Id.*, pp. 77–78.

130. *Dep't of the Interior and Related Agencies Appropriations for 1978: Hearings Before a Subcomm. of the House Comm. on Appropriations*, 95th Cong., 1st Sess., part 2, p. 63. *See also* Comptroller General, note 128 above, pp. 77–78.

131. CERT's main office is at 1999 Broadway, Suite 2600, Denver, Colorado 80202; telephone (303) 297–2378.

132. *See* Cohen, note 118 above, pp. 770–74.

133. *See* 16 U.S.C. Sec. 590a. *See also Management*, note 128 above, p. 10.

134. *See, e.g.*, 25 U.S.C. Secs. 393, 396, and 398.

135. *See, e.g.*, Secretaries of the Dep'ts of Agriculture and Interior, *Study of Fees for Grazing Livestock on Federal Lands* (Washington, DC: Government Printing Office, 1977).

136. *See Management*, note 128 above, p. 10; *Hearings*, note 130 above, pt. 4, pp. 1065, 1084; *U.S. v. Mitchell*, 463 U.S. 206 (1983).

137. 25 U.S.C. Secs. 406, 407, 413. *See* Cohen, note 118 above, p. 776.

138. *Federal Leasing and Disposal Policies: Hearings Pursuant to S. Res. 45, A National Fuels and Energy Policy Study Before the Senate*

Comm. on Interior and Insular Affairs, 92nd Cong., 2d Sess., 651–52 (1972).

139. *See, e.g.,* 25 U.S.C. Secs. 356, 396, 398; 30 U.S.C. Sec. 209; 43 U.S.C. Sec. 31. *See also* Comptroller General, note 128 above, pp. 78–79.

140. *See Hearings,* note 130 above, part 2, p. 63, and part 4, pp. 816–17.

141. *Management,* note 128 above, pp. 82–114.

142. 25 U.S.C. Secs. 2101 *et seq.*

143. 25 U.S.C. Sec. 2102(a).

144. 25 U.S.C. Secs. 450 *et seq.* For a comprehensive analysis of the act, see Cohen, note 118 above, pp. 758–60.

145. 31 U.S.C. Secs. 1221 *et seq.* For further information on this subject, see Cohen, note 118 above, pp. 756–57.

146. 42 U.S.C. Secs. 2991–2d.

147. Cohen, note 118 above, pp. 755–56.

148. *Dep't of the Interior and Related Agencies Appropriations for 1976: Hearings Before a Subcomm. of the House Comm. on Appropriations,* 94th Cong., 1st Sess., part 3, pp. 72–76.

149. *Id.* at 73.

150. 42 U.S.C. Secs. 3721–25, 3731(b), 3781(d).

151. The trust responsibility is the subject of ch. 3.

152. 25 U.S.C. Sec. 175.

153. *See, e.g., Pyramid Lake Paiute Tribe v. Morton,* 499 F.2d 1095 (D.C. Cir. 1974).

154. 42 U.S.C. Secs. 2996 *et seq.*

XVII
The Indian Child Welfare Act

What is the Indian Child Welfare Act?

The Indian Child Welfare Act (ICWA) [1] was passed by Congress in 1978. The act was designed to remedy a shameful situation that existed for many years: the wholesale removal of reservation Indian children by state welfare agencies and state courts. During the mid-1970s, Congress finally investigated this national disgrace. Congress discovered that nearly one-third of reservation Indian children had been separated from their families by state agencies and placed in adoptive families, foster care, or institutions. Most residential placements were to non-Indian homes. These forced separations were disastrous for many of the children involved, their parents, and their tribes.

The evidence also revealed that many state social workers and judges either were ignorant of Indian culture or tradition or were prejudiced in their attitudes; many children were removed from their homes primarily because the family was Indian and poor. The problem was reaching epidemic proportions. In one state, for example, the adoption rate of Indian children was eight times that of non-Indian children. Entire reservations were being depleted of their youth. [2]

The stated purpose of the ICWA is "to protect the best interests of Indian children and to promote the stability and security of Indian tribes and families."[3] The act seeks to protect Indian children, Indian tribes, and Indian culture by limiting the state's powers and by encouraging respect for tribal authority regarding the placement of Indian youth.

The ICWA places such significant restrictions on state courts in resolving reservation custody matters that many states initially contended the act was unconstitutional. However, in 1989 the Supreme Court upheld the constitutional authority of Congress to pass this type of protective legislation for Indians.[4] Opponents of the ICWA have now shifted their focus to narrowing the act's application, and some of these efforts unfortunately have been successful. Congress needs to amend the ICWA in several areas in order to "plug the holes."

What does the ICWA require?

The ICWA establishes specific procedures that state courts must follow in handling Indian child custody matters. To summarize, these procedures are:

1. If the child resides on an Indian reservation[5] or has been made a ward of the tribal court, the tribal court has exclusive jurisdiction. If the child resides off the reservation, the state and the tribal court have concurrent jurisdiction.[6]

2. When the child resides off the reservation and a custody proceeding is initiated in a state court, the court must notify the child's tribe, and the tribe has a right to intervene in the proceeding.[7] If the tribe or either parent requests it, the state court must transfer the case to tribal court unless a parent objects or there exists "good cause" to ignore the request.[8]

3. If the case remains in state court, the court may not terminate parental rights without proof "beyond a reasonable doubt" (or place the child in foster care without "clear and convincing evidence") that continued custody by the child's family "is likely to result in serious emotional or physical damage to the child."[9] In addition, if the child's parent is indigent, the parent has a right to a court-appointed attorney, and separate counsel should be appointed for the child if it is in the child's best interest.[10]

4. Before the state can place an Indian child in a non-Indian adoptive home, the state must give sequential placement preference to (a) the child's extended family, (b) other members of the child's tribe, and (c) other Indian families, unless "good cause" exists.[11] A similar preference exists in foster care placement, with Indian foster homes and tribal institutions being preferred.[12]

5. If the state court proceeding or its placement of an Indian child violates the ICWA, it is subject to invalidation upon the petition of the child's parent, Indian custodian,[13] or tribe.[14]

6. Tribal court custody decisions are entitled to the same "full faith and credit" as state court custody decisions.[15]

7. The state must keep accurate records regarding Indian child placement and make them available to the federal government and the tribe.[16] In addition, when an adopted child becomes eighteen years old, the child must be permitted to discover the biological parents' names and their tribal affiliation.[17]

Thus, the ICWA creates a dual jurisdictional scheme that favors the tribe. If the child lives on the reservation, state courts have no jurisdiction at all. Even if the child lives off the reservation, jurisdiction lies presumptively in the tribe: the tribe can require that the proceeding be transferred to the tribal court, except in cases of "good cause" or objection by either parent. Moreover, the ICWA requires state courts to give preference to Indians whenever they make adoptive or foster care placements.

Does the ICWA apply to voluntary placements?

Yes. Even if both parents of an Indian child consent to having a state court place their child for adoption or in foster care, the ICWA requires that certain steps be followed. The ICWA was intended not only to protect Indian parents but also to protect Indian tribes, and tribes may assert their rights in this situation. Thus, despite the parents' consent, (1) the state court must notify the tribe of its right to intervene; (2) the tribe can seek to transfer the proceeding to tribal court; and (3) even when the case remains in state court, that court must comply with the ICWA's requirements for preferential placement.[18] It is therefore possible, as the Supreme Court held in *Mississippi Band of Choctaw Indians v. Holyfield* (1989),[19] for a tribe to overrule the Indian parents' own desires regarding the placement of their child.

The ICWA also places restrictions on the form of the consent. In order for a consent by an Indian parent or custodian to be valid for foster care placement or for the termination of parental rights, the consent must be in writing and must be recorded before a judge, and the judge must certify that the terms and consequences of the consent were explained to the parent in a language the parent understands.[20] Moreover, the consent is invalid if given prior to, or within ten days after, the child's birth.[21] Consent to temporary foster care placement may be withdrawn by the parent at any time, and the child must then be returned to the parent.[22] Consent for an adoption may be withdrawn by the parent at any time prior to the entry of a final adoption decree,[23] but once the decree is final, it cannot be withdrawn except on proof of duress or fraud in an action filed within two years of the decree.[24]

If an Indian child has been living with an adoptive family for years, can the adoption be invalidated if it violated the ICWA?

It depends. If a state court placed an Indian child in an adoptive home without complying with the ICWA but an adoption decree has not yet been issued, then the parent, custodian, or tribe can have the placement set aside even if many years have elapsed.[25] The proceeding would then be transferred to the tribal court.[26] The tribal court could either place the child back in the same home or make some other placement. For example, if proper notice under the ICWA is not given to an Indian tribe advising the tribe of its right to intervene, a state court decree terminating parental rights can be invalidated.[27]

However, if an adoption decree has already been entered by a state court, a statute of limitations may apply. The ICWA contains only one statutory limitation: a parent who consents to an adoption has only two years in which to claim that the consent was not freely given.[28] Unfortunately, the ICWA does not set any time limits on other types of challenges, nor does it indicate that no time limits apply. Currently, there is a dispute as to whether a state court can apply that state's statutory limitations in ICWA cases.[29] In a recent case, the Alaska Supreme Court imposed Alaska's one-year limitation on withdrawing a valid consent to an adoption.[30] It would be helpful if Congress amended the ICWA to clarify what additional time limits, if any, apply to challenges under the ICWA.

When does the tribe have jurisdiction if the Indian child is born off the reservation?

In determining which court has jurisdiction, legal domicile is more important than location of birth. In the *Holyfield* case cited earlier, both parents had been living on the reservation but left shortly before their twin children were born so that their children would be born off the reservation. The parents then signed consent forms allowing the Holyfields to adopt the twins, and the Holyfields started adoption proceedings in state court. The tribe contended that the children were domiciled for purposes of the ICWA on the reservation and that, consequently, the tribal court had exclusive jurisdiction. The Supreme Court agreed with the tribe. The Court gave the ICWA a broad interpretation consistent with the remedial purpose of the act. Although the children were born off the reservation and had not had any tribal contact, the Court held that the tribal court had exclusive jurisdiction.

Determining the child's legal domicile is an important threshold question because this determines which court has jurisdiction to place the child. When the child lives on the reservation or has been made a ward of the tribal court, the choice is clear: as previously explained, the tribal court has exclusive jurisdiction. If the child is legally domiciled off the reservation, the state court has jurisdiction. However, the state court must transfer the case to the tribal court if requested to do so by a parent, a legal custodian, or the tribe, unless a parent objects or "good cause" exists to deny the request.[31]

It is not always easy to determine a child's domicile, as *Holyfield* illustrates. A child can be living off the reservation at the time the adoption petition is filed and yet still be domiciled on the reservation for purposes of the ICWA,[32] such as when the parents live on the reservation but place the child with someone off the reservation who then files for adoption.[33]

If the Indian child is not enrolled in a tribe, does the ICWA have any application?

Sometimes it does. The ICWA defines "Indian child" as any unmarried person under eighteen years of age who is enrolled in a tribe *or* who is eligible for enrollment.[34] Therefore, if the child is Indian, a state court cannot determine whether the ICWA applies until it finds out from the tribe whether the child is enrolled or is enrollable.

Who needs to be notified when a placement proceeding is commenced in state court?

Three parties are permitted by the ICWA to intervene in a state court custody matter involving an Indian child: the tribe, a parent, or (if there is one) the child's legal guardian.[35] The ICWA requires that the person who commenced the action and who is seeking the placement send a notice to all three of these interested parties and advise them of their right to intervene in the proceeding. The proceeding may not begin until at least ten days after notice has been received, and a twenty-day extension must be granted if requested. The parent, custodian, and tribe have the right to intervene at any point in the proceeding.[36]

Courts have insisted that the act's notice provisions be obeyed. For example, even where it appears that a child would not be eligible for tribal enrollment but the child does have some Indian blood, the tribe must be notified because only the tribe can decide who is eligible for membership.[37] Moreover, notice must be adequate and reasonable. For example, when a state welfare agency knows where a parent lives, placing notice of the court hearing in a newspaper is not sufficient.[38] In any state proceeding in which the identity of a parent or the tribe cannot be determined, the ICWA requires that notice of the proceeding shall be given to the Secretary of the Interior, who has fifteen days to provide the notice to the parent (or legal custodian) and the tribe, if their identities can be determined.[39]

When may a state court deny a request to transfer the proceeding to tribal court?

There are three situations in which a state court may refuse to transfer a custody proceeding to tribal court when requested to do so: the tribal court declines to accept the case, a parent objects to the transfer, or "good cause" exists.[40] Court decisions and Bureau of Indian Affairs (BIA) guidelines indicate that the following situations might constitute "good cause": (1) the tribe, parent, or custodian did not file the request promptly after receiving notice, and the proceeding is in an advanced stage when the request is received;[41] (2) the Indian child is over twelve years of age and objects to the transfer; (3) the evidence necessary to decide the case could not be adequately presented in the tribal court without undue hardship to the parties or the witnesses; or (4) the parents of a child over five years of age are not available, and the child has had little or no contact with the tribe or tribal members.[42]

The burden of proving good cause rests with the party opposing the transfer to tribal court,[43] and it is not an easy burden to satisfy. A child's lack of contact with the tribe is frequently cited as a reason to avoid transfer. However, this cannot constitute good cause in and of itself because otherwise this would encourage the early removal of children from the reservation. It also would overlook the tribe's and the extended family's substantial interest in having these matters decided in tribal court.[44] Even if it might appear to a state court that it is in the child's best interests to live (or to continue living) with a non-Indian adoptive family off the reservation, this is a decision that only the tribal court has the authority to make whenever a proper request to transfer the proceeding has been made.[45] Likewise, geography alone cannot be determinative; a request to transfer should not be denied simply because it would be expensive or inconvenient for off-reservation witnesses to testify in tribal court.[46]

What proof must be shown to terminate parental rights in ICWA cases?

The ICWA provides that parental rights may not be terminated by a state court except "by evidence beyond a reasonable doubt, including testimony of qualified expert witnesses" that continued custody by the parent(s) "is likely to result in serious emotional or physical damage to the child."[47] In addition, it must be shown that "active efforts have been made to provide remedial services and rehabilitative programs" to the family and that these had proved unsuccessful.[48] These are difficult burdens to meet. Indian parents must not be stripped of their parental rights simply because an adoptive family is more secure financially or because the judge disapproves of the tribe's childrearing practices and traditions. However, evidence (especially by Indians who are experts in these matters) that the parent's behavior constitutes abuse, neglect, or abandonment under tribal law or custom can be sufficient to justify the termination of parental rights in a state court provided that remedial services have been tried and failed.[49]

Who is an expert witness for purposes of the ICWA?

As just indicated, in order to justify parental termination, the ICWA requires proof beyond a reasonable doubt, and testimony from expert witnesses is required. Federal guidelines list three categories of experts: (1) a member of the child's tribe who is knowledgeable in tribal childrearing customs; (2) a lay expert who has substantial experience in delivering family care services to Indians and has knowledge of the tribe's cultural standards; (3) someone specially trained in the area in which he or she is testifying (a professional).[50]

Although the ICWA states that there must be "expert witnesses," at least one court has held that one expert is sufficient.[51]

Given the purpose of the act, however, at least one expert should testify about the tribe's customs and standards of child-rearing and its family institutions.

What rights under the ICWA does an unwed father have?

Under the ICWA, each Indian parent must be given notice of a child custody proceeding; each parent may request that the proceeding be transferred to tribal court; and each parent may oppose such a request. However, as defined in the act, a parent "does not include the unwed father where paternity has not been acknowledged or established."[52]

A father may acknowledge or attempt to establish paternity in a variety of ways, such as by signing an affidavit of paternity, marrying the mother, supporting the child financially, or by initiating a paternity lawsuit. Fathers who cannot meet any of these tests have been held by courts not to be a parent for purposes of the ICWA,[53] although these decisions have been criticized.[54]

If a father decides not to establish paternity, and the child's tribal blood comes from the father, the tribe will be unable to participate in the proceeding because the tribe's only link to the child is through the father. The ICWA should be amended so as to allow the tribe the opportunity to establish the father's paternity in these situations.[55]

Must notice be given in emergency custody determinations in state court?

No. The ICWA provides that the notice requirements of the act can be overlooked temporarily when an emergency placement is needed "to prevent imminent physical damage or harm to the child." However, after this initial placement, the court must "expeditiously initiate a child custody proceeding" and provide full notice.[56]

If you wish to appeal a state court custody decision, can the appeal be heard in federal court?

Probably not. If you believe that a state court decision violates the ICWA, you are required to appeal that ruling through the state's appellate court system, and from there to the U.S. Supreme Court. As a general rule, a federal court is never permitted to review a state court's custody decree (even in

ICWA cases) unless it is "fundamentally flawed," a difficult burden to meet.[57] Federal courts also lack jurisdiction to resolve two conflicting tribal court custody decrees.[58]

In what situations does the ICWA not apply?

The ICWA does not apply in several Indian custody situations. For example, it does not apply if the Indian child is not a tribal member or eligible for membership.[59] It also does not apply if the tribe is not recognized by the federal government as an Indian tribe.[60] Thus a state court need not comply with the ICWA if the child's parents are members of a Canadian Indian tribe.[61] The act also does not apply to child custody disputes arising out of divorce or separation proceedings where custody of the child is awarded to one of the parents.[62] The ICWA also does not apply to placements made in juvenile delinquency proceedings when the child has committed an act which, if committed by an adult, would be deemed a crime, unless the proceeding results in the termination of a parental relationship.[63] Moreover, tribes located in so-called Public Law 83–280 states (discussed in chapter 7), can invoke authority under the ICWA only after petitioning the Secretary of the Interior and obtaining the Secretary's permission.[64]

The above exceptions are contained in the ICWA itself. Courts have created a few other exceptions, although they have been criticized for doing so. One court held that it could terminate the parental rights of an unwed Indian father without complying with the ICWA where the mother and the adoptive parents were non-Indian and the child had never lived on the reservation.[65] The court said that the ICWA applied only to "Indian families" and that this was not an Indian family. Using a similar rationale, another court held that the ICWA is not applicable when an Indian child is awarded to the custody of its non-Indian mother in a divorce proceeding, is living off the reservation, and is then adopted by the mother's new spouse.[66] However, the majority of courts have held that the ICWA applies in these types of cases.[67]

Clearly, the ICWA was primarily intended to prevent state courts from placing Indian children in non-Indian, off-reservation homes without providing sufficient protection to the parents' and the tribe's vested interests. The ICWA should be liberally interpreted in order to achieve these goals.

Have state courts obeyed the ICWA?

One reason the ICWA was enacted is because state courts, as Congress noted, "have often failed to recognize the essential tribal relations of Indian people and the cultural and social standards prevailing in Indian communities and families."[68] The ICWA places significant restrictions on state courts. It is now difficult for them to be as discriminatory and as destructive of Indian interests as in the past.

It is not, however, impossible. In fact, in at least two major areas, the ICWA gives an opportunity to state courts to demonstrate opposition to the principles that inspired the ICWA. First, as explained earlier, when an Indian child is not domiciled on the reservation, a state court can refuse to transfer the custody hearing to tribal court if good cause exists. Some state courts have cited to nothing more than the distance state witnesses would have to travel to attend tribal court (which is, of course, the same distance tribal witnesses would have to travel to state court), or to the few contacts a newborn child has had with the reservation (which often is the case for children born off the reservation), as sufficient cause to deny transfer.[69]

Second, the ICWA permits state courts to terminate an Indian's parental rights upon a finding that continued custody by that parent "is likely to result in serious emotional or physical damage to the child."[70] Some state courts have used this somewhat subjective standard as an invitation to unjustly remove Indian children from their parents, especially where the court can claim abandonment. In a recent case, for example, a court held that a fifteen-year-old Indian boy who had fathered a son with a Caucasian girl had abandoned his child, even though the mother and her family had prevented the father from having any contact with the child.[71]

The ICWA is a significant and long-overdue piece of legislation. It is unfortunate that some state courts seem determined to frustrate its application.

NOTES

1. 25 U.S.C. Secs. 1901–63.
2. *See Mississippi Band of Choctaw Indians v. Holyfield*, 490 U.S. 30 (1989). *See also* Comment, *The Indian Child Welfare Act of 1978*, 60

U. Colo. L. Rev. 131 (1989); Tellinghuisen, *The Indian Child Welfare Act of 1978*, 34 S.D.L. Rev. 660 (1989).

3. 25 U.S.C. Sec. 1902. *See Native Village of Venetie IRA Council v. Alaska*, 918 F.2d 797 (9th Cir. 1990).
4. *See Holyfield*, note 2 above.
5. As used in the ICWA, Indian "reservation" means Indian country as that term is defined in 18 U.S.C. Sec. 1151. *See* 25 U.S.C. Sec. 1903(10). "Indian country" is explained in ch. 2, sec. C, of this book.
6. 25 U.S.C. Secs. 1911(a)–(b).
7. *Id.*, Sec. 1912.
8. *Id.*, Sec. 1911(b).
9. *Id.*, Sec. 1912(f) and (e), respectively.
10. *Id.*, Sec. 1912(b). *See In re M.E.M.*, 635 P.2d 1313 (1981); *In re G.L.O.C.*, 668 P.2d 255 (Mont. 1983)
11. 25 U.S.C. Sec. 1915(a). *See In re Bird Head*, 331 N.W.2d 785 (Neb. 1983).
12. 25 U.S.C. Sec. 1915(b).
13. As used in the ICWA, "Indian custodian" means any Indian person who has legal custody of an Indian child under tribal custom or under state or tribal law or who has received temporary custody from a parent of the child. *See* 25 U.S.C. Sec. 1903(6).
14. 25 U.S.C. Sec. 1914.
15. *Id.*, Sec. 1911(d).
16. *Id.*, Sec. 1915(e).
17. *Id.*, Sec. 1917.
18. *Id.*, Secs. 1911–1912. *See Holyfield*, note 2 above, 109 S.Ct. at 1610; *In re Adoption of Holloway*, 732 P.2d 962 (Utah 1986). *But see Catholic Social Services, Inc. v. C.A.A.*, 783 P.2d 1159 (Alas. 1989), *cert. denied sub nom. Cook Inlet Tribal Council v. Catholic Social Services, Inc.*, 110 S.Ct. 2208 (1990) (notice to tribe is not required in voluntary terminations).
19. 490 U.S. 30 (1989). *See also* Tellinghuisen, note 2 above, at 666.
20. 25 U.S.C. Sec. 1913(a).
21. *Id.*
22. *Id.*, Sec. 1913(b).
23. *Id.*, Sec. 1913(c). *See Angus v. Joseph*, 655 P.2d 208 (Or. Ct. App.), *cert. denied*, 464 U.S. 830 (1983).
24. *Id.*, Sec. 1913(d).
25. *See Holyfield*, note 2 above.
26. Of course, the tribe can decline, and a parent can prevent the transfer by objecting to it. *See* 25 U.S.C. Sec. 1911(b).

27. *In re N.A.H.*, 418 N.W.2d 310 (S.D. 1988); *In re Custody of S.B.R.*, 719 P.2d 154 (Wash. App. 1986). *But see Matter of S.Z.*, 325 N.W.2d 53 (S.D. 1982) (court excuses the deficiencies).

28. 25 U.S.C. Sec. 1913(d).

29. *See* Trentadue and DeMontigny, *The Indian Child Welfare Act of 1978: A Practitioner's Perspective*, 62 N.D.L. Rev. 487, 536 (1986).

30. *In re Adoption of T.N.F.*, 781 P.2d 973 (Alaska 1989), *cert. denied sub nom. Jasso v. Finney*, 110 S.Ct. 1480 (1990).

31. 25 U.S.C. Sec. 1911(b). "Good cause" is discussed later in this chapter.

32. *See, e.g., In re Pima County Juvenile Action*, 635 P.2d 187 (Ariz. Ct. App. 1981), *cert. denied*, 455 U.S. 1007 (1982); *In re Baby Child*, 700 P.2d 198 (N.M. Ct. App. 1985), and cases cited in note above.

33. *See Pima County*, note 32 above.

34. 25 U.S.C. Sec. 1903(4).

35. *Id.*, Sec. 1912(a).

36. *Id.*

37. *In interest of H.D.*, 729 P.2d 1234 (Kan. 1986); *In re Junious M.*, 193 Cal. Rptr. 40, 43 n.7 (1983); *In re M.C.P.*, 571 A.2d 627 (Vt. 1989).

38. *Kickapoo Tribe v. Radar*, 822 F.2d 1493 (10th Cir. 1987).

39. 25 U.S.C. Sec. 1912(a).

40. *Id.*, Sec. 1911(b).

41. *See, e.g., In the Matter of the Dependency & Neglect of A.L.*, 442 N.W.2d 233 (S.D. 1989); *In re Robert T.*, 200 Cal. App. 3d 657, 246 Cal. Rptr. 168 (1988); *Matter of Wayne R.N.*, 757 P.2d 1333 (N.M. App. 1988).

42. *See* Guidelines for State Courts; Indian Child Custody Proceedings, 44 Fed. Reg. 67584, 67591 (1978).

43. *Id.*, at 67591. *See In re M.E.M.*, note 10 above, 635 P.2d at 1317.

44. *See, e.g., Junious M.*, note above; *In re Appeal in Cocomino County Juvenile Action*, 736 P.2d 829 (Ariz. 1987). *But see Robert T.*, note 41 above.

45. *See* cases cited in note above. The few courts that have reached a contrary conclusion, such as *In re Robert T.*, note 41 above, are wrongly decided.

46. *See Pima County*, note 32 above. *But see In Interest of J.R.H.*, 358 N.W.2d 311 (Iowa 1984); *Chester County Dep't of Social Services v. Coleman*, 399 S.E.2d. 773 (S.C. 1990).

47. 25 U.S.C. Sec. 1912(f).

48. *Id.*, Sec. 1912(d).

49. *Matter of S.D.*, 402 N.W.2d 346 (S.D. 1987); *In the Matter of M.E.M., Jr.*, 679 P.2d 1241 (Mont. 1983).

50. Guidelines, note 42 above, 44 Fed. Reg. at 67593.

51. *D.A.W. v. State*, 699 P.2d 340 (Alaska 1985). *See also In re T.O.*, 759 P.2d 1308 (Alaska 1988).
52. 25 U.S.C. Sec. 1903(9).
53. *See, e.g., In re Adoption of Baby Boy D*, 742 P.2d 1059 (Okla. 1985), *cert. denied*, 108 S.Ct. 1042 (1988); *In the Matter of Adoption of a Child of Indian Heritage*, 543 A.2d 925 (N.J. 1988).
54. *See* Comment, note 2 above, pp. 165–66.
55. *Id.*, at 166.
56. 25 U.S.C. Sec. 1922. *See D.E.D. v. State*, 704 P.2d 774 (Alaska 1985).
57. *Kickapoo Tribe*, note above; *Kiowa Tribe of Oklahoma v. Lewis*, 777 F.2d 587 (10th Cir. 1985), *cert. denied*, 479 U.S. 872 (1986).
58. *Platero v. Platero*, 10 Indian L. Rep. 3108 (D.N.M. 1983). *See also Thompson v. Thompson*, 484 U.S. 174 (1988).
59. 25 U.S.C. Sec. 1903(4).
60. *Id.*, Sec. 1903(8). The subject of federal recognition is discussed in ch. 15.
61. *In re Reuben, Julio & Rachel Stairwelt*, 17 Indian L. Rep. 5004 (Ill. App. 1989); *In re Wanomi P.*, 264 Cal. Rptr. 623 (Cal. App. 1989).
62. 25 U.S.C. Sec. 1903(1). *See Application of Defender*, 435 N.W.2d 717 (S.D. 1989); *Eastern Band of Cherokee Indians v. Larch*, 872 F.2d 66 (4th Cir. 1989).
63. 25 U.S.C. Sec. 1903(1); Guidelines, note 42 above, 44 Fed. Reg. at 67587.
64. *Id.*, Secs. 1918(a), (b). *See* B.A. Atwood, "Fighting Over Indian Children," 36 *UCLA L. Rev.* 1051, 1073-75 (1989).
65. *Matter of Adoption of Baby Boy L*, 643 P.2d 168 (Kan. 1982).
66. *Johnson v. Howard*, 741 P.2d 1386 (Okla. 1985). *See also Matter of Adoption of DMJ*, 741 P.2d 1386 (Okla. 1985).
67. *See In re J.R.H.*, note 46 above; *In re Custody of S.B.R.*, note 27 above.
68. 25 U.S.C. Sec. 1901(5).
69. *See J.R.H.* and *Coleman*, note 46 above. *See also In the Matter of T.S.*, 801 P.2d 77 (Mont. 1990); *People in Interest of J.J.*, 454 N.W.2d 317 (S.D. 1990).
70. 25 U.S.C. Sec. 1912(f).
71. *In the Matter of Adoption of John Michael Baade*, 462 N.W.2d 485 (S.D. 1990).

XVIII
Judicial Review

This chapter will help individuals obtain a remedy from a court if the tribal, state, or federal government violates their rights. However, even when rights have been violated, there are two major obstacles to obtaining judicial review. First, a court is permitted to hear only those cases the legislature has authorized it to adjudicate. Every court has limits on the cases it can hear. Certain rights can be violated, in fact, without any court being able to hear the case. Second, every government—tribal,[1] state[2] and federal[3]—enjoys "sovereign immunity" from suit. This means that a government may not be sued without its permission. In other words, even if a court is authorized to hear cases involving certain rights, the court must dismiss a case if it is filed against a government that enjoys an immunity from such lawsuits. Congress has the authority to waive a tribe's or a state's sovereign immunity,[4] as well as the federal government's, but unless it does, these governments may be sued only if they have consented to be sued.

A. SUITS AGAINST A TRIBE

As the Supreme Court stated in 1991, Indian tribes "exercise inherent sovereign authority over their members and their territory. Suits against Indian tribes are thus barred by sovereign immunity absent a clear waiver by the tribe or congressional abrogation."[5] Tribal governments enjoy the same sovereign immunity all other governments possess, in order to protect their independence. This immunity can be waived by the tribe[6] or by the United States.[7] However, a waiver of the tribe's sovereign immunity must be "unequivocally expressed"; a waiver may not be implied.[8]

Congress has not waived tribal immunity from suit in general. Congress has passed a few laws that allow a particular type of suit, however. For example, Congress has authorized the Navajo and Hopi tribes to sue one another in federal court to resolve a property dispute between them.[9] Congress has also authorized the filing of lawsuits against the federal, state, and tribal governments concerning hazardous waste disposal.[10] As explained in chapter 14, some courts initially held that the Indian Civil Rights Act of 1968 waived tribal immunity in federal court with respect to a wide range of suits. However, in 1978 the Supreme Court held that this law did not waive tribal sovereign immunity. Similarly, Public Law 83–280 (discussed in chapter 7) and the Indian Self-Determination Act of 1975 (discussed in chapter 16) did not consent to suits against tribal governments.[11]

In short, few controversies against Indian tribes can be heard in federal or state court; these courts lack jurisdiction over such disputes. Courts have dismissed for lack of jurisdiction lawsuits that sought to challenge a tribe's membership requirements,[12] a tribal zoning law,[13] a tribal hunting and fishing regulation,[14] and a tribal bingo ordinance.[15] Courts have also dismissed on sovereignty grounds lawsuits that sought to recover a debt owed by a tribe;[16] to enforce a tribal lease;[17] to determine the ownership of land in which the tribe has an interest;[18] to garnishee tribal assets;[19] to challenge tribal election results or procedures;[20] or to compel a tribe to collect state taxes.[21] The tribe's defense of sovereign immunity, moreover, may be raised in court at any time by the tribe[22] or by the United States acting on the tribe's behalf.[23]

Persons attempting to sue a tribe have used novel but unsuccessful arguments in an effort to overcome the tribe's sovereign immunity. For instance, courts have rejected claims that non-recognized[24] tribes have lost their immunity from suit;[25] that a state government can waive a tribe's immunity;[26] that tribal officials can be sued under a federal law authorizing suits against state officials;[27] that tribes waiving immunity for some claims thereby have waived immunity for other claims;[28] that tribal sovereign immunity does not apply to lawsuits by nonmembers;[29] and that, when a tribe files a lawsuit, it waives its immunity against counterclaims.[30]

Thus, unless a tribe has consented to the type of suit being brought (and some tribes have consented to certain suits), there are few situations in which a judicial remedy can be obtained when the tribe has violated rights. As explained in chapter 14, the U.S. Justice Department is urging Congress to pass a law that would allow federal lawsuits against tribes for civil rights violations. However, it is uncertain whether Congress will waive the tribe's immunity to this extent.

Do tribal corporations share the tribe's immunity from suit?

Some corporations do. When a tribe creates a corporation, the corporation will share the tribe's immunity unless the tribe decides to waive it.[31] Waiving a corporation's immunity can be accomplished by placing a "sue or be sued" clause in the corporate charter, authorizing the corporation to sue and to be sued in its own name.[32] Of course, a tribe does not waive its own immunity when it waives a corporation's immunity.[33]

Being immune from suit may seem advantageous, but for most corporations it is not. Corporations immune from suit have difficulty borrowing money and finding buyers for their goods or services because many people are reluctant to do business with, or lend money to, a corporation that cannot be sued.

What kinds of suits are authorized by the Indian Civil Rights Act?

This subject is discussed in detail in chapter 14. To briefly summarize, the ICRA did not waive the tribe's immunity from suit in federal or state court. However, the act may have waived the tribe's immunity from suit in tribal court; tribal courts have reached differing conclusions on this issue. The ICRA does authorize federal courts, however, to determine whether a person imprisoned by an Indian tribe is being held in violation of the rights conferred by the ICRA.

Can tribal officials be sued individually if they violate a person's rights?

In most situations, no. There are two barriers to these kinds of suits. First, government officials, whether federal, state, or tribal, enjoy the government's immunity from suit whenever they act within the scope of their authority. Thus if an official has been legally authorized to do something, that official cannot be sued if a person is injured in the process because the official enjoys the government's immunity.[34]

In 1978 the Supreme Court suggested that a tribal official "is not protected by the tribe's immunity from suit."[35] This comment has been the source of much debate.[36] However, no court has given this statement a broad application. Rather, most courts have held that tribal officials, like federal and state officials, may not be sued unless they have "acted outside the amount of authority that the sovereign is capable of bestowing."[37] A growing number of federal courts have held, however, that tribal officials *can* be sued when they engage in unauthorized conduct, particularly when they act in violation of federal law. That is, tribal officials enjoy sovereign immunity only when they act within the scope of their valid authority. When they act outside their scope of authority, they can be sued for declaratory and injunctive relief,[38] and perhaps also for damages,[39] although this is not as clear. The Supreme Court needs to resolve this issue.

Even when a tribal official has acted outside the scope of his or her authority, there is a second barrier to suing the officer or the tribe. As previously explained, courts can only adjudicate cases they have been authorized to hear. Federal and state courts have been authorized to hear few types of reservation controversies (see chapters 7, 9, and 14). Therefore, unless the tribe has authorized its own tribal courts to hear these cases, there may be no judicial remedy.[40]

Does sovereign immunity protect a tribe against suits by state governments?

Yes. The Supreme Court has held that a state government has no more right to sue a tribe than an individual does. A state can only sue a tribe if the tribe has consented.[41]

Does sovereign immunity protect a tribe against suits by the federal government?

The few courts that have addressed this question have held that an Indian tribe may not assert a sovereign immunity defense against the United States.[42] The federal government, in other words, may sue an Indian tribe for violations of federal law whether the tribe consents or not.

Does the tribe waive its immunity when it files suit?

Generally, no. Indian tribes do not lose their sovereign immunity when they file suit. Thus someone being sued by a tribe does not necessarily have the right to countersue the tribe.[43] "The perceived inequity" in this situation "must be accepted in view of the overriding federal and tribal interests in these circumstances."[44] Some courts have held that someone sued by a tribe may file a counterclaim against the tribe if the counterclaim arises out of the same transaction as the subject of the tribe's lawsuit and seeks damages not greater than those sought by the tribe.[45] However, these decisions were rendered prior to a 1991 Supreme Court decision which expressly held that "a tribe does not waive its sovereign immunity from actions that could not otherwise be brought against it merely because those actions were placed in a counterclaim to an action filed by the tribe."[46]

B. SUITS AGAINST A STATE

What courts are open to Indians and tribes when a state violates their federal rights?

Indians and tribes have many federal rights. These include those the U.S. Constitution confers on everyone, as well as additional rights from treaties and federal laws. Due to a variety of jurisdictional statutes that Congress has passed, virtually all of these federal rights can be protected in a federal court. State courts must enforce federal rights, too, but they are not well known for protecting Indian rights. Therefore, most Indians and tribes choose federal court.

Four jurisdictional statutes are important in this context. Nearly every violation of federal law committed by a state or state official can be remedied ("vindicated") in federal court because of these four statutes: Title 28, United States Code, section 1331 (written as 28 U.S.C. § 1331), 28 U.S.C. § 1362, 28 U.S.C. § 1353, and 28 U.S.C. § 1343(3).

What jurisdiction is conferred by section 1331?

Section 1331 confers jurisdiction on the federal courts over any civil action which "arises under the Constitution, laws or treaties of the United States." This statute is extremely important to Indians and tribes because it allows federal courts to protect the many federal rights they have under treaties and statutes. In a recent case filed under section 1331, for example, the Supreme Court held that a federal court could order non-Indian trespassers removed from federally protected tribal land.[47] In another case, a federal court ruled that both a tribe and its members can sue a state under section 1331 to enforce a tribe's federal rights.[48]

What jurisdiction is conferred by section 1362?

Section 1362 authorizes federal courts to hear "all civil actions brought by an Indian tribe or band . . . wherein the matter in controversy arises under the Constitution, laws or treaties of the United States." Until this law was passed in 1966, tribes were dependent upon the federal government to file suit on their behalf in its capacity as the tribe's trustee.[49] Now tribes can sue on their own behalf and need not rely on the federal government to protect their interests.[50] Section 1362 allows a tribe, for example, to challenge a state sales tax that violates the tribe's federal rights[51] and to protect land given the tribe by federal treaty or statute.[52] However, in 1991 the Supreme Court held that section 1362 did not waive a state's immunity from suit by an Indian tribe.[53] Thus, the federal government may sue a state on behalf of a tribe because a state has no immunity from suit by the federal government. However, a tribe cannot sue the state (just as a state cannot sue a tribe) without its consent.

Federal court jurisdiction under section 1362 is available, however, only when the tribe is seeking to protect a federal right. A lawsuit which seeks to enforce rights under state law, such as a suit to enforce a private contract, cannot be filed in federal court under sections 1362 or 1331.[54] Moreover, section 1362 is available to Indian tribes but not to tribal corporations, even those owned by the tribe.[55]

What jurisdiction is conferred by section 1353?

Under the General Allotment Act of 1887,[56] thousands of Indians were issued allotments of trust land and became eligible to receive deeds to these parcels. Section 1353 allows Indians to protect their rights in these allotments of land. As the Supreme Court explained in *United States v. Mottaz* (1986),[57] Indians are authorized by section 1353 to bring two types of lawsuits: suits seeking to compel the government to issue an allotment and those seeking to protect the Indian's interest in an allotment once it has been issued. For example, Indians who lease their allotments to a private party can sue for damages under section 1353 when the private party violates the lease.[58] State officials who interfere with an Indian's use or enjoyment of an allotment can also be sued under section 1353.[59]

What jurisdiction is conferred by section 1343(3)?

Soon after the Civil War, Congress enacted a civil rights act (42 U.S.C. § 1983) that prohibits state officials from depriving a person of "any right, privilege or immunity secured by the Constitution of the United States or by any Act of Congress providing for equal rights of citizens." Its jurisdictional counterpart—the statute that authorizes federal courts to adjudicate violations of section 1983—is 28 U.S.C. § 1343(3).

Together, these two laws allow persons to sue a state official who violates their federal rights.[60] Similarly, if a tribal police officer is cross-deputized and is exercising state authority at the time she or he violates a person's federal rights, this officer can be sued under section 1983.[61] If a court finds that federal rights are being violated, it can issue an injunction halting those activities and, in appropriate cases, award money damages for any harm or injury that has been caused.[62] Municipal governments (cities and towns) can be sued under section 1983 in the same way state officials can.[63] Chapter 13 describes some of the cases brought by Indians under sections 1983 and 1343(3) against state officials.

Can the federal government sue a state on behalf of an Indian or tribe?

Yes. The United States is the legal trustee of many Indian and tribal interests, and it can sue a state to protect those interests.[64] Such a lawsuit does not require the consent of the Indian or tribe on whose behalf it is brought.[65] When the United States does file suit, the Indian or tribe usually has the right to retain a lawyer and intervene in the lawsuit in order to protect their interests.[66]

The United States also has the right to give legal assistance to Indians or tribes who sue on their own behalf.[67] If the Indian or tribe should disagree with the position taken by the federal government, the court must accept the government's position as controlling if the lawsuit involves trust property (property owned by the United States and held in trust for an Indian or tribe).[68] In fact, when trust property is involved, the federal government can sue a state even after the tribe has already sued that state and lost. This is because a tribe sues to protect its possessory interest in trust property while the federal government can sue to protect its ownership rights,[69] a different interest.

The United States is not obligated to file a lawsuit on behalf of an Indian or tribe even when the suit seeks to protect federal rights,[70] although a federal law appears to require the government to provide such assistance upon the tribe's request.[71] In 1976 the Comptroller General of the United States issued an opinion[72] authorizing the Secretary of the Interior to reimburse tribes for their attorney's fees when the federal government refuses to provide legal representation in these cases. However, a federal court has held that the Secretary is under no obligation to pay these fees.[73]

Although the United States can sue on behalf of Indians and tribes, this does not prevent Indians and tribes from suing on their own behalf, and a tribe may sue on behalf of its members.[74] If federal trust property is involved in which the tribe has a possessory interest, the tribe can bring suit to protect its interest even if the United States is not a party to the suit.[75] However, the United States will not be bound by the court's decision unless it intervenes in the case.[76]

In summary, Congress has enacted a variety of laws that enable Indians, tribes, and the federal government to sue the state and state officials in federal court to protect their federal rights. Federal courts have the power to issue whatever relief is necessary to protect these rights, including injunctive relief and damages.[77] State officials can even be ordered to undertake activities that are prohibited by state law if these activities are necessary to protect a federal right.[78]

C. SUITS AGAINST THE UNITED STATES

What courts are open to Indians and tribes when the federal government violates their rights?

Hundreds of federal rights have been given to Indians and tribes in federal laws, treaties, executive orders, and agency rulings. At one time or another, almost every one of these rights has been violated by a federal official or by Congress.

Most violations of federal rights are "justiciable," that is, capable of being remedied in a federal court, at least to some extent. As explained earlier, no one can sue the United States unless it consents to be sued. However, Congress has passed a number of laws waiving its sovereign immunity. Today most violations of Indian rights by the federal government are justiciable in a federal court under one or more of these jurisdictional statutes.

Under what circumstances can the United States be sued for money damages?

Several statutes authorize the filing of claims against the United States for money damages. These laws allow a person to recover compensation for injuries suffered when a federal official or Congress violates that person's rights.

The Federal Tort Claims Act[79] (FTCA) is one of the laws by which money damages can be recovered from the federal government. The FTCA waives the federal government's sovereign immunity for "loss of property, or personal injury or death caused by the negligent or wrongful act or omission of any employee of the Government while acting within the scope of his office or employment, under the circumstances where the United States, if a private person, would be liable to the claimant in accordance with the law of the place where the act or omission occurred."

Thus the FTCA allows recovery of damages for most injuries caused by the wrongful or negligent action of a federal official acting within the scope of her or his authority.[80] For example, if the Bureau of Reclamation wrongly floods land,[81] or if a Indian is injured at a federal boarding school due to the negligence of a school employee,[82] or if federal agents wrongly remove property from a house or land[83] or damage that property,[84] or if a person receives inadequate or improper medical care at an Indian Health Service hospital,[85] claims can be filed against the United States for the damages sustained. The claim must first be filed with the federal agency responsible for the harm. But if the agency does not satisfy the claim within 180 days, a lawsuit can then be filed in federal court against the United States.[86] (A claimant has two years from the date the cause of action arose to file a claim with the agency.[87])

The Tucker Act[88] also authorizes certain money claims against the United States. While the FTCA allows recovery for negligent conduct (a "tort"), the Tucker Act allows recovery for a breach of contract or other express or implied obligation by the government. The Tucker Act waives the federal government's sovereign immunity with respect to any action "founded either upon the Constitution, or any Act of Congress, or any regulation of an executive department, or upon any express or implied contract with the United States."[89] An injured party may file a claim against the United States either in the Court of Claims[90] or a federal district court. (However, the government's liability in cases filed in district court is limited to $10,000.)[91] Appeals from the Court of Claims are made to the Court of Appeals for the Federal Circuit, while appeals from a federal district court are made to the court of appeals for the circuit in which the district court is located. The Tucker Act contains a six-year statute of limitations.[92]

The Tucker Act has become especially important to Indians. In recent years, courts have held that Indians can recover damages under the Tucker Act when federal officials mismanage Indian trust resources, such as tribal timber, tribal land, or money deposited in federal Indian accounts.[93] The injured party must show, however, that a federal statute, treaty, or agreement expressly conferred rights that were violated, or created an implied duty to protect the injured party's interests, which duty was ignored. Courts have been liberal in interpreting this requirement. Courts have held that statutes that require federal officials to perform certain tasks for Indians create a trust responsibility to perform those tasks in an efficient and careful manner, the violation of which makes the government liable for damages under the Tucker Act.[94] In *United States v. Mitchell* (1983),[95] for example, the Supreme Court held that federal statutes and regulations that give federal officials comprehensive control over the management of Indian timber resources thereby create a legal duty to manage them wisely. The Court allowed the tribe to obtain damages under the Tucker Act when the government failed to meet this duty.[96]

The Tucker Act contains a major limitation, however. It does not allow tribes to sue the government for a breach of treaty obligations.[97] Prior to 1946, in fact, Congress had not enacted any general law by which tribes could sue the United States for a treaty violation. If the United States broke a treaty and seized Indian land (something that happened frequently), the tribe had no means to sue for damages. A few tribes persuaded Congress to pass special laws authorizing them to sue the United States to recover the value of their stolen property, but most tribes were left with no recourse.

In 1946 Congress filled this void when it passed the Indian Claims Commission Act.[98] This act authorized any "identifiable group" of Indians to file a claim against the United States seeking compensation for the loss of or injury to treaty land or other property the federal government had taken by force, fraud, or mistake or for which the government had paid "unconscionable consideration." (Claims based upon "unconscionable consideration" became known as "moral" claims because, although the government had purchased the tribe's land, the price it paid was ridiculously low.)[99] Under the act, tribes could obtain damages for the loss of their land as well as for the value of resources found on the land, such as water and timber.[100]

The act created the Indian Claims Commission (ICC) to resolve the tribal claims. Tribes had five years in which to file a claim, although this time limit was later extended for a few tribes. Eventually 370 claims were filed, a number of which have yet to be resolved. Once the ICC resolved a claim, both the tribe and the federal government could appeal the ICC's decision to the Court of Claims and then to the Supreme Court. The ICC was abolished by Congress in 1978, and its pending cases were transferred to the United States Court of Claims.

Under the act, after all appeals are exhausted, Congress must appropriate any money awarded to the tribe. The Secretary of the Interior is then required to submit a plan to Congress for disbursing these "judgement proceeds" to the tribe.

Thus far, over eight hundred million dollars has been distributed to tribes under the Indian Claims Commission Act. The size of this figure helps to show how many treaty lands and resources were confiscated from Indian tribes.[101] A graphic description of the confiscation process is contained in *United States v. Sioux Nation of Indians.*[102] This case describes how the Sioux had virtually all of its treaty lands stolen by the federal government in what the Supreme Court labeled a "ripe and rank case of dishonorable dealings."[103]

Under what circumstances can a lawsuit seeking money damages be filed against a federal official?

As explained earlier, government officials acting within the scope of their delegated and lawful authority enjoy the sovereign's immunity from suit and, like the government, cannot be sued for damages without the government's consent.[104] However, when government officials exceed their delegated authority or act under a law the government lacks the power to enact, then the official is not protected by sovereign immunity. In such instances, lawsuits can be maintained against these officials in their individual capacity. Federal officials who engage in conduct that they know or should know is illegal or unauthorized can be sued for damages for injuries caused as a result of their actions.[105]

When can the federal government be sued for declaratory or injunctive relief?

Many disputes with the federal government do not involve a claim for damages. Instead, the relief sought is a declaration of rights and an injunction preventing the government from violating those rights. Suppose the Bureau of Reclamation, for instance, has just announced plans to construct a dam on tribal treaty land, and the tribe wants to prevent the dam from being built. The tribe can sue the bureau and seek a declaration from the court that the tribe has a paramount treaty right to the land and an injunction halting construction of the dam.[106]

The most important relevant statute is the Administrative Procedure Act (APA).[107] The APA authorizes federal courts to review all final decisions of a federal agency, except to the extent that "(1) a statute precludes judicial review, or (2) agency action is committed to agency discretion by law."[108] Thus, the APA gives the government's consent to suits requesting nonmonetary relief from all final decisions of a federal agency, except for those decisions Congress has declared to be conclusive and nonreviewable.[109] Suits seeking relief under the APA can be heard in federal court under 28 U.S.C. § 1331; 28 U.S.C. § 1362 provides an additional jurisdictional basis for APA suits brought by tribes.[110] Both of these jurisdictional statutes are discussed above.

The APA is very important because most activities of the federal government are undertaken through or by a federal agency. The APA allows a claimant to obtain judicial review of these actions when the remedy sought is nonmonetary. The APA authorizes a federal court to set aside any agency action that is "arbitrary, capricious or otherwise not in accordance with law," as well as to compel agency action that is being unlawfully withheld or delayed.[111] In other words, federal courts can prevent agency officials from engaging in an activity that would violate one's rights as well as order them to undertake an activity necessary to preserve one's rights. For example, the Secretary of the Interior can be sued for ignoring a duty to regulate the leasing of Indian land,[112] for ignoring a duty to regulate trade on the reservation,[113] for refusing to recognize a tribal government as required by federal law,[114] for failing to distribute federal benefits to Indians as required by law,[115] for wrongfully interfering in a tribal election,[116] or for wrongfully closing an Indian boarding school.[117]

Unfortunately, a number of federal statutes provide that agency action in certain matters is "final" or "conclusive." In these situations, courts cannot review the agency's decision; judicial review is barred by the government's sovereign immunity.[118] The court can consider whether the statute under which the decision is made is unconstitutional,[119] but the court cannot consider the correctness of the decision.[120] However, unless Congress has clearly and expressly committed a decision to the agency's own discretion, the decision is reviewable by a federal court under the APA.[121]

For example, a federal statute authorizes the Secretary of the Interior to determine the heirs of an Indian who dies without a will.[122] This statute states that the Secretary's decision is "final and conclusive." Even if the Secretary makes an obvious error in determining the heirs, a federal court cannot rectify the mistake.[123] However, the statute that authorizes the Secretary to determine the heirs of an Indian who dies *with* a will does not contain the "final and conclusive" language.[124] Therefore, the Secretary's decisions under this statute are reviewable by a federal court.[125]

In addition to the APA, federal courts can review various Indian and tribal claims under 28 U.S.C. Sections 1331, 1353, and 1362. These statutes permit Indians and tribes to protect their constitutional, treaty, and statutory rights in a wide range of situations.[126]

Even when federal courts are authorized to review a decision by a government agency, a court cannot overturn it unless there has been a clear error in the agency's judgment. In other words, if the agency's record shows that the relevant data were considered, and there is some rational basis for the agency's decision, a court cannot substitute its judgment for the agency's even if a better decision could have been made by the agency.[127] A court's duty is to determine whether the agency's action was arbitrary and capricious and not simply ill-advised.[128]

Must administrative remedies be exhausted before filing a lawsuit against a federal agency?

Generally, yes. Most federal agencies have an appeals procedure. The Department of the Interior, for instance, has several levels of appeals before an agency decision becomes final. A decision by an Interior Department official on the reservation can be appealed to the Area Director, from there to the Commissioner of Indian Affairs, and in cases involving the interpretation of a federal law, from the Commissioner to the Board of Indian Appeals.[129] A court will insist that administrative remedies be exhausted before filing suit unless the delay will cause irreparable harm.[130]

What standards must a court use in reviewing Indian cases?

The Supreme Court has held that the United Sates has "moral obligations of the highest responsibility and trust" toward Indians[131] and must use "great care" in its dealings with them.[132] Consequently, any government action that affects Indian interests must be judged "by the most exacting fiduciary standards."[133]

Because of this high standard of care, Indians have often been successful in challenging government activities. As indicated above, courts have ordered government officials to perform legal obligations they were ignoring as well as to halt injurious activities they were about to undertake. Indians have also obtained damages from the United States when federal officials lost or destroyed their property or failed to manage it properly. Therefore, Indians and tribes should not hesitate to file a lawsuit to protect their rights if the situation warrants it.

NOTES

1. *Santa Clara Pueblo v. Martinez*, 436 U.S. 49 (1978); *Oklahoma Tax Comm'n v. Citizen Band Potawatomi Indian Tribe*, 111 S.Ct. 905 (1991); *American Indian Agric'l Credit Consortium v. Standing Rock Sioux Tribe*, 780 F.2d 1374, 1377–81 (8th Cir. 1985).

2. *Edelman v. Jordan*, 415 U.S. 651 (1974).

3. *U.S. v. Sherwood*, 312 U.S. 584 (1941).

4. *Hutto v. Finney*, 437 U.S. 678 (1978) (state); *Santa Clara Pueblo*, note 1 above (tribal).

5. *Potawatomi Indian Tribe*, note 1 above, 111 S.Ct. at 909 (citation omitted). *See also Santa Clara Pueblo*, note 1 above; *Seneca-Cayuga Tribe of Oklahoma v. Oklahoma*, 874 F.2d 709, 714 (10th Cir. 1989).

6. The case of *U.S. v. U.S. Fidelity & Guaranty Co.*, 309 U.S. 506, 513 (1940), suggested that a tribe cannot waive its own immunity. However, it is now generally agreed that a tribe does possess this power. *See Wichita and Affiliated Tribes v. Hodel*, 788 F.2d 765 (D.C. Cir. 1986); *Native Village of Eyak v. G. L. Contractors*, 658 P.2d 756 (Alaska 1983). *But see* F. Cohen, *Handbook of Federal Indian Law* pp. 325–26 (1980).

7. *Santa Clara Pueblo*, note above; *Potawatomi Indian Tribe*, note 1 above.

8. *Id.*, 436 U.S. at 58. *See American Indian Agric'l Credit Consortium*, note 1 above, at 1377–81; *Pan American Co. v. Sycuan Band of Mission Indians*, 884 F.2d 416 (9th Cir. 1989) (consent to arbitration is not a consent to a lawsuit).

9. *See Sekaquaptewa v. McDonald*, 591 F.2d 1289 (9th Cir. 1979).

10. *See Blue Legs v. BIA*, 867 F.2d 1094 (8th Cir. 1989).

11. *See Three Affiliated Tribes v. Wold Engineering*, 476 U.S. 877, 892 (1986) (P.L. 280); *Evans v. McKay*, 869 F.2d 1341 (9th Cir. 1989) (Self-Determination Act).

12. *Santa Clara Pueblo*, note above.

13. *Trans-Canada Enterprises, Ltd. v. Muckleshoot Indian Tribe*, 634 F.2d 474 (9th Cir. 1980).

14. *People of California ex rel. Dep't of Fish and Game v. Quechan Tribe of Indians*, 595 F.2d 1153 (9th Cir. 1979).

15. *Sycuan Band*, note above.

16. *Wells v. Philbrick*, 486 F. Supp. 807 (D.S.D. 1980); *Ramey Constr. Co., Inc. v. Apache Tribe*, 673 F.2d 315 (10th Cir. 1982); *Bottomly v. Passamaquoddy Tribe*, 599 F.2d 1061 (1st Cir. 1979).

17. *McClendon v. U.S.*, 885 F.2d 627 (9th Cir. 1989).

18. *Lomayaktewa v. Hathaway*, 520 F.2d 1324 (9th Cir. 1975), *cert. denied*, 425 U.S. 903 (1976).

19. *North Sea Products Ltd. v. Clipper Sea Foods Co.*, 595 P. 2d 938 (Wash. 1979).

20. *Goodface v. Goodrope*, 708 F.2d 335 (8th Cir. 1983); *Runs After v. U.S.*, 766 F. 2d 347 (8th Cir. 1985); *Nero v. Cherokee Nation*, 892 F. 2d 1457 (10th Cir. 1989).

21. *Potawatomi Indian Tribe*, note 1 above.

22. *Shortbull v. Looking Elk*, 677 F.2d 645 (8th Cir.), *cert. denied*, 459 U.S. 907 (1982).

23. *Fidelity*, note above.

24. The subject of federal recognition is discussed in ch. 15, sec. E.

25. *Bottomly*, note above.

26. *Id. See also Haile v. Saunooke*, 246 F.2d 293, 297–98 (4th Cir. 1957).

27. *Wells*, note 16 above; *Jicarilla Apache Tribe v. Andrus*, 687 F.2d 1324 (10th Cir. 1982).

28. *Atkinson v. Haldane*, 569 P.2d 151 (Alaska 1977). *See also Boe v. Fort Belknap Indian Community*, 455 F. Supp. 462 (D. Mont. 1978).

29. *Wilson v. Turtle Mountain Band of Chippewa Indians*, 459 F. Supp. 366 (D.N.D. 1978).

30. *Potawatomi Indian Tribe,* note 1 above, 111 S.Ct. at 909.

31. *Namakagon Devel. Co. v. Bois Forte Res. Housing Auth.*, 517 F.2d 508 (8th Cir. 1975); *Hickey v. Crow Creek Housing Auth.*, 379 F. Supp. 1002 (D.S.D. 1974); *North Sea Products*, note 19 above.

32. *See Fontenelle v. Omaha Tribe*, 430 F.2d 143 (8th Cir. 1970); *Rosebud Sioux Tribe v. A&P Steel, Inc.*, 874 F.2d 550 (8th Cir. 1989); *Parker Drilling Co. v. Metlakatla Indian Community*, 451 F. Supp. 1127 (D. Alaska 1978).

33. *Ramey*, note above, and see cases in notes 5 and 28 above.

34. *See U.S. v. Oregon*, 657 F.2d 1009, 1012 n.8 (9th Cir. 1981); *Hardin v. White Mountain Apache Tribe*, 779 F.2d 476 (9th Cir. 1985); *Nero*, note 20 above; *Sahmaunt v. Horse*, 593 F. Supp. 162 (W.D. Okla. 1984).

35. *Santa Clara Pueblo*, note 1 above at 59.

36. *See* Ziontz, *After Martinez: Civil Rights under Tribal Government*, 12 U.C. Davis L. Rev. 1 (1979).

37. *Tenneco Oil Co. v. Sac and Fox Tribe*, 725 F.2d 572, 574 (10th Cir. 1984). *See also Kanai Oil and Gas v. Dep't of Interior*, 671 F.2d 383 (10th Cir. 1982).

38. *See, e.g., Tenneco Oil*, note 37 above; *Wisconsin v. Baker*, 698 F.2d 1323, 1332–33 (7th Cir. 1983); *Burlington No. Railroad Co. v. Blackfeet Tribe*, 924 F.2d 899 (9th Cir. 1991). *Cf., Potawatomi Indian Tribe*, note 1 above, 111 S.Ct. at 912 (Stevens, J., concurring) (suggesting that tribal officials can be sued for declaratory and injunctive relief).

39. *Cf. Potawatomi Indian Tribe,* note 1 above, 111 S.Ct. at 912. (Court notes that it has "never held that individual agents or officers of a tribe are not liable for damages.")

40. *But see Potawatomi Indian Tribe,* note 1 above, 111 S.Ct. at 912–13.

41. *Puyallup Tribe, Inc. v. Washington Dep't of Game,* 433 U.S. 165 (1972); *Wold Engineering,* note above; *Seneca-Cayuga,* note above.

42. *U.S. v. White Mountain Apache Tribe,* 784 F.2d 917, 920 (9th Cir. 1986); *U.S. v. Red Lake Band of Chippewa Indians,* 827 F.2d 380 (8th Cir. 1987), *cert. denied,* 108 U.S. 1109 (1988).

43. *Potawatomi Indian Tribe,* note 1 above; *Squaxin Indian Tribe v. Washington,* 781 F.2d 715, 723 (9th Cir. 1986); *Wichita and Affiliated Tribes v. Hodel,* 788 F.2d 765 (D.C. Cir. 1986).

44. *Wold Engineering,* note 11 above, 476 U.S. at 893.

45. *U.S. v. Agnew,* 423 F.2d 513, 514 (9th Cir. 1970); *A&P Steel,* note 32 above.

46. *Potawatomi Indian Tribe,* note 1 above, 111 S.Ct. at 909.

47. *County of Oneida v. Oneida Indian Nation,* 470 U.S. 226 (1985).

48. *Native Village of Venetie IRA Council v. Alaska,* 918 F.2d 797, 801 (9th Cir. 1990).

49. *See Moe v. Confederated Salish and Kootenai Tribes,* 425 U.S. 463 (1976).

50. *State of Idaho v. Andrus,* 720 F.2d 1461 (9th Cir. 1983), *cert. denied,* 469 U.S. 824 (1984); *Native Village of Venetie,* note 48 above.

51. *Moe,* note 49 above. *See also Knight v. Shoshone and Arapaho Tribes,* 670 F.2d 900 (10th Cir. 1982).

52. *Poafpybitty v. Skelly Oil Co.,* 390 U.S. 365 (1968); *Schaghticoke Tribe of Indians v. Kent School Corp.,* 423 F. Supp. 780 (D. Conn. 1976); *Pueblo of Isleta v. Universal Constructions, Inc.,* 570 F.2d 300 (10th Cir. 1978).

53. *Blatchford v. Native Village of Noatak and Circle Village,* _____ U.S. _____ (1991).

54. *Gila River Indian Community v. Hennington, Durham & Richardson,* 626 F.2d 708 (9th Cir. 1980), *cert. denied,* 451 U.S. 911 (1981).

55. *Navajo Tribal Utility Auth. v. Arizona Dep't of Revenue,* 608 F.2d 1228 (9th Cir. 1979).

56. 25 U.S.C. Secs. 331 *et seq.*

57. 476 U.S. 834 (1986).

58. *Poafpybitty,* note 52 above. *But see U.S. v. Turtle Mountain Housing Auth.,* 816 F.2d 1273 (8th Cir. 1987) (damages for trespass on an allotment cannot be recovered under section 1353).

59. *Cf. Poafpybitty,* note 52 above; *Begay v. Albers,* 721 F.2d 1274 (10th Cir. 1983).

60. *See Procunier v. Navarette*, 434 U.S. 555 (1978); *Golden State Transit Corp. v. City of Los Angeles*, 493 U.S. 103 (1989).

61. *Evans*, note 11 above.

62. *See* cases cited in note 60 above. However, if the state official acted in "good faith," damages are not normally recoverable. *See Procunier*, note 60 above; *Harlow v. Fitzgerald*, 457 U.S. 800 (1982); *Mitchell v. Forsyth*, 472 U.S. 511 (1985).

63. *Monell v. N.Y. City Dep't of Social Services*, 436 U.S. 658 (1978). Municipal governments do not have the "good faith" immunity state officials normally have. *Owen v. City of Independence*, 445 U.S. 622 (1980).

64. *U.S. v. Rickert*, 188 U.S. 432 (1903); *Heckman v. U.S.*, 224 U.S. 413 (1912); *U.S. v. City of Pawhuska*, 502 F.2d 821 (10th Cir. 1974).

65. *Poafpybitty*, note 52 above; *Rickert*, note 64 above.

66. *Arizona v. California*, 460 U.S. 605 (1983); *State of New Mexico v. Aamodt*, 537 F.2d 1102 (10th Cir. 1976), *cert. denied*, 429 U.S. 1121 (1977).

67. *Heckman*, note 64 above; *Wilson v. Omaha Indian Tribe*, 442 U.S. 653 (1979). *See also Arizona v. California*, note 66 above (government's decision is binding on tribe).

68. *Pueblo of Picuris v. Abeyta*, 50 F.2d 12 (10th Cir. 1931).

69. *U.S. v. Candelaria*, 271 U.S. 432 (1926); *Choctaw and Chickasaw Nations v. Seitz*, 193 F.2d 456 (10th Cir. 1951).

70. *Heckman*, note 64 above.

71. 25 U.S.C. Sec. 175.

72. Opinion of the Comptroller General dated Dec. 6, 1976, reprinted in 4 Indian L. Rep. J–2 (1977).

73. *Pyramid Lake Paiute Tribe v. Morton*, 499 F.2d 1095 (D.C. Cir. 1974).

74. *Puyallup Tribe*, note 39 above.

75. *See* cases cited in note 52 above.

76. *See* cases cited in note 69 above.

77. *Bell v. Hood*, 327 U.S. 678, 684 (1946); *Bivens v. Six Unknown Named Agents*, 403 U.S. 388, 396–97 (1971).

78. *Washington v. Washington State Commercial Passenger Fishing Vessel Ass'n*, 443 U.S. 658 (1979).

79. 28 U.S.C. Secs. 1346(b), 2671–80.

80. The FTCA exempts several types of injuries from its coverage, including injuries caused by acts of war. *See* 28 U.S.C. Sec. 2680.

81. *Cf. Dalehite v. U.S.*, 346 U.S. 15, 45 (1953); *Rayonier, Inc. v. U.S.*, 352 U.S. 315 (1957).

82. *Bryant v. U.S.*, 565 F.2d 650 (10th Cir. 1977).

83. *Hatahley v. U.S.*, 351, U.S. 173 (1956).

84. *Red Lake Band of Chippewa Indians v. U.S.*, 800 F.2d 1187 (D.C. Cir. 1986).

85. *Simmons v. U.S.*, 740 F.2d 1023 (9th Cir. 1986); *LaRoche v. U.S.*, 730 F.2d 538 (8th Cir. 1985).

86. 28 U.S.C. Sec. 2675.

87. 28 U.S.C . Sec. 2401(b).

88. 28 U.S.C. Secs. 1491 and 1346(a)(2). *See generally U.S. v. Testan*, 424 U.S. 392 (1976).

89. 28 U.S.C. Secs. 1346(a)(2), 1491. *See U.S. v. Mitchell*, 463 U.S. 206 (1983).

90. 28 U.S.C. Secs. 1491 and 28 U.S.C. Sec. 1505, known as the Indian Tucker Act, which allows claims filed by Indian tribes.

91. 28 U.S.C. Sec. 1346(a)(2).

92. 28 U.S.C. Sec. 2401(a) (district courts), Sec. 2501 (court of claims). The statute of limitations has been liberally construed so as not to bar a meritorious claim. *See Duncan v. U.S.*, 667 F.2d 36 (Ct. Cl. 1981), *cert. denied*, 463 U.S. 1228 (1983). *But see Jones v. U.S.*, 801 F.2d 1334, 1335 (Fed. Cir. 1986), *cert. denied*, 107 S.Ct. 1887 (1987); *Hopeland Band of Pomo Indians v. U.S.*, 855 F.2d 1573 (Fed. Cir. 1988).

93. *Duncan, id.*; *Mitchell*, note 83 above; *Cheyenne-Arapahoe Tribes v. U.S.*, 512 F.2d 1390 (Ct. Cl. 1975); *Manchester Band of Pomo Indians, Inc. v. U.S.*, 363 F. Supp. 1238 (N.D. Cal. 1973); *Navajo Tribe of Indians v. U.S.*, 624 F.2d 981 (Ct. Cl. 1980).

94. *See* cases cited in note 93 above.

95. 463 U.S. 206 (1983).

96. *See also Angle v. U.S.*, 709 F.2d 570 (9th Cir. 1983).

97. 28 U.S.C. Sec. 1502.

98. 25 U.S.C. Secs. 70 to 70v–3. The purpose of the act is discussed in *U.S. v. Dann*, 470 U.S. 39 (1985).

99. *See Minnesota Chippewa Tribe v. U.S.*, 768 F.2d 338 (Cl. Ct. 1986).

100. *See, e.g.*, case cited in note 99 above, and *Northern Paiute Nation v. U.S.*, 10 Cl. Ct. 401 (1986).

101. *See U.S. v. Sioux Nation of Indians*, 448 U.S. 371 (1980). *See also Lipan Apache Tribe v. U.S.*, 180 Cl. Ct. 487 (1967); *Coast Indian Community v. U.S.*, 550 F.2d 639 (Cl. Ct. 1977); *Gila River Puma-Maricopa Indian Community v. U.S.*, 684 F.2d 852 (Cl. Ct. 1982).

102. 448 U.S. 371 (1980).

103. *Id.* at 388, citing *U.S. v. Sioux Nation*, 518 F.2d 1298, 1302 (Cl. Ct. 1975).

104. *Cf. Florida v. U.S. Dep't of Interior*, 768 F.2d 1248 (11th Cir. 1985),

cert. denied, 475 U.S. 1011 (1986). *See also U.S. v. Yakima Tribal Court*, 806 F.2d 853 (9th Cir. 1986), *cert. denied*, 481 U.S. 1069 (1987).

105. *See Larson v. Domestic & Foreign Commerce Corp.*, 337 U.S. 682, 701–2 (1949); *Dugan v. Rank*, 372 U.S. 609, 621–22 (1963); *Florida*, note 104 above; *Bivens*, note 77 above; *Butz v. Economu*, 438 U.S. 478 (1978).

106. *See, e.g., U.S. v. Winnebago Tribe of Nebraska*, 542 F.2d 1002 (8th Cir. 1976).

107. 5 U.S.C. Secs. 701 *et seq.*

108. 5 U.S.C. Sec. 701(A).

109. *U.S. v. Mitchell*, 463 U.S. 206, 227 n.3 (1983); *Coomes v. Adkinson*, 414 F. Supp. 975, 984–85 (D.S.D. 1976).

110. *See Merrion v. Jicarilla Apache Tribe*, 617 F.2d 537, 540 (10th Cir. 1980), *aff'd*, 455 U.S. 130 (1982); *Red Lake Band of Chippewa Indians v. Barlow*, 846 F.2d 474, 476 (8th Cir. 1988). The APA is not itself a jurisdictional statute. *Califano v. Sanders*, 430 U.S. 99 (1977).

111. 5 U.S.C. Sec. 706(1), (2)(A). *See, e.g., Preston v. Heckler*, 734 F.2d 1359 (9th Cir. 1984); *Assiniboine & Sioux Tribes v. Board of Oil & Gas Exploration*, 792 F.2d 782 (9th Cir. 1986).

112. *Coomes*, note 109 above.

113. *Rockbridge v. Lincoln*, 449 F.2d 567 (9th Cir. 1971).

114. *Harjo v. Kleppe*, 420 F. Supp. 1110 (D.D.C. 1976), *aff'd sub nom. Harjo v. Andrus*, 581 F.2d 949 (D.C. Cir. 1978).

115. *Pence v. Kleppe*, 529 F.2d 135 (9th Cir. 1976). *See also Morton v. Ruiz*, 415 U.S. 199 (1974).

116. *Ike v. U.S. Dep't of the Interior*, 9 Indian L. Rep. 3043 (D. Nev. 1982).

117. *Cheyenne-Arapahoe Tribes v. Watt*, 9 Indian L. Rep. 3053 (D. D.C. 1982); *Omaha Tribe of Nebraska v. Watt*, 9 Indian L. Rep. 3117 (D. Neb. 1982).

118. *First Moon v. White Tail*, 270 U.S. 243 (1926); *Johnson v. Kleppe*, 596 F.2d 950 (10th Cir. 1979).

119. *See, e.g., Eskra v. Morton*, 524 F.2d 9 (7th Cir. 1975); *Simmons v. Eagle Seelatsee*, 244 F. Supp. 808 (E.D. Wash. 1965), *aff'd per curiam*, 384 U.S. 209 (1966).

120. *Merrill Ditch-Liners, Inc. v. Pablo*, 670 F.2d 139 (9th Cir. 1982).

121. *Tooahnippah v. Hickel*, 397 U.S. 598 (1970); *Ike*, note 116 above; *Sierra Club v. Hodel*, 848 F.2d 1068, 1075 (10th Cir. 1988).

122. 25 U.S.C. Sec. 372.

123. *First Moon*, note 118 above.

124. 25 U.S.C. Sec. 373.

125. *Tooahnippah*, note 121 above.
126. *See* notes 47–59 above and accompanying text.
127. *Citizens to Preserve Overton Park v. Volpe*, 401 U.S. 402, 415–16 (1971); *Motor Vehicle Mfrs. Ass'n v. State Farm Mutual Automobile Ins. Co.*, 463 U.S. 29, 43 (1983).
128. *See Moopa Band of Paiute Indians v. U.S. Dep't of Interior*, 747 F.2d 563 (9th Cir. 1983), and cases cited in note 127 above.
129. 25 C.F.R. Secs. 2.1 *et seq.*
130. *See, e.g., Faras v. Hodel*, 845 F.2d 202 (9th Cir. 1988); *White Mountain Apache Tribe v. Hodel*, 840 F.2d 675 (9th Cir. 1988).
131. *Seminole Nation v. U.S.*, 316 U.S. 286, 297 (1942).
132. *U.S. v. Mason*, 412 U.S. 391, 398 (1973).
133. *Seminole Nation*, note 125 above, 316 U.S. at 297. *See also Mitchell*, note 89 above.

Appendix A
The Indian Civil Rights Act
(25 U.S.C. §§ 1301–03)

§ 1301. Definitions

For purposes of this subchapter, the term—

(1) "Indian tribe" means any tribe, band, or other group of Indians subject to the jurisdiction of the United States and recognized as possessing powers of self-government;

(2) "powers of self-government" means and includes all governmental powers possessed by an Indian tribe, executive, legislative, and judicial, and all offices, bodies, and tribunals by and through which they are executed, including courts of Indian offenses; and

(3) "Indian court" means any Indian tribal court or court of Indian offense.

§ 1302. Constitutional rights

No Indian tribe in exercising powers of self-government shall—

(1) make or enforce any law prohibiting the free exercise of religion, or abridging the freedom of speech, or of the press, or the right of the people peaceably to assemble and to petition for a redress of grievances;

(2) violate the right of the people to be secure in their persons, houses, papers, and effects against unreasonable search and seizures, nor issue warrants, but upon probable cause, supported by oath or affirmation, and particularly describing the place to be searched and the person or thing to be seized;

(3) subject any person for the same offense to be twice put in jeopardy;

(4) compel any person in any criminal case to be a witness against himself;

(5) take any private property for a public use without just compensation;

(6) deny to any person in a criminal proceeding the right to

a speedy and public trial, to be informed of the nature and cause of the accusation, to be confronted with the witnesses against him, to have compulsory process for obtaining witnesses in his favor, and at his own expense to have the assistance of counsel for his defense;

(7) require excessive bail, impose excessive fines, inflict cruel and unusual punishments, and in no event impose for conviction of any one offense any penalty or punishment greater than imprisonment for a term of one year or a fine of $5000, or both;

(8) deny to any person within its jurisdiction the equal protection of its laws or deprive any person of liberty or property without due process of law;

(9) pass any bill of attainder or ex post facto law; or

(10) deny to any person accused of an offense punishable by imprisonment the right, upon request, to a trial by jury of not less than six persons.

§ *1303. Habeas corpus*

The privilege of the writ of habeas corpus shall be available to any person, in a court of the United States, to test the legality of his detention by order of an Indian tribe.

Appendix B
Public Law 83—280
(18 U.S.C. § 1162, 28 U.S.C. § 1360)

§ 1162. *State jurisdiction over offenses committed by or*
against Indians in the Indian country

(a) Each of the States or Territories listed in the following table shall have jurisdiction over offenses committed by or against Indians in the areas of Indian country listed opposite the name of the State or Territory to the same extent that such State or Territory has jurisdiction over offenses committed elsewhere within the State or Territory, and the criminal laws of such State or Territory shall have the same force and effect within such Indian country as they have elsewhere within the State or Territory:

State or Territory of	*Indian Country Affected*
Alaska	All Indian country within the State
California	All Indian country within the State
Minnesota	All Indian country within the State, except the Red Lake Reservation
Nebraska	All Indian country within the State
Oregon	All Indian country within the State, except the Warm Springs Reservation
Wisconsin	All Indian country within the State, except the Menominee Reservation

(b) Nothing in this section shall authorize the alienation, encumbrance, or taxation of any real or personal property, including water rights, belonging to any Indian or any Indian tribe, band, or community that is held in trust by the United States or is subject to a restriction against alienation imposed by the United States; or shall authorize regulation of the use of such property in a manner inconsistent with any Federal treaty, agreement, or statute or with any regulation made pursuant thereto; or shall deprive any Indian or any Indian tribe, band, or community of any right, privilege, or immunity afforded under Federal treaty, agreement, or statute with respect to hunting, trapping, or fishing or the control, licensing, or regulation thereof.

(c) The provisions of sections 1152 and 1153 of this chapter [see Appendixes C and D] shall not be applicable within the areas of Indian country listed in subsection (a) of this section.

§ 1360. State civil jurisdiction in actions to which Indians are parties

(a) Each of the States or Territories listed in the following table shall have jurisdiction over civil causes of action between Indians or to which Indians are parties which arise in the areas of Indian country listed opposite the name of the State or Territory to the same extent that such State or Territory has jurisdiction over other civil causes of action and those civil laws of such State or Territory that are of general application to private persons or private property shall have the same force and effect within such Indian country as they have elsewhere within the State or Territory.

State or Territory of	Indian Country Affected
Alaska	All Indian country within the State
California	All Indian country within the State
Minnesota	All Indian country within the State, except the Red Lake Reservation
Nebraska	All Indian country within the State
Oregon	All Indian country within the State, except the Warm Springs Reservation
Wisconsin	All Indian country within the State, except the Menominee Reservation

(b) Nothing in this section shall authorize the alienation, encumbrance, or taxation of any real or personal property, including water rights, belonging to any Indian or any Indian tribe, band, or community that is held in trust by the United States or is subject to a restriction against alienation imposed by the United States; or shall authorize regulation of the use of such property in a manner inconsistent with any Federal treaty, agreement, or statute or with any regulation made pursuant thereto; or shall confer jurisdiction upon the State to adjudicate, in probate proceedings or otherwise, the ownership or right to possession of such property or any interest therein.

(c) Any tribal ordinance or custom heretofore or hereafter adopted by an Indian tribe, band, or community in the exercise of any authority which it may possess shall, if not inconsistent with any applicable civil law of the State, be given full force and effect in the determination of civil causes of action pursuant to this section.

Appendix C
The General Crimes Act
(18 U.S.C. § 1152)

§ 1152. *Laws governing*

Except as otherwise expressly provided by law, the general laws of the United States as to the punishment of offenses committed in any place within the sole and exclusive jurisdiction of the United States, except the District of Columbia, shall extend to the Indian country.

This section shall not extend to offenses committed by one Indian against the person or property of another Indian, nor to any Indian committing any offense in the Indian country who has been punished by the local law of the tribe, or to any case where, by treaty stipulations, the exclusive jurisdiction over such offenses is or may be secured to the Indian tribes respectively.

Appendix D
The Major Crimes Act
(18 U.S.C. § 1153)

§ 1153.   Offenses committed within Indian country
   (a) Any Indian who commits against the person or property of another Indian or other person any of the following offenses, namely, murder, manslaughter, kidnapping, maiming, a felony under chapter 190A [18 U.S.C. §§ 2241 *et seq.*, *i.e.*, certain sexual offenses including rape and sexual abuse], incest, assault with intent to commit murder, assault with a dangerous weapon, assault resulting in serious bodily injury, arson, burglary, robbery, and a felony under section 661 of this title [18 U.S.C. § 661, *i.e.*, theft] within the Indian country, shall be subject to the same law and penalties as all other persons committing any of the above offenses, within the exclusive jurisdiction of the United States.
   (b) Any offense referred to in subsection (a) of this section that is not defined and punished by Federal law in force within the exclusive jurisdiction of the United States shall be defined and punished in accordance with the laws of the State in which such offense was committed as are in force at the time of such offense.

Appendix E
"Indian Country"
(18 U.S.C. § 1151)

§ 1151. Indian country defined

Except as otherwise provided in sections 1154 and 1156 of this title, the term "Indian country," as used in this chapter, means (a) all land within the limits of any Indian reservation under the jurisdiction of the United States government, notwithstanding the issuance of any patent, and, including rights-of-way running through the reservation, (b) all dependent Indian communities within the borders of the United States whether within the original or subsequently acquired territory thereof, and whether within or without the limits of a state, and (c) all Indian allotments, the Indian titles to which have not been extinguished, including rights-of-way running through the same.